Interacting Factors Between Physical Health, Mental Health, and A Long Quality Life

BRIAN W. SLOBODA
CHANDRASEKHAR PUTCHA AND SIDDHARTH RANA

BALBOA.
PRESS
A DIVISION OF HAY HOUSE

Balboa Press books may be ordered through booksellers or by contacting:

Balboa Press
A Division of Hay House
1663 Liberty Drive
Bloomington, IN 47403
www.balboapress.com
1 (877) 407-4847

Print information available on the last page.

ISBN: 978-1-9822-3024-1 (sc)
ISBN: 978-1-9822-3027-2 (e)

Balboa Press rev. date: 09/23/2019

Interacting Factors Between Physical Health, Mental Health, and A Long Quality Life

Editors   Chandrasekhar Putcha
                     California State University, Fullerton
                     Department of Civil and Environmental Engineering

                     Siddharth Rana
                     CALTRANS
                     Los Angeles, California

Managing   Brian W. Sloboda
Editor   University of Phoenix, College of Doctoral
                     Studies

List of Contributors

Caroline Bailey
California State University, Fullerton
School of Nursing

Francisco J. Bodán
California State University, Fullerton
School of Nursing

Rebecca Cross Bodán
California State University, Fullerton
School of Nursing

Bhanu Evani
Virginia Commonwealth University
Department of Biostatistics, School of Medicine

Renuka Evani
Chesterfield County, Virginia
County Mental Health Support Services

Richard Hall
University of Phoenix, College of Doctoral Studies

Nalini Kalanadhabhatta
Medical Resident at University of Buffalo

Vivekanand Kalanadhabhatta
Allergist/Immunologist
State University of New York—Downstate (Brooklyn, New York)

Varinder Kaur
Advanced Counseling Services
Canton, Michigan

Sylvia Lindinger-Sternart
University of Providence
Department of Counseling

Maria Matza
California State University, Fullerton
School of Nursing

Nathan Matza
California State University, Long Beach
Department of Health Science

Kenichi Meguro
Geriatric Behavioral Neurology, Tohoku University CYRIC, and the Osaki-Tajiri SKIP Center
Sendai, Japan

Shyamala Mruthinti   Datta ImmunoChem. Inc., USA
                            CEO and Research Director

Aditya Kiran Putcha   Consultant, Entertainment Industries and California State
                            University, Fullerton

Chandrasekhar Putcha   California State University, Fullerton
                            Department of Civil and Environmental Engineering

Viswanath "Vish" Putcha   London School of Economics (LSE)
                            London, United Kingdom

Kamala Rana   Former consultant to the United Nations (Retired)

Siddharth Rana   CALTRANS
                            Los Angeles, California

Ryan Rominger   University of Phoenix, College of Doctoral Studies

Brian W. Sloboda   University of Phoenix, College of Doctoral Studies

Fiona Sussan   University of Phoenix, College of Doctoral Studies

Contents

Foreword

I am delighted to write this foreword, and I immediately accepted the invitation (accompanied by all book materials and chapters) by my old friend and good colleague Brian W. Sloboda. But by no means should this be perceived as a favor to a friend. As a labor economist I know the value of this book's research well. I have conducted research on the health of older populations as well as on the happiness and well-being of immigrants and natives, myself. Besides genuinely caring about the area, I deeply value this volume's contribution to opening our eyes to the interdisciplinary approach to health and well-being and to enriching our knowledge about the intricacies of health and well-being, as we all age. Academics, researchers, students, healthcare practitioners, and policymakers alike can benefit from reading this great book and reflect upon the important message each of the fourteen chapters delivers. This is a book about all of us, our physical, emotional, and social functioning, about the economy, society, the environment and our future.

The ancient Greek saying "a sound mind in a healthy body" is as relevant today as it has been over the millennia. It underlines the importance of a harmonious coexistence of physical health with mental and psychological well-being for a person to be able to enjoy quality of life without limitations or restrictions until the old ages. In the Hippocratic philosophy, the interdependence of mind, spirit, and body were contextualized in the need to also achieve harmony in a person's interactions with his social and natural environment. In this spirit, the World Health Organization (WHO) defines health as "a state of complete physical, mental and social well-being and not merely the absence of disease or infirmity." Mental and physical health are interdependent and highly endogenous. While strong mental health plays a crucial role in maintaining good physical health, mental disorders hold people back from healthy attitudes and activities promoting physical health. And vice-versa, compromised physical health may adversely affect mental health, which in turn affects physical health negatively. Naturally, the CDC documents that among the 10 leading causes of death in the U.S. in 2017, which account for 74% of all deaths, two are related to mental health (Alzheimer's disease and suicide).

Overall, health is an indispensable element of human capital and correlated with education, economic stability, neighborhoods, and social context. The productive benefits of health are recognized in periods of decreasing income inequality and sustained economic growth and are front and center in the 2030 UN Agenda of Sustainable Development Goals. Health is also interlinked with happiness, well-being and the quality of life, perceived by WHO as "a broad ranging concept affected in a complex way by the person's physical health, psychological state, personal beliefs, social relationships and their relationship to salient features of their environment". The environment, defined by WHO as "all the physical, chemical, and biological factors external to a person, and all the related behaviors" not only affects longevity, but also quality of life. Moreover, lifestyle factors can influence a person's risk of dementia, whose debilitating effects impact the everyday lives of those affected and their caregivers. Associated costs of dementia are estimated to be $236 billion for 2016.

It is obvious by now that the book is tackling a multidimensional and interdisciplinary topic and it delivers. The editors, who are also multidisciplinary and have collaborated before in the area of healthcare, have joined forces in undertaking the editing of this book on physical and mental health and quality of life. They have also done a superb job in identifying leading researchers from economics, gerontology, psychology, medicine, nursing, and engineering to provide the state of the art in these timely issues. The chapters analyze, evaluate, and provide insights to the following specific topics, and underscore why this book matters: The relationship between depression and physical health; creativity as a way to longevity; characteristics of longevity; hobbies, spiritual well-being and long quality of life; seniors and sexuality; the immune system in the golden years; decreased physical health, dementia, and the community; anger, meditation, and improved life expectancy; finding better ways to manage dementia such as therapeutic holistic approaches to Alzheimer's Disease through music; mortality, lifestyle and the environment; DALY as a welfare measure; and Parkinson's Disease and its impact on quality of life.

This book is definitely worth reading and having it handy as a reference to these issues that we all face every day. Academics, researchers and the general public will find valuable answers about health and the quality of life in this book. While the importance of "the pursuit of happiness" has been acknowledged in the Constitution, and while mortality and life expectancy constitute indicators of developed nations, physical, mental and emotional health and well-being have been neglected. This book brings mental health to the fore and puts quality of life as it is related to health front and center; as it should be.

Amelie F. Constant
Office of Population Research
Princeton University

Preface

In early 2017 the editors of this research monograph had much discussions about the general idea of longevity, and health. We lamented that some of these books on the market do not show the connection between the physical and mental health and a quality of life. Furthermore, this research monograph has chapters written by three physicians and two nursing professors and their chapters carefully link the factors that lead to a long quality life. In addition, other contributed chapters are written by economists, psychologists, and business administration specialists. So no doubt this research monograph provides a plethora of topics that examine the link of the physical and mental factors that are linked of the longevity of life. These chapters can be read independently of each other based on the reader's interest or as a whole to get the feel of the physical and factors that contribute to quality of longevity of life. Let's provide a brief synopsis of the chapters of this research monograph.

In the first chapter, Rebecca Cross Bodán, Francisco J. Bodán, and Caroline Bailey examine the relationships between clinical depression and physical health continue. There is strong evidence to suggest that those with depression are at a higher risk for developing chronic diseases, e.g, heart failure, coronary artery disease, and diabetes mellitus, compared to those who have never experienced a clinical depression. Conversely, those with certain chronic illnesses are more likely to become depressed when compared to healthy individuals, which can lead to increases in morbidity and mortality when compared to their non-depressed counterparts. In all cases, the presence of depression has the potential to limit both length and quality of one's life.

Chapter 2 by Nalini Kalanadhabhatta and Vivekananda Kalanadhabhatta discuss the normal functions of the immune system from birth through adulthood, followed by changes in the elderly. The role played by immune system in protecting us from infections, autoimmune diseases as well as cancer. They discuss how we can improve the quality of life in trying to modulate the immune system with some insights into new therapies that are on the horizon.

Bhanu Evani and Renuka Evani follows the chapter on the immune system and discuss the brain health. A healthy brain and body play important roles in determining one's Quality of Life (QoL). The brain's health is strongly associated with a healthy heart and its connecting blood vessels. They discuss how we can improve the quality of life in the maintaining of brain health with some insights into new methods to maintain brain health as we age and as a means to maintain longevity.

In the next chapter by Kenichi Meguro, this chapter delves into the importance of health. Health is defined in terms of Quality of Life (QoL) by the World Health Organization (WHO), based on how an individual feel about their life, and accounting for their culture and value systems, and their goals, expectations, standards and concerns. QoL includes items such as physical function and mental health, but health- related QOL is complex, given the multiple chronic diseases and decreased physical function found in many elderly people. This chapter presents some ways to measure QoL.

Next the chapter by Maria Matza and Nathan Matza delves into the topic of sexuality and ageing. The culture of the United States does not comfortably address sexuality as a topic of conversation at any stage of life. Sexuality is not adequately addressed in our educational, medical/health, or social venues. This lack of education is affecting the physical and mental health of the growing number of seniors who are experiencing an increased lifespan and physical ability to engage in intimate relationships. Advances in technology and science are making it possible to live longer; therefore, subjecting seniors to health and social dilemmas that in the past were never addressed. These include physical and mental changes to themselves and their partner because of age or illness; availability of new partners through exposure to social media dating; and risk of exposure to sexually transmitted diseases (STDs).

In the chapter by Shyamala Mruthinti delves into approach in combatting Alzheimer's disease. As means to combat Alzheimer's disease, Shyamala Mruthinti presents yoga, meditation, music and diet as an effective psycho-neuro-immuno- therapeutic holistic approaches in combating Alzheimer's disease (AD), depression, and perhaps other behavioral disorders.

Viswanath Putcha and Chandrasekhar Putcha delve into Parkinson's disease. Parkinson's disease (PD) is the most prevalent neurodegenerative disease among the elderly. It occurs when nerve cells (neurons) in the brain do not produce enough dopamine. The reason that PD occurs, and the neurons become impaired is not known, and there is no cure for the disease. Due to its progressive and chronic characteristics, PD affects quality of life (QoL) not only for patients but also for the people living with and caring for them. The aim of their chapter is to provide various methods to improve quality of life for those dealing with PD.

Ryan Rominger along with Sylvia Lindinger-Sternart and Varinder Kaur prepared a chapter titled Mindfulness and Wellbeing. Their chapter focuses on stress, anxiety, depression, and chronic pain within aging adults. Many aging adults suffer from mental health challenges related not only to usual life stressors (such as economic and relationship challenges) but to physical health challenges, progression through the psyco-social developmental stages into old age, experiencing numerous losses (such as the loss of a spouse or children), and decreased mobility. The authors propose, and review ample research indicating that use of mindfulness-based therapies can greatly reduce stress, anxiety, depression, and chronic pain, reduce the secondary and tertiary effects of the same, and increase overall quality of life.

Fiona Sussan and Richard Hall prepared a chapterthat is based on the prior quality-of-life (QoL) literature that investigated standard of living (i.e., economic status), social status, social support, and psychological well-being as the main drivers of QoL. In light of the urgent need to understand baby boomers and their QoL, in particular medical technology advancement has facilitated longer lives; their chapter proposes physical health as a mediator of the above-mentioned drivers of QoL for senior citizens. They further propose spirituality as a surrogate of mental health directly affects psychological well-being that is linked to physical well-being. Tying mental well-being interrelations to physical well-being has important implications for healthcare practitioners and healthcare policies. They provided a case study that looked at Japan, positing that their proposed model of QoL will vary across cultures.

Kamala Rana in her chapter focuses on the creative aspect. Most people have some ambition, a goal if you will. There are some who want to address a major social issue, and strive to be known. These individuals become community leaders, as they come up with creative solutions to problems.

Some individuals try relentlessly to reach the top of their chosen profession. Sometimes, these people, try to emulate an important person in life. It gives them enthusiasm to perform. These individuals, have a desire to rise high through competition. They are very social, and maintain close ties with family, friends and admirers that gives satisfaction and happiness. In their duty to profession, they have acceptance of high performance. When they face disappointments, they vigorously try to find a new way to find a solution, and don't give up. Therefore, an aspirational urge to scale new heights and to strive harder increases the will to carry on and to live until success is achieved. Longevity is the fruit for those who never quit.

Aditya Putcha in his chapter presents the effect of hobbies on psychological well-being. If creating art and playing sports helps one's psychological well-being and/or leads to longer life expectancies. Some statistical models will be studied in detail and relevant conclusions will be drawn concerning the effects of hobbies on psychological well-being.

Siddharth's Rana in his chapter focus on the important aspects of human facial and other habitual characteristics, which make certain individuals live a long life. He would also elaborate on some individuals who have had meaningful existence in their life, and how they contributed in their own special way. His chapter will also shed some insight on how a person's longevity can have a very gratifying experience for that person and the surroundings.

In the final chapter, Chandrasekhar Putcha and Brian W. Sloboda delve into QALY or the Quality-adjusted life-year.). QALY is a generic measure of the health-outcomes; disease burden that includes both the quality and quantity of life lived. Intuitively, it is a product of life lived and utility value associated with a given state of health. Utility is a subjective value, and the utility data often comes from various specialized surveys. This chapter presented not only the historical overview of the QALY, but specific chronic diseases such as diabetes, cancer, Alzheimer's disease, which do not often measure specific QALYs. This chapter serves as a springboard to subsequent research looking at the estimation of QALYs for specific chronic diseases.

These chapters by esteemed authors of this research monograph highlight the latest research in these topics that can offer new insights for additional research. As a research monograph, *Interacting Factors between Physical Health, Mental Health and A Long Quality Life* offers a unique review of pertinent literature and theories on a topic which affect us all, personally and professionally.

Brian W. Sloboda, Managing Editor
Chandrasekhar Putcha, Editor
Siddharth Rana, Editor

Shedding Light on the Shared and Complicated Relationships Between Depression, Health, and Longevity

Rebecca Cross Bodán, Francisco J. Bodán, and Caroline Bailey

Introduction

Depression, a mood disorder, is one of the most common and costly psychiatric disorders, affecting over 16 million American adults in 2016, with estimated direct and indirect costs above $210 billion, per year (Greenberg, Fournier, Sisitsky, Pike, & Kessler, 2015; NIMH, 2017). Symptoms of depression include dysphoria, irritability, anhedonia, change in appetite, change in sleep patterns, fatigue/lack of energy, feelings of guilt or worthlessness, difficulty concentrating, and suicidality, among others (APA, 2013). While depression can affect anyone, regardless of age, gender, or socio-economic status, there are well-documented risk factors for who is more likely to develop a depressive disorder. These risk factors include: personal or family history of depression; major life change (e.g. birth of a child, divorce); stress or trauma (e.g. poverty, abuse); certain medications or substances (e.g. hormonal contraception, alcohol) or medical conditions (e.g. stroke, heart disease) (NIMH, 2017).

When an individual is experiencing a depressive episode, it becomes difficult to engage in daily life, including work; school; social activities; and self-care behaviors, such as healthy eating and exercise. The impacts on income, school performance and progression, friendships, and health can be far-reaching. There is, in fact, growing data which suggests that the effect of depression goes far beyond the profound impact it can have on quality of life, to also have a negative effect on the quantity of one's life. More specifically, data suggests that those with a history of depression are likely to die earlier than the general population, as a direct result of having depression (Colton & Manderscheid, 2006; Walker, McGee, & Druss, 2015).

While the general population continues to experience an increase in life expectancy, this does not appear to be the case for those with mental illness, including mood disorders (Statistics, 2017). In fact, 8 million deaths a year can be attributed to mental illness worldwide, with nearly 3 million of those deaths specific to depression and other related mood disorders (Walker et al., 2015). To put it another way, those with mood disorders have a mortality rate over 1.8 times greater than the general population (Walker et al., 2015).

A large, longitudinal study found that individuals with depression died on average five years earlier than those without a mood disorder, with a range of 2.5 to 8.7 years, depending upon the cause of death (Kara Zivin et al., 2012). The documented causes of death were both from natural and unnatural (e.g., homicide, suicide, and accident) causes. This translates to 1 to 6 years of potential life lost as a direct result of depression. Compelling results, given that all subjects in this study were within the Veteran's Administration system, eliminating the potential confounders of health care quality and access. These findings suggest that clinicians and researchers should not only focus on treating depression to limit unnatural causes of death but also focus on the treatment and understanding of depression to mitigate the years of potential life lost due to natural causes among depressed individuals.

While depression is associated with higher mortality rates for many common medical disorders, the question as to how and why this is the case remains unanswered. There are a number of possible biological and behavioral possibilities, and perhaps we will one day learn that depression itself is a sort of prodromal symptom to some chronic diseases. Either way, as it stands now, major depression remains underdiagnosed and often undertreated. Perhaps focusing additional attention on the impact depression can have on physical health and longevity will help those with depression and their providers focus on providing evidence-based care, to decrease symptoms, and perhaps resulting in improved health and even longer life.

Depression and Chronic Disease

As alluded to above, depression is intricately related to a variety of chronic diseases. Those with a history of depression are more likely to develop chronic disease (e.g., heart disease, diabetes, and stroke); those with chronic disease are more likely to experience depression; and having a chronic disease with pre-existing or co-morbid depression directly impacts mortality (Kent & Shapiro, 2009; Mills et al., 2018; Whooley, 2006; Yang, Korhonen, Moustgaard, Silventoinen, & Martikainen, 2018). The data supporting this relationship is perhaps strongest when it comes to cardiovascular disease. Those with a history of major depressive disorder have a higher incidence of developing heart disease, while those with heart disease are more likely to become depressed, perhaps even more concerning, those with heart disease and elevated depressive symptoms have a higher rate of mortality compared to those with heart disease and no depression (Jang et al., 2018). The American Heart Association recommend that clinicians caring for those with heart disease, screen for and manage depression when needed (Dupre et al.; Havranek et al., 2015). Hospitalized patients with CVD who have elevated depressive symptoms are more likely to be younger, unmarried, lives alone, when compared to those with lower levels of depressive symptoms (Dupre et al.).

In a longitudinal study of older adults, sub-clinical CVD predicted mortality, depressive symptoms predicted mortality, but the depressive symptoms did not seem to mediate the relationship between sub-clinical depressive symptoms and mortality (Armstrong et al., 2017). While the data supporting the relationship between depression and heart disease is strong, the underlying causes are not. The use of psychotropics can increase the risk for not only obesity, but also insulin resistance and dyslipidemia (Abosi, Lopes, Schmitz, & Fiedorowicz, 2018), all known risk factors for the development of heart disease and type II diabetes mellitus. Interventions that address depression, do not consistently show improvements in mortality in this population, so there is much we have yet to understand (Richards et al., 2017).

Causes of Death

When considering the cause of death for those with depression, most will immediately think of suicide or an injury-related death. While suicide is a serious concern, with approximately 7% of those with a major depressive disorder completing suicide (Isometsa, 2014), the causes of death for most with depression are similar to those of the general population, such as heart disease, cancer, stroke, and lung disease (Zivin et al., 2015). The higher mortality rates for those with depression are maintained, even when controlling for baseline comorbidities. In fact, depression has been associated with a 17% increase in all-cause mortality. Interestingly, those with a history of hospitalization for depression have a lower incidence of mortality than those with depression who have never been hospitalized. Perhaps a consequence of the inadequate treatment many with depression receives in a community setting. Together, these findings highlight the need to have a stronger grasp of the causes and consequences of depression, with the hope of one day improving its treatment, and decreasing mortality rates (Zivin et al., 2015).

Potential Variables Affecting Health and Longevity in Patients with Depression

While the direct links between clinical depression, health, and mortality are eyebrow-raising, the question as to why these relationships exist is still unfolding. As it turns out, depression itself is related to some risk factors that can affect longevity, such as inflammation, physical activity, obesity, disturbances in sleep, social support, adherence to medical treatment, substance use, and poverty. Below is a discussion of these risk factors as they relate to depression, health, and longevity.

Inflammation

The inflammatory, or cytokine, theory of depression postulates that elevations in pro-inflammatory cytokines are both cause and consequence of depression. More specifically, elevations in inflammatory markers have been documented in those with depression; the administration of pro-inflammatory markers to healthy or chronically ill individuals, commonly results in elevations in depressive symptoms; and depression is common in diseases which exhibit high levels of peripheral inflammation (de Beaurepaire, 2002).

Elevations in inflammatory markers in both the periphery, and centrally, are thought to influence depressions' onset, severity, and progression. Elevated serum levels of IL-1, IL-6, TNF-α, CRP, and MCP-1 have been documented in depressed patients, though the results are mixed with IL-8 serum levels, and with IL-6 and MCP-1 levels in the cerebrospinal fluid (Young, Bruno, & Pomara, 2014). Despite data supporting the inflammatory theory, the results remain inconsistent, and there is no specific marker or set of markers that can be reliably used for diagnostic or treatment purposes. This is likely due to the complex nature of depression. With so many affected, and so many potentially causative risk factors, there is likely a role for managing inflammation when it comes to the prevention and treatment of depression, but perhaps we need to understand better what sub-populations of depressed individuals are likely to be affected. Recent research, looking at the depression risk factor of abuse, has shown those who have a history of physical or emotional abuse have increased levels of IL-6, compared to those who never experienced abuse (Munjiza et al., 2018). The rise in IL-6 is correlated to the presence of major depressive disorder in these subjects. We just may find that history and risk factors make a difference in the inflammatory profile.

Knowing that inflammation has a role in both depression and chronic disease, what can be done? The answer for some may be as simple as exercise. There is data to suggest moderate exercise can improve both depressive symptoms and lower levels of pro-inflammatory cytokines, TNF- α and IL-6 (Paolucci, Loukov, Bowdish, & Heisz). Interestingly, subjects in the same study randomized to high-intensity training saw an increase in both depressive symptoms and the same markers, TNF- α and IL-6. These results suggest that exercise may be an important factor when it comes to inflammation in depressed individuals, but intensity matters and may prove itself to be counterproductive.

Cognitive Behavioral Therapy (CBT) may also have a role in improving the inflammatory profile of depressed patients. CBT is a well-studied model of talk therapy, known to be very effective for the management of mild to moderate depression, and in some cases as effective as antidepressant medication (Cuijpers et al., 2013). Though the data is inconsistent at this time, there is enough to suggest that the use of CBT can, in some patients, decreases inflammatory markers among depressed individuals, some of whom have co-morbid chronic illnesses such as heart disease (Doering, Cross, Vredevoe, Martinez-Maza, & Cowan, 2007; Lopresti, 2017; O'Toole et al., 2018). While more work in this area of research is needed, it is incredible even to contemplate that using CBT to change how one thinks and feels, could also have an impact on the inflammatory profile.

Physical Activity

The more you move, the longer you live. While it might not be that simple, regular exercise is thought to limit morbidity, and improve longevity (Kujala, Kaprio, Sarna, & Koskenvuo, 1998; Thompson et al., 2003). The American Heart Association recommends health care providers assess for and promote physical activity, to limit the burden of heart disease and improve health (Lobelo et al., 2018). The data supporting the relationship between exercise and longevity is so strong that in 2008 the U.S. federal government published its first Physical Activity Guidelines (Committee, 2008). The general recommendations were for adults to exercise 150-300 minutes a week at moderate intensity, or 75-150 minutes a week at high intensity. Using these guidelines as a reference, a prospective longitudinal study evaluated the relationship between exercise frequency and intensity and mortality in a group of over 600,000 American adults who participated in the National Cancer Institute's Cohort Consortium (Arem et al., 2015). Those who fell within 1-2 times the minimum exercise recommendations had a mortality rate 31% lower than those who reported no leisure-time exercise. The mortality rate drops to 37% for participants who engaged in 2-3 times the minimum guidelines. While exercising at greater frequency and intensity then the recommended guidelines did not prove harmful in any way, it also did not meaningfully decrease the mortality rate, when compared to those who met the minimum federal recommendations for exercise frequency and intensity (Arem et al., 2015).

The type of exercise may also be important when it comes to improving longevity, particularly as we age. Muscular strength, which naturally decreases with age, is inversely associated with all-cause mortality, a relationship that remains significant even when controlling for other risk major factors such as smoking, body fat, and age (Strasser, Volaklis, Fuchs, & Burtscher, 2018). These findings suggest there may be benefits to incorporating some amount of resistance training into exercise routines when possible. Even for those who have led mostly sedentary lives, increases in muscle filaments can be seen after six weeks of strength training.

Not only can regular exercise increase longevity and improve health, regular leisure-time exercise can also prevent depressive symptoms, and improve, or limit depressive disorders in a wide range of populations (Kuwahara et al., 2018; Murri et al., 2018; Wise, Adams-Campbell, Palmer, & Rosenberg, 2006). For those experiencing a depressive episode, however, it can be incredibly difficult to find the motivation to move. Less sitting and more moving can by itself improve mood, and lower depressive symptoms (Gibson, Muggeridge, Hughes, Kelly, & Kirk, 2017), so while more rigorous exercise may be ideal, simply encouraging those with depression to get up and move may noticeably improve depressive symptoms, though it is unclear if this would have an impact on longevity.

Like its impact on inflammation, the intensity of exercise may also make a difference in its impact on depression. In a study of healthy college-age students, subjects were randomized to three groups, no exercise, moderate exercise, and high-intensity training (Paolucci et al.). Those randomized to the moderate exercise group exhibited the greatest improvement in psychological symptoms, including significant decreases in depression, anxiety, and stress. Those in the high-intensity group showed some decrease in depressive symptoms, along with increases in perceived stress and anxiety. Subjects in the no exercise group exhibited an increase in depressive symptoms, anxiety, and stress. These results point to just how quickly a sedentary lifestyle may impact mood and suggest that moderate intensity training may be the optimal level for improving and preventing depressive symptoms.

Recent studies looking at the impact of formal exercise programs on those with depression have consistently documented an improvement in symptoms when compared to those receiving usual care. These findings are seen both in those with medical co-morbidities in the community and in patients hospitalized for the treatment of severe depression. In a study of breast cancer survivors, moderate exercise was shown to improve depressive symptoms (Carter, Hunter, Norian, Turan, & Rogers, 2017). In a small study of Indian women hospitalized with major depression, a supervised exercise program as an adjunct to care, improved depressive symptoms compared to those receiving usual care. While over symptoms improved, there were no changes in somatic symptoms for those in the intervention group (Roy, Govindan, & Kesavan).

Recommending exercise as part of the treatment plan for depression is an important start, but human nature coupled with the anhedonia or dysphoria inherent to depression can make it difficult for these recommendations to become a reality for many. Incorporating more formalized exercise programs into the plan of care may improve participation in recommended exercise routines, possibly resulting in improvements in both depressive symptoms, overall health, and longevity.

Obesity

There appears to be a reciprocal relationship between obesity and depression; those with obesity are more likely to experience depression than those who are of normal weight, and those with depression are more likely to be obese compared to the general population (Hidese, Asano, Saito, Sasayama, & Kunugi, 2018; Luppino et al., 2010). Like depression, obesity has also been strongly linked to a higher incidence of morbidity and mortality (Rost et al., 2018). The mechanisms linking obesity and depression are not fully understood. There is, however, some evidence that seeking carbohydrates and high-fat foods can increase serotonin levels, a neurotransmitter thought to be in short supply in individuals who are depressed (Wurtman & Wurtman, 2017). This may explain why some with depression have an increase in appetite, often seeking foods higher in carbohydrates and fats, and in many cases resulting in weight gain. Additionally, for those who do seek treatment for their depression and are prescribed a psychotropic medication, weight gain is a known and troubling side effect for a number of common medications (e.g., mirtazapine; tricyclic antidepressants; selective serotonin reuptake inhibitors; and mood stabilizers) used to treat depression (Locatelli & Golay, 2018), in a sense forcing patients to choose between a more regulated mood and weight gain. Knowing that relatively rapid weight gain in already obese individuals can independently increase mortality risk by up to 50% (Myrskyla & Chang, 2009), these side effects are particularly concerning and warrant close attention from clinicians and researchers alike.

Being both depressed and obese is likely to have a further impact on longevity, though the question as to why remains unanswered. Perhaps one explanation, both obesity, and depression are associated with rises in inflammatory markers (Hijmans, 2018; O'Toole et al., 2018). For individuals who have depression and obesity, this is another possible reason for higher mortality rates, as increases in inflammatory markers have been linked to common chronic illnesses such as type II diabetes mellitus and heart disease. While overweight and obesity increase morbidity and mortality, and intensive weight management can lead to weight loss and improve chronic disease indicators such as lower blood glucose in diabetes mellitus (Lean, 2018), weight loss does not necessarily improve mortality rates. In fact, some data suggests mortality rates may increase as overweight or obese individuals lose weight (Sørensen, Rissanen, Korkeila, & Kaprio, 2005). A paradox to say the least, and one area of research and clinical practice where we have more questions than answers. Despite these findings, it is difficult to see the downside of encouraging those with depression to make healthy eating choices and move as much as possible.

Sleep

It is widely accepted that 7 to 9 hours of sleep per night is optimal for overall health. It is also widely known that sleep difficulties are very common in those experiencing depression. Individuals with depression may experience either insomnia (difficulty falling asleep, staying asleep, and/or waking too early) or hypersomnia (sleeping more than recommended or expected). In fact, sleep disturbance is so much a part of depression that it is included in the diagnostic criteria for depressive disorders, and over 80% of depressed individuals may have at least one symptom of insomnia (Poole & Jackowska, 2017). Sleep disturbances may also serve as a prodromal symptom, or leading indicator, that depression is recurring. Conversely, adults who sleep 5 or fewer hours a night and those with primary insomnia disorders are more likely to develop depression, compared to those who do not experience sleep disturbances. Any way you look at it, depression and sleep have a close and uncomfortable relationship.

Recent longitudinal data suggest that, not only is adequate sleep important for optimal function and feeling good but that sleep plays an important and independent role in longevity. In fact, individuals who sleep less than 7 hours, or more than 9 hours on average a night have a higher mortality rate, compared to those who sleep the recommended 7-9 hours (Loprinzi & Joyner, 2018). Those who meet the sleep guidelines have almost a 20% reduction in all-cause mortality compared to those who do not. There is simply no question that regular and adequate sleep is imperative to maintaining health.

In addition to depression, inadequate sleep has also been independently associated with obesity, hypertension, heart disease, cognitive decline, and even sudden cardiac death (Bertisch et al., 2018; Javaheri & Redline, 2017; Sands-Lincoln et al., 2013). Sleep is not always a priority when it comes to depression and chronic disease management but putting a clinical focus on directly addressing sleep with depression management may lead to improvements in health and longevity. Formal exercise programs, for example, have been shown to improve insomnia in patients with chronic pain (Wiklund, Linton, Alfoldi, & Gerdle, 2018). CBT, perhaps the most prominent non-pharmacological treatment for sleep disturbances, is also effective in improving insomnia (Brasure et al., 2016; Wu, Appleman, Salazar, & Ong, 2015). Patients with insomnia who are treated with insomnia specific CBT, have significantly improved sleep, and less reliance on hypnotic medications to fall asleep, stay asleep, and awake feeling refreshed (Wu et al., 2015). These findings hold whether or not the individuals had depression. At this time, sleep is often not regularly assessed by clinicians, and evidence-based sleep interventions, such as CBT are underutilized despite their effectiveness (Koffel, Bramoweth, & Ulmer, 2018).

Substance Use

The impact of the use and abuse of substances such as alcohol, tobacco, and other illicit drugs, on health and longevity, has been well documented (CDC, 2017). The co-morbid presentation of a mood disorder and substance abuse is often referred to as *dual diagnosis*. Persons with a mood disorder are about twice as likely to also have a substance use disorder compared to those without a mental illness (NIDA, 2010).

Use of tobacco products, remains very common in the United States (Lariscy et al., 2013). The relationship between smoking and depression may be particularly pertinent in children. Adolescents who smoke are more likely to develop depression as they become adults, and adolescents who exhibit persistent elevations in depressive symptoms are more likely to smoke as adults (Johnston,

2000). The reciprocal relationship between smoking tobacco and depression is strong. Even though many with depression reach for cigarettes, smokers with depression who can quit exhibit significant improvements in mood (Taylor et al., 2014). Interventions to address depression and smoking and smoking cessation among adolescents may result in improvements in health and longevity as they become adults.

The use of tobacco, alcohol, and other illicit drugs has the potential to cause significant morbidity and mortality. Cancer, chronic respiratory disease, liver failure, and heart disease are just a few of the potential complications. Even after years of use and abuse, health can improve when a person is able and willing to quit. Adequately treating the depression, while addressing the substance use disorder with CBT, group therapy, and/or more intensive residential programs can be effective. A harm reduction, rather than all or nothing approach, can be helpful for many. Unfortunately, up to 50% of patients with a co-morbid mood and substance use disorder will not seek or receive adequate treatment.

Loneliness and Social Support

Loneliness is a relatively common experience for those with depression, perhaps driven by some of the symptoms of depression itself. Anhedonia (loss of interest or pleasure in things one normally enjoys), dysphoria, and irritability can hinder one's ability to initiate and maintain meaningful relationships. The fatigue and feelings of worthlessness may also make it difficult to seek out activities and social situations, negatively impacting one's support network by lacking either formal or informal support. Loneliness is a subjective feeling, not always related to the presence of social contacts. The feeling of loneliness peaks during adolescence, and in older adulthood (Holt-Lunstad & Smith, 2016). One must not be alone to feel lonely, implying that it is the quality, rather than the number of relationships that matter (Perissinotto, Cenzer, & Covinsky, 2012).

In adults 60 years and older, there is a positive correlation between depressive symptoms and levels of loneliness (Aylaz, Akturk, Erci, Ozturk, & Aslan, 2012). In other words, the more depressed one feels, the more loneliness they experience. While variables such as increased age, occupation, and poverty are thought to play a role in levels of loneliness, depression is the strongest predictor of loneliness among older adults (Aylaz et al., 2012). This relationship between depression and loneliness is of particular interest as there is robust evidence to show that social isolation and loneliness are independently associated with morbidity and mortality (Berkman & Syme, 1979; Cacioppo et al., 2002; Luo, 2012; Perissinotto et al., 2012; Teo, 2018). Feelings of loneliness can increase the risk of developing heart disease, type II diabetes mellitus, arthritis, cognitive decline, and suicide (Donovan et al., 2017; Holt-Lunstad & Smith, 2016). While it is not yet clear why loneliness leads to increased mortality, inflammation and lack of sleep seen in individuals who report high levels of loneliness may be associated with the increased mortality rates.

Interventions targeting lack of social support and feelings of loneliness may be particularly pertinent among adolescents and older adults. A recent group CBT intervention targeted at older adults who report feeling lonely has shown promising results (Theeke & Mallow, 2015). The research and clinical interventions in the area of loneliness are in its infancy, but since social interaction is a fundamental part of being human, it will most certainly play an important role for improving longevity in some depressed individuals.

Adherence to medical treatment

Human beings are inherently non-adherent to the medical recommendation, with estimates of 20-80% of those with chronic diseases not following medical advice (DiMatteo, 2004). There is mounting evidence to suggest that depression contributes to the problem of non-adherence across a wide variety of chronic medical conditions, including diabetes mellitus, human immunodeficiency virus, heart disease, and renal disease (Gonzalez et al., 2008; Grenard et al., 2011). Given that poor treatment, adherence has been robustly associated with higher mortality rates in a variety of chronic illnesses; this is yet another risk factor worth exploring as we contemplate the relationships between depression, health, and longevity.

A meta-analysis found that depressed patients' odds of being non-adherent to treatment were 1.8 times those of patients who were not depressed (Grenard et al., 2011). The risk for medication non-adherence in depressed individuals with chronic illness is significantly elevated across type of illness. This increased risk of medication noncompliance may be due in part to hallmark symptoms of depression such as fatigue, negative cognitions, and feelings of hopelessness which may interfere with patient-provider communication (DiMatteo, 2004). Other symptoms of depression, such as social withdrawal and feelings of worthlessness may further decrease motivation for treatment compliance (Tang, Sayers, Weissinger, & Riegel, 2014).

Perhaps not surprisingly, when compared to non-depressed patients with chronic illness, those experiencing depression are more likely to report noncompliance with their medication regiments (Grenard et al., 2011; Sin & DiMatteo, 2014; Tang et al., 2014). Yet, when these depressed individuals' self-reports of medication noncompliance were compared to pharmacy records, the correlation between depressive symptoms and treatment noncompliance while still significant, was reduced in comparison to what patients had indicated on self-report measures (Grenard et al., 2011). This finding may be a result of the negative cognitions, and feelings of low self-worth associated with depression. Others found no difference in treatment compliance between depressed and non-depressed individuals with chronic disease when objective ratings were used (Cukor, Rosenthal, Jindal, Brown, & Kimmel, 2009; Tang et al., 2014). These conflicting findings suggest that depressed patients may be more compliant with their medication regime than they realize.

The overestimation of treatment non-adherence may in some cases instigate a vicious circle in which negative appraisals of their prognosis and response to treatment may consequently contribute to their continued lack of motivation to comply with their ongoing treatment. Addressing this series of related and cumulative barriers to medication compliance is especially relevant to increasing positive response to treatment in patients living with chronic conditions where adherence to medication is critical for increasing longevity (Sin & DiMatteo, 2014).

Several studies have looked at the impact of depression treatment on medication adherence. Treatments that directly targeted depressive symptoms including CBT and treatment with antidepressant medication were found to be more effective in increasing treatment adherence than interventions that targeted general psychosocial support, with individual psychotherapy more effective in increasing treatment compliance than group-based interventions (Sin & DiMatteo, 2014). Other interventions focusing more on case management and individualized education for the management of type II diabetes mellitus, demonstrated success with improved adherence that resulted in lower hemoglobin A1C levels (an indication of diabetes control) and reduction in depressive symptoms compared to those in the control group which received usual care (Bogner, Morales, de Vries, & Cappola, 2012). These findings suggest that pragmatic, individualized interventions for increasing medication compliance in chronically ill individuals with depression may also be effective.

Poverty

Falling into poverty at any point during the life course increases an individual's risk of experiencing mental health problems, chronic illness, and early mortality (Callander, Schofield, & Shrestha, 2013; de Groot, Auslander, Williams, Sherraden, & Haire-Joshu, 2003; Gary-Webb et al., 2011; Mehta, 2016). While the serious consequences of acute onset of poverty on the mental health and illness status of older adults is in need of clinical attention (Lino, Portela, Camacho, Atie, & Lima, 2013; Mehta, 2016; Saito et al., 2014), there is a robust body of literature suggesting that experiencing poverty in childhood affects an individual's developmental trajectory in a manner that greatly increases their risk for both physical and mental illness, specifically depression throughout the life course (Evans, 2016, Wise, 2016). As a result, childhood poverty may have a greater impact on adult mental health and physical health status than experiencing poverty for the first time in adulthood.

Childhood poverty has been shown to predict higher incidences of cardiovascular disease, type II diabetes mellitus, respiratory conditions, osteoporosis, inflammation, and early mortality (Raphael, 2011, Wise, 2016). This marked increase in risk is directly related to the cumulative effects of combined biological, psychological and social factors in the child's ecology on development (Eamon, 2001). Early biological disruptions, which include food insufficiency, have been associated with increased risks of having a chronic disease as an adult (Raphael, 2011; Wise, 2016). The stress of living in poverty has been shown to increase the child's allostatic load. Chronic activation of the hypothalamic-pituitary-adrenal axis related to increases in allostatic load has been linked not only to depression and chronic inflammatory conditions (Evans, 2016, Wise, 2016).

The interaction of poverty and depression is particularly powerful in individuals with chronic health conditions. In fact, individuals with chronic illness are nearly seven times more likely to experience poverty than those who were not ill (Callander et al., 2013). Poverty can also negatively impact one's perception of their health, as was seen in a sample of patients with type II diabetes mellitus (Gary-Webb et al., 2011). Here, those with diabetes living in poverty reported increased perceptions of their limitations in the areas of physical functioning, social function, mental health functioning and overall vitality, compared to those not living in poverty. An important finding as self-perception of health is positively correlated with both psychological distress and health outcomes (Petrie & Weinman, 2012; Williams, Di Nardo, & Verma, 2017). Policies to address poverty are complicated and politically fraught. However, it is hard to imagine significant progress can be made in limiting depression, morbidity, and mortality among low-income individuals, without first addressing the root of the problem.

Implications for Research and Practice

Clinically relevant depressive disorders continue to be underdiagnosed and undertreated. Underdiagnosis is likely related to stigma, a fragmented health care system, and lack of access and resources among underserved communities. The diagnosis and management of depression are frequently left to primary care providers who often are not sufficiently trained, and carry heavy caseloads of complex patients, leaving little time to address what many do not consider a high priority. As the evidence supporting the relationship between depression and longevity grows, it is increasingly important that we move towards action. Action in training health care providers on diagnosis, on evidence-based treatment, and on the consequences of continuing to underdiagnose and undertreat. Action on funding research that focuses on the better understanding of the biological underpinnings and consequences of depression, along with evidence-based treatments that may have a positive impact on morbidity and mortality. For many, the simple act of identifying and sufficiently managing depression maybe enough to improve health outcomes. For others, it may be necessary to target individual risk factors or continue to tailor more directly, and study, interventions to more specifically address the shared complications of depression and chronic illness, such as sleep, loneliness, and inflammation.

Conclusions

Depression is common and costly, with far-reaching impacts on our health care system and society. Only in recent years are we beginning to explore and understand the complex nature of depression, and its relationship to chronic disease and longevity. As researchers continue to study the many facets of depression, and their impact on health, the ultimate goal will be to have a clear picture of who is at risk, how can that risk be mitigated, and when that is not possible, how might clinician's best manage depression as to improve quality of life and limit the negative impact it currently has on health and longevity.

References

Abosi, O., Lopes, S., Schmitz, S., & Fiedorowicz, J. G. (2018). Cardiometabolic effects of psychotropic medications. *Hormone Molecular Biology and Clin Investigation*. doi:10.1515/hmbci-2017-0065.

APA. (2013). *Diagnostic and statistical manual of mental disorders* (5th ed.). Arlington, VA: American Psychiatric Publishing.

Arem, H., Moore, S. C., Patel, A., Hartge, P., de Gonzalez, A. B., Visvanathan, K., . . . Matthews, C. E. (2015). Leisure time physical activity and mortality: A detailed pooled analysis of the dose-response relationship. *JAMA Internal Medicine, 175*(6), 959-967. doi:10.1001/jamainternmed.2015.0533.

Armstrong, N. M., Carlson, M. C., Xue, Q. L., Schrack, J., Carnethon, M. R., Chaves, P. H. M., & Gross, A. L. (2017). Role of late-life depression in the association of subclinical cardiovascular disease with all-cause mortality: Cardiovascular health study. *Journal of Aging Health*, 898264317744921. doi:10.1177/0898264317744921.

Aylaz, R., Akturk, U., Erci, B., Ozturk, H., & Aslan, H. (2012). Relationship between depression and loneliness in elderly and examination of influential factors. *Archives of* Gerontology *and Geriatrics, 55*(3), 548-554. doi:10.1016/j.archger.2012.03.006.

Berkman, L. F., & Syme, S. L. (1979). Social networks, host resistance, and mortality: a nine-year follow-up study of Alameda County residents. *American Journal Epidemiology, 109*(2), 186-204.

Bertisch, S. M., Pollock, B. D., Mittleman, M. A., Buysse, D. J., Bazzano, L. A., Gottlieb, D. J., & Redline, S. (2018). Insomnia with objective short sleep duration and risk of incident cardiovascular disease and all-cause mortality: Sleep heart health study. *Sleep*. doi:10.1093/sleep/zsy047.

Bogner, H. R., Morales, K. H., de Vries, H. F., & Cappola, A. R. (2012). Integrated management of type 2 diabetes mellitus and depression treatment to improve medication adherence: a randomized controlled trial. *Annals of Family Medicine 10*(1), 15-22. doi:10.1370/afm.1344.

Brasure, M., Fuchs, E., MacDonald, R., Nelson, V. A., Koffel, E., Olson, C. M., . . . Kane, R. L. (2016). Psychological and behavioral interventions for managing insomnia disorder: An evidence report for a clinical practice guideline by the American College of Physicians. *Annals of Internal Medicine, 165*(2), 113-124. doi:10.7326/M15-1782.

Cacioppo, J. T., Hawkley, L. C., Crawford, L. E., Ernst, J. M., Burleson, M. H., Kowalewski, R. B., . . . Berntson, G. G. (2002). Loneliness and health: potential mechanisms. *Psychosomatic Medicine, 64*(3), 407-417.

Callander, E. J., Schofield, D. J., & Shrestha, R. N. (2013). Chronic health conditions and poverty: a cross-sectional study using a multidimensional poverty measure. *BMJ Open, 3*(11), e003397. doi:10.1136/bmjopen-2013-003397.

Carter, S. J., Hunter, G. R., Norian, L. A., Turan, B., & Rogers, L. Q. (2017). Ease of walking associates with greater free-living physical activity and reduced depressive symptomology in breast cancer survivors: pilot randomized trial. *Support Care Cancer.* doi:10.1007/s00520-017-4015-y.

CDC. *Alcohol and Public Health: Alcohol related disease impact.* Retrieved from https://nccd.cdc.gov/DPH_ARDI/Default/Default.aspx.

CDC. (2017). *Health effects of cigarette smoking.* Retrieved from https://www.cdc.gov/tobacco/data_statistics/fact_sheets/health_effects/effects_cig_smoking/index.htm.

Colton, C. W., & Manderscheid, R. W. (2006). Congruencies in increased mortality rates, years of potential life lost, and causes of death among public mental health clients in eight states. *Preventing Chronic Disease, 3*(2), A42.

Committee, P. A. G. A. (2008). *Physical activity guidelines advisory committee report.* Washington, D.C.

Cuijpers, P., Berking, M., Andersson, G., Quigley, L., Kleiboer, A., & Dobson, K. S. (2013). A meta-analysis of cognitive-behavioural therapy for adult depression, alone and in comparison with other treatments. *Canadian Journal of Psychiatry, 58*(7), 376-385. doi:10.1177/070674371305800702.

Cukor, D., Rosenthal, D. S., Jindal, R. M., Brown, C. D., & Kimmel, P. L. (2009). Depression is an important contributor to low medication adherence in hemodialyzed patients and transplant recipients. *Kidney International, 75*(11), 1223-1229. doi:10.1038/ki.2009.51.

de Beaurepaire, R. (2002). Questions raised by the cytokine hypothesis of depression. *Brain, Behavior, and Immunity, 16*(5), 610-617. doi:https://doi.org/10.1016/S0889-1591(02)00005-3.

de Groot, M., Auslander, W., Williams, J. H., Sherraden, M., & Haire-Joshu, D. (2003). Depression and poverty among African American women at risk for type 2 diabetes.*Annals of Behavioral Medicine, 25*(3), 172-181. doi:10.1207/S15324796ABM2503_03.

DiMatteo, M. R. (2004). Variations in patients' adherence to medical recommendations: a quantitative review of 50 years of research. *Medical Care, 42*(3), 200-209.

Doering, L. V., Cross, R., Vredevoe, D., Martinez-Maza, O., & Cowan, M. J. (2007). Infection, depression, and immunity in women after coronary artery bypass: a pilot study of cognitive behavioral therapy. *Altneratives Therapies in Health and Medicine, 13*(3), 18-21.

Donovan, N. J., Wu, Q., Rentz, D. M., Sperling, R. A., Marshall, G. A., & Glymour, M. M. (2017). Loneliness, depression and cognitive function in older U.S. adults. *International Journal of Geriatric Psychiatry. 32*(5), 564-573. doi:10.1002/gps.4495.

Dupre, M. E., Nelson, A., Lynch, S. M., Granger, B. B., Xu, H., Churchill, E., . . . Peterson, E. D. (2017). Socioeconomic, psychosocial and behavioral characteristics of patients hospitalized with cardiovascular disease. *The American Journal of the Medical Sciences, 354*(6), 565-572. doi:10.1016/j.amjms.2017.07.011.

Eamon, M. (2001). The effects of poverty on children's socioemotional development: An ecological systems analysis. *Social Work, 46*(3), 256-266. doi:10.1093/sw/46.3.256.

Evans, G. W. (2016). Childhood poverty and adult psychological well-being. *Proceedings of the Nattonal Academies of Sciences U S A, 113*(52), 14949-14952. doi:10.1073/pnas.1604756114.

Gary-Webb, T. L., Baptiste-Roberts, K., Pham, L., Wesche-Thobaben, J., Patricio, J., Pi-Sunyer, F. X., . . . Look, A. R. G. (2011). Neighborhood socioeconomic status, depression, and health status in the Look AHEAD (Action for Health in Diabetes) study. *BMC Public Health, 11*, 349. doi:10.1186/1471-2458-11-349.

Gibson, A. M., Muggeridge, D. J., Hughes, A. R., Kelly, L., & Kirk, A. (2017). An examination of objectively-measured sedentary behavior and mental well-being in adults across week days and weekends. *PLoS One, 12*(9), e0185143. doi:10.1371/journal.pone.0185143.

Gonzalez, J. S., Peyrot, M., McCarl, L. A., Collins, E. M., Serpa, L., Mimiaga, M. J., & Safren, S. A. (2008). Depression and diabetes treatment nonadherence: a meta-analysis. *Diabetes Care, 31*(12), 2398-2403. doi:10.2337/dc08-1341.

Greenberg, P. E., Fournier, A. A., Sisitsky, T., Pike, C. T., & Kessler, R. C. (2015). The economic burden of adults with major depressive disorder in the United States (2005 and 2010). *Journal of Clinical Psychiatry, 76*(2), 155-162. doi:10.4088/JCP.14m09298.

Grenard, J. L., Munjas, B. A., Adams, J. L., Suttorp, M., Maglione, M., McGlynn, E. A., & Gellad, W. F. (2011). Depression and medication adherence in the treatment of chronic diseases in the United States: a meta-analysis. *Journal of General Internal Medicine, 26*(10), 1175-1182. doi:10.1007/s11606-011-1704-y.

Havranek, E. P., Mujahid, M. S., Barr, D. A., Blair, I. V., Cohen, M. S., Cruz-Flores, S., . . . Stroke, C. (2015). Social Determinants of Risk and Outcomes for Cardiovascular Disease: A Scientific Statement From the American Heart Association. *Circulation, 132*(9), 873-898. doi:10.1161/CIR.0000000000000228.

Hidese, S., Asano, S., Saito, K., Sasayama, D., & Kunugi, H. (2018). Association of depression with body mass index classification, metabolic disease, and lifestyle: A web-based survey involving 11,876 Japanese people. *Journal of Psychiatroc Research, 102*, 23-28. doi:10.1016/j.jpsychires.2018.02.009.

Hijmans, J., Diehl, K., Bammert, T., Kavlich, P., Lincenberg, G., Greiner, J., Stauffer, B., & DeSouza, C. (2018). Influence of Overweight and Obesity on Circulating InflammationRelated Microrna. *MicroRNA, 7*. doi:https://doi.org/10.2174/2211536607666180402120806.

Holt-Lunstad, J., & Smith, T. B. (2016). Loneliness and social isolation as risk factors for CVD: implications for evidence-based patient care and scientific inquiry. *Heart, 102*(13), 987-989. doi:10.1136/heartjnl-2015-309242.

Isometsa, E. (2014). Suicidal behaviour in mood disorders--who, when, and why? *Canadian Journal of Psychiatry, 59*(3), 120-130. doi:10.1177/070674371405900303.

Jang, H. Y., Song, Y.-K., Kim, J. H., Kim, M. G., Han, N., Lee, H.-Y., . . . Oh, J. M. (2018). Impact of depression on change in coronary heart disease risk status: the Korean Genome and Epidemiology Study (KoGES). *Therapeutics and Clinical Risk Management, 14*, 121-128. doi:10.2147/TCRM.S149501.

Javaheri, S., & Redline, S. (2017). Insomnia and risk of cardiovascular disease. *Chest, 152*(2), 435-444. doi:10.1016/j.chest.2017.01.026.

Johnston, L., O'Malley, P., & Bachman, J. (2000). *National survey results on drug use from the monitoring the future study. 1975-1999.*

Kent, L. K., & Shapiro, P. A. (2009). Depression and related psychological factors in heart disease. *Harvard Review of Psychiatry (Taylor & Francis Ltd), 17*(6), 377-388. doi:10.3109/10673220903463333.

Koffel, E., Bramoweth, A. D., & Ulmer, C. S. (2018). Increasing access to and utilization of cognitive behavioral therapy for insomnia (CBT-I): A narrative review. *Journal of General Internal Medicine.* doi:10.1007/s11606-018-4390-1.

Kujala, U. M., Kaprio, J., Sarna, S., & Koskenvuo, M. (1998). Relationship of leisure-time physical activity and mortality: The Finnish twin cohort. *Journal of the American Medical Association, 279*(6), 440-444.

Kuwahara, K., Honda, T., Nakagawa, T., Yamamoto, S., Hayashi, T., & Mizoue, T. (2018). Intensity of leisure-time exercise and risk of depressive symptoms among Japanese workers: A cohort study. *Journal of Epidemiology, 28*(2), 94-98. doi:10.2188/jea.JE20170009.

Lariscy, J. T., Hummer, R. A., Rath, J. M., Villanti, A. C., Hayward, M. D., & Vallone, D. M. (2013). Race/ethnicity, mativity, and tobacco use among U.S. young adults: Results from a nationally representative survey. *Nicotine & Tobacco Research, 15*(8), 1417-1426. doi:10.1093/ntr/nts344.

Lean, M., Leslie, W., Barnes, A., Brosnahan, N., Thom, G., McCombie, L., Peters, C., Zhzhneuskaya, S., Al-Mrabeh, A., Hollingsworth, K., Rodrigues, A., Rehackova, L., Adamson, A., Sniehotta, F., Mathers, J., Ross, H., McIlvenna, Y., Stefanetti, R., Trenell, M., Welsh, P., Kean, S., Ford, I., McConnachie, A., Sattar, N., & Taylor, R. (2018). Primary care-led weight management for remission of type 2 diabetes (DiRECT): An open-label, cluster-randomised trial. *Lancet, 391*(10120), 541-551. doi:https://doi.org/10.1016/S0140-6736(17)33102-1.

Lino, V. T., Portela, M. C., Camacho, L. A., Atie, S., & Lima, M. J. (2013). Assessment of social support and its association to depression, self-perceived health and chronic diseases in elderly individuals residing in an area of poverty and social vulnerability in Rio de Janeiro City, Brazil. *PLoS One, 8*(8), e71712. doi:10.1371/journal.pone.0071712.

Lobelo, F., Rohm Young, D., Sallis, R., Garber, M. D., Billinger, S. A., Duperly, J., . . . Joy, E. A. (2018). Routine Assessment and Promotion of Physical Activity in Healthcare Settings: A Scientific Statement From the American Heart Association. *Circulation*. doi:10.1161/CIR.0000000000000559.

Locatelli, L., & Golay, A. (2018). Psychotropic drugs and weight. *Revue Medicale Suisse, 14*(599), 605-609.

Lopresti, A. L. (2017). Cognitive behaviour therapy and inflammation: A systematic review of its relationship and the potential implications for the treatment of depression. *Austrlain New Zealand Journal of Psychiatry, 51*(6), 565-582. doi:10.1177/0004867417701996.

Loprinzi, P. D., & Joyner, C. (2018). Meeting sleep guidelines is associated with better health-related quality of life and reduced premature all-cause mortality risk. *American Journal of Health Promotion, 32*(1), 68-71. doi:10.1177/0890117116687459.

Luo, Y., Hawkley, L., Waite, L., & Cacioppo, J. (2012). Loneliness, health, and mortality in old age: A national longitudinal study. *Social Science Medicine, 74*(6), 907-914. doi:10.1016/j.socscimed.2011.11.028.

Luppino, F. S., de Wit, L. M., Bouvy, P. F., Stijnen, T., Cuijpers, P., Penninx, B. W., & Zitman, F. G. (2010). Overweight, obesity, and depression: a systematic review and meta-analysis of longitudinal studies. *Archives of General Psychiatry, 67*(3), 220-229. doi:10.1001/archgenpsychiatry.2010.2.

Mehta, C. D., A.; Kakrani, V.; Bhawalkar, J. (2016). Economic dependency and depression in elderly. *Journal of Krishna Institute of Medical Sciences University, 5*(1), 100-109.

Mills, J. C., Pence, B. W., Todd, J. V., Bengtson, A. M., Breger, T. L., Edmonds, A., . . . Adimora, A. A. (2018). Cumulative burden of fepression and all-cause mortality in women living with HIV. *Clinical Infectious Diseases*. doi:10.1093/cid/ciy264.

Munjiza, A., Kostic, M., Pesic, D., Gajic, M., Markovic, I., & Tosevski, D. L. (2018). Higher concentration of interleukin 6 - A possible link between major depressive disorder and childhood abuse. *Psychiatry Research, 264*, 26-30. doi:10.1016/j.psychres.2018.03.072.

Murri, M. B., Ekkekakis, P., Menchetti, M., Neviani, F., Trevisani, F., Tedeschi, S., . . . Amore, M. (2018). Physical exercise for late-life depression: Effects on symptom dimensions and time course. *Journal of Affective Disorders, 230*, 65-70. doi:10.1016/j.jad.2018.01.004.

Myrskyla, M., & Chang, V. W. (2009). Weight change, initial BMI, and mortality among middle- and older-aged adults. *Epidemiology, 20*(6), 840-848. doi:10.1097/EDE.0b013e3181b5f520.

NIDA. (2010). *Comorbidity: Addiction and other mental illnesses*. Retrieved from https://www.drugabuse.gov/sites/default/files/rrcomorbidity.pdf.

NIMH. (2017). Major Depression. Retrieved from https://www.nimh.nih.gov/health/statistics/major-depression.shtml

O'Toole, M. S., Bovbjerg, D. H., Renna, M. E., Lekander, M., Mennin, D. S., & Zachariae, R. (2018). Effects of psychological interventions on systemic levels of inflammatory biomarkers in humans: A systematic review and meta-analysis. *Brain Behavor Immunity*. doi:10.1016/j.bbi.2018.04.005.

Paolucci, E. M., Loukov, D., Bowdish, D. M. E., & Heisz, J. J. Exercise reduces depression and inflammation but intensity matters. *Biological Psychology*. doi:https://doi.org/10.1016/j.biopsycho.2018.01.015

Perissinotto, C. M., Cenzer, I. S., & Covinsky, K. E. (2012). Loneliness in older persons: A predictor of functional decline and death. *Archives of Internal Medicine, 172*(14), 1078-1083. doi:10.1001/archinternmed.2012.1993.

Petrie, K. J., & Weinman, J. (2012). Patients' Perceptions of Their Illness:The Dynamo of Volition in Health Care. *Current Directions in Psychological Science, 21*(1), 60-65. doi:10.1177/0963721411429456.

Poole, L., & Jackowska, M. (2017). The epidemiology of depressive symptoms and poor sleep: findings from the English longitudinal study of ageing (ELSA). *Internal Journal of Behavioral Medicine*. doi:10.1007/s12529-017-9703-y.

Raphael, D. (2011). Poverty in childhood and adverse health outcomes in adulthood. *Maturitas, 69*(1), 22-26. doi:10.1016/j.maturitas.2011.02.011.

Richards, S. H., Anderson, L., Jenkinson, C. E., Whalley, B., Rees, K., Davies, P., . . . Taylor, R. S. (2017). Psychological interventions for coronary heart disease. *Cochrane Database Systematic Reviews, 4*, CD002902. doi:10.1002/14651858.CD002902.pub4.

Rost, S., Freuer, D., Peters, A., Thorand, B., Holle, R., Linseisen, J., & Meisinger, C. (2018). New indexes of body fat distribution and sex-specific risk of total and cause-specific mortality: a prospective cohort study. *BMC Public Health, 18*(1), 427. doi:10.1186/s12889-018-5350-8.

Roy, A., Govindan, R., & Kesavan, M. (2018). The impact of an add-on video assisted structured aerobic exercise module on mood and somatic symptoms among women with depressive disorders: study from a tertiary care centre in India. *Asian Journal of Psychiatry*. doi:https://doi.org/10.1016/j.ajp.2017.12.004.

Saito, M., Kondo, K., Kondo, N., Abe, A., Ojima, T., Suzuki, K., & group, J. (2014). Relative deprivation, poverty, and subjective health: JAGES cross-sectional study. *PLoS One, 9*(10), e111169. doi:10.1371/journal.pone.0111169.

Sands-Lincoln, M., Loucks, E. B., Lu, B., Carskadon, M. A., Sharkey, K., Stefanick, M. L., . . . Eaton, C. B. (2013). Sleep duration, insomnia, and coronary heart disease among postmenopausal women in the Women's Health Initiative. *Journal of Womens Health (Larchmt), 22*(6), 477-486. doi:10.1089/jwh.2012.3918.

Sin, N. L., & DiMatteo, M. R. (2014). Depression treatment enhances adherence to antiretroviral therapy: a meta-analysis. *Annals of Behavioral Medicine, 47*(3), 259-269. doi:10.1007/s12160-013-9559-6.

Sørensen, T. I. A., Rissanen, A., Korkeila, M., & Kaprio, J. (2005). Intention to lose weight, weight changes, and 18-y Mortality in Overweight Individuals without co-morbidities. *PLoS Medicine, 2*(6), e171. doi:10.1371/journal.pmed.0020171.

Statistics, N. C. f. H. (2017). *Health, United States, 2016: With chartbook on longterm trends in health*. Hyattsville, MD Retrieved from https://www.cdc.gov/nchs/data/hus/hus16.pdf#015.

Strasser, B., Volaklis, K., Fuchs, D., & Burtscher, M. (2018). Role of dietary protein and muscular fitness on longevity and aging. *Aging Disorders, 9*(1), 119-132. doi:10.14336/AD.2017.0202.

Tang, H. Y., Sayers, S. L., Weissinger, G., & Riegel, B. (2014). The role of depression in medication adherence among heart failure patients. *Clinical Nursing Reearchs, 23*(3), 231-244. doi:10.1177/1054773813481801.

Taylor, G., McNeill, A., Girling, A., Farley, A., Lindson-Hawley, N., & Aveyard, P. (2014). Change in mental health after smoking cessation: systematic review and meta-analysis. *BMJ, 348*, g1151. doi:10.1136/bmj.g1151.

Teo, A., Marsh, H., Forsberg, C., Nicolaidis, C., Chen, J., Newsom, J., Saha, S., & Dobscha, S. (2018). Loneliness is closely associated with depression outcomes and suicidal ideation among military veterans in primary care. *Journal of Affective Disorders, 230*, 42-49. doi:https://doi.org/10.1016/j.jad.2018.01.003.

Theeke, L. A., & Mallow, J. A. (2015). The development of LISTEN: A movel intervention for loneliness. *Open Journal of Nursing, 5*(2), 136-143. doi:10.4236/ojn.2015.52016.

Thompson, P. D., Buchner, D., Pina, I. L., Balady, G. J., Williams, M. A., Marcus, B. H., . . . Metabolism Subcommittee on Physical, A. (2003). Exercise and physical activity in the prevention and treatment of atherosclerotic cardiovascular disease: a statement from the Council on Clinical Cardiology (Subcommittee on Exercise, Rehabilitation, and Prevention) and the Council on Nutrition, Physical Activity, and Metabolism (Subcommittee on Physical Activity). *Circulation, 107*(24), 3109-3116. doi:10.1161/01.CIR.0000075572.40158.77.

Walker, E. R., McGee, R. E., & Druss, B. G. (2015). Mortality in mental disorders and global disease burden implications: a systematic review and meta-analysis. *JAMA Psychiatry, 72*(4), 334-341. doi:10.1001/jamapsychiatry.2014.2502.

Whooley, M. A. (2006). Depression and cardiovascular disease: Healing the broken-hearted. *JAMA : The Journal of the American Medical Association, 295*(24), 2874-2881. doi:10.1001/jama.295.24.2874.

Wiklund, T., Linton, S. J., Alfoldi, P., & Gerdle, B. (2018). Is sleep disturbance in patients with chronic pain affected by physical exercise or ACT-based stress management? - A randomized controlled study. *BMC Musculoskelet Disord, 19*(1), 111. doi:10.1186/s12891-018-2020-z.

Williams, G., Di Nardo, F., & Verma, A. (2017). The relationship between self-reported health status and signs of psychological distress within European urban contexts. *European Journal of Public Health, 27*(suppl_2), 68-73. doi:10.1093/eurpub/ckx008.

Wise, L. A., Adams-Campbell, L. L., Palmer, J. R., & Rosenberg, L. (2006). Leisure time physical activity in relation to depressive symptoms in the Black Women's Health Study. *Annals of Behavioral Medicine, 32*(1), 68-76. doi:10.1207/s15324796abm3201_8.

Wise, P. H. (2016). Child poverty and the promise of human capacity: Childhood as a foundation for healthy aging. *Academic Pediatrics, 16*(3 Suppl), S37-45. doi:10.1016/j.acap.2016.01.014.

Wu, J. Q., Appleman, E. R., Salazar, R. D., & Ong, J. C. (2015). Cognitive behavioral therapy for insomnia comorbid with psychiatric and medical conditions: A meta-analysis. *JAMA Internal Medicine, 175*(9), 1461-1472. doi:10.1001/jamainternmed.2015.3006.

Wurtman, J., & Wurtman, R. (2017). The trajectory from mood to obesity. *Curent Obesity Reports.* doi:10.1007/s13679-017-0291-6.

Yang, L., Korhonen, K., Moustgaard, H., Silventoinen, K., & Martikainen, P. (2018). Pre-existing depression predicts survival in cardiovascular disease and cancer. *Journal of Epidemioligy Community Health.* doi:10.1136/jech-2017-210206.

Young, J. J., Bruno, D., & Pomara, N. (2014). A review of the relationship between proinflammatory cytokines and major depressive disorder. *Journal of Affective Disorders, 169*, 15-20. doi:10.1016/j.jad.2014.07.032.

Zivin, K., Yosef, M., Miller, E. M., Valenstein, M., Duffy, S., Kales, H. C., . . . Kim, H. M. (2015). Associations between depression and all-cause and cause-specific risk of death: a retrospective cohort study in the Veterans Health Administration. *The Journal of Psychosomatic Research, 78*(4), 324-331. doi:10.1016/j.jpsychores.2015.01.014.

Zivin, K., Ilgen, M. A., Pfeiffer, P. N., Welsh, D. E., McCarthy, J., Valenstein, M., ... & Kales, H. C. (2012). Early mortality and years of potential life lost among veterans affairs patients with depression. *Psychiatric Services, 63*(8), 823-826.

The Immune System in the Golden Years

Nalini Kalanadhabhatta and Vivekananda Kalanadhabhatta

Introduction

In the last 100 years, we have seen tremendous advances in science and medicine. We can diagnose and care for chronic illnesses earlier and more effectively than ever before. We have also seen improved health literacy and education via social media with more understanding of the importance of diet, exercise, and smoking cessation. Consequently, the life span of both men and women has been extended. A much larger proportion of people are living into their eighties and nineties, and many centenarians as well.

Longevity requires that we have an immune system that continues to protect us and help us to age in an environment that is constantly changing around us. Jet travel takes us to more places than ever before, exposing us to new microbes and ecosystems that challenge our immune system.

In order to understand how the human immune system works, it is helpful to have a historical perspective. Over millions of years the immune system has evolved from a simple, primitive barrier protection to a complex precisely regulated system involving a cells, proteins, and soluble molecules such as cytokines (messengers that communicate and influence the function of cells).

This chapter reviews:

1. The various components of the innate and adaptive immune system
2. Functions of normal immune system
3. Consequences of dysregulation and its role in disease susceptibility as it pertains to the elderly.

Readers should be aware that this review is meant to enhance their knowledge of the human immune system and that no individual recommendations can be made. The reader should consult their own physician for specific recommendations. Let us now look at the organs, cells and other molecules that play a major role in the body's defense.

Evolution of the Immune System

The immune system is divided into innate and adaptive immunity. Innate refers to the initial line of defense that is present at birth. In its most primitive form, it can be providing a physical and chemical barrier function. Intact skin is a great example of a physical barrier. It serves as an impenetrable barrier to a variety of viruses, bacteria and toxins. We are all too familiar with cuts, wounds or other skin diseases that lead to a breakdown of this barrier and makes us vulnerable to infections. Chemical barriers include hydrochloric acid in our stomach and other antibacterial substances in our body fluids, such as tears and saliva.

The Cells and Soluble Molecules of the Innate Immune System

In order to provide an initial line of defense, the innate immune system must be able to recognize a broad spectrum of microbes and differentiate them from our own cells. There are several molecules and surface receptors that are present on bacteria, for example, that are not present on human cells. Many of these are essential for survival of the organism and hence are preserved through evolution. The innate cells take advantage of this fact through a variety of receptors (known as pattern recognition receptors) that recognize these microbes and use a variety of mechanisms to eliminate them before they can cause disease.

The blood contains white and red blood cells. Some white blood cells can literally swallow and digest microbes (a process called phagocytosis), killing them in the process. These white blood cells include neutrophils (also called polymorphonuclear leukocytes), monocytes and tissue macrophages. These cells internalize and kill the microbes inside specialized spaces with enzymes and oxidative mechanisms. Some cells, called natural killer cells, directly attack and kill virally infected body cells with enzymes and receptors.

Another interesting component of the innate immune system is the complement system. It is so named because it augments the activity of phagocytes and antibodies in killing microbes through the activation of the membrane attack complex that create holes in pathogen cell membranes and calling on phagocytes to clear the debris. There are some microbes that cannot be killed without the help of complement, such as one type of bacteria that can cause meningitis.

The complement system has more than twenty-five proteins that are produced mainly in the liver and many receptors that help with phagocytosis. These proteins also help dilate blood vessels at infection or injury sites so that immune cells can travel to tissues to fight microbes. This blood vessel dilation and immune cell extravasation is part of a process known as inflammation, but more on this later.

Why Do We Need an Adaptive Immune System?

As a first-line of defense, the innate immune system is very effective at fighting everyday invaders whenever they breach our physical and chemical defenses. However, it lacks specificity and memory, requiring other components to fight more complex invaders. This type immunity is carried out by a subset of white blood cells known as lymphocytes. Any substance that can trigger an immune response is called an antigen. It can be a bacterium, virus, toxin, or foreign tissue, as in organ transplant.

The immune system learns to identify an invader by noting certain distinctive characteristics, usually small parts of the antigen. One can think of this as being like fingerprint or retinal scan that is commonly used by law enforcement agencies to identify criminals. Using these distinctive characteristics, the adaptive immune system can respond by creating and mobilizing its different lymphocytes and their components, which is known as specificity.

Some of these lymphocytes that are active in this immune response are stored away as memory cells. These memory cells can respond more quickly, efficiently, and robustly in subsequent encounters with the same antigen. We maximize our immune system response with vaccinations, increasing their ability to respond to those antigens. Those that are vaccinated can recognize and respond to those invaders and better fight infection than those who are not vaccinated. Thus, the adaptive immune system learns to recognize danger, has specific memory and responds better with repeated encounter by the same antigen.

The lymphocytes that carry out the above functions are of two types, T cells and B cells. B lymphocytes produce antibodies when they are transformed into plasma cells by substances secreted by T cells. There are trillions of T and B cells to respond all different antigens that a person encounters during his or her lifetime. Each of these cells respond only to one antigen (Specificity) and can multiply during an immune response to amplify the force of the attack. Since we have such many cells we can virtually respond to every antigen in our environment.

B cells produce different type of antibodies that have different functions: Immunoglobulin G and M fight microbes in blood; Immunoglobulin A protect mucosal surfaces, such as the gastrointestinal tract or respiratory tract, against invaders; Immunoglobulin E plays a role in allergic diseases, like hay fever, allergies, asthma, and eczema. Antibodies attach to outer coat of pathogens, tagging them for ingestion and destruction by phagocytes.

T cells are the orchestrators of the immune response. We can think of T cells as the "conductors" of an immune orchestra, who direct all the other players, or components, to perform together in harmony. Thus, T cells could initiate, conduct, perpetuate, and terminate the immune response for efficient elimination of threat and concurrently protect our own body tissues from harmful effects. T cells are also vital for immune response against viruses, bacteria that live exclusively within our cells, and malignant cells, all of which are usually out of reach for antibodies. These T cells can activate programmed mechanisms within the cell, leading to their destruction.

T and B cells undergo extensive education in thymus and various mucosal lymphoid tissues respectively. They are taught to distinguish "self" from "non-self," or invader. Under normal circumstances, the "self" is protected from attack while pathogens are destroyed. While this is beneficial for most of us, there are select circumstances under which we need to suppress the immune system's destructive ability. In organ transplants, e.g. kidney, heart, liver, patients are given immunosuppressive medications to prevent organ rejection. These medications prevent the immune system from attacking the donor, or foreign, organ, leading to its rejection.

The different parts of the innate and adaptive immune systems do not act in isolation. They co-operate and coordinate to fine tune the response, to protect us from invading antigens and maintain homeostasis and overall well-being. Last but not the least, immune cells are not stationary but are circulating all over the body, surveying and collecting information about invaders. This process is known as immune surveillance. It is very important to detect not only foreign invaders but also recognize cells that are transforming into cancer. This function is diminished when people suffer from immune deficiency from diseases such as HIV and antibody deficiency, making these patients more vulnerable to developing infections and malignancy.

The Elderly: Chronology or Biology

Aging is inevitable. However, not all individuals age to the same degree despite exposure to similar conditions. While we are not clear what exactly drives this process, we do know that aging is influenced by genetics, environmental factors, and learned behaviors. In this context, chronologic age is time dependent while biologic age is influenced by genetics, environmental factors, and lifestyle choices. So, while aging cannot be prevented, it can be ameliorated.

Centenarians represent the best among the elderly in terms of biologic age. They have well preserved functional status well into their eighties and nineties, including their immune systems.

Contrary to popular belief, the aging process begins quite early in life, in the post pubertal years. It is a very slow process and occurs at variable rates throughout life. The genetic influences that dictate this process are probably related to inherited gene variations (genetic polymorphisms). Some such polymorphisms may make an individual less susceptible to disease and decline in organ function so that they may be able to survive to their maximum lifespan.

Beyond the genetic influences on aging, there are environmental factors, such as infections, accidents, and ionizing radiation exposures, as well as behavioral components, such as lifestyle choices, diet, exercise, smoking, and drug use. This category is under our control to an extent. By choosing a healthier lifestyle, one may be able to postpone biologic aging.

Immunosenescence

Immunosenescence refers to the aging of the immune system, both the innate and adaptive components.

In the innate immune system, immunosenescence results in decreased function of phagocytes and natural killer cells that make the elderly susceptible to infections and increased incidence of malignancy. At the same time, there is an imbalance between oxidative and anti-oxidative (redox status) of immune cells that reduces their lifespan and leads to decreased function in the surviving cells.

The T cell pool in the body is influenced by a constant supply of naive (new) cells. T cells are produced in the bone marrow and are transported to the thymus (a gland in the neck, hence the name thymus-derived, or T cells), where they are educated about self and non-self. From puberty into our seventies, the thymus is slowly replaced by fat tissue until only a small amount of thymic tissue is found. This leads to a gradual depletion in the supply of naive cells. Without naive cells, the body is unable to combat new antigens encountered later in life. Mature T cells are those that have already encountered antigens early in life and are still present as long-lived memory cells. These memory cells are still able to mount a response to familiar antigens but cannot combat new antigens. In addition to T cells, antibody production by B-cells is also not as robust as in young individuals, making responses to vaccination less optimal in the elderly.

Consequences of Immunosenescence

The aging of the immune system makes the elderly susceptible to infections, increases organ damage due to chronic inflammation and autoimmunity, and increases the incidence of malignancy. Now let us examine these in more detail.

A) Infections

Pneumonia and influenza (responsible for the flu) are some of the leading causes of disability and death in the elderly. This population is more vulnerable because they have concurrent illnesses, such as diabetes, lung disease, heart disease, liver disease, and kidney disease. In addition to being more susceptible than younger adults, they are also more likely to be hospitalized with prolonged convalescence if they survive. Survival often leads to frailty, organ function deterioration, and an inability to perform simple activities of daily living. The resulting frailty makes individuals vulnerable to falls and serious injuries, such as hip fractures or head injuries, from minor insults in the future and further deterioration. This cycle of illness and minor recovery leads to a progression decline in functional status and overall health.

Although their responses to vaccinations are not as good as younger adults, vaccination reduces morbidity and mortality in the elderly. Therefore, we need to improve the vaccination rates in the elderly to prevent infection from pneumococcal disease, influenza, and herpes zoster.

B) Inflammation

Immune homeostasis is maintained by a balance between pro-inflammatory and anti-inflammatory influences.

Inflammation refers to an injured tissue or organ that has an increased temperature and becomes swollen and red, resulting in pain and decreased in functional ability. Think of someone with a sore throat from an infection. The individual experiences fever, throat pain or has pain while swallowing. This acute inflammation is a beneficial process to contain and/or eliminate infection while repairing the damaged tissue.

Although short-term or acute inflammation is good for the individual, chronic inflammation is harmful. When the immune system must contain chronic infection or attacks the body's own tissues, pro-inflammatory mediators sustain inflammation over prolonged periods of time, which can damage organs and tissues, such as in atherosclerosis or arthritis. Atherosclerosis begins as inflammation of the arteries with gradual narrowing that results in diminished blood supply to the affected organ. When the arteries do not bring enough nutrients to the tissues they supply, it may result in cell death within that organ system. Some well-known examples include heart attacks and strokes.

Despite decreased ability to ingest and destroy harmful microbes, many cells of the innate immune system increase secretion of pro-inflammatory mediators as we age. The elderly has markers of chronic inflammation such as a rise in c-reactive protein and erythrocyte sedimentation rate. Such chronic inflammation results in accelerated disease progression in the elderly.

C) Autoimmunity

Autoimmunity occurs when our own immune system attacks our own cells (self). This can be organ specific or nonspecific, such as the thyroid and in rheumatoid arthritis, respectively. T cells learn not to attack self in the thymus. In the thymic environment, they are brought in contact with every conceivable body tissue and are familiarized with these (Self) cells. Those cells that show excessive or destructive activity against the body's own cells are killed, and only a small portion that recognize our own body tissues and react favorably will be released into the bloodstream. A similar process happens to antibody-producing B cells in lymphoid organs, such as tonsils and lymph nodes.

Unfortunately, this system is not perfect, and some cells escape this protective mechanism, causing autoimmunity under some circumstances. It is conceivable that almost all of us have auto-reactive cells, but only a few of us develop autoimmune diseases. Thus, having autoimmune cells in and of itself is not enough for disease, and many other factors are necessary to develop autoimmunity. Currently there are several antibody-based therapies that are being used to treat autoimmune diseases.

D) Cancer

Malignancy can occur at any age. Some are more common in children while others are more common in the elderly. Common cancers in the older population include colon, lung, prostate, and breast. Like autoimmunity, the causes of cancer are not entirely understood in many circumstances. Some immune factors that contribute to cancer development include decreased immune surveillance, decreased ability to destroy malignant cells, and the existence of some cancers that develop the ability to evade the immune system.

We now have many cancer therapies, both in use and in development, that maximize the advantages of our immune system and its ability to target specific antigens, known as immunotherapy. Some of these therapies attach anti-cancer medications to antibodies so that they exclusively target malignant cells without destroying surrounding normal cells. Many new T cell-based immunotherapies are also being developed.

What Can We Do?

We can all agree that aging is inevitable, and death is the ultimate truth. However, we can postpone our biologic age and make this journey as healthy as possible. There are many factors under our control and making better choices will make our lives healthier and happier, maintain effectiveness of our immune system into our golden years. We have included some of those choices in the following list of do's and don'ts. The list is by no means exhaustive but is dynamic as our knowledge expands and lead to new and better alternatives.

1. Include fruits and vegetables, antioxidants, and follow a healthy diet as per your physician.

2. Maintain an active lifestyle, and exercise regularly under the guidance of your physician.

3. Prevent sedentary habits and obesity. Obesity can itself cause increased inflammation.

4. Follow the guidelines, and get vaccinated against preventable diseases, such as pneumonia and influenza.

5. Get regular medical checkups to prevent and/or diagnose chronic conditions early before they lead to complications.

6. Modify behaviors, such as smoking, drug use, and excessive alcohol consumption.

It is our sincere hope that we have provided some insight into the functions of the normal immune system and dysregulation in the elderly. We have provided some technical references below for further reading.

Acknowledgements: The authors are grateful to M.R. Murali, MD and Yashodhara Kirtane, MD for their review and critique of the subject matter.

References

De la Fuente, M. (2008). Role of neuroimmunomodulation in aging. *Neuroimmunomodulation 15, 213-223.*

Peakman, M. & Vergani, D (2009). *Basic and clinical immunology*, Second Edition.

Pfister, G & Savino, W (2008). Can the immune system still be efficient in the elderly? An immunological and immunoendocrine therapeutic perspective. *Neuroimmunomodulation 15,* 351-364.

Yanes, R.E., Gustafson, C.E., Weyand, C.M., & Goronzy, J.J. (2017). Lymphocyte generation and population homeostasis throughout life. *Seminars in Hematology 54,* 33-38.

Healthy Brain and Quality of Life in the Aging Population

Bhanu Evani and Renuka Evani

Introduction

The United States is projected to experience a rapid growth in its older population between 2010 and 2050. By 2030 nearly one in five U.S. residents will be 65 or older. The baby boomers are largely responsible for this increase in the older population. U.S government records (2017) show that the average life expectancy is 78.8 years, i.e. (81.2 years. for females and 76.4 years. for males). According to United Nations World Population Prospects (2015 Revision), the worldwide life expectancy at birth (2010-2015) was 71.5 years, i.e. (72.7 years. for females and 60.3 years. for males). Much of the recent improvement in both the death rates and life expectancy, is attributable to reductions in deaths from such major illnesses as heart disease, cancers and stroke. Science has managed to enhance longevity considerably, although this longevity may not always be accompanied by good health and independent living.

Aging for living organisms is as inevitable as dying. A healthy brain and body play important roles in determining one's Quality of Life (QoL). The brain's health is strongly associated with a healthy heart and its connecting blood vessels. The blood vessels perfuse the brain with blood carrying oxygen and nutrients to the cells, while removing carbon dioxide and waste away from the cells and play an important role in controlling blood pressure.

A reader interested in brain health can visit the Brain Health website maintained by the National Institute of Aging (NIA), which is one of the National Institutes of Health (NIH). There is a strong interplay between a healthy heart and healthy brain, and we need to set the stage for the healthy heart to get to the healthy brain. The American Heart Association defines target levels for seven cardiovascular health factors: smoking, body mass index, physical activity, diet, blood pressure, cholesterol, and glucose. These "Life's Simple 7" guidelines are:1) Stop smoking; 2) Lose weight; 3)

Get active; 4) Eat better; 5) Manage blood pressure; 6) Control cholesterol; and 7) Reduce blood sugar. Each of the seven guidelines can be met with lifestyle changes.

Smoking cigarettes has a high risk for developing cardiovascular diseases, COPD, cancers and several other illnesses. To break the smoking habit, smoking cessation programs, as well as over the counter products like Nicorette gum or prescription medications like the Nicotine patch, Bupropion and Varenicline, are available to reduce nicotine dependence. These medications work well when combined with psychosocial interventions.

Aging is generally associated with increases in fat deposition in the various tissues, such as the heart, liver, skeletal muscle, and bone marrow. It is the visceral fat accumulation (around the organs) rather than the subcutaneous fat (under the skin), that is detrimental to health. Body fat is associated with increased secretion of free fatty acids, an elevation of cholesterol levels, and a reduction in insulin's effectiveness at controlling high blood sugar levels. Losing excess weight, getting active and eating healthy are closely linked. The trio help to reduce the burden on the heart and blood vessels, while managing normal blood pressure, cholesterol and blood sugar levels.

Schneider et al. (2010) researched different measures of obesity for incident cardiovascular events and mortality. They recommend age-dependent cut-offs for risk assessments as *waist-to-height ratio* (0.5 for <40 years and 0.6 > 50 years) to be the better predictor of cardiovascular risk and mortality, followed by *waist circumference* (102 cm for men and 88 cm for women as normal)and *waist-to-hip ratio* (0.95 for men and 0.88 for women as normal), rather than the current standard of Body Mass Index (BMI = 25 kg/m^2 as normal for the Caucasian population but can be different based on ethnicity). BMI does not distinguish between overweight due to muscle vs. fat accumulation. The age associated increases in fat deposits within the upper and central body accelerate in post-menopausal women.

Food we eat is turned into plasma glucose (blood sugar) by our bodies and the insulin hormone secreted by the pancreas enables glucose uptake into the peripheral tissues. Over time, persistent, elevated levels of blood sugar damage the heart, kidneys, eyes, and peripheral nerves. The term "metabolic syndrome" is used to group risk factors that include high blood pressure, high blood sugar, unhealthy levels of cholesterol and abdominal fat. When these risk factors combine, they increase the risk of blood vessel and heart disease, leading to heart attacks and strokes. Metabolic syndrome been shown to increases the risk of becoming diabetic. Sustained programs that improve nutrition/weight-loss were found to relieve depression, lower the risk of diabetes (Type 2), decrease gastroesophageal reflux/heartburn, reduce high blood pressure, reduce high cholesterol, reduce osteoarthritis of the weight-bearing joints, reduce skin breakdown /ulcers (pressure sores), reduce sleep apnea/respiratory problems, and reduce urinary stress incontinence, in the aging population. The healthy diets popular over the past few decades are:

- the DASH diet (promoted by NIH) to reduce hypertension, which is rich in fruits, vegetables, whole grains, and low-fat dairy foods, includes meat, fish, poultry, nuts, and beans.
- the Mediterranean diet has vegetables, fruits, nuts, seeds, legumes, potatoes, whole grains, breads, herbs, spices, fish, seafood and extra virgin olive oil, poultry, eggs, cheese and yogurt, but no red meat.
- the Vegan diet excludes meat, eggs, dairy products and all other animal-derived ingredients.
- the Pescatarian is like the vegetarian diet but the difference being that it includes seafoods like fish and shellfish.
- the Lacto-Ovo-Vegetarian diet focuses on eggs for protein, dairy products – cheese, milk, yoghurt, and grains, pulses, legumes, nuts, seeds, vegetables, fruits, fungi, algae, yeast but no meats or seafood.
- Other diets that are popular include the Atkins (a diet high in proteins and fat but low in carbohydrates, intended for weight loss); the South Beach diet (which emphasizes eating high-fiber, lean protein, low-glycemic carbohydrates and unsaturated fats, both having categories of "good" or "bad"); Keto diets which put the body in a state of ketosis and the ketones burn body fat to produce energy as opposed to producing energy from serum glucose; Paleolithic diet consists of low-carbs and high-proteins - promoting meat, fish, vegetables, fruit, roots and nuts but excluding grains, legumes, dairy products, salt, refined sugar, and processed oils; several other diets are also popular.

Arteriosclerosis is the age-related stiffening of the arteries where the elasticity of the arteries gradually decreases and arterial rigidity increases, making it hard for the autonomic system to control blood pressure and provide the necessary blood supply to the organs (ischemia). High levels of cholesterol and triglyceride contribute to fatty plaque buildup on arterial walls, clogging arteries. Gardener et al. (2016) showed that as people age, ideal cardiovascular health promotes less decline in the domains of the brain's processing speed, its executive function (planning, setting goals, responding to problems and being persisting on tasks), and episodic memory (events from past personal experiences tied to places and times).

The normal aging process involves several changes in the brain. Age-related cognitive decline and cognitive deficits show considerable individual variability. In older subjects, post-synaptic nerve cells require greater stimulation for the long-term potentiation to activate the learning and long-term memory. The cognitive control process that enables the inhibition of irrelevant information and the learning based on contextual cues declines with age. The ability to perform multiple cognitive tasks and the cognitive processing speeds decrease as age increases. Cognitive executive functions, such as working memory and planning, also decline with aging. The reaction time in tasks slows down with age due to a conflict between visual stimulus and the required appropriate motor response. Verbal and visual memory decline even in the absence of clinical presentation of any dementia (Baltimore Longitudinal Study of Aging (1958-). Problems with speech production and a reduced speech rate occur with aging. Normal aging is also associated with decreases in sensory and motor functions like hearing over the phone or in a crowd, visual accommodation like presbyopia, decreased visual acuity, decreased taste and smell, and decreased fine motor skills with a slowed motor response. These are some aspects of normal aging.

An annual physical exam with the primary care physician and a follow-up on the doctor's recommendations in terms of nutrition and medications is strongly recommended. When the elderly encounter medical, psychological, social, or behavioral conditions that are more extreme than what one might expect due to normal aging, professional help should be taken from a primary care physician, a psychiatrist or a licensed therapist. For mild psychological conditions like stress, relationship problems, mild depression or anxiety, one can seek therapy. For severe depression and anxiety, the therapy may be combined with psychotropic medications.

The physiology of aging affects medications and therefore a fundamental knowledge of pharmacokinetics (drug absorption, distribution, metabolism and its elimination) and pharmacodynamics (breakdown of drugs in the body) helps understand how medications are processed through the body. An elderly person is more susceptible to polypharmacy (multiple drugs to treat one condition or disease), poor adherence to treatment regimens, and drug-induced adverse events. Decrease in lean body mass and increased adipose tissue in the elderly leads to an altered volume of distribution of lipid-soluble drugs, effectively increasing their elimination half-life. The kidney's and liver's drug clearance rates and the gastrointestinal tract's drug absorption efficiency decline with age. These altered pharmacokinetics result in increased or decreased concentrations of free drugs in the blood plasma of elderly patients.

Several forms of therapies are available in practice – supportive therapy, psychodynamic (insight-oriented) therapy, interpersonal therapy and cognitive behavioral therapy to name a few. Cognitive-Behavioral Therapy (CBT) can be recommended for anxiety, depression, grief or a neurocognitive disorder. The goal of the therapeutic relationship (Kazantzis et. al, 2017) between the therapist and the client during CBT is to effect a change in the client's (maladaptive) beliefs and/or perceptions through a collaborative use of cognitive and behaviorally focused interventions, Socratic dialogue, recorded observations, and experimentations. The Beck Institute for Cognitive Behavioral Therapy founded by Aaron T. Beck, MD and daughter Judith S. Beck, PhD, is a useful training and resource center.

Traditionally, psychiatry as a branch of medicine has dealt with mental illness through diagnosis and treatment, to which Jeste (2015) and his associates propose including the concept of positive psychiatry. It is the science and practice of psychiatry that seeks to understand and promote well-being through assessment and interventions involving positive psychosocial characteristics. They propose positive psychiatry as having four main components: 1) positive mental health outcomes/well-being; 2) positive psychosocial characteristics including resilience, optimism, social engagement, spirituality/ religiosity, and compassionate wisdom; 3) the biology behind positive psychiatry constructs; and 4) including preventive interventions.

Some common reversible mental health issues like depression, anxiety disorders, and the more complex neurocognitive disorders, their risk for disease, clinical presentations, and treatments are presented next.

Depression

Prevalence studies in depression have shown that 14% to 20% of the elderly in the community have depression. World Health Organization (2017) updated fact sheet states that unipolar depression occurs in 7% of the general older population and it accounts for 5.7% of Years Lived with Disability (YLDs) among those 60+ years old. Other types of depression include bipolar disorder with depression, depression secondary to medications, depression due to medical illnesses, and depression associated with neurological disorders, age-related losses or reactions to grief.

Okereke O.I. in the textbook "Prevention of Late Life Depression; (2015)" lists demographic, social, psychological and behavioral risk factors for late-life depression. The main risk factors discussed are being female, loss of spouse or significant other, major adverse or stressful life event, loneliness, along with lifestyle/ behavioral risk factors like: Smoking, Alcohol consumption, Obesity, Activity level and Diet. Some of these risk factors are modifiable while others may not, but interventions might mitigate their impact. The population of depressed older adults exhibits substantial heterogeneity, with respect to the age at onset, influence of genetic factors, existing medical comorbidities, and increased variability in neurocognitive disease outcomes.

Measurement of function in late-life depression (LLD) must relate to activities of daily living (ADL) and social functioning, while using validated instruments to diagnose LLD. Elderly with depression may have symptoms that may be difficult to distinguish from symptoms of dementia. The clinical picture is sometimes referred to as pseudodementia. Patients with depression not related to cognitive dysfunction generally have prominent depressive symptoms, more insight into their symptoms than do demented patients, and often have a history of depressive episodes (Kaplan & Sadock, 2017).

Milder forms of depression may respond to Cognitive Behavior Therapy or supportive therapy. More severe symptoms of depression may need antidepressants. The medications may include selective serotonin reuptake inhibitors (SSRI) like citalopram, sertraline, etc. (Geriatric depression, BCMJ Bonnie S Wiese, 2011). Other medications may include Bupropion or Mirtazapine. Although tricyclic/tetracyclic antidepressants (TCAs) and monoamine oxidase inhibitors (MAOIs) may be effective in the elderly, their side effect and safety profiles are suboptimal and thus are not recommended in late-life. The choice of antidepressant is based on its side effect profile and drug-to-drug interactions (Rothschild, 2012). In the evidenced-based guide to antidepressant medications, Drs. Liptzin and Hobgood review the use of antidepressant medications in geriatric patients (with dementia, stroke and Parkinson's disease), and their age-specific side-effects. Dr. Rothschild discusses the challenges in treatment of major depressive disorders, bipolar depression, psychotic depression and treatment-resistant depression when prescribing antidepressants and the any associated risk of suicidality, albeit in patients below the age of 24 years.

In adults, there is evidence supporting the integrated treatment for comorbid depression and Substance Use Disorders (SUDs). The substance use/abuse in the older population is usually alcohol, pain medications and sedative hypnotics (anti-anxiety, sleep-inducing). A meta-analytic review showed that the integrated treatment for these comorbidities has significant effects on the percent of abstinent days reported at post-treatment, compared to the single-focus treatment (e.g. treatment as usual and 12-step programs) (Babowitch & Antshel, 2016). These integrated treatments often include CBT, Motivational Enhancement Therapy (MET) and newer approaches, such as Acceptance and Commitment Therapy (ACT).

Anxiety Disorders

Anxiety disorders are common amongst the elderly and are often accompanied by depression with worsening physical, cognitive and functional impairments. Prevalence studies of anxiety disorders have shown that 17.1% of the elderly have anxiety disorders, with an overall and lifetime prevalence of 18.6%. The prevalence rates for specific anxiety disorders include 6.9% for generalized anxiety disorder, 3.2% for obsessive compulsive disorder, 2.8% for social phobia, 1.9% for post traumatic disorder, and 0.4% for panic disorder (Kirmizioglu, Geri Psychiatry, 2009). Milder symptoms may respond to Cognitive Behavior Therapy (CBT) alone. For more severe symptoms, evaluation by a psychiatrist for possible initiation of the Selective Serotonin Reuptake Inhibitors (SSRI) or Serotonin Norepinephrine Reuptake Inhibitors (SNRI), is recommended provided all medical conditions or medications causing anxiety are ruled out. Valium or other benzodiazepines and beta-blockers, must be avoided if possible as they reduce alertness, increase confusion and may put the elderly at risk for unsteady gait or falls. A comorbidity of anxiety disorders with SUDs in the elderly aggravates anxiety, and an integrated treatment approach is recommended.

Neurocognitive Disorders

The National Institute of Neurological Disorders and Stroke (NINDS.NIH.gov) describes dementia as: Dementia is the loss of cognitive functioning—the ability to think, remember, problem solve or reason—to such an extent that it interferes with a person's daily life and activities. Dementia ranges in severity from the mildest stage, when it is just beginning to affect a person's functioning, to the most severe stage, when the person must depend completely on others for basic activities of daily living. Functions affected include memory, language skills, visual perception, problem solving, self-management, and the ability to focus and pay attention. Some people with dementia cannot control their emotions, and their personalities may change. Signs and symptoms of dementia result when once-healthy neurons (nerve cells) in the brain stop working, lose connections with other brain cells, and die. While everyone loses some neurons as they age, people with dementia experience far greater loss. Unlike dementia, age-related memory loss is not disabling. The causes of dementia can vary. Many people with dementia have both Alzheimer's disease and one or more closely related disorders that share brain scanning or clinical (and sometimes both) features with Alzheimer's disease. When a person is affected by more than one dementia disorder, the dementia can be referred to as a mixed dementia. Some people may have mixed dementia caused by Alzheimer's-related neurodegenerative processes, vascular disease-related processes, or another neurodegenerative condition.

World Health Organization (Fact sheet updated 2017) estimated that 50 million people worldwide are living with dementia with nearly 60% living in low-income and middle-income countries. The total number of people with dementia is projected to increase to 82 million in 2030 and 152 million in 2050. According to the Merck Manual approximately 5% of people aged 65 to 74 years and 40% over the age of 85 years have some form of dementia. Dementia is not a normal process of aging (UCSF Memory and Aging Center). Risk factors for dementia include advancing age, stroke, high blood pressure, poorly controlled diabetes, and a thickening of blood vessel walls (atherosclerosis). Other dementias include frontotemporal disorders, vascular dementia, and Lewy body dementia.

Alzheimer's disease (AD) is a sub-type of the neurocognitive disorder (dementia). AD is characterized by the progressive accumulation of neuritic plaques of amyloid-beta (Aβ) followed by intracellular neurofibrillary tangles. In a healthy brain, the normally produced Amyloid precursor protein fragments get broken down and get eliminated, but in Alzheimer's disease, these fragments accumulate to form hard, insoluble plaques. Beta-amyloid protein deposition has been found to increase with age. Although amyloid plaques are particularly associated with dementias like Alzheimer's, amyloid deposits are also present in individuals without any overt neuropathology and appear to be a feature of normal aging. Other conditions or diseases such as Creutzfeldt-Jakob disease, Huntington 's disease, and Chronic Traumatic Encephalopathy (CTE) can also cause dementia or dementia-like symptoms accompanied by the less predictable non-cognitive symptoms in behavior and personality. The behavioral and psychological symptoms of dementia present significant distress and a poor QoL for both the dementia patients and the caregivers (Ryu et al., 2011).

Psychological and behavioral changes that are the early warning signs of a neurodegenerative disease in the elderly are listed in the Merck Manual. At first, the differences between normal aging and symptoms of early dementia may be hard to spot. Some of the common psychological and behavioral changes are:

→ Forgetting things that just happened
→ Forgetting where things are
→ Having trouble finding the right word to say and difficulty understanding what others say
→ Forgetting to pay bills
→ Having more trouble than usual with numbers
→ Getting lost when driving in familiar areas
→ Being more emotional, e.g. quickly switching from being happy to sad

During diagnosis, it is important to have collateral information from the family, a good clinical evaluation and supporting medical work-up like complete blood-count, comprehensive metabolic panel, lipid profile, thyroid panel, B12 and Folic acid levels, Rapid Plasma Reagin (RPR) test for syphilis, HIV testing, EKG, and head imaging studies to assist in ruling-in or ruling-out neurocognitive disorders. A combination of non-pharmacological and pharmacological interventions is recommended for managing the behavioral problems and symptoms of dementia. Advice of a geriatric psychiatrist or physicians with a sub-specialty in elderly populations should be sought for medical treatment.

Once the condition is diagnosed, the treatment of mild to moderate dementia could be with psychotropics like anticholinesterase inhibitors namely, Donepezil and others like Rivastigmine which will slow down the degenerative process for a couple of years and have been found to be useful in controlling behavioral problems. Cholinesterase inhibitors are designed to combat impairment of cholinergic neurons by slowing degradation of acetylcholine after its release at synapses. Memantine prevents overstimulation of the N-methyl-D-aspartate (NMDA) subtype of glutamate receptors, which may contribute to the pathogenesis of AD and other neurodegenerative conditions by causing excitotoxicity. Both drugs are often administered together for added benefit and to reduce the side effects of the Cholinesterase inhibitors. A high degree of clinical expertise is needed to appropriately recognize and manage the neuropsychiatric symptoms in dementia patients.

Currently, we have no cure for most types of dementia, of which Alzheimer's is the most common form of dementia in the elderly above the age of 75 years. Taking care of an Alzheimer's patient can be demanding over the long-term. A dementia patient needs to be in safe, familiar, and stable surroundings. Their living environment must be extra safe with electrical equipment having self-shutting capability and detectors installed on doors to prevent the patient from wandering off. The patient could wear an identification bracelet or a medical alert button that can be easily activated in an emergency. People with dementia usually do best in familiar surroundings, and any changes to the immediate environment are usually disturbing. Establishing a regular routine for bathing, eating, sleeping, and other activities can give the patient a sense of stability. Regular contacts with the same, familiar people also help keep the person calm and stable. Family members and caregivers can always announce their presence, make supportive comments as to where they are, and talk about whatever is going on in the immediate environment each time they meet with the person.

Current Research and Trends

"Understanding how the brain processes information and how it lays down memories and retrieves them will be instrumental for understanding brain health, and ultimately, preventing brain disease," said NIH Director Francis S. Collins, M.D., Ph.D. Launched in 2013, the BRAIN Initiative (**B**rain **R**esearch through **A**dvancing **I**nnovative **N**eurotechnologies') is a large-scale effort to push the boundaries of neuroscience research and equip scientists with insights necessary for treating a wide variety of brain disorders such as Alzheimer's disease, schizophrenia, autism, epilepsy, and traumatic brain injury. NIH's efforts are focused on the development of new tools and technologies to understand neural circuit function and capture a dynamic view of the brain in action. The aim is to have the BRAIN Initiative spur progress in neuroscience much like the NIH's Human Genome Project did for genetics." said Joshua A. Gordon, M.D., Ph.D., director of NIH's National Institute of Mental Health.

Patients with an inherited form of Alzheimer's disease carry mutations in the presenilin proteins or in the amyloid precursor protein. These mutations result in the increased production of the longer form of Aβ and are associated with early-onset, autosomal dominant Alzheimer's disease. Earlier research had shown that three *APoE* alleles are expressed in humans: *APoE ε4* allele, the single most important genetic risk factor for Alzheimer's disease; *APoE ε3* allele which is neutral, and *APoE ε2* allele that is protective. A person's genetics carrying even a single copy of the *APoE ε2* allele appears to reduce the risk of developing Alzheimer's. Researchers believe that genetic testing is useful for studying Alzheimer's risk in large groups of people but that it is not recommended for determining any one person's risk.

Scientists funded by the National Institutes of Health have discovered a potential strategy for developing treatments to stem the disease process in Alzheimer's disease. It's based on unclogging and removal of toxic debris that accumulates in patients' brains, by blocking activity of a little-known regulator protein called CD33. "Too much of CD33 protein's regulator activity appears to promote late-onset Alzheimer's by preventing support cells from clearing out toxic plaques, a key risk factor for the disease", explained Rudolph Tanzi, Ph.D., of Massachusetts General Hospital and Harvard University (2013), a grantee of the NIH's National Institute of Mental Health (NIMH) and National Institute on Aging (NIA). Future medications that impede CD33 activity in the brain might help prevent or treat the disorder. Since increased CD33 activity in the microglia has impaired the beta-amyloid clearance in late onset Alzheimer's, Dr. Tanzi and colleagues continue the search for agents that can cross the blood-brain barrier and block CD33 protein's regulator activity.

Kadmiri et al. (2018) discuss diagnostic biomarkers in the cerebrospinal fluid (CSF) samples as t-tau, phospho-tau and Aβ1-42 peptide, in predicting MCI's progression to AD. Blood is an attractive source of biomarkers for AD, but the sensitivity and specificity of blood markers for detecting AD remain lower than those biomarkers from CSF. However, the assessment in the CSF requires a spinal tap which is not a trivial task and is difficult to implement in clinical practice. Most of the new drug candidates are targeted on inhibiting Aβ production and its aggregation. We want the reader to be aware that despite extensive worldwide research, no definitive diagnostic methods and cures are available as of now. The existing AD treatments are only targeting the symptoms; however, the future is hopeful because of ongoing research in this field.

Other Biological and Social Considerations of Normal Aging

Research in chromosomal telomere lengths associated with aging shows promise in identifying causal factors affecting brain health. Elizabeth Blackburn, who shared the 2009 Nobel Prize for Physiology and Medicine, studied the single-cell organism and found that the ends of chromosomes (telomeres) contain a short DNA sequence with several repeats named telomeres whose length maintenance is essential for cell longevity. Telomere DNA protects the chromosomes and their aberrant attrition is associated with cell aging and eventual cell death. Every time the cell divides, and the DNA is copied, some of that DNA from the ends gets worn down and some of that telomere DNA shortened.

The research team discovered a new enzyme that synthesizes telomeres and named it telomerase. They showed a causal relationship between the telomerase and the enzyme's telomere synthesizing capability by subtracting that enzyme from the single-celled *Tetrahymena* which literally defied the aging process. What they discovered was inevitable cell death in the absence of the telomerase enzyme. Without telomerase the chromosomes are shortened each time the cell divides to generate new cells. Chromosomes that have their telomeres severely shortened send a signal instructing the cell's death. A few phenotypical examples of shortened telomeres are skin cell death causing wrinkles in our skin; pigment cells death causing greying of the hair; immune cells death increasing the risk of falling sick. However, if telomeres are synthesized to abnormally long sequences, the natural process of cell death does not take place, and it initiates uncontrolled cell multiplication, resulting in certain cancers. Therefore, abnormal telomerase enzyme activity increases the risk of diseases and cancers, often associated with aging.

The social aspect of aging can play an important part in delaying or averting age-related mental illnesses. A strong family, community, and neighborhood provides an essential social network which can enhance a person's QoL. A higher socioeconomic status (SES) in the elderly increases their QoL, since it determines where they live, their access to health care facilities and the possible assistance that is available to them in conducting their activities of daily living. Social support consisting of family and friends is an important component to having a high sense of external control on outcomes, during a health crisis. In a systematic review and meta-analysis of longitudinal cohort studies on social relationships associated with the risk of dementia, low social participation (RR=1.41 (95% CI 1.13-1.75)), less frequent social contact (RR=1.57 (95% CI 1.32-1.85)) and more loneliness (RR=1.58 (95% CI 1.19-2.09)) were found to be statistically significant with incident dementia (Kuiper, et al. 2015). Poor social interactions could therefore be added to low educational attainment, physical and intellectual inactivity and late-life depression, which are the well-established risk factors for late-life dementia. Further studies are needed to understand older persons who live harmoniously in large social communities and their QoL.

Knowing these interacting physical and mental health factors and having the goal to improve one's quality of life during the later years, it is most important that we continually assess an aging person, especially when there is a significant change in that person's life. Some significant events that could lead to feelings of loss or regret are unemployment, loneliness, heart-break, an accident, deterioration in health, a disability, harm or loss of a dear one's life. In the text "On Grief and grieving." (Kübler-Ross & Kessler, 2014) discusses the well-established five stages of grief as discussed as being denial, anger, bargaining, depression and acceptance. These five stages are a part of the framework that makes up our learning on how to live with any significant loss. The grieving process does not follow some linear timeline and is a unique experience for every grieving individual, in that, not everyone goes through all five stages or in a prescribed order.

Summary

An elderly person transitioning from a normally aging brain through an increasing Cognitive Impairment into a progressively advanced Alzheimer's disease will need years of nurturing and caregiving to preserve that patient's QoL. The best that one can hope to accomplish is to provide a safe, stable and familiar environment with appropriate mental stimulation. It is best to start promoting a healthy heart and a healthy brain throughout early life, since the underlying anatomical and pathophysiologic changes in dementia begin many years before clinical symptoms emerge. Finding cures for neurocognitive disorders associated with Alzheimer's, Parkinson's, Huntington's and Creutzfeldt-Jakob's diseases and the like, is hopeful because of the enormous research efforts and funding that has been committed to finding their cures and treatments. The portal "ageing-map.org/atlas" provides access to the latest scientific research on human ageing-related physiological, pathological and psychological changes.

References

American Psychiatric Association (2013). Diagnostic and Statistical Manual of Mental Disorders DSM-5 (5th ed.). Washington D.C.: American Psychiatric Publishing.

Blazer, D.G. & Steffens, D.C.(Eds.). (2012). *Essentials of geriatric psychiatry* (2nd ed.). Virginia: American Psychiatric Publishing.

Croce, E.A., Jaramillo, S., Cruz-Ortiz, C. & Camfield, K. (2017). Pharmacological management of anxiety disorders in the elderly. *Current Treatment Options in Psychiatry 4*, 33-46.

Deary, I.J. et. al (2009). Age-associated cognitive decline. *British Medical Bulletin 92*(1), 135–152. doi.org/10.1093/bmb/ldp033.

El Kadmiri, N., Said, N., Slassi, I., El Moutawakil, B. & Nadifi, S. (2018). Biomarkers for Alzheimer's disease: Classical and novel candidates' review. *Neuroscience 370*, 181-190.

Gardener, H., Wright, C.B., Dong, C., Cheung, K., DeRosa, J., Nannery, M., …, Sacco, R.L. (2016). Ideal cardiovascular health and cognitive aging in the Northern Manhattan Study. *Journal of the American Heart Association: Cardiovascular and Cerebrovascular Disease. 5(*3), e002731.

Gracie, A., Serrano-Pozo, A., Parrado, A.R., Lesinski, A.N., Asselin, C.N., Mullin, K.,…,Tanzi, R.E. (2013), Alzheimer's disease risk gene CD33 inhibits microglial uptake of Amyloid Beta. *Neuron 78*(4), 631-643.

Hales, R.E., Yudofsky, S.C. & Roberts, L.W. (Eds.). (2014). Textbook of Psychiatry DSM-5 Edition (6th ed.). Washington D.C.: American Psychiatric Publishing.

Health Related Quality of Life (HRQoL) and Well Being. Office of Disease Prevention and Health Promotion. Accessed on February 2, 2018 from https://www.healthypeople.gov/2020/topics-objectives/topic/health-related-quality-of-life-well-being.

Huang, Y.A., Zhou, B., Wernig, M., & Sudhof, T.C. (2017). APoE2, APoE3 and APoE4 Differentially Stimulate APP Transcription and Aβ Secretion. *Cell 168*, 427-441

Jeste, D.V. (2015). Positive psychiatry: The time has come. *The Journal of Clinical Psychiatry 76*(6), 675-83.

Kuiper, J.S., Zuidersma, M., Oude Voshaar, R.C., Zuidema, S.U., van den Heuvel, E.R., …, Smidt, Nynke (2015). Social relationships and the risk of dementia: A systematic review and meta-analysis of longitudinal cohort studies. *Ageing Research Reviews, 22*, 39-57.

Mirza S.S., Ikram, M.A., Bos, D., Mihaescu, R., Hofman, A. and Tiemeier, H. (2017). Mild cognitive impairment and risk of depression and anxiety: A population-based study. Alzheimer's Dementia: *The Journal of the Alzheimer's Association, 13*(2), 130-139

Passarino, G., De Rango, F. & Montesanto, A. (2016). Human longevity: Genetics or lifestyle? It takes two to Tango. *Immunity & Ageing. 13*, 12.

Rothschild, A.J. (2012). *The evidence-based Guide to antidepressant medications.* American Psychiatric Publishing, Washington D.C.

Sadock, B.J., Sadock, V.J. & Ruiz, P. (Eds.). (2017). Kaplan & Sadock's Comprehensive Textbook of Psychiatry (10th ed.). Philadelphia: Wolters Kluwer.

The Brain Research through Advancing Innovative Neurotechnologies® (BRAIN) INITIATIVE. National Institutes of Health (NIH). Accessed on February 2, 2018: https://www.braininitiative.nih.gov/index.htm.

The Digital Ageing Atlas, the Portal of Ageing-related Changes. Digital Ageing Atlas; http://ageing-map.org/atlas/.

Vincent, G.K. and Velkoff, V.A. (2010). The Next Four Decades. The Older Population in the United States: 2010-2050. Population Estimates and Projections. Accessed on February 2, 2018: https://www.census.gov/prod/2010pubs/p25-1138.pdf.

Wragg, M., Hutton, M., Talbot, C., et al. (1996). Genetic Association Between Intronic Polymorphism in Presenilin-1 Gene and Late-onset Alzheimer's Disease. *The Lancet 347*(9000), 509-512.

A Comprehensive Psychosocial Intervention Combined with Drug Treatment for QoL in Alzheimer Patients

Kenichi Meguro

Introduction: QOL and the Bio-Psycho-Socio-Spiritual Model of Health

Health is defined in terms of Quality of Life (QoL) by the World Health Organization (WHO), based on how an individual feel about their life, and accounting for their culture and value systems, and their goals, expectations, standards and concerns (WHO, 2017a). QoL includes items such as physical function and mental health, but health- related QoL is complex, given the multiple chronic diseases and decreased physical function found in many elderly people. Health is also defined by the WHO based on complete physical, mental and social well-being, rather than simply the absence of disease or infirmity (WHO, 2017b), and this is the basis of the Bio-Psycho-Socio-Spiritual (BPSS) model.

Group Reminiscence with Realty Orientation

Patients with Dementia

In reminiscence therapy, recall of past experiences is encouraged to promote intra- and interpersonal activity that may improve well-being and QoL (Gragnon, 1996; Woodrow, 1998; Hodgson, 1999; Grasel et al. 2003). Therefore, this therapy focuses on discussion of activities from the past, usually through stimulation using prompts such as photographs, household contents, and other items from the past. This therapy is supported by the relatively well-preserved remote memory in patients with AD (Zec, 1993). Reality orientation (Gragnon, 1996; Grasel et al. 2003; Onder, 2005) is also used in patients with dementia as a psychosocial intervention, since these patients are often disoriented. Orientation information, such as time and place, is thought to improve understanding of surroundings, which may promote senses of control and self-esteem. This therapy is usually used in combination with reminiscence therapy (Onder, 2008).

We previously used cognitive and behavioral parameters to evaluate the effects of group reminiscence (GR) in 60 patients with Vascular Dementia (VaD), (Ito, et al., 2007). These patients were randomly assigned to a GR arm, a social contact (SC) arm, and a control (CL) arm. GR and SC sessions of one hour were given once weekly for three months for the GR and SC arms, respectively, while the CL arm received supportive care only. The primary outcome was defined as improved cognitive function and behavior, but the absence of significant improvements suggested that the hypothesis of a benefit of GR in patients with VaD was incorrect.

The dropout rate was higher in the SC arm compared to those in the GR and CL arms because the SC subjects told us that the intervention was boring. The content in the SC arm was 50 minutes of group discussion on social issues such as health and disease management, current hot topics, and daily living, including recreation and meals in facilities. In contrast, older residents in the GR arm enjoyed talking about their memories, and the absence of this discussion in the SC arm led to boredom.

A secondary analysis of emotional ratings for the GR and SC arms was performed using a scale of "very enjoyable," "enjoyable," "normal," "boring," and "very boring". For the GR arm, 76% of subjects felt that the intervention was very enjoyable or enjoyable, whereas only 27% gave these answers for the SC arm. The subjects were placed in "Enjoyable" and "Boring" groups, independent of the GR and SC arms, and the "Enjoyable" group was found to have had a significant improvement on the MOSES scale compared with the "Boring" group.

We have previously described a patient with dementia with improvement of their mental inner world after a psychosocial approach, despite no marked change in MMSE (Mini Mental State Exam) score (Gragnon, 1996). In contrast to clinical trials of drugs, a randomized controlled trial (RCT) design is difficult for psychosocial approaches, and caution regarding "superficial" interpretation is needed. Instead, a patient-reported outcome (PRO) Meguro (2013) may be better for examination of a psychosocial intervention.

People with Mild Cognitive Impairment

GR and Reality Orientation (RO) are common psychosocial interventions for patients with dementia, while a PRO has been found to be useful for qualitative evaluation of the reminiscence approach in such patients (Meguro, 2013). Therefore, we investigated the effects of GR-RO for patients with mild cognitive impairment (MCI) using the PRO as a cluster RCT design (Nakamura, 2016).

Of 295 community-dwelling people assessed as CDR 0.5 in our prevalence study, a psychosocial intervention study was performed for 127 people who met the inclusion criteria and gave consent to participate (Meguro, 2015; Nakatsuka, 2015). As a PRO, the subjects were asked to write about their impressions after psychosocial intervention (Nakamura, 2016). Ultimately, 94 subjects (39 GR-RO, 23 physical activity (PA), 32 cognitive training (CT)) completed the study (Nakamura, 2016).

We retrospectively analyzed the PRO of impressions of the nonpharmacological interventions of GR-RO, OA, and CT subjects, with categorization of the descriptions into "impression with content" and "reminiscence with life review". Writing on memory loss was also analyzed, and the life review content was focused on in the GR-RO group. Compared with the PA and CT groups, the GR-RO patients reminisced through life review and discussed their own memory problems. The order of events was accurate in their autobiographical memories. There was a significant time effect between the two-family involvement groups in QoL scores, and post-intervention QOL scores were significantly better than those obtained before the intervention (Nakamura, 2016)

These results suggest that GR-RO for patients with MCI stimulates life review and increases self-awareness of memory deficits, without confusion of the order of events. Thus, GR-RO may improve self-esteem and develop self-awareness (Nakamura, 2016). Reminiscence in subjects with MCI may stimulate remote memory and enrich inner life through a review of the life of the patient. Thus, GR-RO may stimulate remote memory and increase self-awareness of memory deficits, which we consider to be healthy self-recognition, with subsequent improvement of self-esteem and growth of self-awareness. In this study, the patients with MCI had an intact order of events in remote memory and were able to recall autobiographical memory in reminiscence therapy. RO in this study may have affected awareness of SCI. The patients did not have deficits in order of events in memories of their childhood and did not confuse childhood and recent memories. This suggests that patients with MCI do not exhibit deficits in the order of events that are related to basal forebrain function (Nakamura, 2016).

In a study of autobiographical episodic memory, patients with MCI had significantly lower scores than healthy elderly individuals for recall of adolescent, middle age, and recent memories, but not for childhood and early adulthood memories (Barnabe, et al., 2012). Deficits in emotional autobiographical memory are found in prodromal and mild AD patients compared with controls, but memory specificity remains. Impaired emotional autobiographical memory due to right amygdala-hippocampal atrophy also occurs in these patients (Philippi et al, 2015). Our hypothesis for the effect of reminiscence therapy is that triggers such as verbal cues and old photographs are reminders of autobiographical memories, with or without emotion. Recall of remote memories, which are often images of old scenes, increases spontaneous verbal output (writing and talking) considerably (Nakamura, 2016).

These results suggest that GR-RO in subjects with MCI can stimulate life review and increase self-awareness of memory deficits without confusion of the order of events, and this in turn may improve self-esteem and develop self-awareness (Nakamura, 2016). The relationship of evocation of autobiographical memory with spontaneous writing requires a further study using brain function analyses.

Evidence for use of a Comprehensive Approach

We examined the effect of donepezil and psychosocial intervention in combination on cognitive function and QoL for patients with AD (Meguro, et al, 2008). Donepezil was given with or without the psychosocial interventions described above. There was no group effect for MMSE changes, but QoL-AD changes showed a significant group effect with a time by group interaction.

We have shown that psychosocial intervention stimulates the frontal lobe in patients with dementia (Akanuma, et al, 2011), and that the parietal lobe is associated with logical judgment (Inoue et al. 2012). Thus, a combined approach with symptomatic drug treatment may directly stimulate attention function and may also affect judgment function indirectly through observation of the behaviors of other subjects. To examine this hypothesis, 52 patients with AD underwent GR-RO and received donepezil. CBF(Cerebral Blood Flow) was assessed with ECD SPECT (Electrical Circular Dichroism Spectra). Comparisons were performed between responders and non- responders based on MMSE scores, and between those with good and poor memories of the intervention content. CBF in the frontal lobe was significantly higher in responders, and CBF in the parietal lobe (especially on the left side) was significantly higher in those with a good memory. Areas like those affected by the psychosocial intervention were directly stimulated by donepezil, which suggests compatibility of the drug and the intervention. The parietal lobe was also stimulated indirectly, suggesting an indirect effect of the intervention based on logical judgment function.

Long-Term Effect: QALY

QALY and Dementia

Analyses of health economics of diseases such as Alzheimer's disease (AD) are based on QoL scales, such as the quality-adjusted life-year (QALY), and health state utility values (HSUVs). HSUVs use a scale of health related QoL (HRQOL) scored as 0 for death and 1 for complete health (Ikegami et al.

2001). Cost-effectiveness in economic evaluation of healthcare is analyzed using a cost-effectiveness ratio based on HSUVs. The QALY combines HRQOL and survival benefit; that is, HSUVs are multiplied by lifetime under the relevant conditions. For example, if the HSUV for Cerebro Vascular Disease (CVD) is 0.60 and the lifetime for CVD is 10 years, QALY is 0.60 × 10 = 6. Therefore, analysis of healthcare economics requires estimation of HSUVs based on disease and severity of injury (Kasai, et al, 2013).

AD is the most common type of dementia, and there are about twice as many cases of AD with CVD compared to AD without CVD (i.e., 'pure' AD) in Japan, with rates of 44% and 19%, respectively, of all dementia cases (Meguro et al, 2002). Many patients with AD with CVD also have impaired activities of daily living (ADL) due to low physical activity, in addition to the effects of AD, and may be admitted to nursing facilities or require more long-term care. Evaluation of the effects of pharmacotherapy including anti- dementia drugs requires estimation of HSUVs based on the level of ADL impairment and the outcomes of AD. Thus, we estimated HSUVs in AD with inclusion of ADL.

A PubMed search was used to find studies on QALY and HSUVs based on ADL levels in AD. HSUVs in AD patients were estimated based on independent walking and eating (ADL level A), some problems with walking, but sitting without assistance (ADL level B); and confined to bed (ADL level C). These three ADL levels correspond approximately to the stages of mobility on the EQ-5D (Japanese EuroQol Translation Team, 1998; The EuroQol Group, 1990).

The literature search found no reports on HSUVs associated with the level of physical activity of patients with AD. Using published data and the mobility subscale of the EQ-5D, the HSUVs of pure AD and AD with CVD for ADL levels A, B, and C were estimated to be 0.61 and 0.58, 0.53 and 0.28, and 0.19 and 0.05, respectively (Kaisai et al, 2013). This is the first estimation of HSUVs related to the physical activity level of patients with AD.

These results may be more accurate than previous estimations of HSUVs, and suggest that analysis of healthcare economics of dementia in Japan may be improved by accounting for the extent of ADL, in addition to the severity of AD. For example, galantamine shows a good therapeutic effect on cognitive functions and ADL abilities in patients with AD combined with CVD, as well as for AD alone (Erkinjuntti et al. 2002; Kurz et al, 2003; Erkinjuntti et al. 2008). Improved evaluation of drug efficacy requires identification of patients with AD alone and AD with CVD, and the ADL level should be included in the evaluation. More AD patients have CVD and low levels of physical ADL in Japan, compared to AD patients in the EU and USA. Health policy decisions for dementia require more information than the direct effect of drug treatment on AD, and the effects of ADL should be considered in the decision-making process for dementia care in Japan (Kaisai, et al, 2013).

Long-Term Effect and QALY

Cognitive impairment or dementia with advancing age is a negative predictor of survival (Maier, 1999), which may be due to decreased biological vitality (Johnson, et al, 2008) and to a multifactorial phenomenon that is dependent on events over the entire lifespan (Backman & McDonald, 2006). A recent systematic review (Brodaty, 2012) showed that many factors are associated with survival after diagnosis of dementia, with life expectancy depending on age at diagnosis, gender, dementing diseases, and severity.

There are no curative drugs for neurodegenerative diseases such as AD or dementia with Lewy bodies (DLB), but symptomatic drugs such as cholinesterase inhibitors (ChEIs) or memantine may delay disease progression. A comprehensive approach with psychosocial interventions can improve QOL (Nakamura, et al, 2016), but the ultimate outcome of drug therapy should be based on life expectancy. Lopez et al. (2002) found that ChEIs can delay the time to nursing home residence without an apparent effect on life expectancy, whereas a Swedish mega-data analysis (Nordström, et al., 2013) showed that ChEIs were related to a lower risk of death.

Based on this background, we retrospectively analyzed the influence of donepezil on life expectancy after onset of AD and on special nursing home (SNH) residency (Meguro et al, 2014), in cases that also received comprehensive therapy with psychosocial interventions Nakamura et al, 2016; Meguro et al, 2012; Meguro et al, 2010, 2017, 2009). Medical records and death certificates were analyzed for outpatients at the Tajiri Clinic at the Osaki-SKIP Center. The entry criteria were a diagnosis of dementia based on DSM-IV criteria and diagnostic criteria for AD, VaD, and DLB; medical treatment for >3 months; and follow up until <1 year before death. Of 390 subjects with available data, 275 had a diagnosis of dementia that met the entry criteria. Of the 100 patients with AD, the lifetime expectancies after onset were 7.9 in 52 patients who had taken donepezil, and 5.3 years in 48 who had not received the drug due to treatment before donepezil was introduced in Japan in 1999. There was also a significant drug effect with a significant covariate effect of SNH residency. Other covariates did not reach a significant level.

The effects on concomitant CVD and VaD (Vascular Dementia) were analyzed in a further study (Meguro, et al, 2015). Of 390 subjects, 275 had dementia that met the entry criteria (67 with pure AD, 33 with AD and CVD, 110 with VaD). SNH residence and donepezil both had positive effects on life expectancy in patients with pure AD, whereas donepezil only had this effect in those with AD and CVD.

Donepezil has recently been indicated for treatment of dementia with DLB, but its effect on life expectancy is unclear. Therefore, we analyzed the effects of donepezil on DLB in 510 subjects using medical records and death certificates (Meguro et al, 2018). Of these subjects, 360 had a diagnosis of dementia that met the entry criteria, and 51 patients had DLB. The lifetime expectancies after onset of DLB were 6.4 years in 23 patients who had taken donepezil and 3.6 years in 28 patients treated prior to the introduction of donepezil in Japan in 1999, showing a significant drug effect. However, in contrast with previous AD data, no significant effect of SNH residency was found.

These retrospective studies are limited by a lack of randomization, but the results showed a positive effect of donepezil on life expectancy after onset of AD and indicated the importance of CVD prevention. Decreased mortality due to reduction of concomitant diseases such as pneumonia may be important in this finding. A favorable health economics outcome is suggested by the similar life expectancies for patients taking donepezil at home and those not taking donepezil in a SNH. For DLB, the lower life expectancy compared with that of AD and the lack of an effect of SNH residency suggest greater cholinergic deficiency in DLB compared to that in AD.

Objective Cognitive Impairments and Subjective Quality of Life

Many elderly people with cognitive dysfunction may experience decreased health and QoL. Basic QoL includes physical function and mental health; with physical health and, to a lesser extent, psychological health, social relationships, and environment, being of most importance in elderly people. The short version of the WHO Quality of Life (WHOQOL-BREF) scale is a brief questionnaire used to assess international QoL in young and elderly people, using physical health, psychological health, social relationships, and environment domains (The WHOQOL Group, 1998; Saxena et al, 2001; Tazaki and Nakane, 2007). The WHOQOL-BREF has good reliability and validity for dementia (Lucas-Carrasco et al, 2011). Muangpaisan et al. (2008) found that subjects with MCI had a significantly lower psychological subscale on the WHOQOL- BREF compared to normal subjects.

CDR (Clinical Dementia Rating) and WHOQOL-BREF are standardized scales to assess everyday life of elderly people with dementia. Objective cognitive impairments such as memory and home and hobbies impairments in daily living are included on the CDR (Hughes et al, 1982; Morris et al, 1993), whereas the WHOQOL-BREF assesses subjective QoL using the domains listed above The WHOQOL Group, 1998; Saxena et al, 2001; Tazaki and Nakane, 2007). However, the relationship between objective cognitive impairments and subjective QoL has not been investigated in very mild dementia. Therefore, we explored the relationships between subjective (WHOQOL-BREF) and objective (CDR) results in elderly community-dwelling people to examine possible early detection of dementia and to identify the most important QoL domain for elderly people in Japan (Kaisai et al, 2018).

A total of 403 people aged ≥75 years living in Tome City, Northern Japan, were invited to participate in the study (Akanuma et al, 2016; Liu et al, 2017), 188 agreed to participate, and 178 completed the WHOQOL-BREF. These people included 66 CDR 0 (healthy), 86 CDR 0.5 (possible dementia or MCI), and 26 CDR ≥1 (dementia) cases. All CDR 1 cases met DSM-IV criteria for dementia (American Psychiatric Association, 1994). Clinical examinations, blood tests, neuropsychological tests, and magnetic resonance imaging (MRI) were also conducted in this study (Kaisai et al, 2018).

Using Pearson correlation analysis, there were significant negative correlations of all CDR subscales with the WHOQOL-BREF physical domain, of the CDR subscale of memory impairment with the WHOQOL-BREF physical and psychological domains, and of the CDR subscale of home and hobbies with all WHOQOL-BREF domains ($p<0.05$) (Kaisai et al, 2018). These results suggest that Japanese elderly people may confuse objective cognitive impairment with subjective physical health, and that objective home and hobbies impairment affects all categories of QOL in the elderly (Kaisai et al, 2018).

In this study, the CDR scale was used for evaluating objective cognitive impairments, including those for memory, orientation, judgment, community affairs, home and hobbies, and personal care; and all CDR subscales were significantly correlated with the physical health domain of the WHOQOL-BREF. Memory impairment is the most frequent and severe symptom of dementia, specifically in AD, and was correlated with subjective poor scores in the WHOQOL-BREF psychological and physical domains. Elderly people who actually had objective cognitive impairments may also subjectively have had physical complaints such as knee pain or fever. Thus, these people had confusion between objective cognitive impairments and subjective physical health.

In a study of patients with hip fractures and dementia, we found that fear of falling, a psychological risk factor for falling, reflected both physical function and cognitive impairments (Kaisai et al, 2017). Thus, fear and concern of falling may also reflect both physical and cognitive impairments in patients with dementia (Kaisai et al, 2017). A potential cultural effect may also be present in these results. For example, elderly Japanese people would view a massage as benefiting both the body and mind, whereas elderly Western people might view it as benefiting the body only. In this study, some individuals may have subscribed to the idea of "mind-body unity," a term from Japanese Zen Buddhism (Yuasa, 1987)., and some elderly people in Japan follow the philosophy of Eastern Mind-Body Monism, in contrast to Mind-Body Dualism in Western countries. The physical area overlaps the mental area in Eastern Mind-Body Monism, and the body is centered in this theory. The brain may be in the body, but the boundaries among the mind, body and brain are loose. In contrast, in Mind-Body Dualism, the mental area is separate from the body area.

Next, when elderly people had objective home and hobbies impairment, they subjectively felt a decline in all QOL domains. After retirement, most elderly people are concerned with activities related to their home and hobbies. However, those with very mild/mild dementia exhibited disabilities of complicated instrumental activities of daily living (IADL) in the home, such as shopping and food preparation (Kobayashi, et al, 2016; Ouchi et al, 2016). Cognitive impairments, including executive dysfunction, decreased complicated IADL in patients with very mild dementia (Ouchi et al, 2016), regardless of the intensity of physical activity (Kobayashi, et al, 2016). This suggests that rehabilitation of and care for dysfunctions of activities related to home and hobbies in elderly people with very mild dementia are required through physical, psychological, social, and environmental support (Kaisai et al, 2018).

Another possibility is that people with very mild/mild dementia may have anosognosia or may over- or underestimate true cognitive impairment, with an imbalance between subjective and objective cognitive complaints, especially in patients with VaD (Tezuka et al, 2013). Patients with dementia may misunderstand their cognitive and physical impairments, and elderly people with cognitive impairments may not be aware of their disabilities; that is, self-awareness is required to recognize impairments. Age may also affect these issues, but our patients were all aged ≥75 years, and thus age was not a factor (Kaisai et al, 2016). The neural basis of the mechanism underlying disabilities of behavior and subjective and objective awareness of cognitive impairment requires further investigation.

In conclusion, patients with very mild/mild dementia may confuse cognitive impairment and physical disabilities, and subjective physical complaints related to cognitive impairments in Japanese elderly people may assist in early detection of very mild dementia. Further studies that involve memory clinics and all departments that care for elderly people, including orthopedics, are required for early detection, rehabilitation, and long-term care for dementia (Kaisai et al, 2016). International studies are also required to compare objective and subjective cognitive impairments in patients with dementia.

Acknowledgements: I am grateful to Dr Mari Kasai and the staff at the Geriatric Behavioral Neurology, Tohoku University CYRIC, and the Osaki-Tajiri SKIP Center.

References

Akanuma K, Meguro K, Meguro M, Sasaki E, Chiba K, & Ishiim H. (2011). Improved social interaction and increased anterior cingulate metabolism after group reminiscence with reality orientation approach for vascular dementia. *Psychiatry Research: Neuroimaging*, 192(3), 183-187.

Akanuma K, Nakamura K, Meguro K, Chiba M, Gutiérrez Ubeda SR, Kumai K, Kato Y, Oonuma J, Kasai M, Nakatsuka M, Seki T, Tomita H, Tome Project Members. (2016). Disturbed social recognition and impaired risk judgement in older residents with mild cognitive impairment after the Great East Japan Earthquake of 2011: The Tome Project. *Psychogeriatrics. 16*,349-354.

American Psychiatric Association (1994). *Diagnostic and statistical manual of mental disorders* (DSM-IV), 4th Edition. Washington, DC: American Psychiatric Association.

Backman L & MacDonald SWS. (2006). Death and cognition: Synthesis and outlook. *European Psychologist.* 11, 224-235.

Barnabe A, Whitehead V, Pilon R, et al. (2012). Autobiographical memory in mild cognitive impairment and Alzheimer's disease: A comparison between the Levine and Kopelman interview methodologies. Hippocampus, 22, 1809- 1825.

Brodaty H, Seeher K, Gibson L, (2012). Dementia time to death: A systematic literature review on survival time and years of life lost in people with dementia. Int Psychogeriatr. 24, 1034-1045.

Bruce E, & Hodgson S, Schweitzer P. (1999). *Reminiscence with people with dementia: A handbook for carers.* London, Age Exchange.

Erkinjuntti T, Gauthier S, Bullock R, Kurz A, Hammond G, Schwalen S, Zhu Y, & Brashear R. (2008). Galantamine treatment in Alzheimer's disease with cerebrovascular disease: responder analyses from a randomized, controlled trial (GAL-INT-6). *Journal of Psychopharmacology, 22,* 761–768.

Erkinjuntti T, Kurz A, Gauthier S, Bullock R, Lilienfeld S, & Damaraju CV. (2002). Efficacy of galantamine in probable vascular dementia and Alzheimer's disease combined with cerebrovascular disease: a randomised trial. *Lancet*, 359.

Gragnon D.L. (1996). A review of reality orientation, validation therapy, and reminiscence therapy with the Alzheimer's client. *Physical & Occupational Therapy in Geriatrics, 14*, 61-77.

Grasel E, Wiltfang J, & Kornhuber J. (2003). Non-drug therapies for dementia: An overview of the current situation with regard to proof of effectiveness. *Dementia and Geriatric Cognitive Disorders. 15*, 115-125.

Hughes C.P., Berg L., Danziger W.L., Coben LA, & Martin R.L. (1982). A new clinical scale for the staging of dementia. *British Journal Psychiatry, 140*, 566-572.

Ikegami N, Fukuhara S, & Ikeda S. (2001). QOL evaluation handbook for clinical diagnosis (in Japanese). Tokyo, Igaku Shoin, 45–49.

Inoue K, Meguro K, Akanuma K, Meguro M, Yamaguchi S, & Fukuda H. (2012). Impaired memory and executive function associated with decreased hippocampal and frontal blood flow in CDR 0.5 status: The Osaki-Tajiri Project. *Psychogeriatrics, 12*(1), 27-33.

Ito T, Meguro K, Akanuma K, Ishii H, & Mori E. (2007). A randomized controlled trial of the group reminiscence approach in patients with vascular dementia. *Dementia* and *Geriatric Cognitive Disorders. 24*, 48-54.

Japanese EuroQol Translation Team. The development of the Japanese EuroQol Instrument.(1998). *Journal of Health Social Care in the Community*, 8, 109–123.

Johnson JK, Lui LY, & Yaffe K. (2007). Executive function, more than global cognition, predicts functional decline and mortality in elderly women. *The Journal of Gerontology, Series A:Biological Sciences and Medical Sciences, 62*,1134-1141.

Kasai M, Meguro K, Ozawa H, Kumai K, Imaizumi H, Minegishi H, Oi H, Oizumi A, Yamashiro M, Matsuda M, Tanaka M, Itoi E. (2017). Fear of falling and cognitive impairments in elderly people with hip fractures. *Dementia and Geriatric Cognitive Disorders Extra, 7*, 386-394.

Kasai M, & Meguro K. (2013). Estimated quality-adjusted life-year associated with the degree of activities of daily living in patients with Alzheimer's disease. *Dementia and Geriatric Cognitive Disorders Extra, 3*, 482-488.

Kasai M & Meguro K. (2018). Patients with very mild dementia may confuse objective cognitive impairments with subjective physical health of quality of life: The Tome City Project in Japan. *Front Psychology, 8,* 533.

Kobayashi Y, Takahashi Y, Seki T, Kaneta T, Amarume K, Kasai M, Meguro K. (2016). Decreased physical activity associated with executive dysfunction correlates with cognitive impairment among older adults in the community: A retrospective analysis from the Kurihara Project. *Dementia and Geriatric Cognitive Disorders Extra. 6,* 350-360.

Kurz A.F., Erkinjuntti T., Small G.W., Lilienfeld S., & Damaraju C.R. (2003). Long-term safety and cognitive effects of galantamine in the treatment of probable vascular dementia or Alzheimer's disease with cerebrovascular disease. *European Journal of Neurology. 10,* 633–640.

Liu Y.C., Meguro K, Nakamura K, Akanuma K, Nakatsuka M, Seki T, Nakaaki S, Mimura M, & Kawakami N. (2017). Depression and dementia in old-old population: history of depression may be associated with dementia onset. The tome project. *Frontiers in Aging Neuroscience,* 9, 335.

Lopez O.L., Becker J.T., Wisniewski S., Saxton J., Kaufer D.I., & DeKosky S.T. (2002). Cholinesterase inhibitor treatment alters the natural history of Alzheimer's disease. *The Journal of Neurology, Neurosurgery, and Psychiatry, 72,* 310-314.

Lucas-Carrasco R, Skevington SM, Gomez-Benito J, Rejas J, & March, J. (2011). Using the WHOQOL-BREF in persons with dementia: A validation study. *Alzheimer Disease and Associated Disorders. 25,* 345–351.

Maier H, & Smith J. (1999). Psychological predictors of mortality in old age. T*he Journal of Gerontology: Social Sciences. 54,* 44-54.

Meguro K, Akanuma K, Meguro M, Kasai M, Ishii H, & Yamaguchi S. (2015). Lifetime expectancy and quality-adjusted life-year in Alzheimer's disease with and without cerebrovascular disease: Effects of nursing home replacement and donepezil administration -A retrospective analysis in the Tajiri Project. *BMC Neurology. 15,* 227.

Meguro K, Akanuma K, Meguro M. (2013). Patient-reported outcome is important in psychosocial intervention for dementia: A secondary analysis on RCT of group reminiscence approach data. *Dementia and Geriatric Cognitive Disorders Extra, 3*(1), 37-38.

Meguro K, Ishii H, Yamaguchi S, Ishizaki J, Shimada M, Sato M, Hashimoto R, Shimada Y, Meguro M, Yamadori A, & Sekita, Y. (2002). Prevalence of dementia and dementing diseases in Japan: the Tajiri Project. *Archives of Neurology, 59,* 1109– 1114.

Meguro K, Kasai M, Akanuma K, Meguro M, Ishii H, & Yamaguchi S. (2014). Donepezil and life expectancy in Alzheimer's disease: A retrospective analysis in the Tajiri Project. *BMC Neurology, 14,* 83.

Meguro K, Kumai K, Takada J, Chida K, Kato Y, & Yamaguchi S. (2018). Lifetime Expectancy in Dementia with Lewy Bodies: Effects of Donepezil Administration and Special Nursing Home Replacement. A Retrospective Analysis in the Tajiri Project. The *Journal* of *Alzheimer's Disease and Parkinsons, 8,* 1.

Meguro K, Tanaka N, Kasai M, Nakamura K, Ishikawa H, Nakatsuka M, Satoh M, & Ouchi Y. (2012). Prevalence of dementia and dementing diseases in the old-old population in Japan: the Kurihara Project. Implications for Long-Term Care Insurance data. *Psychogeriatrics, 12,* 226-34.

Meguro K. (2017). Cholinesterase inhibitors are compatible with psychosocial intervention for Alzheimer disease patients suggested by neuroimaging findings. *Psychiatry Research: Neuroimagingm 259,* 29-33.

Meguro M, Ishizaki J, & Meguro K. (2009). Collage technique may provide new perspectives for Alzheimer patients by exploring messages from their inner world. *Dementia & Neuropsychologia, 3,* 299-302.

Meguro M, Kasai M, Akanuma K, Ishii H, Yamaguchi S, & Meguro K. (2008). Comprehensive approach of donepezil and psychosocial interventions on cognitive function and quality of life for Alzheimer's disease: The Osaki- Tajiri Project. *Age & Ageing. 37*(4), 69-473.

Meguro M, & Meguro K. (2010). Activated thalamic glucose metabolism after combined donepezil and psychosocial intervention. *British Journal of Neuroscience Nursing,* 6,176-180.

Morris J.C. (1993). The Clinical Dementia Rating (CDR): Current version and scoring rules. *Neurology, 43,* 2412-2414.

Muangpaisan W, Assantachai P, Intalapaporn S, & Pisansalakij D, (2008). Quality of life of the community-based patients with mild cognitive impairment. *Geriatrics & Gerontology International, 80–85.*

Nakamura K, Kasai M, Nakai M, Nakatsuka M, Meguro K. (2016). The group reminiscence approach can increase self-awareness of memory deficits and evoke a life review in people with mild cognitive impairment: The Kurihara Project data. *Journal of the American Medical Directors Association, 17*, 501-507.

Nakatsuka M, Nakamura K, Hamanosono R, Takahashi Y, Kasai M, Sato Y, Suto T, Nagatomi R,& Meguro K. (2015). A cluster randomized controlled trial of non- pharmacological interventions for old-old people assessed as "0.5" of the Clinical Dementia Rating: The Kurihara Project. *Dementia and Geriatric Cognitive Disorders Extra,* 5, 221-232.

Nordström P, Religa D, Wimo A, Winblad B, & Eriksdotter M, (2013). The use of cholinesterase inhibitors and the risk of myocardial infarction and death: a nationwide cohort study in subjects with Alzheimer's disease. *European Heart Journal, 24*, 2585-2591.

Onder G, Zanetti O, Giacobini E, Frisoni GB, Bartorelli L, Carbone G, Lambertucci P, Silveri MC, & Bernabei R. (2005). Reality orientation therapy combined with cholinesterase inhibitors in Alzheimer's disease: randomized controlled trial. *British Journal of Psychiatry*, 187, 450-455.

Ouchi Y, Kasai M, Nakamura K, Nakatsuka M, & Meguro K. (2016). Qualitative Assessment of Instrumental Activities of Daily Living in Older Persons with Very Mild Dementia: The Kurihara Project. *Dementia and Geriatric Cognitive Disorders Extra, 6,* 374-381.

Philippi N, Botzung A, Noblet V, et al. (2015). Impaired emotional autobiographical memory associated with right amygdalar-hippocampal atrophy in Alzheimer's disease patients. *Frontiers in Aging Neuroscience*, 7, 21.

Saxena S, Carlson D, & Billington R: WHOQOL Group. (2001). World Health Organization quality of life. The WHO quality of life assessment instrument (WHOQOL-BREF): the importance of its items for cross-cultural research. *Quality of Life Research. 10*, 711-721.

Tazaki M, & Nakane Y. (2007). A Guide to WHOQOL-26. Revised version. 2007, Tokyo, Kaneko Shobo.

Tezuka K, Meguro K, Akanuma K, Tanaka N, Ishii H, & Yamaguchi S. (2013). Overestimation of self-reported activities of daily living in vascular dementia patients with a right hemisphere lesion. *The Journal of Stroke & Cerebrovascular Diseases. 22*, 9-14.

The EuroQol Group. (1990), EuroQol – a new facility for the measurement of health- related quality of life. *Health Policy*, 199–208.

The WHOQOL Group. (1998). Development of the World Health Organization WHOQOL-BREF quality of life assessment. *Psychological Medicine, 28*, 551-558.

Woodrow P. (1998). Interventions for confusion and dementia 3: Reminiscence. *British Journal of Nursing 7*, 1145-1149.

World Health Organization. (2017a). Constitution of WHO principles. Health is a state of complete physical, mental and social well-being and not merely the absence of disease or infirmity. (June 10, 2017). http://www.who.int/about/mission/en/.

World Health Organization. Introducing the WHOQOL instruments. (2017b). (June 10, 2017). http://depts.washington.edu/seaqol/docs/WHOQOL_Info.pdf.

Yuasa, Y. (1987). The Body: Toward an Eastern Mind-Body Theory, ed. T. P. Kasulis and trans. N. Shigenori and T. P. Kasulis (Albany, NY: State University of New York Press).

Zec RF. (1993). Neuropsychological functioning in Alzheimer's disease. In: Parks RW, Zec RF, Wilson RS, eds, *Neuropsychology in Alzheimer's disease and other dementias*. Oxford: Oxford University Press, 3-80.

Seniors and Sexuality: A Topic Concerning Total Health and Quality of Life

Maria Matza and Nathan Matza

Introduction

The culture of the United States is not comfortable in addressing sexuality as a topic of conversation at any stage of life, however science and human nature dictates that sexuality is a normal and manifested throughout the lifespan. Traditionally, U.S. society continues to express reticence in addressing sexuality at every stage of life, but advocacy efforts to provide health promotion and disease prevention persist. Consider the historical events from the pioneering dedication for women's rights and birth control of Margaret Sanger in 1916, which lead to the founding of Planned Parenthood, to the obstructive federal funding efforts of Presidents Reagan and G.W. Bush for abstinence only education. It was not until the Obama Administration that federal support was allocated for comprehensive sexuality education (Huber & Firmin, 2014). Sexuality education was limited, unscientific, and biased prior to the 1990s until the AIDS epidemic gave this type of education critical importance. Sexuality education should be shared throughout the lifespan as today's seniors enjoy a more active and engaged life, and sexual activity should be included as a measure of their quality of life (Dominguez & Barbagallo, 2016).

Sexuality is not limited to the few moments involved in sexual activity. Rather, it is about the essence of a person. It is expressed in how one does everything, including how one dresses, expresses, listens, moves, and benefits from a quality life. The lack of awareness about the importance of sexual integration into the ordinary sphere of senior life is affecting the physical and mental health of the growing number of seniors who are experiencing an increased lifespan and physical ability to engage in intimate relationships. Advances in technology and science are making it possible to live longer, therefore subjecting seniors to health and social situations that in the past were not addressed. These include physical and mental changes to themselves and their partner because of age or illness; availability of new partners through exposure to social media dating; and risk of exposure to sexually transmitted infections (STIs). This lack of awareness extends to the public, policy makers, health providers, social service providers, and even to older adults.

This chapter will focus on sexuality related to older adults with emphasis on demographics, normal physical changes related to aging, chronic illness and those effects on sexuality and sexual function. Also, this chapter will address partner availability, including LGBTQ couples, safe sex practices, sexually transmitted infections, and HIV risk. Sexuality in the aging population is often negated by health care providers, social service providers, and all forms of media, therefore this chapter opens the door for further education, research, and policies around normal aging and sexual function. Resources related to addressing the sexuality needs of seniors will be provided to health care providers, social agencies, and policy makers, but most importantly as a resource for seniors.

Demographics

There is no clearly defined age when an American becomes a senior citizen. Some may consider themselves seniors when invited to join AARP, qualify for Medicare, or officially receive a pension (Brandon, 2010). In the United States, persons who are of standard retirement age, usually after age sixty are referred to as senior citizens or seniors. These terms refer to the life stage of old age, although it is imprecise to identify the final stage of a normal life span. In a 2010 Del Webb survey 96 percent of current 50-year-olds don't consider themselves senior citizens and only slightly over half (56 percent) of 64-year-olds say the term senior citizen applies to them (Brandon, 2010). In a Pew Center telephone research survey (2009) only 33% of respondents reported that no longer being sexually active was a marker of old age (Pew Social Trends, 2009).

The Centers for Disease Control and Prevention (CDC) predicts that the number of Americans 65 and older will increase from about 40 million (2010) to over 71 million in 2030. (CDC, 2012). The Baby Boomer generation (those born between 1946 and 1964), is considered the largest generation of children born in American history and represents a group of people still sexually active but facing numerous obstacles (Marasco, 2014). The U.S. Census Bureau data (2014-2060) predicts that the Baby Boomers will surpass 100 million by 2060 (Colby & Ortman, 2015). Other populations of seniors that are invisible, and therefore often ignored are underserved seniors with disabilities, those that identify as LGBTQ, and racially and ethnically diverse seniors.

Normal Physiology in Aging

Sexuality has profound implications for human health. Sexual desires and behaviors include psychological and biological aspects, but also social and cultural dimensions affecting all ages of life. Sexuality is more than intercourse; it is the essence of a person. Sexuality for seniors, is often blurred with preconceptions and prejudgments such as the belief that older persons are asexual, abnormal, inappropriate, or even immoral in their behaviors. It is true that normal aging may result in normal physiologic changes that alter sexual functioning and frequency, but research shows that despite normal physiologic changes, many elders continue to maintain and enjoy sexual activity (Dominguez & Barbagallo, 2016).

Knowledge about the interconnectedness between sexual health, quality of life, and aging is recognized but the research is limited. What is identified in the literature is that many seniors strive to continue to have a healthy, active sex life well into the 8th or 9th decade of life (Traeen, Hald, Graham, Enzlin, Janssen, Lunden, Kvalem, et al., 2017; Lindau, et al., 2007). Desire (arousal) is not necessarily absent with aging (Dominguez & Barbagallo, 2016) and should not be confused with libido. After all, if one feels satisfied with their sex life, the aspects of one's sexuality can be difficult to separate from one another. It is a normal physiologic change that libido and arousal do decrease with age (McNicoll, 2008). Libido refers to an individual's baseline interest in sex and may be referred to as sexual appetite. Arousal refers to an individual's physiological response to sexual stimuli. Physical manifestations include vaginal lubrication, and increased blood flow to the penile tissues, the labia, clitoris, and vagina (Yarber & Sayad, 2016).

The desire to have an intimate sexual relationship lasts throughout the lifetime, but sexual expression and frequency may be altered due to the physical and functional limitations of aging. Physiologically, age affects sexual function by prolonging the excitement phase and requiring a longer period of stimulation in order to achieve orgasm in both men and women. The refractory period between orgasms is also longer in both men and women. The term "refractory period" refers to a period immediately following stimulation during which a nerve or muscle is unresponsive to further stimulation (Yarber & Sayad, 2016).

Related to normal physical anatomy and physiology are the psychological or functional facts that older adults may be hesitant or simply too tired to engage in regular sexual acts. Fatigue is a common complaint of busy youth and younger adults, and just as their younger counterparts, older couples need to plan on a date and time to become intimate. It should be noted that too much alcohol can cause difficulties in getting and maintaining an erection in men and delayed orgasm in women (National Institute on Aging, 2017). Open communication with the partner and mutual strategies are essential and will help in boosting self-esteem. Dealing with body image due to normal aging may leave a man or woman feeling less sexy, spontaneous, and more self-conscious in sexual encounters and activity which can fuel relationship conflicts and resentment, creating discord. These changes are due to aging, decreased or fluctuating hormone levels, and gravity. The aging process is associated with body reshaping, reduction in tone and muscle mass, weight gain, and skin wrinkling, but remarkably, preliminary research has not recorded a radical increase of body dissatisfaction with age (NGEAU, 2015). During the seventh decade, women seem to make a parallel adjustment to body ideal, comparing themselves to friends and family and not to models and media celebrities. At this time a woman's role is linked to her role in relation to her family, career, and community, making the link between body satisfaction and appearance not as significant. Predictors of self-esteem are connected functional health and healthy weight. Men, on the other hand are generally satisfied with their body image before age 50; at age 50 there is concern for a desired or lost body ideal. After age 60, there is less difference between genders and sexual functionality is the major priority of intimate partner couples (Grogan, 2012).

On a positive note, population-based surveys find that half or more of healthy older men report no sexual difficulties, but physical health problems and depression are risk factors for erection problems in older men (Traeen, et al., 2017). It is a popular myth that sexual problems are linked to normal aging, that there is no remedy, and so why bother to bring up the subject to a health care provider? Seniors need to be empowered to seek a provider who has been trained to address issues of sexuality in an unbiased, empathetic, and non-judgmental manner (McNicoll, 2008). Treatments and medications are available to treat these concerns; however, seniors should be made aware that many treatments and medications for chronic medical conditions may have side effects that cause reduced sex drive or erectile dysfunction (ISSM, n.d.).

For women, post-menopausal changes and lower levels of testosterone may lead to decreased sexual desire and frequency. Vaginal dryness and dyspareunia (pain with sexual intercourse) may ensue because of anatomical changes to the vagina which shortens, or narrows, and the vaginal walls become stiff. Decreased vaginal lubrication impacts sexual function for many women. Drugs that may enhance sexual function in post-menopausal women do exist, but are often prescribed off-label, as research studies have not been conducted for complete safety and efficacy on this age group. A personal lubricant, either water based, or silicone based, can dramatically improve vaginal moisture and facilitate pleasurable intercourse.

In August of 2015, a new medication, ADDYI™ (Flibanserin), a medication approved for the treatment of pre-menopausal women with hypoactive sexual desire disorder (HSSD) was approved by the FDA. As clinical trials were solely conducted with pre-menopausal women, ADDYI™ is not approved for older women. This drug has many restrictions, including abstinence from alcohol and side effects including low blood pressure, fainting, nausea, dizziness, and sleepiness (addyi.com, n.d.; Margo, 2015). Flibanserin must also be taken daily for a month before it is effective.

Drugs created to treat erectile dysfunction in men such as Viagra™ (sildenafil) have not been approved for use by women but are utilized by some women, either as off-label prescription or personal use. Women using sildenafil have the same side effects as men, including headaches and nasal congestion but sildenafil does increase blood flow to female genitalia, although it does nothing to enhance arousal in women. Basson and colleagues concluded that in a research study studying the effects of sildenafil in both estrogenized or estrogen deficient women, genital physiological effect of Viagra™ was not perceived to improve sexual response in women; more research is needed to find any correlation like the erectile response improvement in men (Basson, McInnes, Smith, Hodgson, & Koppiker, 2004).

As women age, testosterone levels are naturally reduced, and supplemental testosterone may be prescribed with careful monitoring as and it must be carefully monitored. Hormone replacement therapy (estrogen/progesterone) is available to correct decreased hormonal levels but may be contraindicated because of potential risk due to family medical history or co-morbidity. Therefore, the use of a vaginal lubricant or sex toys are methods to greatly improve the sex life for the older woman. Sexual activity may be altered to include mutual masturbation, use of mechanical devices, or simply hugging and kissing. Women outlive men, and/or divorce their partners or spouses, affecting availability of a partner, and therefore significantly reduces sexual activity. Marasco found that in older women, who are actively pursuing to maintain an active sexual life, the most common sexual behaviors in this group of older females include receiving and giving oral sex, vaginal intercourse, as well as solo and partnered masturbation (Marasco, 2014).

Chronic Illness

Life expectancy and better medical care will result in older individuals with chronic diseases living longer, therefore the effects of chronic illness and subsequent treatments affecting sexuality and quality of life must be addressed. Chronic illnesses affect a person's daily life, are ongoing and usually last a year or more. Although, chronic illnesses are usually preventable, they are generally incurable and require ongoing medical attention (AARP, 2009). The most common chronic conditions that affect sexual functioning are arthritis, cancer, cardiovascular (heart) disease, depression, diabetes, erectile dysfunction, and incontinence. Many of these conditions are interrelated, as they can exacerbate conditions either with symptoms or treatment. These are described below.

Arthritis

Many people over 50 have chronic bone conditions such as osteoporosis, back problems, or arthritis. These conditions may be related to each other. For example, osteoporosis may lead to back problems or to a catastrophic hip fracture; likewise forms of rheumatoid arthritis or osteoarthritis can lead to a hip replacement surgery. Arthritis is the leading cause of disability in the United States. One out of four adults are diagnosed with some form of arthritis, is found commonly in both genders, and nearly 50% of American adults over age 65 deal with this condition. Arthritic symptoms that are common to both genders include decreased range of motion (ROM), pain, stiffness, and swelling of joints. Uncontrolled chronic pain can curtail sexual activity in older adults as joint pain can make sexual activity uncomfortable or difficult to achieve due to the need to bend, stretch and reach during intercourse and other sexual activities. Weight gain (caused by not exercising due to arthritic pain) exacerbates joint pain, therefore it is advisable to engage in water type exercises, modified yoga, and other exercises that require gentle bending and stretching. Exercise will provide relief and may reduce the need to rely on oral analgesics for pain relief. Rest, warm baths, changing position or timing of sexual activity can be helpful (National Institute on Aging, 2017).

Erectile Dysfunction

Dominguez & Barbagallo (2016) describe the most common sexual disorders and/or roadblocks for men as erectile dysfunction, delayed ejaculation and reduced sexual interest (Dominguez & Barbagallo, 2016). Erectile dysfunction impacts spontaneity and intimate sexual intercourse. The Urology Care Foundation defines erectile dysfunction (ED) as difficulty to get or keep an erection that is firm enough for sex and ED affects as many as 30 million men in the U.S. (Urology Care Foundation, 2018). Most men have problems with erections from time to time, but when this happens more than half of the time, then ED is present. Health problems that limit blood flow or cause damage to nerves in the penis and stress or emotional reasons can also cause ED. It should be noted that erectile dysfunction can serve as an early warning of a more serious illness. Heart disease, high blood pressure and high blood sugar can all cause ED. Finding and treating the cause(s) of ED can help older adults, as well as younger men, to improve overall health and well-being (Mayo Clinic, n.d.).

Prior to 1998, men suffering from erectile dysfunction had very limited treatment opportunities (Lariviere & Wolff, 2015). Most of the treatments were invasive and included injections, penile prostheses, penis pumps, or vascular reconstructive surgeries. The most common drug was Alprostadil, a penile suppository applied into the urethra or injected into the penis 10 minutes before the erection was needed (Lariviere & Wolff, 2015). Yohimbe is a natural plant extract used as an aphrodisiac and sexual performance enhancer for both genders; it was a popular sexual stimulant prior to the introduction of Viagra. In its natural state Yohimbe is safe but dietary supplements of prescription-strength active ingredients of Yohimbe are potentially dangerous. Yohimbe can cause high blood pressure, anxiety, racing heartbeat, and headaches; at high doses it can cause heart failure or death (Harvard Health Men's Watch, 2015).

In 1998, Viagra (sildenafil) was approved by the FDA for use by men (Dominguez & Barbagallo, 2016) and the United States is the highest user of this drug per capita of any country in the world (Lariviere & Wolff, 2015). Viagra (sildenafil) has become a lifestyle drug that affects quality of life and can be a great help if men use it in conjunction with regular health examinations and visits with health care providers to rule out any other health problems. The most common side effect in taking sildenafil is flushing and nasal congestion. Sildenafil is contraindicated with nitrate containing medicines such as nitroglycerine tablets, sprays, or patches or any other nitrates as blood pressure may suddenly fall to dangerous levels. Men should consult with their health care providers before using any medications, but especially if they have a history of high blood pressure and are being managed with hypertensive drugs, have insufficient hepatic (liver), compromised renal (kidney) function, or use alpha blockers (e.g. doxazosin) for prostate problems. Caution should be taken if alcohol is used simultaneously as alcohol use decreases getting an erection, temporarily lowers blood pressure, and may cause dizziness and fainting. Men with anatomical penile deformities such as angulation, cavernous fibrosis, or Peyronie's disease should be closely monitored by their provider as they may encounter penile strain. Sudden partial or total vision loss in one or both eyes needs to be reported immediately as loss can be partial or complete. Erections lasting more than four hours (priapism) are rare but must receive immediate medical attention to prevent tissue damage and permanent loss of ability to have an erection.

It is important to understand the indirect effects of Viagra on nontarget groups such as partners. The effects of Viagra on males has been researched, but little research has been conducted to study how the lifestyles of partners is affected positively or negatively using this drug or increase in risky sexual behavior (Lariviere & Wolff, 2015). A qualitative study conducted in New Zealand in 2003 explored women's heterosexual experiences and concerns about the downside of Viagra (Potts, Gavey, Grace, & Vares, 2003). Three key dimensions were identified by women about use of Viagra by male partners: the neglect of women by the pharmaceutical industry and health providers; the physical and psychosocial aspects of the impact on relationship when Viagra is used; and broader socio-cultural impact on understanding male and female sexuality in older individuals (Potts, et al, 2003). To summarize the implications of this study, more attention needs to be paid to partners' perspectives, desires and the dynamics of each individual relationship.

Cardiovascular Disease (CVD)

Sexual activity is equivalent to mild to moderate exercise in the range of 3 to 5 METS. METS are metabolic equivalents which translate to climbing 2 flights of stairs or walking briskly for a short duration (Hellerstein & Friedman, 1970) and considering an individual's capacity to perform physical activity (Levine, Steinke, Bakaeen, Bozkurt, Cheitlin, Conti, Foster, … Stewart, 2012.)

Decreased sexual activity and function are common in patients with CVD and often interrelated to anxiety and depression. CVD can result in hardening or narrowing of the arteries and decreased blood flow, consequently impacting arousal, libido, and orgasm for both men and women. A history of having experienced a myocardial infarction (MI), commonly called a heart attack, can impede sexual functioning in couples; there may be hesitation to have sexual intercourse for fear of having another MI. Studies have repeatedly shown that sexual activity following a MI is relatively safe (Dahabreh & Paulus, 2011). Recent guidelines from the American College of Cardiology and the American Heart Association recommend that physicians counsel patients about resuming sexual activity following an MI (Abramsohn, Decker, Garavalia, Garavalia, Gosch, Krumholz, Spertus, …Tessler Lindau, 2013; Levine, et. al., 2012; Steinke, Bakaeen, Bozkurt, Cheitlin, Conti, Foster, …Stewart, 2012). Older adults should have their health care provider rule out any coexisting problems related to cardiac function and sexual activity with a comprehensive history and physical examination (Levine et. al., 2012; National Institute on Aging, 2009). Depending on an individual's medical history and physical function, providers may counsel older adults towards counseling, cardiac rehab, medications, diet, and/or exercise. Patients with unstable symptoms should be treated first before engaging in physical activity. Exercise testing can provide additional information as to the safety of sexual activity. It is ideal that conversations about sexuality and cardiac rehabilitation between client and provider be initiated following a cardiac event; studies show that there are major gaps in communication between provider and patient, especially among older female patients as the women who discussed sex with their physicians initiated the conversation themselves (Abramsohn, et al., 2013). It is also important to involve partners in discussions following first MI as studies show a decrease in partner's sexual function. Providers, including nurses, need to provide sensitive encouragement, along with clear and practical information about sexuality to older adults (Arenhall, Erikksson, Nilsson, Steinke, & Fridlunds, 2018).

Strokes

Stroke is a leading cause of disability that can impair physical, linguistic, cognitive and sexual function (Park, Ovbiagele, & Feng, 2015). Normal sexual function relies on a complex network of central and peripheral nervous system pathways involving autonomic (sympathetic/parasympathetic), spinal, and somatic nervous systems. However, little is known about the impact of stroke on sexual activity or which specific psychological or organic factors contribute to SD after stroke. Strokes are the result of death to brain cells due to lack of oxygen flow from a cerebrovascular accident (CVA) from a clot or thrombus, or from a cerebral hemorrhage (brain bleed). The result of a stroke may result in a variety of neurologic changes that range from paralysis to weakness, causing degrees of immobility, and usually affecting one side of the body. Depending on the location in the brain where the insult to the brain occurred, will determine function and rehabilitation potential. Strokes can affect the areas of the brain that control arm and leg movements, thus preventing couples from achieving the sexual positions they are used to using and enjoying.

Sexual dysfunction after a stroke can present as decreased libido, impotence or inability to ejaculate in males or decreased libido, lack of vaginal lubrication, arousal problems or orgasmic dysfunction in females. It is also affected by a variety of psycho-social factors, the most prominent being depression, fear, and fatigue which materialize in behaviors of low self-esteem, uncertainty of relationships, preoccupation with finances, and difficulty accepting a life with a disability (Park, et., al., 2015; Rosenbaum, et., al. 2014). Libido may be adversely affected by medication meant to manage post stroke issues such as high blood pressure and depression. Strokes may affect genital sensation, leading to numbness, or there may be a failure to recognize one's own genitals or other parts of their body (agnosia) (Karaahmet, Gurcay, Avluk, Umay, Gundogdu, Ecerkale, & Cakci, 2017).

Sexual satisfaction can change dramatically after a stroke. Research studies measuring satisfaction pre and post stroke find scores dropping from 90% to less than 50%, respectively (Rosenbaum, Vadas, & Kalichman, 2014.) Other studies measured post stroke dissatisfaction in males to be greater than in females (Park, et al, 2015). After a stroke, there may be a temporary interruption in sexual activity that serves as time to adapt to necessary modifications and accommodations. One study showed that 80% of men who report erectile dysfunction after a stroke regain function a few months later (Karaahmet, et. al., 2017). However, post-stroke, many couples endure sexual problems for years after, due to fear of initiating another stroke, immobility, depression, and damage to area of the brain that control or effect sexual function. The scientific literature describes hyposexuality after stroke as common, but in some rare cases, a stroke may increase sexuality or unusual or inappropriate sexual behavior. If the stroke affects the hypothalamus, the area that controls the sex hormones, this can affect a person's sex drive. Hypersexuality after stroke is commonly associated with temporal lobe lesions, subthalamic or bilateral thalamic infarction.

Of all post-stroke disabilities, sexual dysfunction is the most under-recognized (Park, et, al., 2015). Understandably stroke patients are often embarrassed to discuss sexuality issues with their physicians, but even people that are wheelchair-bound still have sexual feelings and desires. Patient reticence and physician ignorance have arguably led to a relative neglect of sexuality informed post-stroke interventions. There is a critical need to provide education and the skills about sexuality for providers and rehabilitation professionals in order to be able to address this issue with post-stroke patients and their partners.

Diabetes

Diabetes Mellitus (DM) is a common chronic condition in the United States with an estimated lifetime risk of 32.8% in men and 38.5% in women (Copeland, Brown, Creasman, Van Den Eden, Subak, Thom, et. al., 2012). Among men, diabetes is a recognized risk factor for sexual dysfunction with prior research documenting an over threefold increased risk of erectile dysfunction in diabetic men compared with nondiabetic men; ED is known to occur in approximately 50% of men with diabetes prior to age 60 (Whitehouse, 2009). The effects of diabetes on sexual function among women is not fully understood and little research on women has been conducted (Maiorino, Bellastella, & Esposito, 2017; Copeland, et. al., 2012; Whitehouse, 2009). Some researchers report a wide variety of issues related to sexual function in diabetic women with strong link to psychological factors associated with stress and especially coexisting depression (Mayo Clinic, 2011; Giraldi & Kristensen, 2010). There are two major effects on sexual function in women with diabetes. The first is due to vascular changes in the urogenital lubrication tissues affecting genital lubrication and the second is neuropathy affecting genital arousal response. The global effects of diabetes on overall health, physical and mental functioning, and interpersonal relationships affects the woman's interest, satisfaction, and ability to participate in sexual activity. It has been hypothesized that sexual dysfunction in women with diabetes mellitus exists due to hyperglycemia or high blood sugars which lead to reduced hydration of mucous membranes (vaginal tissue) and therefore poor lubrication and painful intercourse (dyspareunia). Hyperglycemia is also associated with urinary tract infections, yeast infections

It is important to understand the role that medications play in sexual dysfunction. Diabetes is usually accompanied by comorbidities that are managed pharmacologically. There are more than 200 medications that can cause or directly contribute to sexual dysfunction in adults of any age. Medications that have the most side effects include, but are not limited to cardiovascular drugs, anti-hypertensives, and psychotropic drugs. Older adults may attribute sexual dysfunction to aging rather than medication-interaction, therefore a review of all prescribed, over the counter, and herbal/natural supplements should be assessed by a provider or clinician for possible side effects or harmful interactions (Whitehouse, 2009).

Incontinence

Urinary incontinence is a common among 15 to 55 % of all women (Lains Mota, 2017). According to the North American Menopause Society, urinary leakage during intercourse is estimated to affect up to a quarter of women with incontinence (North American Menopause Society [NAMS], 2018). The main risk factors for developing urinary incontinence are vaginal childbirth and increased age (NAMS, 2018). UI is also associated with obesity, pelvic surgery, perception of self-image, and chronic disease (Felippe, Zambon, Girotti, Shulze Burti, Rosenblatt Hacad, Cadamuro, & Almeida, 2017; Lains Mota, 2017; National Institute of Diabetes, Digestive, and Kidney Disease [NIDDK], n.d.). Incontinence or loss of bladder control or leaking of urine is more common in older women and may be associated with aging, pelvic surgery, hormonal influence, perception of self-image, and chronic disease. At perimenopause and at menopause estrogen levels are reduced and may cause thinning of the lining of the urethra which is the short tube that passes urine from the bladder out of the body. The pelvic muscles surrounding the urethra may weaken with the aging process and cause pelvic relaxation. As a result, women at midlife and beyond are at increased risk for urinary incontinence. It is a symptom that affects the quality of life of women mainly in their social, familiar and sexual domains (Lains Mota, 2017).

The most prevalent form of urinary incontinence is associated with stress, (SUI) followed by mixed urinary incontinence (MUI), and urge urinary incontinence (UUI). SUI is caused by weak pelvic floor muscles is present pre-menopause, and usually does not worsen with menopause. The most common symptoms of SUI are leakage of urine with coughing, laughing, sneezing, or lifting of heavy objects. Urge incontinence (UII) is frequently termed as overactive bladder and is caused by overly active or irritated bladder muscles. The most common symptom is the frequent and sudden urge to urinate, with occasional leakage of urine (NAMS, 2018). Pressure on the abdominal area during sex could be embarrassing and force many women to avoid sex (NIH 2017). The fear of odor from incontinence during sexual intercourse, compounded by the unpredictability and chronicity, promotes anxiety and damages self-esteem in women. Those women living with UI are more likely to be sexually abstinent than continent women (Lains Mota, 2017). Furthermore, women with UI showed less sexual desire, sexual comfort, and sexual satisfaction than their counterparts despite having a similar frequency of sexual activity (Felippe, et. al., 2017).

There are several treatment options for UI. Conservative treatment may begin with pelvic floor muscle training (Kegel Exercise) to the simple practice of urinating right before intercourse (NAMS, 2018). Pharmacological treatment then onto pharmacological treatment, and surgical procedures. Research has been conducted on conservative and surgical treatment options in relation to female sexual function; there is limited research on pharmacological management and its effect on sexual function.

Surgical Procedures Affecting Sexuality

Surgery and complications from surgery can be worrisome for people throughout their lives, especially for the older adult. For both men and women, reproductive surgical procedures are especially disconcerting. Communication and support are always important in maintaining a relationship, and chronic illness tests partners, friends, and family. Not all reproductive surgical procedures are for cancer management, but many surgeries are for the treatment of different types of malignancies, including breast, uterine, ovarian, or cervical cancers. The most common surgeries encountered are hysterectomy (with or without removal of the ovaries) and breast surgery for breast cancer. Mastectomies are no longer the only surgical option in the treatment of breast cancer; today there are fewer radical procedures offered. Nonetheless, breast cancer survivors who have undergone a lumpectomy or simple mastectomy report satisfaction with their sex lives to be between 70 to

73% before treatment but after treatment their satisfaction dropped between 50 to 56%. Of those participants who have undergone as simple mastectomy report feeling less attractive after surgery (Davis, Meneses, & Hilfinger Messias, 2010). Persons diagnosed with any type of cancer may be offered different treatment options depending on type, site, and stage of the cancer. With or without surgery they may be treated with combinations of chemotherapy and radiation. All these options have implications on sexuality, self-image, and pain from skin sensitivity following radiation to neuropathy caused by various chemotherapy agents. Those having undergone breast surgery may be affected by decreased mobility and use of affected upper extremity or extremities. Depending on the type of tumor, men or women may not have the option for hormone replacement therapy. For women, symptoms such as vaginal dryness, itching, and dyspareunia maybe exacerbated. Physically and psycho-socially these diagnosis and treatment affect an older person's sexual desire. Non-hormonal treatments may be sought. Breast reconstruction is also available and is an option for the older woman.

There are numerous support groups and educational programs offered by the American Cancer Society and the Susan J. Komen Organization is available for women facing a breast cancer diagnosis (https://ww5.komen.org/BreastCancer/AboutBreastCancer.html.). Communication among partners, family, and friends are significant in recovery, survivorship and quality of life. City of Hope National Medical Center offers online guidance for patients and their partners (Blitz, 2016). It is important for seniors to address fears and issues of sexuality with their health care providers. It is equally important for providers to be prepared to answer these questions or at least to refer to programs that provide guidance and support.

Prostate Cancer

After skin cancer, prostate cancer (PC) is the most common cancer among men and the second leading cause of cancer death, after lung cancer (American Cancer Society [ACS], 2018).

The ACS estimates that 1 in 9 men will be diagnosed in their lifetime. PC develops mainly in older men and in African-American men. About 6 cases in 10 are diagnosed in men aged 65 or older, and it is rare before age 40. The average age at the time of diagnosis is about 66. The good news is that because of the slow progression of PC, many men diagnosed do not die from the disease (ACS, 2018; Canalichio, Jaber, & Wang, 2015; Graeffen & Schlomm, 2012). In fact, more than 2.9 million men in the United States who have been diagnosed with prostate cancer at some point are still alive today (ACS, 2018). Because of the chronic nature of the disease and the extended time from premalignant lesion to clinically relevant cancer, treatment should focus not only on survival but also on quality of life and sexual health (Canalichio, Jaber, & Wang, 2015).

Treatment options are dependent on stage at time of diagnosis. Because of the slow progression of PC watchful waiting or active surveillance may be initiated in the early stages. In active surveillance the cancer is monitored closely by physician visits that include prostate specific antigen (PSA) blood test and digital rectal exam (DRE) about every 6 months. If results change, treatment options are offered. This includes monitoring of PSA levels. Watchful waiting describes a less intensive follow up with fewer tests and reliance on symptoms to determine if treatment is needed. Active treatment options include surgery, radiation therapy, cryotherapy (cryosurgery), hormone therapy, chemotherapy, vaccine therapy, and bone-directed treatment. A prostate cancer dedicated website provided by the ACS offers definitions, guidance and resources. It is offered at the end of this chapter under resources.

Treatment decisions should be made after considering the health status and life expectancy of the individual patient. Due to increased life expectancy, the incidence of prostate cancer is expected to rise, making effective management of this high-risk senior patient group increasingly important (Canalichio, et. al., 2015). Radical prostatectomy (RP) can increase survival and decrease the risk of metastatic progression. Surgical and postsurgical complications are affected more by comorbidity than by age. If eligible, the patient should be offered radical prostatectomy as a potentially curative treatment, without a rigid restriction to a certain chronological age (Graefen & Schlomm, 2012). The risk of PC affects a high proportion of men over 70 years of age, who are likely to have high-risk disease and without intervention, a substantial risk of prostate-cancer-specific death (Graefen & Schlomm, 2012). Male sexual health is affected by therapies currently available for PC. It is important for providers to have individualized discussions with their patients to explain the risks associated with all treatment options. Advanced age may increase the likelihood of incontinence following radical prostatectomy (Graefen & Schlomm, 2012) and erectile function will be less effected if a patient has preoperative potency, is younger, or is having a nerve-sparing surgery. There is often a delayed recovery of erectile function up to 2 years following RP. Options for penile rehabilitations are available, however this will depend on the patient, his partner, and the willingness and ability of the provider to communicate these options.

Availability of Partners

Estimates from the U.S. Census Bureau project that in 2050 the population aged 65 and over is projected to be 83.7 million, almost double from the 2012 estimate of 43.1 million (Ortman, Velkoff, & Hogan, 2014). The baby boomers are largely responsible for this increase in the older population, as they began turning 65 in 2011. By 2050, the surviving baby boomers will be over the age of 85. The changing sex structure among the older population will also have social and economic consequences. Although female life expectancy has long exceeded male life expectancy, resulting in women outnumbering men in the older age groups, the gap between men and women is expected to narrow by 2050 due to increased life expectancy for both groups (Ortman, et., al, 2014). The longevity gap between the sexes may be narrowing, but women will continue to outlive men, therefore the share of women living alone tends to be higher than that of men. Lindau and colleagues found the impact of age on spouse availability or other intimate partner was much more prevalent among women (Lindau, Schumm, Laumann, Levinson, O'Muircheartaigh, & Waite, 2007). Their data revealed that 78% of men 75 to 85 years, compared to 40% of women in the same age group reported having an intimate partner or spouse. This difference was explained by the fact that among older adults, men would marry women younger than themselves, and men die earlier as compared to women (Lindau, et. al., 2007).

Spouses may be able to continue to care for each other, and there may be a demand for aging in place, assisted living arrangements, or institutional care for couples. Couples going into assisted living or institutions are confronted with numerous factors that impact privacy and sexual activity. (Palacios-Ceña, Mártinez-Piedrola, Pérez de Heredia, Huertas Hoyas, Carrasco Garrido, & Fernández de las Peñas2016; Mahieu & Gastmans, 2015). Other than the physical limitations associated with normal aging and chronic conditions, divorced or widowed seniors may be left without a sexual partner, or seniors may find themselves admitted to a long-care facility. Barriers to sexuality exist in institutional settings where the medical model of safety and physical care supersede other needs. Some of these barriers are lack of privacy, negative attitudes from staff, family, and themselves about sexual activity in seniors, criticism or gossip from other residents, lack of a partner, cognitive decline (dementia), and physical limitations (Palacios- Ceña, et., al., 2016). LGBTQ seniors may no longer feel comfortable disclosing their preference and therefore someone who came out years before, may find themselves going "back in the closet" (Spring, 2015).

For those seniors who find themselves divorced or widowed, they may choose to live independently in senior communities where socialization may be readily available and partners accessible. Older adults may not be aware of sexual health risks as they no longer are concerned with contraception and pregnancy and may not consider STIs as a threat to their health. Sexuality education and avoidance of risky behavior should be reintroduced at this stage of life.

Older adults may turn to online dating over more traditional methods of establishing romance and relationships because they have fewer natural social institutions available to find a partner and are more finite in their expectations as they no longer are focusing on future goals (Stephure, et. al., 2009). Although there is little research in the area of online dating and seniors, a Canadian survey published in 2009 reported that online dating may increase rather than decrease with age (Stephure, Boone, MacKinnon, & Deveau, (2009). In searching online there are multiple dating websites intended for use by seniors or adults 50+: SilverSingles; Elite Singles; Match; eHarmony; and even AARP offers a site (http://www.datingadvice.com/online-dating/best-dating-sites-for-over-50). Even with the multitude of sites, Internet users 55 years of age and older are substantially underrepresented among visitors to online dating sites.

LGBT Older Adults

The National Institutes of Health (NIH) defines "sexual and gender minority" as an all-inclusive term for the federal government. Not only does the label include lesbian, gay, bisexual and transgender populations; but it also includes other non-binary individuals that identify or have gender expressions, or reproductive development that fluctuates from cultural, societal or physiological norms (NIH, 2017).

For decades LGBTQ individuals have suffered various forms of discrimination. From the transformative 1969 Stonewall riots in New York City, when gay men were harassed and arrested while socializing in bars, to numerous discriminatory practices and vicious attacks on transgender persons in the 2000s (NTDS, 2016). On June 26, 2015, same-sex marriage was established in all 50 states as a result of the ruling of the Supreme Court of the United States in the landmark civil rights case of Obergefell v. Hodges. The habits, behaviors and health, of the older LGBTQ adult as related to sexuality remains nearly unknown, or as some state, "the invisible of the invisible minority" (Dworkin, 2006). Recent studies indicate that there are more than 39 million people in the U.S. age 65 years or older and about 2.4 million seniors identify as lesbian, gay, bisexual, transgender, and/or questioning (LGBTQ). This unique older adult population will increase from 12.8 % to an estimated 19 % by 2030 (Choi & Meyer, 2016). Compared to cisgender older adults, LGBTQ older adults have worse mental and physical health. Cisgender is described as perception of gender identity where individuals' experiences of their own gender agree with the sex they were assigned at birth (Yarber & Sayad, 2016). LGBTQ older adults have higher rates of risks for mental health issues, disease, disability, depressive symptoms often associated with victimization and stigma (Mustanski, Andrews, & Puckett, 2016).

Most importantly, since LGBTQ individuals often frequented bars as a haven for socialization, studies revealed that LGBTQ older adults have higher prevalence of smoking, excessive alcohol and drug use and risky sexual behaviors compared to non-LGBTQ adults (Choi & Meyer, 2016). They live with high rates of stress facing various levels of discrimination in their daily lives and Hunt (2012) reports that LGBTQs have astoundingly higher rates of substance abuse. Gay and transgender individuals smoke up to 200 percent more than heterosexual peers; have twenty-five percent alcohol abuse compared to 5 to 10 % of the general population. Men that have sex with men (MSM) are 3.5 times more likely to use marijuana and 9.5 times more likely to use heroin than men who do not have sex with men (Hunt, 2012).

Besides the life-long need to address sexual orientation and gender identity, LGBTQ older adults often suffer health care disparities such as lack of insurance coverage and finding sensitive and culturally competent health care providers. Tragically, less than one in four older LGBTQ adults reveal their sexual identity which leads to inappropriate screening and treatment related to sexual health. Identifying the specific sexual behavior practices of the LGBTQ older adult is limited or non-existent (Hillman, 2016). Lindau and colleagues completed a study of 3005 U.S. adults (1550 women and 1455 men) ages 67-85 years of age to determine the sexual behaviors of older adults. They concluded that many older adults are still sexually active. Women were less likely than men to have an intimate partner or spouse, and sexually related problems were infrequently discussed with physicians (Lindau, Schumm, Laumann, Levinson, O'Muircheartaigh, & Waite, 2007). These findings are based on national data that indicate that older adults "still desire sex" and are engaging in sexual activity with spouses or other intimate partners.

Data on LGBTQ older adult's sexuality is very limited; and subgroups within the LGBTQ population is even more understudied. Little is known about transgender and bisexual intersectional groups. Examples would be older Asian transmen, Black lesbians, or Hispanic transwomen. Policies should focus on older LGBTQ individuals and should be recognized by the Older Americans Act (OAA) as a social group with the "greatest social need." The Older Americans Act of 1965 was the first federal initiative aimed at providing comprehensive services for older adults (OAA, 1965), and should provide the impetus to yield culturally prepared training offered to social workers, medical professionals and psychological experts to help this subgroup with support, especially dealing with sexual disparities.

STIs and HIV Risks

The 2016 Surveillance from the Centers for Disease Control (CDC) estimates that the incidence of STIs is more than 20 million new STIs in the U.S. each year. The Centers for Disease Control and Prevention (CDC) reports significant increases in STIs between 2010 and 2014 among adults 65 and over: chlamydia infections increased by about 52 percent; syphilis infections rose by about 65 percent; and gonorrhea cases increased by more than 90 percent. Is Viagra™ to blame or are American Baby Boomers living longer, healthier lives? Is the availability of partners or a lack of sex education in older adults accounting for such a dramatic increase in STIs (Berkeley Wellness, 2016, CDC 2015)?

Sexually transmitted infections (STIs) have been significant in the battle for public health. Despite efforts to educate providers and the public about STIs, entire cultural and ethnic groups continue to endure stigmatization and ostracism. In recent years gonorrhea rates have been historically low, syphilis infections were very close to elimination, and new advances in prevention and screening has reduced chlamydia infections. However, that progress stopped around 2016 as CDC surveillance studies identified a rise in condom-less sex; the increased use of dating websites and apps; more sensitive laboratory detection; and funding cuts to public health clinics (Belluz, 2017). Reported cases of syphilis continue to climb, and antibiotic resistant gonorrhea strains have become a major concern. Additionally, women are often asymptomatic to STIs and face undiagnosed infections putting them at risk for increased morbidity (CDC, 2016). Older women are at increased risk for HIV and other STI infections because of vaginal dryness and the thinning vaginal wall creates an environment conducive to injury and infection. In 2011, the *Orlando Sentinel* reported CDC data about syphilis and chlamydia among older adults outpacing the nation's average. Among all age groups nationwide, reported cases of syphilis increased 60 percent between 2005 and 2009, while in the 55 to 64 age group it increased 70 percent. Meanwhile, the incidences of chlamydia rose 27 percent among all ages, and double that among those age 55 to 64 (Jameson, 2011). In the Sunbelt where retirees have formed large communities, the rise was even more dramatic. In Arizona's Maricopa and Pima counties, where retirees have formed large communities, reported cases were up 87 percent among those 55 and older in those counties. Central and South Florida, Palm Springs, and other senior Meccas reflect similar data (Jameson, 2011).

While the overall prevalence of HIV in the U.S. population had decreased by the late 2000s, older adults have been significantly impacted by the virus. HIV/AIDS education and media attention have LGBTQ youth using PrEP or PEP as prophylaxis in HIV-free youth. Pre-exposure prophylaxis (or PrEP) is when people at very high risk for HIV take HIV (injection drug users, unprotected sex with numerous partners, men that have sex with men) medicines daily to lower their chances of getting infected. A combination of two HIV medicines (tenofovir and emtricitabine), sold under the name Truvada®, is approved for daily use as PrEP to help prevent an HIV-negative person from getting HIV from a sexual or injection-drug-using partner who's positive. Studies have shown that PrEP is highly effective for preventing HIV if it is used as prescribed. PrEP is much less effective when it is not taken consistently (CDC, 2015b). LGBTQ youth are aware of these preventative strategies, however older people in the United States are not educated about these preventative methods or may already be infected and have late stage HIV infection at the time of diagnosis (CITE). This lack of knowledge leads to new infection or to late treatment and immune-system damage to an already compromised senior. Many health care providers do not include questions about sexual activity in their history and examination, losing an opportunity to test older people for HIV infection. Additionally, older people may mistake HIV symptoms for those of normal aging or symptoms of a cold or flu (CDC, 2015b).

Many older people are sexually active, including those living with HIV, and may have the same HIV risk factors as younger people, including ignorance about HIV prevention, multiple partners, or infection from a new sex partners. In 2015 the CDC reported that persons aged 50 and over accounted for 17% (6,725) of the 39, 513 HIV diagnoses in 2015 in the United States. People aged 50 to 54 accounted for 45% (3,010) of the diagnoses among people aged 50 and over. Among people aged 50 and over, Black/African Americans accounted for 43% of all new HIV diagnoses in 2015. Whites accounted for 36%, and Hispanics/Latinos accounted for 17%. Among people aged 50 and older, 49% of new HIV diagnoses in 2015 were among gay and bisexual men, 15% were among heterosexual men, 23% were among heterosexual women, and 12% were among persons who inject drugs. From 2010 to 2014, HIV diagnoses among all people aged 50 and over decreased by 10%. However, in 2014, 40% of people aged 55 and older had late stage infection (AIDS) at the time of primary HIV diagnosis (CDC, 2015b).

For the older adults, numerous factors compound their risk for STIs. Researcher McDaniel explains that men using ED drugs plus post-menopausal women who no longer fear pregnancy, are the perfect formula for unprotected and risky sexual activity. It is significant that fewer older men are available, so women to please and maintain a partner may have risky unprotected sex. Older adults are now using on-line dating and thus are relatively unfamiliar with the sexual history of the new partner. Baby Boomers came from the sexual revolution of the 1960s/1970s and are now reverting to the previous risky sexual behavior of their youth. Many older adults married without ever receiving any form of standardized sex education. Now divorced or widowed, they are faced with new relationships and are susceptible to the same communicable diseases as other single people. Seniors are often embarrassed to discuss sexual issues with their health care providers and likewise providers have not been trained to routinely assess for sexual activity in their senior patients (McDaniel, 2014).

Media Influences

The term ageism was first used by the American gerontologist Robert Butler in 1968. He characterized it as "Ageism allows the younger generations to see older people more different than themselves; thus, they subtly cease to identify with their elders as human beings" (Minichiello, Hawkes, & Pitts, 2011, p. 184). Supported by medical authority in its treatment of old age and by social norms that equate old age with physical and mental decline, elders are metaphorically and patently institutionalized by American society. The world worships youth, and conversely, aging is represented with a negative body image of frailty, disability, and dependence. Many of these stereotypes and myths stem from fears about the aging process and its associated outcomes. The association between aging and ill health has also been prominent in commercial advertising, even in advertising campaigns deemed as accurate representations of the aged (Minichiello, et. al., 2011)

Often the general population, and especially major media sources, have portrayed the elderly as asexual, non-sexual, or as a source of ridicule. For many Americans, the thought of parents or grandparents showing an interest in sexual activity is appalling, especially if in assisted living or skilled nursing facility. Situation comedies, stand-up comedians, and others use humor to focus on the sexual activities of older Americans. A recent report from Harvard University simplifies three common myths about sex for the older adult (Harvard, 2017).

Myth 1: Only the young are sexually attractive.

The culture we live in exalts youth. Turn on the TV or open a magazine and you'll be barraged with images of supple skin, firm flesh, and beautiful models with lustrous locks. But if your mirror is reflecting a different picture these days, you may feel like the party is going on without you.

The reality: Older can be quite sexy.

Sure, thinning hair, laugh lines, and a paunchy midriff are no picnic. But think back on what it was that made you attractive in your younger years. Was it your soulful brown eyes, your crooked smile, or maybe your infectious laugh? Chances are, those attributes are still as appealing as ever. In fact, a 1999 survey conducted by the AARP and *Modern Maturity Magazine* revealed that the percentage of people age 45 and older who consider their partners physically attractive "increases with age" (AARP, 1999).

Myth 2: Sexuality in later life is undignified.

Whether it's the white-haired grandmother fussing with her knitting or the loveable old grandpa puffing on a pipe, society is inclined to desexualize older adults. When older adults do express their sexuality, it's often viewed with derision — for example, the stereotype of the "dirty old man."

The reality: It's healthy for older adults to express their sexuality.

People are living longer and remaining healthier. And they are more vigorous than ever before. Former President George H.W. Bush took his last skydiving dive to celebrate his 90th birthday, John Glenn returned to space at age 77, and Carol Sing forged a new world record at 57 by becoming the oldest woman to swim the English Channel. In 2016, Daljinder Kaur, a woman from India gave birth at age 70! While issues of sperm motility, morphology and concentration may result in older men; men are still able to impregnate women into their 90s! (Harris, Fronczak, Roth, et al., 2011). With this trend toward later-life vitality, why shouldn't seniors be allowed to cast off outdated and ill-fitting stereotypes in order to express their normal, healthy sexual appetites?

Myth 3: Men and women lose their ability to perform sexually after a certain age.

Vaginal dryness and erectile difficulties loom large as you hurtle past 50. You may be feeling that you should just listen to what your body is trying to tell you: Sex is a thing of the past (Harvard, 2017). Once again, myths can be replaced by many sexually active people who exercise and help minimize pain from their arthritic bodies.

Most surprisingly from the AARP study was that the myths about sex among the elderly is opposite from what is portrayed. The study used a multivariate analysis called CART (Classification and Regression Trees) which impacts overall life satisfaction and sexual satisfaction in men and women. The important measures in the analysis were: feeling that difficulties were getting so high they could not overcome them; feeling that things were going their way; feeling happy during the past seven days; overall health; having a spouse or partner who is a skillful lover; having an exciting spouse; and having a spouse or partner who is a best friend (AARP, 1999).

For females, the factors that most affect their satisfaction with their sex life included: having a partner who is imaginative about sex; whether or not feel that people dislike her; having an exciting partner; whether or not enjoy sex; feeling that sex is critical to a good relationship; feeling that sex is important to the overall quality of life; feeling that partner understand her needs; and whether or not feel that sex is for younger people.

For males, the factors that most affect their satisfaction with their sex life included: whether they were happy in the last seven days; overall health; and feeling that their spouse or partner is romantic and feeling that their spouse or partner is sensitive to their moods. Thus, this data contradicts so many popular stereotypes that women only want romance and a sensitive partner. It is quite the opposite. Men do want romance, and women do want imaginative and exciting sex (AARP, 1999).

Conclusion

Baby Boomers are largely responsible for the dramatic demographic change related to age forecasted in the U.S. population. By 2050, the population of seniors aged 65 and over will double to 83.7 million (Ortman, et. al. 2014) and today's seniors are demanding a better quality of life than experienced by prior senior generations. Advances in technology and science are making it possible to live longer, therefore subjecting seniors to health and social situations that in the past were not addressed. This chapter provided an opportunity to examine many of the areas that impact sexuality and its importance to a total quality life. What stands out to the authors of this chapter is the lack of awareness about the importance of sexuality in senior life. This awareness is shared with everyone, including seniors, health and social service providers, and policy makers. In 2016, the state of California enacted the California Healthy Youth Act which mandates a revised curriculum of comprehensive sexuality education for middle and high school youth (CDE, 2017). It is critical that this communication and skill-based education be shared with older adults, so they may continue to enjoy a holistic, safe, and high-quality life. After all, sexuality is so much more than sexual activity, it is the essence of a person.

References

AARP. (2009). 1. Chronic Conditions Among Older Americans. AARP Public Policy Institute beyond 50.09. Retrieved from https://www.aarp.org/health/medicare-insurance/info-03- 2009/beyond_50_hcr.html

Abramsohn, E., Decker, C., Garavalia, B., Garavalia, L., Gosch, K., Krumholz, H., Spertus, J. A., Tessler Lindau, S. (2013). "I'm not just a heart, I'm a whole person here": A qualitative study to improve sexual outcomes in women with myocardial infarction. *Journal of the American Heart Association,* 2, 1-11.

Addis, I.B., Van Den Eeden, S.K., Wassel-Fyr, C.L., Vittinghoff, E., Brown, J.S., & Thom, D.H. (2006). Sexual activity and function in middle-aged and older women. *Obstetrics & Gynecology,* *107,* 755-764.

Advocates for Youth. (n.d.). *Sexual Health Education for Young People with Disabilities* Research and Resources for Educators, Retrieved from http://www.advocatesforyouth.org/publications/publications-a-z/2559

Addyi.com. (n.d.) Retrieved from http://www.addyi.com.

American Cancer Society. (2018). *Prostate Cancer.* Retrieved from https://www.cancer.org/cancer/prostate-cancer.html

APA, (2001-2003). Aging and Human Sexuality Resource Guide. Retrieved from http://www.apa.org/pi/aging/resources/guides/sexuality.aspx

Arenhall, E., Eriksson, M, Nilsson, U. Steinke, E. E., & Fridlund, B. (2018). Decreased sexual function in partners' after first myocardial infarction. *European Journal of Cardiovascular Nursing,* 00, 0,1-6.

Belluz, J. (2017). 5 reasons why 3 STDs are roaring back in America. Retrieved from https://www.vox.com/science-and-health/2017/9/27/16371142/2016-record-year-syphilis-gonorrhea-chlamydia.

Berkeley Wellness Newsletter. (2016). University of California. Retrieved from http://www.berkeleywellness.com/self-care/sexual-health/article/seniors-sex-and-stds

Basson, R., McInnes, R., Smith, M., Hodgson, G., & Koppiker (2004). Efficacy and safety of sildenafil citrate in women with sexual dysfunction associated with female sexual arousal disorder. *Journal of Women's Health & Gender-Based Medicine. 11*(4).

Blitz, C. (2016). Supporting a Partner with Breast Cancer. Retrieved from http://www.breastcancer.org/community/podcasts/partners-20160209.

Brandon, E. (2009). When Does Old Age Begin? *U.S. News.* Retrieved from https://money.usnews.com/money/blogs/planning-to-retire/2009/07/02/when-does-old-age-begin

Brito, J. (2017). Are There Side Effects to Masturbation? *Medical News Today.* Retrieved from https://www.medicalnewstoday.com/articles/320265.php

Butler, R. N., & Lewis, M. I. (2002). *The new love and sex after 60 (3rd ed.).* New York: Random House Publishing Group.

California Department of Education [CDE]. (2017). *Comprehensive Sexual Health & HIV/AIDS Instruction.* Retrieved from https://www.cde.ca.gov/ls/he/se/

Canalichio, K., Jaber, Y., & Wang, R. (2015). Surgery and hormonal treatment for prostate cancer and sexual function. *Translational Andrology and Urology, 4*(2), 103-109.

Centers for Disease Control and Prevention (CDC) (2012). Retrieved from https://wonder.cdc.gov/population- projections.html

Centers for Disease Control and Prevention (CDC). (2015). *Sexually Transmitted Disease Surveillance 2014.* Retrieved from https://www.cdc.gov/std/stats14/surv-2014-print.pdf.

Centers for Disease Control and Prevention (CDC) (2015b). *Diagnoses of HIV infection in the United States and Dependent Areas.* Retrieved from https://www.cdc.gov/hiv/pdf/library/reports/surveillance/cdc-hiv-surveillance-report-2016- vol-28.pdf

Centers for Disease Control and Prevention (CDC) (2016). *2016 Sexually Transmitted Diseases Surveillance.* Retrieved from https://www.cdc.gov/std/stats16/foreword.htm#ref-

Chambers, L., Wilson, M., Rueda, S., Gogolishvili, D., & Shi, M. (2014). Evidence informing the intersection of HIV, aging, and health: A scoping review. *Aids & Behavior, 18*, 4, 661-675.

Choi, S., & Meyer, I. (2016). LGBT Aging: A Review of Research Findings, Needs and Policy Implications. *The Williams Institute*. UCLA School of Law.

Dhingra, I., De Sousa, A., & Sonavane, S., (2016) Sexuality in older adults: Clinical and psychosocial dilemmas. *Journal of Geriatric Mental Health, 3*, 31-139.

Dominguez, L., & Barbagallo, M. (2016). Ageing and sexuality. *European Geriatric Medicine. 7*(6), 512-518.

Dworkin, S. (2006). The aging bisexual, the invisible of the invisible minority. In Douglas Kimmel, Tara Rose, & Steven David (Eds.) *Lesbian, Gay, Bisexual and Transgender Aging: Research and Clinical Perspectives.* New York: Columbia University Press. 36-52.

Francis, Pope. (2016) *The Joy of Love. (*AMORIS LÆTITIA). Retrieved from https://w2.vatican.va/content/dam/francesco/pdf/apost_exhortations/documents/papa-

Gallo, J. J., Bogner, H. R., Fulmer, T., & Paveza, G. J. (2006). *Handbook of Geriatric Assessment, 4th Edition.* Sudbury, MA: Jones and Bartlett Publishers.

Galinsky, A. (2012). Sexual touching and difficulties with sexual arousal and orgasm among U.S. older adults. *Archives of Sexual Behavior. 41*(2). *875-890.*

Giraldi, A., & Kristensen, E. (2010). Sexual dysfunction in women with diabetes mellitus. *Journal of Sex Research* 47,2-3.

Graefen, M., & Schlomm, T. (2012). Is radical prostatectomy a useful therapeutic option for high risk prostate cancer in older men? *The Oncologist, 17 (suppl.1),* 4-8.

Grogan S. (2012). *Body image: Understanding body dissatisfaction in men, women, and children.* New York, NY: Routledge.

Harris, I., Fronczak, C., Roth, L., & Meacham, R. (2011). Fertility and the aging male. *Reviews in Urology,13,4,* 184-190.

Harvard (2015). Yohimbe supplements found to be dangerously strong. *Harvard Men's Health Watch, Harvard Health.*

Harvard (2017). Attitudes about Sexuality and Aging. *Harvard Medical School*. Retrieved from https://www.health.harvard.edu/staying-healthy/attitudes-about-sexuality-and-aging

Hillman, J. (2016). Sexuality and sexual health among older LGBT adults: Preparing for a culturally competent practice. *The Gerontologist. 56*(3).

Huber, V., & Firmin, M. (2014). A history of sex education in the United States since 1900. Retrieved: http://digitalcommons.cedarville.edu/psychology publications/180/

Hunt, J. (2012). *Why the Gay and Transgender Population Experiences Higher Rates of Substance Use*. Center for American Progress. Retrieved from https://www.americanprogress.org/issues/lgbt/reports/2012/03/09/11228/why-the-gay-and-transgender-population-experiences-higher-rates-of-substance-use.

Inelman, E. M., Gasparini, G., & Enzi, G. (2005). HIV/AIDS in older adults: A case report and literature review. *Geriatrics, 60*(9), 26-30.

ISSM. (n.d.). What are some side effects of erectile drugs. International Society for Sexual Medicine. Retrieved from http://www.issm.info/sexual-health-qa/what-are-some-side-effects-oferectile-dysfunction-drugs/

Kuhn, D. (2002). Intimacy, sexuality, and residents with dementia. *Alzheimer's Care Quarterly, 3*(2), 165-176.

Levine, G., Steinke, E., Bakaeen, F., Bozkurt, B., Cheitlin, M., Conti, J., Foster, E., Jaarsma, T., Kloner, R., Lange, R., Lindaus, S., Maron, B., Moser, D., Ohman, E., Seftel, A., & Stewart, W. (2012). Sexual activity and cardiovascular disease: a scientific statement from the American Heart Association. *Circulation, 125,* 1058-1072.

Lee, S. (2015). Effects of smoking on menopausal age: results from the Korea national health and nutrition examination survey, 2007 to 2012. *Journal of Preventative Medicine & Public Health. 48*(4), 216-224.

Lichtenberg, P.A. & Strzepek, D.M. (1990). Assessments of institutionalized dementia patients' competencies to participate in intimate relationships. *The Gerontologist, 30*(1), 117-120.

Lindau, S., Schumm, P., Laumann, E., Levinson, W., O'Muircheartaigh, C., & Waite, L. (2017). A study of sexuality and health among older adults in the United States. *New England Journal of Medicine, 357,* 762-774.

McDaniel, D. (2017). Sex and seniors-STDs: a new reality for the elderly. Retrieved from https://www.huffingtonpost.com/derrick-y-mcdaniel/sex-and-seniors-stds-a-ne_b_9619778.html

Mahieu, L., & Gastmans, C. (2015). Older residents' perspectives on aged sexuality in institutionalized elderly care: a systematic literature review. *International Journal of Nursing Studies,52,* 1891-1905.

Marasco, V. (2014) Perceived facilitators and barriers to intimate relationships of persons ages 65 and older. Master's Thesis, University of Nebraska ProQuest Publishing. Ann Arbor, MI.

Margo, J. (2015). Pill promises to find women's lost libido. *The Australian Financial Review, 26,* 38.

Mayo Clinic (n.d). Erectile Dysfunction. Retrieved from https://www.mayoclinic.org/diseases-conditions/erectile-dysfunction/symptoms-causes/syc-20355776.

Mayo Clinic (2011). *Erectile Dysfunction and Diabetes: Take Charge Today.* https://www.mayoclinic.org/diseases-conditions/erectile-dysfunction/in-depth/erectile-dysfunction/art-20043927.

Messinger-Rapport, B. J., Sandhu, S. K., & Hujer, M. E. (2003). *Sex and sexuality: Is it over after 60. Clinical Geriatrics, 11* (10), 45-53.

MetLife Mature Market Institute. (2006). *Out and Aging: The MetLife study of Lesbian and Gay Baby Boomers.* Retrieved from https://www.tandfonline.com/doi/abs/10.1080/15504280903472949

Mustanski, B., Andrews, R., & Puckett, J. (2016). The effects of cumulative victimization on mental health among lesbian, gay, bisexual, and transgender adolescents and young adults. *American Journal of Public Health106,* 3, 527–533.

National Association of Social Workers. (2003). *The Aging of HIV.* Retrieved from https://www.socialworkers.org/LinkClick.aspx?fileticket=u7moIMQSJoY%3D&portalid=0

National Council on Aging. (1998). *Healthy Sexuality and Vital Aging.* Retrieved from http://www.ncoa.org/attachments/SexualitySurveyExecutiveSummary%2Epdf

National Institute on Aging. (2009). *Sexuality in Later Life*. Retrieved from https://www.nia.nih.gov/health/sexuality-later-life.

National Institute on Aging. (2017). Age Page: *Sexuality in Later Life*. Retrieved from https://order.nia.nih.gov/publication/sexuality-in-later-life

National Institute of Health (NIH). (2017). *The NIH SGM Research Coordinating Committee (RCC)*. Retrieved from https://dpcpsi.nih.gov/sgmro/sgm-research-coordinating-committee.

National Transgender Discrimination Survey (NTDS), (2016). *U.S Transgender Survey*. Retrieved From https://transequality.org/issues/national-transgender-discrimination-survey.

Older Americans Act (OAA) (1965). Retrieved from https://legcounsel.house.gov/Comps/Older%20Americans%20Act%20Of%201965.pdf

Ortman, J.M, Velkoff, V.A., & Hogan, H. (2014). *An aging nation: The older population in the United States*, U.S. Department of Commerce, Economics and Statistics Administration U.S. Census Bureau, 1-28.

Palacios-Ceña, D., Mártinez-Piedrola, R.M., Pérez de Heredia, M., Huertas Hoyas, E., Carrasco

Garrido, P., & Fernández de las Peñas, C. (2016). Expressing sexuality in nursing homes. The experience of older women: a qualitative study. *Geriatric Nursing, 37*, 470-477 http://doi.org/10.1016/j.gerinurse.2016.06.020

Pew Trends (2009). Growing Old in America: Expectations vs. Reality. Retrieved: http://www.pewsocialtrends.org/2009/06/29/growing-old-in-america-expectations-vs-reality/

Potts, A., Gavey, N., Grace, V.M., & Vares, T. (2003). The downside of Viagra: women's experiences and concerns. *Sociology of Health & Illness, 25*, 7, 697-719.

Spring, L. (2015). Older women and sexuality-are we still just talking lube? *Sexual and Relationship Therapy, 30*, 1, 4-9. http://dx.doi.org/10.1080/1481994.2014.920617.

Susan J. Komen, (n.d.). *About Breast Cancer*. Retrieved from https://ww5.komen.org/BreastCancer/AboutBreastCancer.html

Syme, M., & Cohn, T (2014) Examining aging sexual stigma attitudes among adults by gender, age, and generational status. *Aging and Mental Health.* Retrieved from https://www.ncbi.nlm.nih.gov/pubmed/25703148

Traeen, B., Hald, G., Graham. C., Enzlin, P., Janssen., E., & Kvalem, L. (2017). Sexuality in older adults (65+)—An overview of the literature, Part 1: Sexual function and its difficulties. *International Journal of Sexual Health. 29*(1), 1-10.

Wallace, M. (2007). *Sexuality Assessment for Older Adults.* Retrieved from http://www.gnjournal.com/article/S0197-4572(08)00275-9/abstract

WebMD. (2007). *Sex Therapy for Erectile Dysfunction.* Retrieved from http://www.webmd.com/erectile-dysfunction/guide/sex-therapy-erectile-dysfunction

WebMD. (2004). *Sexual Problems in Women - Topic overview.* Retrieved from http://www.webmd.com/sexual-conditions/tc/sexual-problems-in-women-topic-overview

WebMD. (2004). *Sexual Problems in Men – Topic overview.* Retrieved from http://www.webmd.com/sexual-conditions/guide/mens-sexual-problems

Worthington, J. (n.d.) Help for Ed after Prostate Surgery. Prostate Cancer Foundation. Retrieved from https://www.pcf.org/c/help-for-ed-after-prostate-surgery-the-basics/.

Yang, H., Suh, P. & Kim, S. *Effects of smoking on menopausal age: Results from the Korea national health and nutrition examination survey, 2007 to 2012.* Retrieved from https://www.ncbi.nlm.nih.gov/pmc/articles/PMC4542296/

Yarber, W., & Sayad, B. (2016). *Human sexuality: Diversity in contemporary America. 9th Edition,* New York, NY: McGraw Hill.

Resources for Seniors and Providers

The American Psychological Association (APA) has prepared an extensive collection of articles on human sexuality for the elderly. Topics include sexuality for middle-aged and older women; changes in sexual functions; relationship and erectile function; men's sexual health after midlife; sexual desire in later life; medications that contribute to sexual disorders; and clinical perspectives on sexual issues in nursing homes. The electronic enabled links below describe many of these sources. Several of these organizations also hold conferences and workshops throughout the year. Information for older adults and their families include:

- Sex, Romance, and Relationships: AARP Survey of Midlife and Older Adults
- American Association of Sex Educators, Counselors, and Therapists (AASECT)
- American College of Obstetricians and Gynecologists (ACOG)
- American Social Health Association (ASHA)
- Association for the Treatment of Sexual Abusers (ATSA)
- The World Professional Association for Transgender Health, Inc (WPATH)
- International Academy of Sex Research (IASR)
- International Association for the Treatment of Sexual Offenders (IATSO)
- International Society for the Study of Women's Sexual Health (ISSWSH)
- Kinsey Institute for Research in Sex, Gender, and Reproduction
- Age Page: Sexuality in Later Life (Spanish) National Institute on Aging
- National Vulvodynia Association (NVA)
- North American Menopause Society (NAMS)
- Annotated Bibliography: Sexuality in Middle and Later Life Sexuality Information and Education Council of the United States (SIECUS)
- APA Psychologist Locator
- Society for the Scientific Study of Sexuality (SSSS)
- World Association for Sexual Health (WAS)

Other Chapter Sources

Senior sexual health: The effects of aging on sexuality

Bradford, A., & Meston, C. M. (2007). In L. VandeCreek, F. L. Peterson Jr., & J. W. Bley (Eds.), *Innovations in clinical practice: Focus on sexual health* (pp. 35-45). Sarasota, FL.

This chapter offers an overview of the influence of aging on the sexual lives of men and women.

Sexuality in midlife and later life couples

Burgess, E. O. (2004). In J. H. Harvey, A. Wenzel, & S. Sprecher (Eds.), *The handbook of sexuality in close relationships* (pp. 437-454). Mahwah, NJ: Lawrence Erlbaum Associates Publishers.

This chapter explores how aging influences sexual behavior with an emphasis on physiological changes for older adults.

Golden sexuality: Sex therapy for seniors

Davis, L. M. (2007). In L. VandeCreek, F. L. Peterson Jr., & J. W. Bley (Eds.), *Innovations in clinical practice: Focus on sexual health* (pp. 261-276). Sarasota, FL: Professional Resource Press/ Professional Resource Exchange.

Sex therapist Davis dispels the myth that older adults are not interested and reviews therapeutic methods available to help older adults return to a vibrant sexual life.

The aging bisexual: The invisible of the invisible minority

Dworkin, S. H. (2006). In D. Kimmel, T. Rose, & S. David (Eds.), *Lesbian, gay, bisexual, and transgender aging: Research and clinical perspectives* (pp. 37-52). New York, NY: Columbia University Press.

This chapter clarifies issues related to the bisexual older adult. Discussions include gender orientation, gender identity, couples, marriage and families impacting the lives of bisexuals.

Sexuality in the lives of aging lesbian and bisexual women

Garnets, L., & Peplau, L. A. (2006). In D. Kimmel, T. Rose, & S. David (Eds.), *Lesbian, gay, bisexual, and transgender aging: Research and clinical perspectives* (pp. 70-90). New York, NY: Columbia University Press.

A review of available research on the sexuality of aging lesbian and bisexual women is addressed in this chapter. Topics include empirical studies and factors affecting the lifespan of lesbian and bisexual women.

Sexuality at midlife and beyond

Johnson, B. (2007). In M. S. Tepper, & A. F. Owens (Eds.), *Sexual health Vol 1: Psychological foundations* (pp. 291-300). Praeger perspectives: Sex, love, and psychology. Westport, CT: Praeger Publishers/Greenwood Publishing Group.

With women 65 and older outnumbering male counterparts by nearly 30%, this chapter explains the demographic changes in the U.S. older adult population (Baby-Boomer) population and the impact on sexual relationships.

Sex therapy with aging adults

Leiblum, S. R., & Segraves, R. T. (2000). In S. R. Leiblum, & R. C. Rosen (Eds.), *Principles and practice of sex therapy* (3ʳᵈ ed.) (pp. 423-448). New York, NY: Guilford Press.

This chapter discusses recent technological advances and medical developments that have allowed clinicians to utilize numerous pharmacological and therapeutic options available related to the sexual changes in aging men and women.

Later life sexuality

Sharpe, T. H. (2006). In R. D. McAnulty, & M. M. Burnette (Eds.), *Sex and sexuality, Vol 1: Sexuality today: Trends and controversies* (pp. 133-151). Westport, CT: Praeger Publishers/Greenwood Publishing Group.

In this chapter, Sharp discusses some of the unique factors and/or tasks facing the older adult dealing with the awkwardness and embarrassment associated with sexual intimacy.

Sexual changes in the aging male

Siegel, L. A., & Siegel, R. M. (2007). In A. F. Owens, & M. S. Tepper (Eds.), Sexual health Vol 2: *Physical foundations (pp. 223-255). Praeger perspectives*: Sex, love, and psychology. Westport, CT: Praeger Publishers/Greenwood Publishing Group.

This chapter focuses on the many sexual changes that occur in men as they get older and addresses some special considerations, such as illness and disease, grief and loss, divorce, self-perception, and sexual identity. Treatment options are explored to help men return to normal sexual activities.

Gay men and aging: Sex and intimacy

Wierzalis, E. A., Barret, B., Pope, M., & Rankins, M. (2006). In D. Kimmel, T. Rose, & S. David (Eds.), *Lesbian, gay, bisexual, and transgender aging: Research and clinical perspectives* (pp. 91-109). New York, NY: Columbia University Press.

The authors of this chapter provide an overview of literature related to gay men and discusses issues related to intimacy and life span sexual identity. An examination of cultural considerations, and sexual transmitted infections is also included.

Recommendations and Sex Education for Seniors

Sometimes people just need a 'to do list' to help change their behaviors and improve their lives. This could also apply to improving one's sex life. While it may be difficult for couples to face (literally face) their partners and talk about sexual details; the suggestions below can dramatically improve sexual intimacy.

1. **Communication:** Talk to your partner. Talking about sex is one of the most difficult tasks for all couples; but if each can explain in a relaxed comfortable environment what they like or dislike, intimate partner improvements can result. Many would be very embarrassed to have this type of conversation but talking can express feelings and offer suggestions to improve intimacy. Some may find it easier to write down notes to themselves, or chat on the computer or even send text messages to relay an idea.

2. **Choose the Right Time**: In recent years Viagra™ has been a major help for many men facing erectile dysfunctions; however, a man can't simply say he took the pill and is now ready. His female partner still needs to be in the mood. Some enjoy 'pillow talk,' others can improve their communication on long road trips. Find a comfortable place and time with emphasis on privacy.

3. **Talk During Love Making**: Erogenous zones may vary from one person to another. Instead of assuming your partner likes certain stimulation, it helps to simply ask. "Does that feel good?" "Do you like it when I do this?" If talking is still too embarrassing, simply show your partner by moving his or her hand to the area that you find pleasurable. This is a time that 'talking dirty' could also greatly enhance intimacy.

4. **Avoid Criticism:** Don't focus on the negative problems and most importantly do not share any of the sexual issues with friends or others. Make sex a very enjoyable, personal and sacred act between you and your partner. Instead of focusing on specific mechanics, use sentences such as, "I would like it if you …" or, "How about we try doing…" If there are mistakes gently describe them to your partner, again, in a safe and private environment, and not necessarily right after sex.

5. **Try Something New:** Boredom often arises because sex was done in the same place, the same time in the same positions for many years. Redecorating the bedroom, removing any clutter, kid's (or grandkids), toys laundry etc. can prepare an inviting environment. An enjoyable meal, or a bath or shower together before sex can also help. Go very slowly, (even slower than that!) the longer you are relaxing with your partner in bed, the more enjoyable the sexual act will become. Kissing and cuddling during sex can be very sexy. Try having sex at a hotel or some other location. Have sex outdoors!

6. **Limit Alcohol and Eliminate Tobacco**: Many couples enjoy alcohol to help relax and lower inhibitions; but alcohol is a depressant drug and excessive use can cause medical harm to the

liver and stomach; and most importantly can cause erectile problems in men. Smoking not only is related to cancer heart disease and a plethora of other diseases; it also can limit blood flow to the penis and vascular tissues. Stop smoking for better sex. Studies have even shown that female smokers may develop earlier menopause. (Yang, Suh, Kim, & Lee, 2015).

7. **Exercise and Eat Healthy:** Sex requires lots of movement, bending, stretching, and reaching to be comfortable. Arthritis and joint and muscle pain can make sex very uncomfortable or awkward, and even embarrassing. Regular exercise, even taking long walks, swimming or doing water aerobics, yoga or dancing can prepare the body for comfortable sex. A healthy diet higher in plants and lower in fats can prevent obesity, diabetes, heart disease, stroke and elevated cholesterol.

8. **Masturbate:** Women oftentimes have been taught that masturbation is dirty, nasty or only something that boys and men do. Firstly, masturbation is a way to have sex with someone you truly trust! Both women and men can benefit from masturbation for numerous reasons. Secondly, women can be very specific on how to stimulate the clitoris or clitoral hood to feel the stimulation that they enjoy. That information can be discussed or shown to their partner. For men, masturbation can be a way to find out how to practice sexual stimulation and deal with erectile problems. Both men and women can also benefit from masturbation if partners are unavailable or ill. Moreover, masturbation has been shown to reduce stress, enhance sleep quality, boost concentration, elevate mood, relieve menstrual cramps, alleviate pain and improve sex (Brito, 2017; Yarber & Sayad, 2016).

9. **Watch Dr. Lindsey Doe's You-Tube Videos:** Dr. Lindsey Doe is a professional sex therapist and expert on a wide variety of sexuality education. She publishes over 220 *Explanation* videos that are short, specific and very entertaining (Sexplanations). Many of the topics can help couples of all ages. She includes topics ranging from anatomy and physiology of males and females to prevention of STIs, sex for the disabled, pornography, sexual identity, urinary tract infections consent and sex toys. Couples can benefit immeasurably by watching her videos and having open honest discussions. Her videos are truly outstanding.

Yoga, Meditation, Music & Diet are an Effective Psycho-Neuro-Immuno- Therapeutic Holistic Approaches in Combating Alzheimer's Disease (AD), Depression, and Other Behavioral Disorders

Shyamala Mruthinti

Introduction

Alzheimer's disease (AD) is a progressive neurodegenerative dementia disorder affecting nerve cells located within higher cortical centers that ultimately result in impaired cognition, including a gradual decline in memory, judgment, and communication. Our brain has about 100 billion neurons which form highly complex network for transferring information to other neurons, via 1000 trillion synaptic connections. Although neurons are not directly connected, they pass the information via neurotransmitters, which are chemical messengers responsible for receiving and passing on the information from different parts of the brain, muscles and other organs of the body. Our mind carries memories and other information back and forth via well-knit neuronal tracs traversing across the brain. Alzheimer's disease (AD) is caused by neuronal degeneration and loss of synapses to signify that, AD is a "neuronal disintegration and synaptic loss disorder" rather than memory loss disorder; as memory is not an organ gene, protein or neuron to be lost or degenerated nor memories are stored in the brain. AD is characterized pathologically by the deposition of long-lived proteins in brain tissue, both extracellularly as senile plaques containing an abnormally cleaved 1-42 amino acid amyloid beta (Aβ) peptide fragments and intracellularly as phosphorylated tau protein in neurofibrillary tangles. Less is known regarding the nature of the neurotoxicity induced by the presence of amyloid peptides, although, the generation of oxidative free radicals, immune-like responses, and inflammation have been suggested to play a key role. One age-dependent process that appears to fit with the modes of potential neurotoxicity is the non-enzymatic reactions of amino acids with sugars to form insoluble, irreversible Schiff base end products collectively known as "advanced glycation end products or AGEs". AGEs have been

95

implicated in the chronic complications of diabetes mellitus and have been reported to play an important role in the pathogenesis of AD (Sasaki et al., 1998). AGEs are perilous due to four main characteristic features which are: a) they are insoluble, b) they are irreversible, c) they clog blood vessels and d) they can bind with neighboring proteins easily to alter and destroy its very essential function leading to tissue and organ destruction and are like vagabonds with no role in the body and are like bad guys with an agenda to destroy good tissue, arteries and organs in the body. Also they can clog the very small blood vessels (microvascular system) throughout the body, especially in the kidneys, eyes, heart, and brain, which may contribute to the risk of various diabetic complications. High temperature cooked food containing-AGEs are more palatable and adds flavor and taste to the food which are more harmful than useful for overall health of body and brain. More harm is done to the body and brain by AGE receptor "RAGE", which is a single transmembrane multi-ligand receptor molecule belonging to the immunoglobulin superfamily; that binds to a broad repertoire of ligands and mediates responses to cell damage and stress conditions (Riehl et al., 2009). RAGE transports Aβ from blood to the brain, to and fro and is responsible in preventing wound healing and long term sustenance of inflammation leading to damage and death of cell or neuron (Deane et al., 2003). RAGE plays a key role not only in Diabetes and AD, but in several other diseases such as: cancer, stroke, atherosclerosis, arthritis, and neurodegenerative disorders. Our studies have shown that AGE-receptor RAGE trigger series of cyclic events leading to autoimmunity, inflammation and oxidative damage and death of major neurons responsible for memory and cognitive functions of the brain (Mruthinti et al., 2003, 2004, 2006, 2006, 2007, Wilson et al., 2009 and Webster et al., 2012). Autopsied brain tissue sections revealed two major hallmarks of AD-pathogenesis: 1) senile plaques containing deposits of 1-42 amino acid amyloid-β (Aβ) peptide fragment, which is abnormally cleaved from its parent β-amyloid precursor protein (β-APP) and: 2) strings of tau protein containing neurofibrillary tangles that form inside cells. Our research data derived from human and primate blood and brain autopsied samples, AD-transgenic mouse models and in-vitro neuronal cell culture models, have strongly suggested that Aβ by itself is non-immunogenic, but upon binding with AGE receptor RAGE; transforms as an immunogenic Aβ-RAGE complex antigen-molecule to trigger autoimmune, inflammatory cascade of cyclic events leading to oxidative damage and death of neurons (Mruthinti et al., 2003, 2004, 2006, 2006). Our studies have shown that, anti-RAGE and anti-Aβ specific immunoglobulin (IgG) levels increase proportionately and their levels also positively correlate with mini mental score(MMSE), Clinical Dementia Rating (CDR) scores as well as index scores on the Repeatable Battery for the Assessment of Neuropsychological Status (RBANS) in domains associated with cortical function. The close relationship between titers for Aβ and RAGE IgGs suggests the possibility that the antibodies are being produced in response to a common mechanism or protein complex linked to the disease (Mruthinti et al., 2004, Wilson et al., 2009, Webster et al., 2012). Individuals with AD were significantly older, they had significantly lower Mini-Mental State Examination (MMSE) scores, and they exhibited significantly higher mean plasma RAGE and Aβ- IgG levels than control individuals (Wilson et al., 2009). Our earlier studies involving in vitro cell culture models and AD-transgenic mice (confirmed by samples from monkeys and humans), strongly supports the hypothesis that antibody against Aβ-RAGE complex can be more effective treatment strategy for AD than vaccination with Aβ-42 alone. Aβ42 binding to RAGE does not fully explain the selective vulnerability of cholinergic basal forebrain neurons in Alzheimer's disease. The α7 subtype of the nicotinic acetylcholine receptor (α7nAChR) is expressed on basal forebrain neurons that play a role in memory and cognitive function. Indeed, the expression of α7nAChR protein is significantly diminished in the cerebral cortex of Alzheimer's disease patients. To assess the cell surface expression levels of major receptor binding sites in presence of AGEs, we have incubated differentiated neuronal cultures of PC-12 or IMR-32 cells with bovine serum albumin–advanced-glycation-end-product (BSA-AGE) or with carboxy-methyl-lysine (CML). We have shown that AGE treatments have indeed induced significant concentration-dependent increases of APP (amyloid precursor protein), RAGE, and α7-subtype of the nicotinic acetylcholine receptor (α7-nAChR) as measured by flow cytometer, RT-PCR, Western blot and ELISA techniques (Mruthinti et al., 2006).

AD was diagnosed in 1907, and from past 30+ years the long-held concept of "beta amyloid (Aβ42) hypothesis" has been abandoned, due to 100 percent failure rate. Biogen and its partner, Japan's Eisai, shocked the world by halting the Phase III studies in April 2019 and series of failures of Aβ42-targeting drugs had disappointed investor's enthusiasm. Several biotech companies during a panel discussion at the CNBC Healthy Returns conference in New York on May 21, 2019 argued that: they don't yet have the technology or understanding of AD, to find a cure for the disease. They said *"With Alzheimer's, we don't even really know the very first layer, so the probability that you're going to find the right target and hit it, is going to be unlikely; unless we can get that first level of understanding the disease".*

It is time for a radical new approach to prevent and cure AD, after more than 100 drug trials which have failed to cure or revert AD-pathogenesis. Researchers are wondering "if they got it all wrong" in understanding AD pathogenesis according to ABC news of 24th September, 2018. There have been more setbacks and failures than treatment successes. For AD sufferers, brain inflammation ignites a neuron-killing to ignite "Forest Fire" (Weintraub, 2019).

Currently there is no cure for AD and if not intervened, it can reach an epidemic proportion striking every 65 year old adult by 2050. When all doors are closed for AD cure, Holistic approaches using Yoga, Meditation, Music and Diet seem to give a ray of hope as an ideal, safe and effective alternative approaches to combat AD.

AD can be prevented by using Complementary Holistic Approaches using Ayurvedic Medicine which includes a) internal purification process followed by b) healthy diet, c) herbal remedies, d) music therapy, e) yoga, and f) meditation.

Ayurveda is derived from the Sanskrit words ayur (life) and veda (science or knowledge). Ayurveda translates to knowledge of life. Ayurveda, a natural system of medicine, originated in India more than 3,000-5,000 years ago. We are 3-Dimensional figures encompassing body-mind and spirit or consciousness and modern medicine and our treatment strategies should include all 3 dimensions as well as the environment in which we live and grow. What we breathe, eat, think, speak and listen impacts overall health of our body mind and spirit. Modern medicine often treats patients mostly looking at the symptoms of the disease and/ or aftermath of the disease process (like amyloid plaques in the brain which are not cause of AD, but aftermath of disease process). Ayurvedic medicine on the contrary, incorporates not only all three dimensions of human life which includes body-mind and spirit or consciousness, but also includes prakriti or nature and environment in which we live; and the prana or breath force which is the life energy force with which we are born and which we leave back to the atmosphere when we die. Ayurveda treatment starts with an internal purification process, followed by a special diet, herbal remedies, massage therapy, yoga, and meditation to ultimately bring a balance between the body, mind, spirit, and the environment. The concepts of universal interconnectedness, the body's constitution (prakriti), and life forces (doshas) are the primary basis of ayurvedic medicine. *"The soil is more important than the seed"* concept underlies several Ayurvedic treatment strategies. Max Lugavere and Paul Grewal's recent book entitled "Genius Foods", which is a *New York Times* best seller quotes that: *our immune systems have become chronically activated in response to our poor diets, unhealthy lifestyles, stress, depression and lack of exercise to cause neurodegenerative diseases.*

AD is a Synaptic Loss Disorder rather than Memory Loss Disorder

My premise is that AD is a synaptic loss disorder caused by inflammation and oxidative stress rather than a memory loss disorder; because memories are related to the mind, which is not an organ, gene, protein or a neuron to be lost or degenerated. Mind is often equated with consciousness, a subjective sense of self-awareness which exists beyond the body. Mind is more subtle and it's most mysterious aspect is consciousness or awareness, which can take any form from the experience of pain, agony, happiness to self-consciousness. Yoga philosophy explains that you are the mind, which is the spirit without the body. Mind is transparent and all pervasive like air and sky and uses neurons for its function traversing via neuronal network to load and unload memories across the brain.

Memories are not stored in the brain but exists in the cosmic space of infinite consciousness. Our brain is like a TV screen on which movies and images are seen when TV is turned on, but none of the images are stored inside TV screen (Sheldrake, 1987). Memories cannot be retrieved due to loss of synaptic connections between neurons in the brain, like movies and images cannot be viewed when TV is destroyed. As we age, several factors influence the disruption of neuronal network to destroy memory and cognitive functions. While modern medicine focuses on swallowing a pill for quick remedy, the holistic approach emphasis on what we eat, breathe, drink, think and listen reflects our overall well-being.

Yoga

Yoga is a Sanskrit word meaning "union of the body, mind and spirit or soul." Yoga combines the physical postures or asanas with the mental conscious breathing patterns through various kriya-yoga exercises which teaches correct way of inhale and exhale methods and ultimately bodily exercises practiced with focus, attention and skill to relax and strengthen muscles, joints, organs, arteries and veins. Yoga lower blood pressure, and alleviates arthritis, back pain and boost heart and mental health.

Meditation

Meditation is diverting the mind from outward to inward to become consciously aware and be in tune with one's own essential pure self which is universal in nature; where individuality is lost into universality of oneness. In meditation, the senses are controlled bringing the wandering mind to a focus which is "breath." In meditation one learns to silently observe one's own thought processes and just like the clarity of water is more visible when muddy water settles down, similarly in meditation when flocking thoughts are settled down, situations and problems of life are resolved when understood with clarity of the mind. Meditation helps in removal of mental blocks, negative thinking, unrealistic facts and fears to cause stress and anxiety. Mindfulness training programs such as Cognitive Based Compassion Training (CBCT) can help overcome depression. Compassion meditation may reduce stress-induced immune and behavioral responses, which relates to better health and well-being (Carlson et al., 2003). CBCT has been shown to reduce neuroendocrine, inflammatory and behavioral responses to psychosocial stress that have been previously linked to the development of mental and physical disease (Corina Aguilar-Raab et al., 2018). As a result, mindfulness meditation is increasingly incorporated into mental health interventions, and theoretical concepts associated with it have influenced basic research on psychopathology. Preliminary evidence suggests that mindful meditation can improve attention, memory, executive function, processing speed, and general cognition seem to be working through Amygdala, the brain center that processes emotional stimuli (Desbordes et al., 2012). Moreover, studies have shown that meditation influences brain structure and function, particularly in areas involved in attentional control, self-awareness, and emotion-regulation (Boccia et al., 2015).

Music Therapy (MT)

MT is an effective, non-pharmacological psycho-neuro-immuno therapeutic method to treat Alzheimer's, depression, attention deficit disorder (ADD) and other behavioral disorders. Music has a long history of healing physical and mental illnesses. Many clinical findings indicate that music reduces blood pressure in various patients and attenuates symptoms in various types of diseases, such as epilepsy, Parkinson's disease (PD), senile dementia and attention-deficit/hyperactivity disorder (ADHD). Music might regulate and/or affect various brain functions through dopaminergic neurotransmission and might therefore be effective for rectification of symptoms in various diseases that involve memory and cognition. Recent studies conducted at Indian Institute of Technology (IIT) says that: music activates, sustains and improves attention; suggesting that "Melody can rid you of malady" (The new Indian Express, Dec 8th, 2018). Their study shows that music not only refreshes the mind but also takes care of the heart, relieves the tension and increase, focus, attention and grasping power of the brain.

Patanjali Yoga sutras, which are a collection of 196 Indian sutras (aphorisms) on the theory and practice of yoga, compiled prior to 400 CE by Sage Patanjali who synthesized and organized knowledge about yoga & meditation from ancient vedic traditions. There are 72,000 *naadis* (nerves) in our body. The word *nadi* comes from the Sanskrit root word "nad" meaning channel, stream or flow. Evidence is mounting that music can help people concentrate and help bring best out of them. *Ragas*, the musical tunes, were shown to restore lost connectivity between neurons and boosts immune system and improves overall health of the body and mind (Music can rejuvenate and prompts neurons to traverse towards each other to re-join and reconnect the lost synapses. Several lines of evidence suggest that the lost memory is regained in some coma patients after listening to music (Sun & Chen, 2015). The therapeutic potential of music in various neurocognitive and other disorders is being experimented at the music therapy center at Datta Yoga Center, Mysore, India based on the compositions of the music healer and composer His holiness Dr. Shri Ganapati Sachidananda Swamiji composed > 2,000 musical tunes specific for each disease type (www. nadaragasagara.org). For children with attention deficit hyperactivity disorder known as ADHD, music therapy improves attention and focus, reduces hyperactivity, makes them happy, strengthens their self-esteem and enhances their interpersonal/social skills. Above all music develops inter-connectedness, love and compassion between fellow humans and renders inner joy, peace and blissful state of mind.

In conclusion, MT can be considered a non-pharmacological intervention which has the potential effects to reduce cognitive decline, improve neuropsychiatric symptoms and behavioral symptoms of AD (Herholz, et al., 2013). In addition to lyrics, the music involves rhythms with long-lasting creation of musical impressions in the mind. Music therapy can protect cognition of AD especially autobiographical and episodic memories, psychomotor speed, executive function, and global cognition (Fang et al. 2017). For well-being of our body, mind and behavior, holistic approaches involving Yoga-Meditation & Music as psycho-neuro-immuno therapeutic strategies are simple, safe and effective treatment methods in curing diseases, improving attention, memory as well as establishing a violence-free peaceful society in the world (Mruthinti, 2016).

Curcumin as an anti-inflammatory and neuroprotective agent preventing amyloid plaques

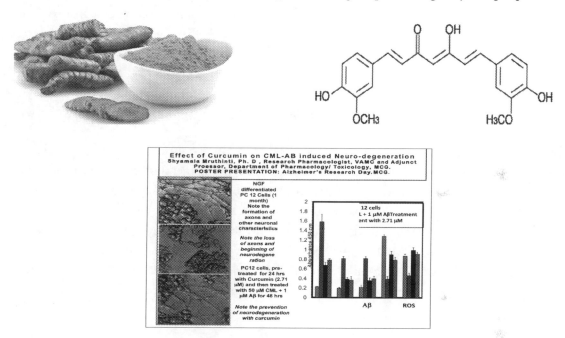

Turmeric which is used in India from thousands of years as a spice in food, as skin-protectant as well as beautifying agent, for rituals in the temple, wound healing antiseptic cream, as good omen for bride and groom and during birth of a child as well as on the dead bodies; thus, signifying its importance from birth to death. Recently curcumin has received interest from both the medical/ scientific world and from culinary enthusiasts, as it is the major source of the polyphenol curcumin. It aids in the management of oxidative and inflammatory conditions, metabolic syndrome, arthritis, anxiety, and hyperlipidemia. Turmeric is used in curry powder, as well as in ancient traditional medicinal practices such as Ayurveda and Chinese traditional medicine (Zhang et al., 2018). Curcumin also possesses potent antioxidant and cholesterol lowering properties (Qin et al., 2017). Inflammation is one of the underlying causes of neuronal damage in AD, a process possibly initiated in response to the amyloid peptide, Aβ. Curcumin has been shown to block the formation of and/or disaggregate amyloid plaques (Yang et al., 2005). Our earlier studies showed that curcumin can help reestablish neuronal connectivity in the cultured cells challenged with inflammatory compounds.

When PC-12 cells were differentiated with nerve growth factor (NGF), they establish strong intricate neural-like network, characteristic of neurons in the central nervous system. Addition of carboxymethyl-lysine (a type of inflammatory compound derived from AGEs) disrupted the neuronal network and cells begin to die due to upregulation of apoptosis, the programed cell death, characteristic of neurons in AD brains. Addition of curcumin not only prevented the apoptosis but also facilitated reconnection of axons forming a healthy neural network (Mruthinti, 2008). Our data presented in the poster indicates that curcumin has the potential to prevent synaptic connection loss, reduce inflammation and inhibit ROS production to prevent neurotoxic effect of beta amyloid and AGE adducts such as CML and BSA-AGEs. These observations open an alternative non-pharmaceutical safe and effective disease preventing strategies to combat AD and several other disorders.

Conclusions

In brief, the holistic approaches incorporate four-dimensional state of well-being of our body, mind, spirit, and five senses. Thus, these approaches such as yoga, meditation and music need to be integral part of healthcare delivery as well as normal wellbeing. Overwhelming evidence point to the enormous benefits of meditation, particularly cognitive based compassion meditation. Similarly, music therapy renders soothing effect on the body and mind of patients and their caregivers to cope with stress and anxiety. Music improves memory, cognition, intellect and learning / grasping power of the brain. Music gives inner joy, peace, love and harmony with self and others, adding key ingredients such as curcumin, renders protection from inflammation and improves cognitive functions.

Research Support and Funding Source:

Research Grant Funded to Dr. Shyamala Mruthinti as Principal Investigator (P.I)

1.Hemoglobin A1c Project: MCGRI ($ 20,000) (1990)

2.Ovarian Cancer : American Cancer Society ($ 15,000) 1992

3.Ovarian Cancer : BRSG, MCG ($ 10,000) 1994.

4.VISN-7 Career Development Award for Alzheimer's disease($ 100,000) 2000-02

5. MERIT review grant for Alzheimer's disease ($700,000) (2006-2010)

6. Parkinson's Foundation Grant ($ 25,000) (2009-2010).

Acknowledgements:

1. I acknowledge late Dr. Jerry J Buccafusco who was has rendered support and guidance as Mentor and colleague from 2000-2010 to pursue my research goals.
2. I acknowledge my husband Dr.Swamy S Mruthinti who has motivated and supported me for 40 years by collaborating and sharing my passion for science.
3. I acknowledge my daughters Professor Harshita Kamath, Dr. Navyata Mruthinti and Miss. Namrata Mruthinti for giving me inspiration and encouragement rendered for my career pursuits.

References

Aguilar-Raab, C., Jarczok, M. N., Warth, M., Stoffel, M., Winter, F., Tieck, M., ... & Ditzen, B. (2018). Enhancing social interaction in depression (SIDE study): Protocol of a randomised controlled trial on the effects of a Cognitively Based Compassion Training (CBCT) for couples. *BMJ Open, 8*(9), e020448.

Basta, G., Lazzerini, G., Massaro, M., Simoncini, T., Tanganelli, P., Fu, C., ... & De Caterina, R. (2002). Advanced glycation end products activate endothelium through signal-transduction receptor RAGE: a mechanism for amplification of inflammatory responses. *Circulation, 105*(7), 816-822.

Brownlee, MD, M. (1995). Advanced protein glycosylation in diabetes and aging. *Annual Review of Medicine, 46*(1), 223-234.

Carlson, L. E., Speca, M., Patel, K. D., & Goodey, E. (2003). Mindfulness-based stress reduction in relation to quality of life, mood, symptoms of stress, and immune parameters in breast and prostate cancer outpatients. *Psychosomatic Medicine, 65*(4), 571-581.

Deane, R., Du Yan, S., Submamaryan, R. K., LaRue, B., Jovanovic, S., Hogg, E., ... & Zhu, H. (2003). RAGE mediates amyloid-β peptide transport across the blood-brain barrier and accumulation in brain. *Nature Medicine, 9*(7), 907.

Kametani, F., & Hasegawa, M. (2018). Reconsideration of amyloid hypothesis and tau hypothesis in Alzheimer's disease. *Frontiers in Neuroscience, 12*, 25.

Khalsa, D. S., & Perry, G. (2017, March). The four pillars of Alzheimer's prevention. In *Cerebrum: The Dana forum on brain science*. Dana Foundation.

Lavretsky, H., Epel, E. S., Siddarth, P., Nazarian, N., Cyr, N. S., Khalsa, D. S., ... & Irwin, M. R. (2013). A pilot study of yogic meditation for family dementia caregivers with depressive symptoms: effects on mental health, cognition, and telomerase activity. *International Journal of Geriatric Psychiatry, 28*(1), 57-65.

Lorenzo, A., Yuan, M., Zhang, Z., Paganetti, P. A., Sturchler-Pierrat, C., Staufenbiel, M., ... & Yankner, B. A. (2000). Amyloid β interacts with the amyloid precursor protein: a potential toxic mechanism in Alzheimer's disease. *Nature Neuroscience, 3*(5), 460.

Moss, A. S., Wintering, N., Roggenkamp, H., Khalsa, D. S., Waldman, M. R., Monti, D., & Newberg, A. B. (2012). Effects of an 8-week meditation program on mood and anxiety in patients with memory loss. *The Journal of Alternative and Complementary Medicine, 18*(1), 48-53.

Mruthinti, S., Hill, W. D., Swamy-Mruthinti, S., & Buccafusco, J. J. (2003). Relationship between the induction of RAGE cell-surface antigen and the expression of amyloid binding sites. *Journal of Molecular Neuroscience, 20*(3), 223-232.

Mruthinti, S., Buccafusco, J. J., Hill, W. D., Waller, J. L., Jackson, T. W., Zamrini, E. Y., & Schade, R. F. (2004). Autoimmunity in Alzheimer's disease: increased levels of circulating IgGs binding Aβ and RAGE peptides. *Neurobiology of Aging, 25*(8), 1023-1032.

Mruthinti, S., Schade, R. F., Harrell, D. U., Gulati, N. K., Swamy-Mruthinti, S., Lee, G. P., & Buccafusco, J. J. (2006). Autoimmunity in Alzheimer's disease as evidenced by plasma immunoreactivity against RAGE and Aβ42: Complication of diabetes. *Current Alzheimer Research, 3*(3), 229-235.

Mruthinti, S., Capito, N., Sood, A., & Buccafusco, J. J. (2007). Cytotoxicity of Aβ 1-42, RAGE23-54, and An Aβ-RAGE complex in PC-12 Cells. *Current Alzheimer Research, 4*(5), 581-586.

Mruthinti S., Sood, H.., Swamy-Mruthinti & Buccafusco, J. (2006). The induction of surface Aβ-binding proteins and enhanced cytotoxicity in cultured PC-12 and IMR-32 cells by AGEs. *Neuroscience 142*, 463-473.

Mruthinti S., Capito, & Buccafusco, J. (2007). Cytotoxicity of Aβ1-42, RAGE23- 54 & Aβ-RAGE complex in PC-12 cells. *Current Alzheimer's Research*, 581-586.

Mruthinti, S. (2013). RAGE-Aβ complexes play a crucial role in triggering inflammatory, autoimmune related cascade of cyclic events leading to AD-pathogenesis. *Journal of Alzheimers Disease and Parkinsonism, 3*, 4.

Mruthinti S. (2016). Psycho-Neuro-Immno-Therapeutic holistic approaches involving Yoga-Meditation & Music are simple, safe and effective treatment methods in curing diseases, improving attention, memory as well as establishing a violence-free peaceful society in the world. Science of Consciousness Conference, Arizona.

Mruthinti, S. (2017). Mind Training Programs Like CBCT is Beneficial In: A. Combating Behavioral Disorders, B. Sharpening Human Intellect and Wisdom and C. Improving Health, Peace, Love and Compassion for Self and Others: Invited Speaker: Science of Consciousness, (June 5-10, 2017).

Riehl, A., Németh, J., Angel, P., & Hess, J. (2009). The receptor RAGE: Bridging inflammation and cancer. *Cell Communication and Signaling*, *7*(1), 12.

Särkämö, T., Tervaniemi, M., Laitinen, S., Forsblom, A., Soinila, S., Mikkonen, M., ... & Peretz, I. (2008). Music listening enhances cognitive recovery and mood after middle cerebral artery stroke. *Brain*, *131*(3), 866-876.

Sasaki, N., Fukatsu, R., Tsuzuki, K., Hayashi, Y., Yoshida, T., Fujii, N., Koike, T., Wakayama, I., Yanagihara, R., Garruto, R., Amano, N. and Makita, Z. (1998). Advanced glycation end products in Alzheimer's disease and other neurodegenerative diseases. *The American Journal of Pathology*, 153(4), 1149-1155.

Schmidt, A.M & Stern, D. (2000). RAGE: A New Target for the Prevention and Treatment of the Vascular and Inflammatory Complications of Diabetes. *Trends in Endocrinology and Metabolism. 11*(9), 368-375

Sun, J., & Chen, W. (2015). Music therapy for coma patients: preliminary results. *European Review of Medical Pharmacological Sciences*, *19*(7), 1209-18.

Webster, S. J., Mruthinti, S., Hill, W. D., Buccafusco, J. J., & Terry, A. V. (2012). An aqueous orally active vaccine targeted against a RAGE/AB complex as a novel therapeutic for Alzheimer's disease. *Neuromolecular Medicine*, *14*(2), 119-130.

Wilson, J. S., Mruthinti, S., Buccafusco, J. J., Schade, R. F., Mitchell, M. B., Harrell, D. U., ... & Stephen Miller, L. (2009). Anti-RAGE and Aβ immunoglobulin levels are related to dementia level and cognitive performance. *Journals of Gerontology Series A: Biomedical Sciences and Medical Sciences*, *64*(2), 264-271.

Parkinson's Disease and Its Impact on Quality of Life

Viswanath Putcha and Chandrasekhar Putcha

Introduction

Parkinson's disease (PD) is the most prevalent neurodegenerative disease among the elderly. It occurs when nerve cells (neurons) in the brain do not produce enough dopamine. The reason that PD occurs, and the neurons become impaired is not known, and there is no cure for the disease. Due to its progressive and chronic characteristics, PD affects quality of life (QoL) not only for patients but also for the people living with and caring for them. The aim of this chapter is to provide various methods to improve quality of life for those dealing with PD.

Studies have shown that the symptoms of PD usually appear when fifty percent or more of the dopamine neurons in the midbrain have been lost. Symptoms begin gradually and typically worsen over time (National Institute of Environmental Health Sciences, 2018). Figure 1 shows how neurons are transmitted to receptor cells.

Figure 1. The transmission of neurons to receptor cells in healthy patients and those with Parkinson's disease. Source: National Institute of Environmental Health Sciences (NIEHS).

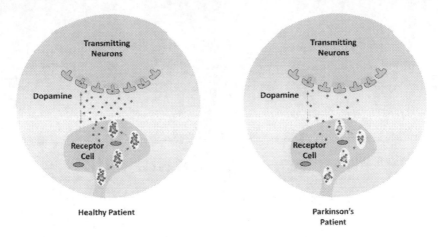

PD is a complex disease that can cause a variety of symptoms, including shaking, rigidity, slowness of movement, and difficulty walking. As the disease progresses, cognitive and behavioral problems may arise. Other symptoms include sleep and emotional problems, depression, difficulty with coordination and speech, severe fatigue, balance problems, and pain, all of which have a significant impact on the patient's QoL (Opara, 2003). Medications to alleviate PD's symptoms also have some of these side effects. The four most common early symptoms of PD are tremors (shaking or trembling in hands, arms, legs, face, and jaw), stiffness or rigidity of the limbs and trunk, slowness of movements, and difficulty with balance, speech, and coordination. It is important to remember that individual symptoms like imbalance or muscle stiffness may be caused by other conditions.

How Prevalent Is Parkinson's Disease?

PD is the second most common age-related neurodegenerative disorder after Alzheimer's disease. An estimated seven to ten million people worldwide have PD, and men are one-and-a-half times more likely to develop it than women (Naqvi, n.d).

It is relatively rare for a person under fifty years of age to develop PD—an estimated four percent of people with PD are diagnosed before age fifty. Approximately 60,000 American are diagnosed with PD each year, but this number does not include the cases that go undetected. An estimated seven to ten million people worldwide are living with PD ((Parkinson's Association of Carolinas, n.d.).

Approximately one percent of people over age sixty in industrialized countries are living with PD (deLau & Breteler, 2006) one in two hundred between ages sixty and sixty-nine, one in one hundred between ages seventy and seventy-nine, and one in thirty-five over age eighty. PD is more prevalent in developed countries, but that trend is starting to change. Figure 2 shows the prevalence of PD in 2005 in the world's most populous countries, as well as a projection of the prevalence in 2030 (Tanner, Brandabur, & Dorsey, 2008).

Figure 2. Distribution of individuals with Parkinson disease by Country from 2005 to 2030*

*Among individuals over 50 in the world's ten most and Western Europe's five most popular nations

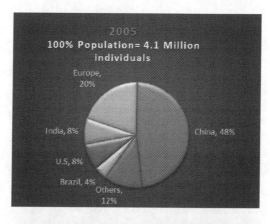

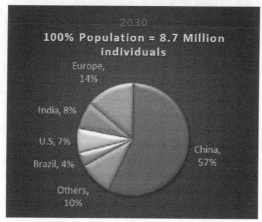

The Financial Burden of Parkinson's Disease

The lack of treatment options to change the trajectory of PD's progression, combined with the age of patients, creates a serious economic burden for patients. In 2010 people with PD in the United States incurred medical expenses of approximately $14 billion ($22,800 per patient), $8.1 billion higher than those without PD. The burden of chronic conditions such as PD is projected to grow substantially over the next few decades, as the size of the elderly population grows (Kowal Dall, Chakrabarti, Storm, & Jain, 2013)

The combined direct and indirect costs of PD—including treatment, social security payments, and lost income due to the inability to work—are estimated to be nearly $25 billion per year in the United States alone. In a survey conducted in twenty-eight European countries, PD was classified as the fourth most expensive disease among the twelve most prevalent and costly neurologic disorders (Bovolenta, Sônia, de Azevedo Silva, Arb Saba, Borges, Ballalai Ferraz, & Felicio, n.d.).

What Is Quality of Life (QoL)?

QoL describes the general well-being of individuals and societies, considering life satisfaction in physical health, family, employment, education, wealth, religion, finances, and the environment.[9] It is relevant in a wide range of fields, including politics, employment, international development, and healthcare.

Quantifying Quality of Life

Clinicians and policymakers are recognizing the importance of measuring health-related quality of life (HRQL) to inform patient management and policy decisions. Self- or interviewer-administered questionnaires can be used to measure cross-sectional differences in QoL between patients at a single point in time (discriminative instruments) or longitudinal changes in HRQL for a patient during a period (evaluative instruments). Both discriminative and evaluative instruments must be valid and have a high ratio of signal to noise (reliability and responsiveness, respectively). Reliable discriminative instruments reproducibly differentiate between persons. Responsive evaluative measures detect important changes in HRQL during a period, even if those changes are small. HRQL measures should also be interpretable—that is, clinicians and policymakers must be able to identify differences in scores that correspond to trivial, small, moderate, and large differences (Guyatt, Feeny, & Patrick, 1993).

QoL is a multidimensional construct that affects at least three broad domains: physical, mental, and social (Oara, Brola, Leonardi, & Blaszczyk, 2012). Tools are available to measure QoL in patients with PD. The major factors that affect QoL for patients with PD are emotional well-being, interpersonal relationships, material well-being, personal development, physical well-being, self-determination, social inclusion, rights, social stigma, cognition, communication, bodily discomfort, fatigue, and sleep disorders. Awareness about the emotional side effects of PD can help both patients and their caregivers significantly improve their QoL (Thompson, 2009).

Quality of Life and Emotional Health

People with PD may show signs of depression, denial, anxiety, and apathy. Mood changes are a common result of biochemical changes, the medications used to counteract PD, and a natural reaction to loss of control of the body (Thompson, 2009).

Depression

Many people with PD experience depression: it is estimated that at least fifty percent of those with PD will also experience some form of depression during their illness. Depression may be a result of the emotional challenges that come from living with PD (Parkinson's disease, n.d.) or the chemical changes that occur in the brain as a result of the disease. Some symptoms of depression and PD may overlap, including low energy, weight loss, insomnia or excessive sleep, slowed motor function, and diminished sexual function. Thus, depression may be overlooked if symptoms develop after a PD diagnosis has been made. Additional symptoms that distinguish depression from PD include consistent low mood that lasts most days for at least two weeks; suicidal thoughts; pessimistic thoughts of the future, the world, or the self; and a sharp increase or decrease in appetite.

Denial

According to an article published in the website *what-when-how Parkinson*, denial of a difficult situation is a normal human coping mechanism. It allows a person to process information subconsciously while continuing the usual activities of living. For many people, a diagnosis of PD is a shock, even if it is anticipated or provides a much-needed explanation for their symptoms. Denial is the mind's way of dealing with this shock. Acceptance is the necessary next step in developing a healthy perception of the situation. It may occur gradually or in stages, depending on the way the person processes challenges. Accepting and acknowledging the reality of a PD diagnosis initiates realistic expectations about treatment and prognosis (What- When – How; Denial and Acceptance, n.d).

After diagnosis, the emotional components of PD are often neglected as the focus turns to treatment and the physical challenges of the disease. This emphasis can leave the patient and his or her family members feeling confused and alone as they come to grips with what the diagnosis means in terms of health and life plans. Denial helps protect them from the emotional stress of these feelings.

Typically, a PD diagnosis is confirmed when symptoms respond to anti-Parkinson's medications. Although there is no conclusive diagnostic test for PD, similar conditions do not respond to treatment with dopamine agonists or Levodopa. For many people, this is the point at which the reality of the diagnosis begins to sink in and the transition to acceptance begins. For others, however, the remission of symptoms brought on by treatment feeds denial. They may continue to seek opinions from different medical specialists. Many people with PD experience numerous cycles of denial and acceptance throughout the course of the disease, often in response to the ebb and flow of their symptoms. These cycles can help them to cope with the challenges of changing and unpredictable circumstances (What- When – How; Denial and Acceptance, n.d).

Sometimes family members struggle with denial and acceptance related to a loved one's diagnosis for the same reasons as the person with PD. Their attitudes can increase emotional stress for the patient, particularly when he or she has moved from denial to acceptance, but the family member has not.

On his website Fighting Parkinson's Drug Free, Howard Shifke points out that accepting a PD diagnosis is the first step in fighting the disease. It can be difficult to think about recovery plans because this forces the patient to discard the conventional protocol for PD and take recovery into his or her own hands Shifke (2013). Shifke recommends the following acceptance affirmations for people with PD:

- "I accept that I have Parkinson's disease."
- "I accept that I can do something about it."
- "I accept responsibility to do something about it."
- "I accept that I have the power to heal myself and that I am healing myself."
- "I accept that I am recovering every day I do something positive in furtherance of my recovery."
- "I accept that I am worth it."

Some denial ("I deny that I have Parkinson's disease") is unhealthy. If a person cannot accept a PD diagnosis, then he or she will do nothing to fight it and the disease will get worse. Healthy denial is also possible. Shifke recommends the following denial affirmations for people with PD:

- "I deny that Parkinson's is incurable"
- "I deny there is nothing I can do to recover from Parkinson's."
- "I deny that unless I am taking medication or having brain surgery, I am doing nothing for my Parkinson's."
- "I deny that I am not worth it."

On days when symptoms seem worse and fear creeps in, it is difficult to maintain acceptance and denial affirmations. Shifke encourages PD patients:

Remember that the journey you are on is life, not Parkinson's. Parkinson's is just something happening in the journey called life, so you deal with it while you are living your life to its fullest. Every road has bumps; it is how you view the bump that matters. Some people see the bumps as roadblocks to life; I preferred to see the bumps as nuisances that made me slow down and navigate more carefully. While I am slowing down and navigating more carefully, I am noticing many beautiful things that I had been missing. So, my Parkinson's bumps in the road became such a blessing. They became mere signs to follow that I needed to pay more attention to healing my life. And when I finish healing my life, my soul, mind and body I do not need any more messages or signs and they left Shifke (2013).

Anxiety

Researchers believe that depression and anxiety related to PD may be due to the underlying changes in brain chemistry and circuitry caused by the disease itself (Anxiety and Depression with Parkinson disease, n.d.). According to the National Foundation for Parkinson's disease, there are different forms of anxiety common in PD: generalized anxiety disorder, anxiety attacks, social avoidance, and obsessive-compulsive disorder.

Generalized Anxiety Disorder

Generalized anxiety disorder is characterized by feelings of nervousness and thoughts of worry and fear that are present most of the time. The worry exceeds normal levels and often feels out of control. Physical symptoms are common and include butterflies in the stomach, trouble breathing or swallowing, racing heart, sweating, and increased tremors.

Anxiety Attacks

Anxiety attacks usually start suddenly and manifest as a sense of severe physical and emotional distress. A person having an anxiety attack may feel as if he or she cannot breathe or is having a heart attack. A common worry is that a medical emergency is happening. Anxiety attacks usually last less than an hour. Sometimes they can last for longer periods of time.

Social Avoidance

As the name implies, those who suffer from social avoidance avoid social situations due to fear of exhibiting PD symptoms (i.e., tremors, trouble walking) in public. Exposure to social situations can lead to severe anxiety, which goes away when the person leaves the social setting.

Obsessive-Compulsive Disorder

People with OCD may be plagued with persistent, unwelcome thoughts or images, or by the urgent need to engage in certain rituals. For example, they may be obsessed with germs or dirt and wash their hands over and over, or they may be filled with doubt and feel the need to check things repeatedly. Such repetitive behaviors are often performed with the hope of preventing or alleviating obsessive thoughts. However, performing these rituals provides only temporary relief while avoiding those increases anxiety.

Anxiety affects up to forty percent of people with PD and has various causes. There are some common fears and worries related to anxiety in patients with PD (Parkinson.org, n.d.). One is a fear of being unable to function, particularly during a sudden "off" period. This sometimes always causes the patient to feel a need to be with someone and to fear being left alone. Another is a fear of being embarrassed, perhaps when others notice the patient's symptoms of PD in public.

Many of the brain pathways and chemicals linked with depression in patients with PD are also likely related to anxiety. PD patients have abnormalities in GABA, a brain chemical closely connected to anxiety (and the target of one class of antianxiety medications). In some cases, anxiety in people with PD is directly related to changes in motor symptoms. People who experience "off" periods can develop severe anxiety, sometimes to the point of full-blown anxiety attacks.

Beyond medication, which is recommended for certain anxiety disorders, there are many other treatments for anxiety. Psychotherapy can help a person focus on the changes in thinking and behavior that occur with anxiety. A therapist can also provide support, understanding, and education for a person struggling with anxiety. It may be helpful to attend therapy alone, as a couple or family, or in a group. Another therapeutic approach for improving mood and anxiety is exercise. All basic forms of physical activity can be helpful, including walking, stretching, yoga, tai chi, and dance. In addition, relaxation techniques, massage therapy, acupuncture, aromatherapy, meditation, and music therapy can all alleviate anxiety.

Apathy

According to Pluck & Brown (2002), patients with PD had significantly higher levels of apathy than equally disabled osteoarthritic patients. Furthermore, among patients with PD, levels of apathy appear to be unrelated to disease progression. PD patients with the highest levels of apathy were not more likely to be depressed or anxious than those with the lowest levels of apathy, though they did show reduced hedonic tone.

Measuring Quality of Life in Patients with Parkinson's disease

In health research and clinical practice, measurement instruments are used to assess the health status of individuals, usually with the objective of making a diagnosis or predicting future developments (predictive measures), to evaluate changes in health status over time (evaluative measures), or to discriminate between patients (discriminative measures). Measurement involves the assignment of values to variables and can be performed with various types of instruments, including questionnaires, structured interviews, tests, and rating scales (Marinus, and van Hilten, 2007).

An overall aim for treatment of PD is to lower the negative impact of the disease on the functioning and QoL of patients. Therefore, a measurement of functioning and QoL must be included in evaluations of the effectiveness of treatment (Opara, Brola, Leonardi & Błaszczyk, 2012). Subjective factors related to QoL in PD patients include perception of symptoms; level of fitness; self-image; satisfaction with family life, work, and finances; interactions with other people; social support; and life in general. Objective factors include the clinical picture of the disease, social status, social and living conditions, and the number and intensity of social contacts. The scales used to assess QoL in PD may use either subjective or objective indicators or both (Brooks, 1996).

When using questionnaires for measurement, they may be completed by the patient in person or over the telephone, by family members or other close friends, or by health professionals. The most desirable and reliable is an assessment by the patient, especially when the subjects of measurement are the subjective aspects of QoL. QoL scales for patients with PD could be divided into universal (generic) and specific to the disease.

Generic Questionnaires

Among the generic questionnaires related to disease, those used for the assessment of QoL in patients with PD are the Medical Outcome Study 36-Item Short Form Health Survey (SF-36), EuroQol (EQ-5D), Sickness Impact Profile (SIP) Life Satisfaction Questionnaire (LSQ), WHOQOL BREF, and Quality of Well-Being Scale (QWBS) (Opara, Brola, Leonardi & Błaszczyk, 2012; EuroQoL 1990; Brooks, 1996;

The WHOQOL Group Development 1998; Skevington, Loft, O'Connell, 2004; Kaplan, Bush, Berry, 1976; de Boer & Wijker, 1996; Canter, de la Torre & Mier, 1961; Diamond & Markham, 1983; Fahn & Elton, 1987; Jenkinson, 1995).

Questionnaires Specific to Parkinson's disease

There are two commonly used questionnaires for measuring the QoL of patients with PD: the 39-Item Parkinson's disease Questionnaire (PDQ-39) and Parkinson's disease Quality of Life Questionnaire (PDQL).

PDQ-39 is a thirty-nine-item questionnaire with questions about PD-specific HRQL over the last month. It is used to help assess how often patients experience difficulties across the eight QoL dimensions: activities of daily life, attention and working memory, cognition, communication, depression, functional mobility, social relationships, and social support. PDQ-39 offers a patient-reported measure of health and QoL. It is the most frequently used PD specific health status measure and can be used by health and social care professionals to explore the wider impact of PD on QoL and to observe any changes following treatment.

Determining Quality of Life Scores

According to Brola, Leonardi, & Błaszczyk (2012), QoL scores are usually supplemented by a study of cognitive function and depression, since these factors significantly affect QoL and provide important context for the interpretation of test results. Scoring QoL in patients with PD, especially when done for scientific purposes, requires measurements of functional status and fatigue because, in addition to depression and cognitive impairment, these are the most important determinants of QoL in patients with PD

Fatigue is one of the most common symptoms of PD and is associated with reduced QoL. According to recent literature, fatigue in patients with PD has been increasing. Fatigue can be defined as uncontrollable apathy, lack of energy, feelings of exhaustion with no link to depression, or muscle weakness. It is a problem that is frequently underestimated in patients with PD, even though as many as every third patient considers it the most disabling symptom of the disease (as manifested in the HRQL measured with PDQ-39 and SF-36). Indeed, Hitten observed excessive fatigue in forty-eight percent of patients with PD. Fatigue is independent of the motor and nonmotor symptoms of PD, and it may be related to the medications for PD (Friedman & Friedman, 1993; Herlofson & Larsen, 2003; Hitten, van Hoogland, & van der Velde 1993; Karlsen, Larsen, & Tandberg, 1999).

Improving Quality of Life

The website of the Parkinson's Foundation is a great source of information on living with PD. It encourages those with PD to improve their QoL by working through their feelings, embracing hope, building a network, diet and exercise, and spirituality.

PD symptoms and treatments can influence mood. Depression and anxiety affect up to fifty percent of people living with PD and, along with stress, can cause disease symptoms to worsen, leading to decreased QoL. Tending to emotional health keeps this cycle at bay. Accepting and successfully navigating feelings of anger, sadness, grief, or even denial is important. Counseling sessions— alone, as a couple or family, or in a group—can provide support, understanding, and education for those affected by PD. A PD support group can also offer a venue for those with PD to share their experiences with others.

It is also important for patients with PD to focus on and nurture the positive aspects of their life in order to change their emotional outlook. Embracing positives—for example, family, friends, or a new or favorite hobby—can offer a respite when life is difficult. Those with PD must trust themselves to handle any challenges that their diagnosis brings. Reflecting on past trials they have weathered can give them confidence in their capability to withstand future tests (Parkinson's Foundation n.d.).

People with PD must not underestimate the impact of a strong support network. It is important to share feelings and needs with family, friends or neighbors whomever you may want to share. Bigger your aid network, the better. People often want to help but may need your direction. For those with PD, a network of people and groups to provide emotional support and help with basic needs such as transportation or meal preparation is crucial, as it prevents any one person from taking on too many responsibilities and becoming overwhelmed (Parkinson's Foundation n.d.).

Healthy behaviors—including attention to diet, meal planning, and regular moderate exercise— can also improve emotional well-being. Having a meal plan in place can reduce worry and ensure healthy eating, and regular exercise—including yoga, tai chi, and boxing—can improve PD symptoms and mental health.

Focusing on the deeper meaning of life and embracing faith or moral-based core values can offer patients with PD comfort. Trust in a divine power or greater outside influence or plan may ease acceptance of the things they cannot control and allow them to free their mental energy to focus on the things they can. Spirituality means something different for everyone. Beyond religion, prayer, meditation, and acts of service such as volunteering help people with PD find strength, inner peace, happiness, and a deeper connection to the divine or their community. Such actions also help to minimize stress.

Conclusion

PD is a neurodegenerative disease that progresses over time without proper medication and good care. The QoL of patients with PD and their families can be adversely affected by the disease and the toll it takes on emotional well-being, sleep, and energy of the patients.

The first step in treating PD is acceptance of the diagnosis. Next, patients must develop an understanding of the consequences of the disease—both physical and psychological. Family and friends of those with PD must be sure to engage them in positive conversations and avoid discussions of the matters that worry them.

There are two commonly used tools for measuring QoL in patients with PD: PDQ-39 and PDQL. Those with PD should use these tools to stay informed about changes in their QoL. To improve QoL for patients with PD and their loved ones, it is important to work through feelings, embrace hope, build a support network, prioritize proper diet and regular exercise, and engage in spiritual activities.

References

Barcaccia, B. (2013) Retrieved from: https://www.forbes.com/sites/iese/2013/09/04/quality -of-life-everyone-wants-it-but-what-is-it/#6d97174a635d

Brooks, R., & Group, E. (1996). EuroQol: the current state of play. *Health Policy, 37*(1), 53-72.

Canter G, de la Torre R, & Mier, M. (1961). A method for evaluating disability in patients with PD. *Journal of Nerve Mental Disease, 133,* 143.

de Boer, AGEM & Wijker, W. (1996). Quality of life in patients with Parkinson's disease: Development of a questionnaire. *The Journal* of *Neurology, Neurosurgery, and Psychiatry.* 61, 70–74.

deLau, L.M.L, & Breteler, M.M.B. (2006). Epidemiology of Parkinson's disease. *The Lancet Neurology 5* (6).

Diamond, SG & Markham, CH. (1983). Evaluating the evaluations: or how to weigh the scales of Parkinson's disability. *Neurology. 133,* 1089.

EuroQol, G. (1990). EuroQol--a new facility for the measurement of health-related quality of life. *Health Policy (Amsterdam, Netherlands), 16*(3), 199.

Fahn, S. R. L. E. (1987). Unified Parkinson's disease rating scale. *Recent development in Parkinson's disease.*

Friedman, J. & Friedman, H. (1993). Fatigue in Parkinson's disease. *Neurology. 43,* 2016–2018.

Guyatt G,H., Feeny D.H., & Patrick D.L. (1993). Measuring health-related quality of life. *Annals of Internal Medicine, 118,* 622–629.

Herlofson K,, & Larsen J.P. (2003). The influence of fatigue on health-related quality of life in patients with Parkinson's disease. *Acta Neurologica Scandinavica.* 107, 1–6.

Hitten J.J., van Hoogland G., & van der Velde E.A. (1993). Diurnal effects of motor activity and fatigue in Parkinson's disease. *The Journal of Neurology, Neurosurgery, and Psychiatry. 56,* 874–877.

Howard (2013), Fighting Parkinson Drug free. Retrieved from: https://www.fightingparkinson sdrugfree.com/2013/07/24/fighting-parkinsons-and-acceptance-and-denial/.

Jenkinson C, & Peto, V. (1995). Self-reported functioning and well-being in patients with Parkinson`s disease: Comparison of the short-form health survey (SF-36) and the Parkinson`s disease questionnaire (PDQ-39). *Age Ageing. 24*, 505–509.

Kaplan, R.M., Bush, J.W,, & Berry, C.C. (1976). Health status: Types of validity and the Index of WellBeing. *Health Services Research. 11*, 478–507.

Karlsen K, Larsen J.P. & Tandberg E. (1999). Fatigue in patients with Parkinson's disease. *Movements Disorders, 14*, 237–241.

Kowal, S. L., Dall, T. M., Chakrabarti, R., Storm, M. V., & Jain, A. (2013). The current and projected economic burden of Parkinson's disease in the United States. *Movement Disorders, 28*(3), 311-318.

Marinus, J., & van Hilten, J. J. (2007). Clinimetrics and movement disorders. *Parkinsonism and related disorders. Amsterdam, The Netherlands: VU University Press*, 551-558.

National Institute of Environmental Health Sciences, Retrieved from https://www.niehs.nih.gov/ health/topics/conditions/parkinson/index.cfm

Naqvi, Erum, Parkinson's News Today, https://parkinsonsnewstoday.com/parkinsons-disease-statistics/.

National Parkinson Foundation; Parkinson.org

Opara, J. (2003). Current possibilities of evaluation of quality of life in Parkinson disease. *Neurologia i neurochirurgia polska, 37*, 241-250.

Opara, J. A., Brola, W., Leonardi, M., & Błaszczyk, B. (2012). Quality of life in Parkinsons Disease. *Journal of Medicine and Life, 5*(4), 375.

Parkinson's Association of Carolinas, Statistics for Parkinson's disease. Retrieved from: http://www. parkinsonassociation.org/facts-about-parkinsons-disease/.

Parkinson's disease. Retrieved from: https://www.healthline.com/health/parkinsons-and-depression.

Pluck, G. C., & Brown, R. G. (2002). Apathy in Parkinson's disease. *Journal of Neurology, Neurosurgery & Psychiatry, 73*(6), 636-642.

Skevington S, Lofty M, & O'Connell, KA. (2004). The World Health Organization's WHOQOL-BREF quality of life assessment: Psychometric properties and results of the international field trial. A report from WHOQOL Group. *Quality of Life Research*, 299–310.

Tânia M Bovolenta, Sônia Maria Cesar de Azevedo Silva, Roberta Arb Saba, Vanderci Borges, Henrique Ballalai Ferraz, and Andre C Felicio; NCBI - Average annual cost of Parkinson's disease in São Paulo, Brazil, with a focus on disease-related motor symptoms

Tanner, C. M., Brandabur, M., & Dorsey, E. R. (2008). Parkinson disease: A global view. *Parkinson Report, 1*, 9-11.

Thompson, D. (2009). Everyday Health. When Parkinson's disease affects mood.

Whoqol Group. (1998). Development of the World Health Organization WHOQOL-BREF quality of life assessment. *Psychological Medicine, 28*(3), 551-558.

What- When – How; Denial and Acceptance – Parkinson's disease; Retrieved http://what-when-how.com/parkinsons-disease/denial-and-acceptance-parkinson%E2%80%99s-disease/.

Mindfullness and Well-Being

Varinder Kaur, Sylvia Lindinger-Sternart, and Ryan Rominger

"Aging is not lost youth but a new stage of opportunity and strength."

Betty Friedan

Introduction

If only we could maintain the optimism toward aging exemplified by Betty Friedan's quote above. For most, aging brings many joys including children and grandchildren, gaining competence in work and family life, opportunities to travel or pursue interests, and less concern for meeting expectations imposed by social norms. However, for others aging brings stresses and strains indicative of the 'slings and arrows of outrageous fortune,' as Hamlet repines in Shakespeare's play of the same name. The slings and arrows in this case include increasing physical, social, and mental health challenges. As with earlier stages of development, those in late adulthood remain susceptible to stress, anxiety, depression, and chronic pain. The Center for Disease Control released two briefs regarding mental health among the elderly in America (CDC, 2008, 2009). The briefs make it clear that while most elderly report positive mental health, roughly 20% of those 55-years or older experience some type of mental health challenge (CDC, 2008, 2009).

The CDC additionally provides a review of three programs which have been developed to help increase mental health among the aging. These three programs include the Improving Mood-Promoting Access to Collaborative Treatment (IMPACT), Program to Encourage Active Rewarding Lives for Seniors (PEARLS), and Identifying Depression, Empowering Activities for Seniors (Healthy IDEAS) (CDC, 2009). Each of these programs has components of a team-based approach (broadening the mental health team beyond the primary care physician), a community or social approach (activating both social engagement of the individual and social supports to help the individual), and helping the individual better understand mental health challenges (CDC, 2009).

The last component, increasing understanding, includes psychoeducation regarding the effects of stress, anxiety, depression, and other mental health challenges. It also includes helping the individual to become more aware of when she or he is experiencing mental illness, and when to reach out for help. This is where mindfulness can become *especially important*, as mindfulness allows an individual to better reflect upon internal states.

Below we provide a discussion of the history of mindfulness, the emergence of mindfulness therapies, and a more in-depth review of research on stress, anxiety, depression, and pain management within the context of mindfulness therapies. Each section will contain both general information and research as well as information specific to the aging. You may choose to focus on one specific 'in-depth' area such as anxiety, or you may choose to follow the flow of the chapter. However, the sections strive to open an ongoing discussion of how treating stress, anxiety, depression, and pain management might be greatly improved through the integration of mindfulness-based interventions.

"Pain is not just a 'body problem', it is a whole-systems problem." Jon Kabat-Zinn

Mindfulness

Mindfulness has been defined in any ways, with different foci depending on the source. The word mindfulness originally stems from the Pali word "sati that means practicing awareness, attention, and recalling" (Bodhi, 2000). Mindfulness describes a state of consciousness that focuses on one's moment-to-moment experience and is developed through meditation practice (Kabat-Zinn, 2005). Mindfulness means "paying attention in a particular way: on purpose, in the present moment, and non-judgmentally" (Kabat-Zinn, 1994, p.4). Langer & Moldoveanu (2000) define mindfulness as paying attention to novel stimuli, whether trivial or important, which leads to the subjective experience of a heightened state perceived as wakefulness and involvement in the present moment. Brown et al. (2013) indicated that mindfulness is composed of two essential components: "an open attention to one's present experience and a non-judgmental, accepting attitude toward whatever one encounters" (p. 96), where experience refers to not only what is occurring in the person's external environment, but also to what the person is sensing internally such as bodily sensations, emotions, or ideas. Mindfulness can also be defined as paying attention to whatever comes to ones' senses (Brown et al., 2013).

Consistent meditation practice reduces the individual's reactive attention to what is happening in the moment. Maintaining the highest mastery and integrity of mindfulness is considered by many a way of being, seeing, of unearthing the dimensionality of our humanity. Siegel (2011) agreed that mindfulness helps people train their mind so that they pay attention to their own intentions and become aware of their awareness in a manner that is nonjudgmental and nonreactive. This last component, being aware of awareness, is a key component to develop what psychologists call *metacognition*, or thinking about thinking.

The integration of mindfulness practice in daily life is the definitive challenge, and meeting that challenge fosters a life-long engagement to growth, development, and maturation. This challenge has critical implications for how mindfulness-based interventions are taught. To view the concept of mindfulness for the practicality would be a betrayal on the hidden dimensions that rest at the core of authentic meditative experience. Understanding of human nature and the mind/body connection has significant implications for health and disease across the lifespan. The contention, then, is that mindfulness-based interventions can help people lower their stress level by freeing themselves from the grip of two critical processes that lie at the root of stress and many other emotional problems: the tendency to overthink, ruminate, or worry too much about some things; and a tendency to avoid, suppresses, or pushes away other things (Teasdale et al., 2014).

Kabat-Zinn (2005) also describes pure awareness as reflected in deep silence and openheartedness, which are qualities developed at the core of mindfulness-based interventions. These qualities can be experienced alone or when practicing with others. The cultivation of this way of being may transcend symptom reduction and learning new coping mechanism. It is believed to expresses the wisdom inherent in being human, particularly as humans can engage in *metacognition*. People are capable of learning mindfulness and use it, but it must be cultivated through regular practice so that it becomes more reliable and efficient (Kabat-Zinn, 2006). If mindfulness is not practiced or nurtured regularly, one can get carried away by a flow of thoughts, by his or her busy schedules, and by thinking about the past or the future (Kabat-Zinn, 2006). The simple skill to concentrate on one's own breathing and stay in the moment will shift a person's attention and involve gaining awareness and increased acceptance. According to Kabat-Zinn (2005) acceptance of things as they are will create compassion toward one's nature, limits, emotions, and thoughts.

History of Mindfulness

Human beings have been imparting and practicing mindfulness skills as a means of easing psychological suffering for at least 2,500 years (Teasdale, 1999; Williams, Duggan, Crane, & Fennell, 2005). In terms of historical context, there is no distinct origin of mindfulness. According to Miller, Fletcher, & Kabat-Zinn (1995), while the practice is strongly tied to the teachings of the Buddha, others have pointed out that mindfulness practices date back thousands of years before the Buddha's time, with its roots in ancient yogic practices. Although mindfulness originated from Eastern spiritual teachings, the practice of relating to one's experience in the present moment with acceptance and full awareness is by no means limited to a religious tradition (McWilliams, 2014).

Friedman (2010) notes that many monotheistic religious traditions have contemplative practices like that of mindfulness.

Buddha chose the pragmatic approach in his teachings and addressed human conditions as a present embodied reality rather than focusing on worldly issues or worrying about life after death (Kwee, 2010). Buddha employed a non-authoritarian approach to teaching and proposed the way of living as a person's direct experience of self with his or her own efforts independent of any faith, belief, or authority (Mikulas, 2010). Buddha's teachings focused on the free examination of the utility of his teachings without blindly following what he taught (Mikulas, 2007). Buddha also stated that the human mental process is a source of suffering, but it so too does it possesses the practical ways to overcome human dysfunctions (McWilliams, 2014). He believed the nature of an uncultured human life was frustration, dissatisfaction, and suffering; and he proposed that the core reason of dissatisfaction and frustration is the misalignment between desires and expectations, leading to suffering (McWilliams, 2014).

Buddha taught that suffering does not occur because of due to metaphysical sources, but because of sensory or mental experience (Guang, 2010). According to Buddhism, the source of the problem lies in the human craving for pleasure, the desire for sensory gratification and self-preservations, the thirst to become important, expectations, attachment to perceptions, opinions, self-image, reified beliefs and views, and the wish to exist forever (McWilliams, 2014). A key Buddhist tenet, the problem is explained as "attachments take the form of greed, passion, or lust (what one must have), anger, hatred or malice (what one must destroy or avoid), and ignorance, delusion or false belief (not understanding the illusory nature of mental projections)" (McWilliams, 2014, p. 118).

While there are many types of Buddhism (such as Zen and Dzogchen), one general Buddhist perspective on mental health is that it considers a person as a combination of five attributes: physical body, sensations, perceptions and cognitions, predispositions and volitions, and consciousness (Kalupahana, 1992). In other words, Buddhism does not view the person, the self, and all phenomena as independent existing entities, but as an interconnected and interdependent (Ronkin, 2009).

Extrapolating from the teachings of Buddha, mental health issues arise because of confusion, dependence, impermanence, and treating conventional beliefs and concepts as ultimate truth (Ekman, Davidson, Ricard, & Wallace, 2005). Impermanence, or the propensity for change, is defined as a universal aspect of life most noticeable when using developmental lifespan viewpoint, where one is born, matures into adulthood and old age, and then eventually dies (Weisman & Smith, 2001). Everyday people experience impermanence in their relationships, jobs, family, housing, studies, families, and health, which are often in changing states (Weisman & Smith,

2001). The impermanence can be stressful even if it is pleasant or unpleasant because one needs to get constantly adapted to it (Weisman & Smith, 2001).

Brief History of Mindfulness in Psychology

Kabat-Zinn (1994) is one of the first and most well-known scholars who integrated mindfulness into Western healing practices. Jon Kabat-Zinn (1982) introduced mindfulness in the western culture in the form of a mindfulness-based stress reduction (MBSR) program, which played a crucial role in the growth and acceptance of mindfulness in the clinical area. MBSR was originally created for stress reduction and alleviation of chronic pain (Slyter, 2012). MBSR has continued to develop and change, with some teachers incorporating other components of Buddhist practice that suit the Western countries' needs and mindsets (Rapgay & Bystrisky, 2009).

Additionally, MBSR spawned other types of mental health interventions. For instance, mindfulness-based cognitive therapy (MBCT) developed by Segal, Williams, and Teasdale (1990) has emerged from the work of Kabat-Zinn's MBSR program. MBCT was initially developed to help prevent relapse in depression (Segal et al., 1990). The modern version of mindfulness incorporated into Western countries includes features such as: attention and acceptance; more cognitive in nature instead of perceptual in nature; focus on present moment; awareness without any reaction to it; and reduced emphasis on goal-, phase-, or process- oriented attainments (Rapgay & Bystrisky, 2009). A term more recently adopted when discussing the wide variety of therapies which incorporate mindfulness is *Mindfulness-Based Therapies (MBT)*. MBT include mindfulness-based cognitive therapy, acceptance-commitment therapy, and dialectical behavior therapy, among others (Felder, Aten, Neudeck, Shiomi-Chen, & Robbins, 2014; Kangas, 2014).

A neuroscientific perspective describes brain areas which are affected by mindfulness meditation. For example, the anterior cingulate cortex, posterior cingulate cortex, insula, and thalamus seem to play a significant role in the concepts of mindfulness meditation and consciousness (Manuello, Vercelli, Nani, Costa, & Cauda, 2016). It appears that mental training can change the function and the structure of the brain. This can be described as an example of top-down control of our brain, which induces rewiring and creating new neural circuits, key components of neuroplasticity. Neuroplasticity can be understood in that the mind is like the body, and regular focused mental activity will promote brain and mental health. It is now believed that the growth of new neurons in the brain continues until we die. Practicing mindfulness meditation can, for example, strengthen the prefrontal cortex which leads to faster recovery in the amygdala, allowing the brain to return to the pre-stress levels ('baseline') after experiencing stress or negative emotions. Additionally, there is a positive relationship between the hours of meditation and the pace with which the amygdala recovers after stress – the more a person meditates, the quicker the return to pre-stress levels within the brain (Paulson, Davidson, Jha, & Kabat-Zinn, 2013). In conclusion, mindfulness approaches may be an effective method to prevent and even treat stress, anxiety, depression, and experiences of pain.

Meta-Analysis Research on Mindfulness

So much research is generated each year on the effects of MBT that it now becomes prudent to review meta-analysis of groups of studies. A meta-analysis is a specific type of study which reviews several other studies based on their similarity. The similarities usually include having a similar topic, similar research methods, and similar data (such as error variance, power, or effect sizes) which are reported by the authors. Through meta-analysis researchers may theoretically draw a more solid conclusion about the effectiveness of an intervention due to the increased overall number of study participants, based on a review of many studies which were conducted on the topic. However, one caution is that a meta-analysis is only as strong as the criteria for including studies with high validity and parsing out poorer studies, those which do not clearly describe interventions, or those which fail to report key statistical elements (such as effect size).

Within the past five years, several meta-analyses have been completed on mindfulness therapies. Khoury et al. (2013) reviewed 209 studies (a total of 12,145 participants) which used mindfulness-based therapy (MBT) as an intervention and which met the meta-analysis inclusion criteria. Results indicated a moderate effect size when compared pretest to posttest or against treatment as usual, waitlist, or other psychological treatments. The authors noted that MBT was equally as effective as cognitive behavioral therapies. Khoury, Sharma, Rush, & Fournier (2015) later conducted a meta-analysis including 29 studies (n=2,668 participants) which investigated the effects of MBSR on nonclinical (healthy) participants. The studies assessed levels of stress or anxiety (along with other conditions), and results indicated that MBSR had a large effect on stress, and moderate effect on anxiety, depression, distress, and quality of life. The authors also reported a small effect on burnout. This meta-analysis supports a prior meta-analysis which investigated the general health benefits of MBSR (Grossman, Niemann, Schmidt, & Walach, 2004).

Grossman et al. (2004) reviewed 64 empirical studies which used MBSR to alleviate physical, psychosomatic, and psychiatric disorders, 20 of which met criteria for inclusion into the meta-analysis (1,605 participants total). Results indicated that MBSR demonstrated moderate effect size (0.5) for a wide range of problems, including pain, cancer, heart disease, depression, and anxiety. A more recent MBT study focusing on health-care was conducted by Gotink et al. (2015). In their study, Gotink et al. (2015) reviewed 187 studies, of which 23 (with 8,683 total participants) met the criteria for inclusion. The authors focused primarily on MBSR and MBCT, and the studies demonstrated significant improvement on depressive symptoms, anxiety, stress, quality of life, and physical functioning. MBT, and specifically MBSR, has also been used with breast-cancer patients. Zainal, Booth, and Huppert (2013) conducted a meta-analysis of 9 studies, representing 470 patients within two RCT, one quasi-experimental case study, and six single group pre-test post-test studies. Results of the meta-analysis indicated that for breast-cancer patients, MBSR demonstrated moderate to high levels of effect size with significant results on stress, depression, and anxiety.

More population-specific and disorder-specific meta-analyses have also been conducted. Norton, Abbott, Norberg, and Hunt (2014) investigated the effects of mindfulness and acceptance-based treatments (MABTs) on social anxiety disorder. The analysis included 9 studies (3 MBSR, 2 ACT, and 2 MAGT) with a total of 380 participants. The authors concluded that MABT participants demonstrated significant improvement on social anxiety disorder, generally equal to that of cognitive-behavioral therapy. Taylor, Cavanagh, and Strauss (2013) chose to focus on the use of mindfulness within the perinatal period for women and couples. Their meta-analysis contained 17 studies (n=595) which met inclusion criteria, with eight using randomized controlled design (RCT) and nine using uncontrolled designs. Pre-to-post analysis demonstrated significant decreases in anxiety, stress, and depression with small to medium effect sizes (Taylor et al., 2013). However, when comparing between groups at post-intervention, the mindfulness intervention was not maintained, and the effect sizes were minimal. Qualitative data reported in the 17 studies was mixed. Some women were quite positive about the mindfulness intervention, while others reported already having significant support and resources. Men, on the other hand, reported that the mindfulness intervention helped decrease stress, increase connection between father and child, and helped fathers embody the father role (Taylor et al., 2013).

While Taylor et al. (2013) focused on couples and perinatal stress, Yoon, Slade, and Fazel (2017) choose to investigate the effectiveness of psychotherapy within the prison population. After narrowing the meta-analysis to 37 studies which used RCT (2,761 prisoners from 7 countries), results indicated that CBT and mindfulness-based therapies had the most evidence for success on psychiatric disorders (depression, anxiety, PTSD/trauma, and somatization) (Yoon, Slade, & Fazel, 2017). Finally, two meta-analysis focused on the use of mindfulness-based therapies with adolescents and children. Montgomery et al. (2013) conducted a review of 296 articles focused on use of MBT with adolescents, of which 15 met the criteria for use in a meta-analysis (i.e., included an appropriate method and data to calculate effect sizes). The 15 studies included RCT, quasi-experimental, and single group pre-test/post-test designs, and the authors did not report the total number of adolescents within the 15 studies. General results indicated that there was a medium to large effect size for psychological wellbeing, school attendance, medication use, and pain management (Montgomery et al., 2013). A more recent review conducted by Kallapiran et al. (2015) studied the effects of mindfulness on mental health within children and adolescents. Within this meta-analysis, 15 studies met the criteria for inclusion, and results indicated that MBSR and MBCT were more effective than non-active controls on improving stress, anxiety, and depression, acceptance and commitment therapy was comparable to active treatments on depression and quality of life, and 'other' mindfulness-based interventions also demonstrated effectiveness for anxiety and stress, but not depression (Kallabiran et al., 2015). Clearly, MBT has demonstrated significant improvement on several disorders, with several different populations, with at least a moderate effect size.

General Mindfulness Research and the Elderly. There are two types of research which become important when extending mindfulness research conclusions to older adults. First, some research has focused upon diseases which older adults might be more likely to have. For example, Tovote et al. (2017) studied the effects of cognitive behavioral therapy (CBT) versus MBCT for treating depression within 91 patients (mean age of 53-years-old) who had diabetes. Managing diabetes can be complex, and the effects of diabetes include both physical and mental challenges. The authors used a randomized controlled trials approach, with 34 participants completing the MBCT intervention and 33 completing the CBT (treatment as usual) intervention. Results indicated that *both* CBT and MBCT were effective in treating depression within this population.

Another group of research has more directly focused on the use of MBT with the elderly. Perez-Blasco et al. (2016) studied the effects of mindfulness and self-compassion on the ability to adjust to stressful situations among 45 elderly adults (mean age was 63.5 years old). The participants were randomly assigned to the intervention or a wait-list control, where the intervention's focus was on a combination of MBCT and the Mindful Self-Compassion Program (Perez-Blasco et al., 2016). Results demonstrated a significant improvement in resilience and other anti-stress components. Helmes & Ward (2017) focused on the use of MBCT for anxiety among 52 older adults within a residential care facility (mean age was 83 years old). These authors also used a randomized control, with the treatment group receiving MBCT while the control group engaged in activities within the facility. Helmes & Ward (2017) found that the MBCT group demonstrated significant improvements on anxiety measures, while the activities group did not. These two studies, which specifically focused on older or elderly populations, demonstrate that MBTs can be effective with older adult populations. Now we move to addressing the specific areas of *stress, anxiety, depression,* and *pain management*.

Mindfulness and Stress

Theories and Impacts of Stress

Stress is a very common experience, and many have felt it at some point in life. Historically, literature reveals that there are different types of stresses including stimulus-based (Holmes & Rahe, 1967), response-based (Selye, 1956), stimulus-response interaction based (Lazarus & Folkman, 1984), as well as perceived stress (Largo-Wight, Peterson, & Chen, 2005).

Stress as a stimulus and stress as response. One of the types of stress defined by Holmes and Rahe (1967) included stress as a stimulus, which is a result of pressure. The more pressure there is, the more likely the recipient will fail to resist. Pressure here often refers to external pressures, or external stimuli.

Another type of stress defined by Selye (1956) is stress as a response to noxious or aversive stimuli such as extreme temperatures, electric shocks, or food deprivation. According to Selye (1956), stress occurs in three stages of physiological reaction to noxious events: the alarm stage, resistance stage, and exhaustion stage. At the first stage, the body responds with an alarm reaction once it is alerted; at the second stage, the body responds with an automatic activity as it prepares to deal with the stress; at the third stage, the system can become damaged and collapse if stress surpasses the capacity of the body to respond.

It was found that purely stimulus or response-based definitions of stress possess some limitations. Butler (1993) discussed the limitations of stimulus-based definition, which suggest that internal collapse is unavoidable when the external stimulus becomes too great, irrespective of the characteristics of the internal responses. The limitation of the response-based definition includes the assumption that the psychological responses could be insidious as well as alarm-based depending upon the specific characteristics of the person suffering the stress (Butler, 1993). The response-based definition also suggests that at some stage, the collapse or exhaustion becomes unavoidable if the stress persists, which doesn't focus on the magnitude of stress as an external stimulus (Butler, 1993). Both stimulus-based and response-based definitions lack in considering other stress determining factors such as cognitive factors including thoughts, beliefs, or attitudes as well as the perceived demands and the perceived resources that some individuals experience (Butler, 1993).

Stress as a stimulus-response interaction. Therefore, the third type of stress offered by Lazarus & Folkman (1984) as a stimulus-response interaction has more clinical value (Butler, 1993). According to Lazarus & Folkman (1984), the process of stress includes both internal and external factors such as the personal characteristics and contextual circumstances of an individual as well as the interaction between them. The definition of stress as a stimulus-response interaction explains that the perceived demands and the perceived resources of an individual determine the amount of stress experienced by an individual (Lazarus & Folkman, 1984).

Perceived stress. Perceived stress is defined as an assessment of a situation or stimulus as intimidating by an individual even though it is not actually threatening (Largo et al., 2005). Perceived stress includes both actual threat (for example, a grizzly bear running at you) as well as threats which are more internal (worrying about paying monthly bills). Some of the negative effects of perceived stress on the physical health include high blood pressure, decreased immune system function, recurrences of herpes virus, increased susceptibility to infection, cancer, coronary heart disease, autoimmune disease, and stroke (Largo et al., 2005). According to Ekpenyong, Daniel, & Aribo (2013), there is no universal definition of stress as the effects of stress may vary depending upon the ways it is assessed, or the ways it is coped with by different people from different ethnic, cultural, and socio-economic backgrounds.

The difference between perceived stress and other types of stresses include avoidable stressors such as lack of sleep, excessive smoking, relationship issues, self-esteem issues, or pushing oneself physically beyond one's limits (Martino, 2009). There is high tendency of avoidable stressors to fall under perceived stress as compared to other types of stresses, because perceived stress results from the story one tells oneself which might not be true (Martino, 2009). The stress response to those things that one imagines produces the same negative effect on the physical and mental health as that of other types of stresses by producing same powerful stress-chemicals in the body (Martino, 2009).

Some stressors are perceived as positive or good and help enliven us, such as the birth of a newborn, a graduation ceremony, going out on first date, a job promotion, public speaking, a job interview or a family vacation (American Psychological Association, 2016; Kaplan & Sadock, 1998). Other stressors may be perceived as negative, distressing, or bad. Negative stressors affect our mental and physical health in a negative way. For instance, these stressors include the hospitalization of a close family member, accidents, financial burden, marital issues, physical illness, or work pressure (Yeager & Roberts, 2003). All stressors are not bad, and some stressors are inherent to living a meaningful life. Too much stress comprising multiple stressors without effective coping strategies, however, may be detrimental to one's mental health as well as one's mental and physical health. Stress can become chronic if experienced over a long period of time (American Psychological Association, 2016).

Rumination and stress. Rumination and stress are directly related to each other and one can cause the other (Slavich, O'Donovan, Epel, & Kemeny, 2010). Robinson and Alloy (2003) introduced the concept of stress-reactive rumination as an extended version of the previously described rumination. Robinson and Alloy (2003) described stress-reactive rumination as an inclination to ruminate on negative conclusions following stressful life events. Literature distinguishes between rumination as a maladaptive behavior and mindful self-awareness as an adaptive ruminating behavior (Teasdale, 1999; Watkins & Teasdale, 2004). The maladaptive rumination or depressed rumination involves thinking and analyzing stressful life events and feelings, whereas the adaptive rumination or mindful self-awareness includes direct and non-evaluative experiential awareness in the present moment (Teasdale, 1999; Watkins & Teasdale, 2004). Where maladaptive rumination hinders the problem-solving ability, enhances the depressive symptoms, and over generalization of the autobiographical memory of an individual (Watkins & Teasdale, 2004), mindful self-awareness enhances one's openness to solve problems related to various life events (Treynor, Gonzalez, & Nolen-Hoeksema, 2003).

One of the major factors that cause rumination is experiencing stress. Stressful life events not only cause rumination regarding those events, but also rumination about other areas of an individual's life (Nolen-Hoeksema, 1994). A negative state of mind might lead to fixation on discrepancies between one's goals and one's current state leading to rumination about how to reduce such discrepancies (Carver & Scheier, 1981; Martin & Tesser, 1996). Chronic or uncontrollable stressors that cannot be resolved lead to ongoing rumination as a result of discrepancies between one's current state of mind and his or her goals or desired state of mind (Watkins, 2008). The rumination may be due to weakened self-regulation, or the ability to engage in self-control over one's behavior (Baumeister, Gailliot, DeWall, & Oaten, 2006). The limited self-regulation ability of an individual may cause impairment to one's ability to get engaged in active coping or problem solving, which increases the likelihood of engagement in rumination (Nolen-Hoeksema, Wisco, & Lyubomirsky, 2008). The rumination can also be caused by a variety of other cognitive mechanisms following stressful life events such as focusing on negative thoughts and feelings and autobiographical memory for previous negative events (Scher, Ingram, & Segal, 2005; Segal & Ingram, 1994).

Stress and the Body/Mind. The physiological response to stressful life events affects the physical health in a variety of ways (Yeager & Roberts, 2003). For instance, a series of biochemical reactions as a result of stressful life events can affect the major organ systems of the body (Yeager & Roberts, 2003). Cannon (1927) described the response to a perceived stressful or emergency event as the fight or flight response. According to Cannon (1927), body activates resources to protect an individual either by getting away fast or by fighting. Some of the neurochemicals, specifically serotonin, norepinephrine, and dopamine, are affected due to the triggered complex chain reaction that is experienced while responding to neurochemical messages. As a result of this chain reaction, the body produces larger quantities of chemicals such as adrenaline, cortisol, and other hormones, which causes an increased heart rate and blood pressure, dilated pupils, sweating, a heightened muscle preparedness, and alertness (Yeager & Roberts, 2003). These bodily responses are the survival mechanisms, which are presumed to have been present since the beginning of humankind (Chrousos & Gold, 1992; Haddy & Clover, 2001; McEwen, 1995). While these bodily responses protect human beings from a dangerous or challenging situation, they slow down the non-essential body functions such as our digestive and immune system because of the full concentration on rapid breathing, blood flow, alertness and muscle use during fight or flight mode (Nordqvist, 2015). Over time, repeated engagement of the sympathetic and parasympathetic systems, linked to the flight, fight, or freeze response, leads to degradation of the bodily systems.

It has been found that stress may lead to several mental health issues as a result of developing unhealthy coping mechanisms. Research supports the idea that stress is one of the significant factors contributing to drug or alcohol use and relapse vulnerability (Bamberger & Bacharach, 2006; Sinha, 2008). A review of the literature supports the conclusion that long-term exposure to stress may lead to unhealthy coping mechanism such as alcohol dependence. Perceived stressors are found to be more stressful for individuals suffering from neuroticism, because of their high tendency to develop substance abuse when exposed to high stress level (Colemean & Trunzo, 2015). The term neuroticism is defined as one of the personality traits in the five-factor model of personality (Digman, 1990), which could be one of the major factors in contributing the development of drug use and abuse (Colemean & Trunzo, 2015). For instance, the children who score high on the neuroticism possess high tendencies to develop substance abuse (Colemean & Trunzo, 2015).

Along with the physical and mental consequences of stress, there are few emotional effects as well. For example, stressful life events may lead to emotional abuse among college students (Colemean & Trunzo, 2015). Other psychological and emotional problems caused by stress include anxiety, frustration, worrying, irritability, anger, uncertainty, and lack of confidence (Antai-Otong, 2001; Zautra, 2003), increased muscle tension, reduced energy, and emotional distress (Almeida, 2005; Brown & Harris, 1989).

Stress and the Elderly. Stress, especially chronic stress, among the elderly can have particularly negative effects (Zimmerman et al., 2016). Zimmerman et al. (2016) investigated the hippocampal subfield volumes (volume of the brain in the hippocampus region, a region responsible for healthy adaptation to stressful events) among 116 patients over the age of 70 by using an MRI scan. The authors found that individuals who reported greater amounts of perceived lifetime stress had more brain deterioration, or smaller hippocampal volume, than those who reported less perceived stress. It appears be that chronic stress within adults, as with other animals, has a long-term negative impact upon our physical brain, especially that part of the brain responsible for dealing with stress.

Short-term stress has a negative impact upon brain activity. Adorni et al. (2018) studied the effects of a stressful experience upon 18 healthy elderly adults (mean age of 70). The participants also completed an anxiety assessment. The authors used near-infrared spectroscopy (NIRS) along with electrocardiography (ECG) and cognitive assessments during the stressful event to measure brain functioning. Results indicate that the stressful event had a negative impact upon response times, and the more anxious a participant reported the larger the negative effect on response times. Accuracy also decreased and was lower the higher the reported anxiety. Regarding brain function, the right pre-frontal cortex demonstrated activation, and was positively correlated with anxiety levels (or, in other words, the higher the anxiety score, the more the PFC was activated) (Adorni et al., 2018).

Research on Mindfulness and Stress

Nyklicek & Kuijpers (2008) indicated that the increase in mindfulness level reduces the impact of stress, which improves the quality of life and increases the sense of vitality. Nyklicek & Kuijpers (2008) conducted a study with 40 women and 20 men with the symptoms of distress and found the evidences for a mediation effect of general mindfulness in the case of perceived stress, quality of life, and partially on vital exhaustion. A total of 60 participants were randomly distributed into an intervention group that would receive the MBSR training and a waiting-list control group that would receive MBSR after the intervention group finished their training. The randomization was blind, but group assignment was not blind except for assessment of the outcomes, which was achieved by sending questionnaires to the participants by post. The inclusion criteria included people responding that they felt distressed at least regularly or often upon asking about how often they felt distressed or if they had a psychological disorder that was present for at least past two months. The exclusion criteria included serious psychopathology such as suicidal ideation, and insufficient understanding of the Dutch language as the sessions were held in Dutch. The measures included questionnaires on psychological wellbeing, quality of life, and mindfulness, which were used before and after the intervention. The psychological wellbeing was assessed by using the constructs such as perceived stress, vital exhaustion, positive affect, and negative affect. Maastricht Questionnaire was used to assess the vital exhaustion, which is defined as a feeling of being dejected or defeated, increased irritability and unusual fatigue. The negative affect characterized by fatigue and malaise, and the positive affect characterized by energy and sociability were assessed by the Global Mood Scale. The World Health Organization Quality of Life-Brief questionnaire was used to measure the quality of life. This questionnaire was used to obtain contentment in the different domains such as physical health, psychological health, social relationships, environment, and general quality of life. The mindfulness skills were assessed by the combination of the Mindful Attention Awareness Scale and two subscales of observe and accept without judgment from the Kentucky Inventory of Mindfulness Skills. In addition to these questionnaires, participants were asked at each intervention session that how many times they practiced at home according to the instructions during the past week. Repeated measures multiple analysis of variance (MANCOVAs) was conducted to produce the results. Results indicated stronger reductions of perceived stress and vital exhaustion and stronger elevations of positive affect, quality of life, as well as mindfulness in comparison with the control group. It was concluded that the increased mindfulness level might at least partially mediate the positive effects of mindfulness-based stress reduction intervention.

There are several benefits of mindfulness such as improving emotional stability of secondary school students (Huppert & Johnson, 2010), fostering inner knowing, improving emotional strength, and incorporating moral and spiritual vision (Bazzano, 2014). The use of mindfulness by educators in the field of education has been considered as marginalized by contemporary instrumentalist conceptions of the educational task (Siegel, 2007; Burnett, 2011). The direct and practical links between educational tasks and mindfulness strategies at all levels are among the biggest advantages of mindfulness for educators (Hyland, 2015). Mindfulness has many benefits for educators as well as students; for instance, benefits for educators include improving focus, enhancing classroom environment, increasing responsiveness to student need. The benefits for students include readiness in learning, reducing anxiety, strengthening concentration, and enhancing social and emotional learning (Schoeberlein & Sheth, 2009). While mindfulness has been shown to be effective in a few areas as discussed above, this study focuses on the psychological benefits of mindfulness among graduate counseling students such as alleviation of stress among counseling students and enabling them to use mindfulness as an intervention with their clients.

Roberti, Harrington, & Storch (2006) discussed that college students face enormous stress due to various issues such as unexpected breakups, demanding academic work, uncertainty about the future, difficulties in interpersonal relationships, dating problems, self-doubt, family issues, or making difficult decisions about their future. Smith (2007) identified several effective acute stress management techniques used to alleviate stress such as relaxation techniques including stretching exercises, progressive muscle relaxation, breathing exercises, meditation, mindfulness, imagery, and visualization. Few studies in the literature indicates that the mindfulness reduces stress and compulsive thinking, improve concentration, increase focus, enhance clarity, and induce a state of calm among college students (Chiesa & Serretti, 2009; Hanstede et al., 2008; Christopher & Maris, 2010). Literature indicates that the significant greater awareness of bodily sensations helps college students in recognizing situations triggering unhelpful emotions, which helps them getting engage in emotional self-regulation (Fonow, Cook, Goldsand, Buke-Miller (2016). One population that has historically reported high levels of chronic stress is counseling students (Rizzolo, Zipp, Stiskal, & Simpkins, 2009). There are high chances for graduate counseling students to develop chronic stress because they are expected to perform well in their academic courses in addition to their requirement to get involved with client care (Rizzolo et al., 2009).

There are few studies in the literature that include the examination of the potential applications of mindfulness practices to the training of counselors and psychotherapists. Christopher, Christopher, Dunnagan, & Schure (2006) used a focus group at the end of the semester with graduate counseling students who took a semester long mindfulness course. Christopher et al. (2000) asked several questions to the students such as 1) Why did you take this course? 2) What do you like the most about the class? 3) What is the first thing that comes to mind when you consider the course? 4) What did you like least about the class? 5) What are the strengths and weakness associated with the class organization? After analyzing the responses of students, it was found that the students noticed physical, emotional, mental and spiritual changes in themselves along with increased patience, awareness, consciousness, and ability to focus. Students also discussed that the course changed their conceptualization of working with their clients.

Schure, Christopher, & Christopher (2008) analyzed four different cohorts' experiences at the end of the semester-long course (Christopher & Maris, 2010). The students were asked four questions: 1) How you see your life changed over the course of this semester due to the inclusion of mindfulness practices? 2) What is your favorite mindfulness practice and why? How has it affected you? 3) How the course has affected your sessions with your clients, both in terms of being in the room and thinking about the treatment? 4) How can you integrate any of the learned practices from class into your clinical work with your clients? The students indicated changes in the physical, emotional, mental, spiritual, and interpersonal aspects. Students reported positive impact of yoga in terms of increased awareness of body, increased flexibility and energy, increased mental clarity and concentration. Students also reported the positive influence of mindfulness practices on the work with their client such as increased comfort with silence, increased attention to therapeutic process, and improvement in viewing the therapy. Student also showed their willingness to integrate mindfulness training in their therapeutic sessions, continuing mindfulness exercises in their personal lives, and incorporating class ideas to their therapeutic sessions. Students also reported changes due to Qi gong such as increased energy, increased sense of mind or body or emotion connection, increased feelings of centeredness, increased sense of fluidity. This study offered future implications for integrating mindfulness practices including recommending specific practices, integration of class ideas, continuing personal practice, and incorporating practices in therapy.

Chrisman, Christopher, & Lichtenstein (2009) conducted a study in which they asked students to discuss their experience of starting qigong at the beginning as well as at the end of the semester long course. The students indicated some of the experiences after the first session including relaxation, feelings of calmness, a sense of being grounded, and positive changes in energy level, balance, and body temperature. The students in this study also reported increased sense of calmness and mental focus. Most of the students described that initially they judge themselves for their ability to learn something new, but later their judgmental attitude dissipated quickly. After fifteen weeks of practicing qigong, students reported the same initial themes along with the awareness of group energy and a sense of synchrony and harmony within the group.

Christopher, Chrisman, & Trotter (2009) conducted the semi-structured interview with students after they completed their mindfulness course two to six years previously. The interview explored many areas of mindfulness experienced by the students, such as the most important things they learned in the class, the effect of the class on their personal life in the areas of awareness, relationships, and interactions with others, health, and psychological development. For instance, some of the questions related to their professional life included the ways in which they think about the clients' issues, ideas about the therapeutic process, considering mindfulness as a healing process, comfort level while introducing mindfulness techniques to their clients, and any negative consequences from mindfulness experience. Some other questions included what self-care practice they often use, how did the class influence the practices, do they attribute changes to the class, have these changes stayed with them since they took the class. The result of this study indicated the positive influence on students' personal and professional lives. For instance, the personal improvement was reported in terms of increased physical, emotional, and mental health along with improved interpersonal relationships. The influence on professional life included incorporating mindfulness practices into their clinical practice, increased awareness and acceptance of themselves as a therapist and of their clients, improved therapeutic relationship with clients, and shaping theoretical and conceptual framework. Therefore, increasing the probability that graduate students in counseling programs are mindful could increase their counseling skills and mindfulness level, and decrease their stress level, as well as benefit their clients both directly and indirectly. The implications for the mindfulness training included teaching counseling student's self-care that can be helpful in preventing burnout, compassion fatigue, and vicarious traumatization.

Literature reveals that including mindfulness related courses in the master level counseling programs leave positive impact on the counseling skills of future counselors (Schure, Christopher, & Christopher, 2008). Schure et al. (2008) conducted a four-year qualitative study that included teaching hatha yoga, meditation and qigong to counseling graduate students in a 15-week, 3-credit mindfulness-based stress reduction course resulted into a positive physical, emotional, mental, spiritual, and interpersonal changes and substantial effects on their counseling skills and therapeutic relationships. At the end of the course students were asked to write a journal assignment which includes answering four questions in writing such as sharing their experience regarding any change in their lives during the course of the semester, their learning from the class, the effects of those learning on their lives, any effect of those learning on their clients' lives in the room and thinking about the treatment, any plans on integrating their learning from the class into their clinical practice or career plans. Students were not provided with the direction on the length of their answers. Students were offered with the option of not having their responses used in the study, but no students chose wanted to withhold their data.

The results showed that all students did not experience all the themes. Most of the students indicated the positive effects of the course on the physical, emotional, mental, spiritual, and intellectual aspects of their lives. For instance, under the theme of physical aspect, the respondents indicated the positive benefits of yoga such as promoting flexibility, strength, and balance; getting sick less frequently, improving immune systems, and increasing awareness and sensitivity to their bodies.

Schure et al. (2008) also found that there were emotional changes among students in terms of accepting and letting go of negative thoughts and emotions. The theme of interpersonal changes was reported in terms of increased capacity related to changes in perception, attitude, mental clarity, and enhanced listening abilities. According to Schure et al., (2008), this result of interpersonal changes can be helpful for students in their counseling sessions in order to stay more comfortable sitting in silence with their clients and stay more focused on the therapeutic process. Overall, students reported positive implications for integrating the course concepts into their personal and professional life. Most of the students showed their willingness to integrate mindfulness practices into their future profession. Schure et al. (2008) reported the benefits for counseling students, which includes gaining new ways of relating to their emotional life, becoming less reactive to stress related or anxiety-provoking events such as during clients' crisis or painful situations, becoming more present and connected with themselves, their clients, and their supervisors.

Anxiety and Mindfulness

Palpating heart, sweating, vision narrowing, feeling feint, repetitive thoughts about harm, looking for the nearest escape route, or physiological symptoms like upset stomach or bodily pain and recurrent indigestion. One might even feel that death is imminent, either through heart attack or some other catastrophic malady. These symptoms, and more, are common for those who suffer anxiety in many of its forms. At times the symptoms come on unexpectedly, and other times they occur in the presence of a specific item or situation. Either way, clinical levels of anxiety are believed to affect about 19.1% of the adult population each year, or an estimated 44 million people in 2017 in the United States (Harvard Medical School, 2007; U.S. Census Bureau, 2017). Among adolescents, lifetime prevalence of anxiety skyrockets to 31.9%, with 38% of female and 26.1% of male adolescents reporting struggles with anxiety (Harvard Medical School, 2007).

So, what is the big deal about anxiety? Anxiety has very real effects on the body. Anxiety contributes to increased stress, strain on the sympathetic and parasympathetic system, and cortisol levels (Arbel et al., 2017). In a very real sense, anxiety is a form of worrying and includes cognitive preoccupation, rumination, distraction, and physical stress. Those who experience anxiety also wish it to end, often as quickly as possible. People who do not have access to mental health services may try to self-medicate through drugs, alcohol, sex, or other risky behaviors. For example, Hill et al. (2017) note that men who report higher anxiety also report less condom use during sexual encounters. Thus, anxiety has a very real impact, both direct and indirect, on the health and wellbeing of the person experiencing it. In a similar fashion, those who are family or friends of someone with anxiety may also feel the effects due to the self-medication or overcompensation needed to deal with the disorder.

However, what about those with sub-clinical levels of anxiety? While incidence and prevalence reports are focused on those who have been diagnosed with anxiety, many more people experience brief periods of worrying or anxiety, or simply do not seek mental health assistance (and thus go undiagnosed). And with so many people suffering from anxiety, it is no wonder that Business Insider claimed anxiety is an epidemic (Kelley, July 17, 2012), or that HuffPost calls America the United States of Anxiety (Deterline, August 4, 2017) and *The New York Times* refers to America as The Prozac Nation and United States of Xanax (Williams, June 10, 2017).

Anxiety and the Elderly

Anxiety is a concern among the elderly, as adult onset anxiety does occur and may manifest in different ways than early onset anxiety (CDC, 2008). Anxious elders may be concerned about falling while alone, worry about family members, and worry about unstable financial or medical situations. Additionally, anxiety may be found in elderly whether they are living independently or within an assisted living facility. Bendixen and Engedal (2016) studied the presence of anxiety among 473 elderly (mean age was 75.1 years of age) admitted to a geriatric psychiatry department. The authors found that those admitted had a variety of mental health concerns: 65.3% depression, 38.8% dementia, 33.3% mania, and 28% psychosis (Bendixen & Engedal, 2016). The authors also found that anxiety was increasingly comorbid among those who were female and who were depressed.

Herrera, Montorio, & Cabrera (2017) in turn studied the effect of anxiety upon memory within older adults. The authors recruited 102 older adults (with a mean age of 67.29 years) with either high or low trait anxiety. Participants engaged both recognition and autobiographical memory tests, and results indicated that elders with higher trait anxiety remembered fewer positive pictures and remembered life experiences with more negative valence. Thus, those with high anxiety had poorer memory, and when they did remember life events there was more of a negative emotional tone to the memories. Those with less anxiety, however, had better memory and remembered more positive life experiences.

Mindfulness and general anxiety disorder. Often, when anxiety hits it can be difficult to pinpoint the exact cause. A good analogy (which one author, Ryan Rominger, uses with clients) is that of filling a coffee cup (I happen to often have a tea or coffee during sessions, so it makes for a useful visual analogy). We each have our own personal 'coffee cup' for stress and anxiety. If we are using positive coping strategies or our life is going well, our cup might only be a quarter full. However, if we have lots of changes, work or family stress, health problems, are routinely discriminated against, encounter numerous social barriers or difficulties, then our cup might be close to full daily. Then, we might encounter an experience (news of a family member being sick, a difficult review at work, a child who encounters a bully at school) and suddenly we find we are during full-blown anxiety overload. Our cup is flowing over. While the experience may not have normally put us into such a state, because of our ongoing daily stress and anxiety, our cup was already full – or our mental, physiological, and emotional system was already taxed to its limit. This constant anxiety, especially if it is occurring for longer than 6 months, leads to constant worrying, results in restlessness, being easily tired, difficulty concentrating, irritability, muscle tension, and sleep disturbance, and all of this is causing difficulties on a day to day basis, could mean that one has a *generalized anxiety disorder* (APA, 2013). The label, noted as GAD, simply means that one is constantly struggling to cope with the anxiety and it has been a bit too much for one to deal with, especially with one's current set of coping strategies. This is where mindfulness enters the picture. Mindfulness is another coping strategy, or set of strategies really, that can help a person manage the daily anxiety and 'anxiety attacks.'

It appears that most 'anxiety' and mindfulness research has occurred within the general premise of generalized anxiety disorder (GAD), or at a minimum 'general' anxiety. While practitioners have been reporting the effects of mindfulness practices and therapies (MBT) on anxiety (Kabat-Zinn, 1990), formal research on the topic had had mixed results. Most report decreases on anxiety measures; however, a few studies have pointed out that MBT are not more effective than cognitive behavioral therapy (but are, nonetheless, still effective). Millstein et al. (2015) studied the effects of mindfulness within acceptance-based behavior therapy and applied relaxation interventions for 81 participants who had GAD randomly selected to receive either ABBT or AR. Results indicated that participants receiving a mindfulness intervention significantly decreased their anxiety, as well as decreased interpersonal problems associated with anxious behaviors (Millstein et al., 2015). Similarly, Hoge et al. (2015) studied the effects of MBSR on general anxiety disorders among 38 participants randomly assigned to either an MBSR or an attention control class. While Hoge et al. (2015) were focused on analysis for mechanisms of change, their results noted that those who received MBSR decreased on GAD scores. Idusohan-Moizer et al. (2015) studied the effects of

MBCT, rather than MBSR, upon anxiety scores. The authors recruited 15 participants who had intellectual disability, had depression, anxiety, or both, and who had histories of self-harm. MBCT improved anxiety, depression, self-compassion, and compassion for others, with the largest impact on anxiety (Idusohan-Moizer et al., 2015).

More recently, Blake et al. (2016) investigated the effects of a group MBCT program on anxiety and sleep disorders among 144 high school students. Participants were randomly assigned either the MBCT or a study skills group. Those who received the group MBCT intervention had lower levels of anxiety as well as less sleep disorders than the active control group (Blake et al., 2016). Another study which used the group format was Evans et al. (2016), who worked with primary care patients who exhibited depression and anxiety. Of those who attended more than one visit (*n*=19), results indicated a significant decrease from pre-test to post-test on anxiety and depression with small to medium effect sizes. However, as the authors note, while efficacy studies attempt to maximize internal validity, this study was focused on external validity (executing the program in a live setting with comorbid diagnoses while intersecting other healthcare programs), and thus comparison to other MBT efficacy studies should be taken lightly (Evans et al., 2016).

One such efficacy study was conducted by Sundquist et al. (2017). Sundquist et al. (2017) investigated the effects of mindfulness-based group therapy (MGT) on a broad range of psychiatric symptoms. The authors recruited 215 participants from 16 primary care clinics in Sweden. The RCT design compared the participants' symptoms from the start of the study (pre-test) to scores after they had completed the 8-week group (post-test), and compared between the MGT group and a treatment as usual group (TAU). Participants in both groups demonstrated a significant decrease in symptom severity, including decreases in anxiety and depression, and significant increases in mindfulness. The MGT group demonstrated a slightly higher increase with respect to mindfulness at the post-test, but the increase was not greater than the TAU group.

Mindfulness and social anxiety disorder. People with social anxiety disorder often find themselves feeling nervous while in the midst of others. However, for those with a clinically diagnosable disorder, the nervousness goes beyond simple nerves to feelings of outright fear of being judged while being observed by others, performing in front of others, or simply being in large crowds or groups (such as in school, at the mall, or in airports) (APA, 2013). Additionally, one might feel afraid of showing anxiety in front of others, the fear is out of proportion to the actual threat, and the social settings are either avoided or managed through some compensating behavior, all of which may cause serious distress within the individual (APA, 2013). Social anxiety disorder can impact a person's desire to engage social activities with friends or family, leading to reclusive behavior and a reduced social support network. For those who experience SAD in a school or work setting, the effects can greatly impact school or work performance, and ultimately lead to decreased grades, lack of advancement in the workplace, and even job loss.

Koszycki et al. (2016) studied the effects of mindfulness-based therapy, which included compassion meditation and mindful exposure, on social anxiety disorder among 39 clients seeking treatment. Participants were randomly assigned to either a wait-list control group, where they did not receive treatment for a period of time, or the mindfulness intervention. Those who were in the mindfulness intervention had significantly less anxiety, depression, better social adjustment, enhanced self-compassion, and increased mindfulness characteristics (Koszycki et al., 2016). The changes were maintained at a 3-month follow-up, demonstrating that the effects lasted beyond the therapy intervention. The authors concluded that the combined compassion and mindfulness intervention was very effective in treating SAD. In a more recent study, Hjeltnes et al. (2017) investigated the effect of a standard 8-week MBSR training on SAD within a college setting. Fifty-three participants joined the study, although only 45 completed the 8-week training. Participants completed pre-test and post-test measures related to SAD, psychological distress, mindfulness, self-compassion, and self-esteem, and reported significant reductions in SAD and psychological distress as well as increases in mindfulness, self-compassion, and self-esteem. The effect sizes ranged from moderate to large, indicating that MBSR could be an effective tool for facilitating health and well-bing for college students suffering SAD (Hjeltnes et al., 2016).

Mindfulness and panic. Few recent studies have specifically addressed the use of mindfulness with people who have panic disorders. Panic disorders are characterized by sudden bursts of fear that peak within minutes, and the person generally experiences at least four of the following: palpitations or a pounding heart, sweating, shaking, shortness of breath, feelings of choking, chest pain or discomfort, abdominal distress or nausea, dizziness, faintness, or lightheadedness, chills or heat flash, numbness or tingling (often in the extremities), fears of losing control or going crazy, and fears of dying (APA, 2013). Those with panic disorder may have a comorbid diagnosis of other types of anxiety, such as generalized anxiety. Often individuals will have a variety of mild, moderate, and severe attacks, with anxiety about another occurring between panic attacks. The goal of mindfulness would be to facilitate a more non-judgmental awareness of bodily reactions and sensations so as not to escalate into a panic attack when one feels sensations which might be associated with panic (for example, heavy breathing after exercising, which can be mistaken for the onset of a panic attack). Additionally, mindfulness practices may provide an immediate coping strategy, through breath awareness, which may help disrupt the trajectory and severity at panic onset.

Almost a decade ago, Kim et al. (2009) studied the effects of adding an 8-week MBCT program to pharmacotherapy treatment for panic disorder and generalized anxiety disorder. Forty-six participants were randomly assigned to either the MBCT adjunct or an anxiety education adjunct, with participants' anxiety, depression, and symptoms measured before the start of the program and at the end of the program. Participants in the MBCT group demonstrated a significant decrease, as compared to the education group, on all scales of anxiety and depression. Kim et al. (2009) concluded that MBCT would be a valuable addition to treat panic disorders (as well as GAD). A year later B. Kim et al. (2010) published a similar study investigating the effects of adding MBCT to pharmacotherapy for 23 individuals with panic disorder. This single-group study tracked phobia, anxiety, and depression at weeks 2, 4, and 8, with the participants showing significant decreases in panic and anxiety by the end of the study (B. Kim et al., 2010).

One recent study did investigate the use of mindfulness practices with individuals who have panic in association with asthma. Kraemer, McLeish, and Johnson (2015) recruited 56 young adults who self-reported physician diagnosed asthma. The participants were a subset of a larger study using college students (*n*=431). Kraemer et al. (2015) found that participants who had greater use of the mindfulness skill of 'acting with awareness' demonstrated fewer panic symptoms and anxiety sensitivity. Thus, considering the effects of mindfulness on general anxiety, and Kraemer et al.'s (2015) findings regarding panic within asthma sufferers, it appears that mindfulness may be a viable intervention to help facilitate a decrease in anxiety and panic for this population, and potentially panic within the larger panic disorder population.

Mindfulness and Depression

Historical documents written by philosophers, healers, and writers have described the long-standing existence of depression as a problem of human beings' health. Depression was initially called "melancholia" and appeared to be the most identifiable mental disorder over a 2,500-year history. The earliest narratives of melancholia appeared in ancient Mesopotamian texts in the second millennium B.C. and medical texts in ancient Greece described it as deep sadness and its core features of hopelessness, sorrow, emptiness, despair, discouragement, despondency, and sorrow. The symptoms have included loss of appetite, sleeplessness, irritability, fatigue, restlessness, fear of death, repetitive focus on negative ideas, lack of pleasure in previously enjoyed activities and social detachment (Horwitz, Wakefield, & Lorenzo-Luaces, 2016). The first historical understanding of depression was related to a spiritual or mental illness rather than a physical problem (Barry, 2013).

Hippocrates described melancholia in his Aphorisms as a distinct disease with specific mental and physical symptoms, which he characterized all "fears and despondencies" if they last a long time. He believed that melancholia was caused by too much black bile in the spleen and treated his patients with bloodletting, bathing, and exercise. In contrast, the Roman philosopher Cicero argued that melancholia was a mental problem and caused by grief, fear, and violent rage (Bound, 2006).

In 1917, Freud described the state of melancholia in this paper *Mourning and Melancholia* as a problem of loss. He explained that such a loss results in severe melancholic symptoms more severe than mourning as the world is viewed negatively and the ego itself compromised. Freud defined how both mourning and depressive symptoms involve an involuntary abandonment of object cathexis. He explained that the abandonment is forced and thus, experienced as a painful process that will be repressed and may develop a response of self-hate and self-destructive behavior. The ego denies the loss and replace it with a substitute object such as a hallucination, a fantasy, or imaginary. Freud suggested psychoanalysis to resolve unconscious conflicts and reduce the need for self-destructive thoughts and behavior (Lear, 2014).

Carhart-Harris, Mayberg, Malizia, & Nutt (2008) hypothesized in their article that reduced volumes found in postmortem and neuroimaging studies of depression are related to the influence of repression. They described that most severe reductions have been found with single photon emission computed tomography (SPECT) images in Cg25, which was postulated to exert the major repressive force. Considering the history of depression, topics such as repression, consciousness and unconsciousness are now investigated within neuroscience.

The last decade, depression research has identified many factors that can contribute to the development of depression. The biopsychosocial model developed by cardiologist Dr. George Engel suggests that biological, psychological, and social factors are associated with each other regarding cause disease or to promote health. He postulated that the mind and the body are not separate rather they connect and dependent on each other. Engel concluded that illness and wellness is influenced by the individual's physical, mental, and social status (Engel & Engel, 2002).

Depression can be developed by many factors that appear to be independent but are related. For instance, a person can have a body reaction to social or mental stress. On the other hand, physical problems can cause depressive symptoms and thus all factors should be considered when forming a complete explanation of depression. The link between physical, mental, and social factors should be considered when treating depression and promoting well-being.

Depression as a Disorder

Depression is one of the most prevalent emotional disorders and has a persistent effect on individuals' lives. According to the WHO (2017), depression is the largest contributor to disability across the globe. Depression is also the main cause to the almost 800,000 deaths per year through suicide (WHO, 2017). Not only has the treatment of depression but also suicidal depression required attention on alleviating symptoms. Most people who experienced an episode of depression are at risk for future depressive symptoms. Therefore, one of the most important goals is to reduce risk of relapse in individuals who have experienced depression in the past.

Depression is characterized by persistent sadness, loss of energy, worthlessness, loss of interest in activities that individuals normally enjoy, accompanied by a change in appetite, sleep, reduced concentration, guilt, indecisiveness, restlessness, hopelessness and suicidal ideation (APA, 2013). Depression impacts individual, social, and biological functioning of those individuals and often reduces their ability to control daily life. Negative thinking encompasses usually a depressive person's views of the personal past, the current self, the world, and the future. As a response, depressive individuals reduce activities, cope with ruminative thinking, avoid social interactions that consequently limit enjoyable events and positive feelings. These mental health symptoms go together with dysregulation of physical systems, whit symptoms of fatigue and problems with concentrating. Depressive symptoms range in terms of their severity from mild to severe and their duration from months to years. Many depressed individuals describe is as painful as they often remain passive and in significant numbers this increases hopelessness with the risk of suicidal ideation. At its most severe stage, depression can lead to suicide in individuals. Depression is treatable with mental health counseling or antidepressant medication or a combination of both.

The prevalence of depression in Western countries is very high. According to World Health Organization (WHO) (2017) over 300 million people are estimated to suffer from depression at a global level. The estimated numbers present that 4.4 % of the world's population struggle with depression and it does affect individuals of all ages, from all societal categories; however, poverty, unemployment, life events such as relationship losses, physical diseases and drug problems increase the risk of becoming depressed (WHO, 2017).

Figure 1. Cases of Depressive Disorder (322 million), by WHO Region

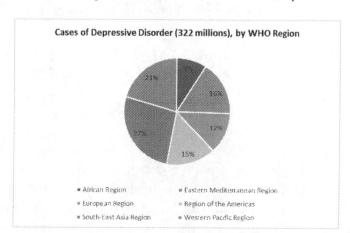

Source: WHO (2017)

Of the estimated 322 million depressed individuals worldwide, current prevalence of depression in the United States is around 15%, similar to Europe with 12%. South-East Asia Regions are estimated having 27%, Western Pacific Region 21%, Eastern Mediterranean Region 16%, and African Region 9% of depressed cases across the globe. These rates are projected to increase worldwide by the year 2020. In 2015, suicide was one of the top 20 leading causes of death and accounted for close to 1.5% worldwide (WHO, 2017).

Depression and the Elderly

The most common mental health challenge among the elderly is depression, which not only leads to suffering within the individual but can also complicate the treatment of other acute or chronic diseases. Elderly depressed adults may be less likely to socialize, eat healthy, follow prescription routines, and will visit the doctor's office more often (CDC, 2008, 2009). While more elderly women report current or lifetime diagnosis of depression, older males have the highest rate of suicide of all gender and age groups (CDC, 2009).

Likely because depression arises most often for older adults, many more studies have been completed with this population. Semino et al. (2017) used network analysis to study the connections between neurological functioning, cognitive functioning, depression, and other risk factors for depression. The authors recruited 264 patients (mean age of 72.95 years) from a hospital ward for geriatric psychiatry. Patients had to have been admitted with either depression or cognitive impairment. The network analysis indicated that the most pivotal 'nodes' associated with depression were 'hopelessness' and 'loss of energy' (Semino et al, 2017). The authors additionally concluded that if cognitive impairment was limited, then interventions should focus on limiting social withdrawal in order to decrease depression. However, if cognitive impairment was higher, it would be important to address patient feelings of anxiety and complaints of memory loss in order to decrease depression. Put plainly, if an elderly person was showing signs of difficulty with thinking tasks, depression is more likely if the person is also anxious and has memory loss. If an elderly person was not having trouble with thinking tasks, then a primary focus could be engaging in social activities to help ameliorate depression.

However, physical activity and social engagement can be difficult, especially if other medical problems are present. The importance of physical activity is even more evident in the next two studies. Holmquist et al. (2017) studied 2,084 individuals who turned 70 within the general community of Umeå, Sweden to determine risk factors for depression within this population. The authors discovered a 'high-risk' cluster which demonstrated high levels of obesity, type 2 diabetes, and very low levels of physical activity. The authors further concluded that elderly individuals with low levels of physical activity and functional performance were at a high risk for depressive symptoms. The results are additionally echoed in another study by Santo and Daniel (2018), who studied optimism within 66 residents (mean age of 80.85 years) of long-term care homes within Portugal. The authors found that "optimism was low and associated with failure to do physical exercise, urinary incontinence, increased anxiety, depressive symptoms and feelings of loneliness, and reduced satisfaction with life and positive affect" (Santo & Daniel, 2018, p. 5). To increase optimism and satisfaction with life, then, one would focus on helping elderly to engage physical exercises and decreasing anxiety, depression, and loneliness. Incidentally, Takahashi et al. (2016) also found that social participation (which would combat loneliness) was impacted by the psychological stress of incontinence as well as the trouble engaging in physical exercises.

Research on Depression and Mindfulness

A meta-analysis by McCarney, Schulz, & Grey (2012) evaluated the effectiveness of mindfulness-based therapies in decreased symptoms of depression. The results of 11 studies showed a significant mean reduction score in depressive symptoms that were measured by the Beck depression inventory (BDI). Bieling et al. (2012) investigated the presence of metacognitive skills, acquired in mindfulness-based cognitive therapy (MBCT) in 84 clients who used medication to prevent relapse of depression. The randomized trial assessed symptom variables of depression, changes in mindfulness, rumination, and refocusing of thoughts. The findings showed that MBCT may be effective through the underlying reinforcement of shifting the focus and curiosity. This can assist individuals to reduce their depressive symptoms of rumination and negative thoughts.

A study by Rosselló, Zayas, & Lora (2016) evaluated the effect of mindfulness meditation on depression, anxiety, anger, and stress symptoms. Participants documented the daily minutes of their practiced mindfulness meditation. Pre and post assessment showed a significant decrease of depression, anxiety, anger, and stress. Results also showed a significant increase of mindfulness and strong positive relationships were found between minutes meditating and depressive thoughts. Mindfulness meditation appears to be a favorable practice to reduce symptoms of depression. Dutt, Wahl, & Rupprecht (2018) examined the negative impact of elevated awareness of age-related losses on depression. The result showed that mindfulness buffered this negative effect on depressive symptoms (Dutt, Wahl, & Rupprecht, 2018).

Few studies have investigated prevention relapse for substance use disorders (SUDs). Roos, Bowen, & Witkiewitz (2017) used mindfulness-based relapse prevention (MBRP) for SUDs to assess moderators. Their findings showed that MBRP seems to be an effective treatment to prevent SUDs relapse among clients with severe levels of SUD symptoms and depression.

Farb et al. (2018) conducted the first study to compare the effect of relapse prevention with Mindfulness Based Cognitive Therapy (MBCT) and Cognitive Therapy (CT) to increase symptom self-management that is linked to relapse of depression. The result showed that both interventions were equally effective to help individuals to develop cognitive skills for regulating negative thoughts and emotions. Mindfulness-based cognitive therapy (MBCT) can be applied as a class-based program to prevent relapse or return of major depression. Coelho, Canter, & Ernst (2013) described MBCT as an additional benefit to normal care in clients with 3 or more previously experienced depressive episodes.

Individuals who have a history of suicidal thinking and depression may benefit from mindfulness training to focus on the moment and reduce negative thinking. Participants of a randomized controlled trial were assigned to the four following groups: mindfulness-based cognitive therapy (MBCT), cognitive psychoeducation (CPE) without meditation, treatment as usual (TAU), and an active control group. The results showed that MBCT can lower the correlation between depressive symptoms and suicidal ideation and therefore reduce the risk for relapse to suicidal ideation.

Nationality and culture can influence distress level when disclosing personal mental health issues and mindfulness can have a protective function. A study by Bergfeld & Chiu (2017) investigated if factors (trait mindfulness, coping strategies, and social support) may mediate minority stress and depression. The researchers confirmed that all three protective factors partially mediated the correlation between minority stress and depression and called for more research in this area. A study by Kahn, Wei, Su, Han, & Strojewska (2017) investigated mindfulness and cultural context as moderators of the correlation between distress disclosure, life satisfaction, and depression. Their sample involved college students from Taiwan and European Americans and the result showed a significant interaction effect of mindfulness and distress disclosure on life satisfaction and depression in Taiwanese participants but not in European Americans. Minority groups such as gay men struggle often with depression and anxiety because of experienced discrimination and stigma. Mindfulness is known to promote resilience when challenging life events occur. Loyns (2016) investigated the impact of dispositional mindfulness on mental health and self-esteem in 369 gay-identified men. The findings showed that mindfulness appears to decrease the negative impact of discrimination and stigma in this population. The author suggested to provide mindfulness training in the community and mental health agencies to support vulnerable populations with the impact of discrimination and stigma.

Psychological distress is prevalent in cancer clients and mindfulness meditation can reduce it. There is increased evidence that meditation practice has positive effects on physical and mental health. A randomized study by Bränström, Kvillemo, & Moskowitz (2012) found a larger increase of mindfulness in the group of cancer patients who attended an 8-weeks mindfulness training. The findings also revealed a significant reduction in posttraumatic stress symptoms of avoidance in the intervention group compared to the control group. Nevertheless, this study did not find differences in perceived stress, depression and other outcomes.

Boyle, Stanton, Ganz, Crespi, & Bower (2017) investigated mindfulness meditation and the influence on emotion regulation abilities of participants. Their specific focus was to evaluate the effects of emotion regulation through mindfulness meditation and self-kindness on depressive symptoms in breast cancer survivors. The results showed that self-kindness and mindfulness together mediated intervention effects on perceived stress in women with breast cancer. Previous research has shown that pro-inflammatory cytokines have been associated with depression. Pro-inflammatory cytokines can be measured in the salivary of individuals. Walsh, Eisenlohr-Moul, & Baer (2016) have investigated the effects of a 4 weeks Mindfulness-Based Intervention (MBI) on salivary pro-inflammatory cytokines related to depression. The 64 participants were assigned to an intervention and control group and salivary cytokines and depressive symptoms were conducted in pre- and post-assessments. The results showed that mindfulness interventions reduced both the pro-inflammatory cytokines and depressive symptoms but the MBI predicted larger reductions in salivary pro-inflammatory cytokines. However, the study revealed that reduced salivary cytokines were not linked to changes in depression in the mindfulness group.

A meta-analysis by Yoon, Slade, & Fazel (2017) evaluated the efficacy of mental health interventions in prisons. The researchers analyzed 37 studies and found the highest level of effectiveness in Cognitive Behavioral Therapy (CBT) and mindfulness-based trials. They concluded that CBT and mindfulness-based therapies are effective for prisoners to reduce depression and anxiety. Mindfulness has shown positive effects in various populations.

A randomized study by Benn, Akiva, Arel, & Roeser (2012) resulted in significant positive changes such as reduced stress and anxiety and increased mindfulness, self-compassion, and personal growth in parents and educators of children with special needs. There is lack of research on the impact of mindfulness in children with autism. Jones, Hastings, Totsika, Keane, & Rhule (2014) evaluated whether mental distress in parents of children with autism could be positively influenced by mindfulness. The authors explored whether acceptance and mindfulness mediated the relationship between parental distress and child behavior. 71 mothers and 39 fathers of children with autism participated and reported their own mental health well-being and their child's behavioral problems. Acceptance mediated for maternal anxiety, stress, and depression, and for paternal depression. The findings showed significant mediation effect of general mindfulness and mindful parenting on maternal anxiety, stress, and depression. These results suggest mindfulness may be helpful for parent and caretaker support.

Consideration mediation effects, some researchers suggest that specific aspects of mindfulness act as the vehicle driving changes, and thus attempt to identify correlated variables describing the impact of mindfulness interventions on mental health. However, many are limited to redundant clarification and do not refer to the mind-body connection that mindfulness concentrates on. Lo, Ng, Chan, Lam, & Lau (2013) investigated the concept of stagnation, which stems from Chinese medicine, and the mechanism of mindfulness practice. The researchers identified 82 individuals with depressive and anxiety symptoms and randomized them to either a Compassion-Mindfulness Therapy (C-MT) training or a waitlist control group. The results showed a significant reduction in depression, anxiety, and stagnation as well as other measures such as physical distress and daily functioning and affect. The study supported the proposition that stagnation mediates the changes in mindfulness practices and the researchers described their findings as a new evidence to body-mind nondualism and treatment opportunities.

One specific method of mindfulness is kindness-based meditation (KBM) that fosters kindness in a conscious way. A meta-analysis by Galante, Galante, Bekkers, & Gallacher (2014) evaluated the effect of KBM on health and well-being. The researchers included 22 studies and found that KBM moderately decreased self-reported depression and increased mindfulness, compassion, and self-compassion. Although the results of the analysis were inconclusive, the authors suggested that KBM presented health benefits for individuals and communities through its impact on well-being and social relations.

Mindfulness-based cognitive therapy (MBCT) has a positive impact on individuals' mental health. Geschwind, Peeters, Drukker, van Os, & Wichers (2011) examined in their randomized controlled trial the impact of MBCT on positive feelings in the moment and the use of natural rewards in daily life. The findings represented a significant increase of positive feelings and activity enjoyment. Participants also showed a significant increase in their ability to boost positive feelings in the moment by practicing pleasant activities. The authors concluded that the clients' improved positive emotions through MBCT may foster resilience against depression.

Mindfulness-based cognitive therapy (MBCT) has been suggested as a mental health method to reduce chronic depression. Michalak, Schultze, Heidenreich, & Schramm (2015) investigated in a randomized controlled trial the effect of three interventions groups on 116 participants with chronic depression. The applied interventions were mindfulness-based cognitive therapy and a group version of cognitive behavioral analysis system of psychotherapy (CBASP) compared to the group who received treatment as usual (TAU). The results showed equal effectiveness of the MBCT and TAU, whereas CBASP showed significantly reduced depressive symptoms in participants. The researchers suggested future studies to examine whether the interpersonal focus of CBASP may have played a role to show a superior effect on clients with chronic pain.

Finally, many individuals in midlife experience crisis accompanied by depression, which may influence the well-being negatively and fasten the aging process. Sometimes mental health distance services are welcomed as they are anonymous and easy to access. Zautra, Davis, Reich, Sturgeon, Arewasikporn, & Tennen (2012) examined whether phone-based interventions with automated mindfulness and mastery messages would impact the daily performance positively in middle-aged depressed community members. A randomized controlled trial was conducted to investigate the impact of a brief, daily practice targeting either personal control/mastery (MC) or mindful awareness/acceptance (MA) compared to a control group that received only tips for healthy lifestyle (HT). Seventy-three participants received a brief in-person orientation to the interventions before they received prerecorded automated messages via phone according to their group of MC, MA, or HT. Every evening, participants completed an online diary that described the outcome measures on a daily base. The results showed a positive impact of all three interventions but only the mindful awareness/acceptance intervention demonstrated higher scores associated with self-reported physical health. MA had the most robust effect on Individuals with moderate depression compared to the other interventions. The authors suggested more research to provide accessible mindfulness interventions to older people who struggle with mental health problems.

Mindfulness and Pain Management

Pain is prevalent across the world as the World Health Organization found that every 1 in 10 adults has diagnosed chronic pain (Goldberg & McGee, 2011). In the United States, chronic pain is estimated at 11 % to 18 % of American adults (Clarke, Black, Stussman, Barnes, & Nahin, 2015); the prevalence in Europe is around 20% (Breivik et al., 2006), and between 34% - 41% in low and middle-income countries (Jackson et al., 2016).

In 2017, the World Health Organization (WHO), which sets the global institution health policy standards, has proposed a new definition of chronic pain as a condition. Now, chronic pain will be expected to be included for the first time in the World Health Organization International Classification of Diseases (ICD 11). The recognition of chronic pain by the ICD is usually followed by governments when they are adjusting their health systems (SIP, 2017). Chronic Pain is defined as "unpleasant sensory and emotional experience associated with actual and potential tissue damage or described in terms of such damage. Chronic pain is pain that persists or recurs for longer than 3 months" (ICD-11 Beta Draft, [Mortality and Morbidity Statistics], 2018).

The Global Burden of Disease study (2015) has stated the six most common causes for chronic pain as the following: (1) low back pain, (2) neck pain, (3) migraine, (4) other musculosketal disorders, (5) osteoarthritis, and (6) medication overdose headache. The major causes for pain were found with minor variations in both the United States and Europe (Global Burden of Disease

Study Collaborators et al., 2015). It is estimated that 126.1 million adults reported pain in the last three months, more specifically 25.4 million adults experience daily (chronic) pain (level 3) and 25.3 million adults reported a lot of pain (level 4) in the United States. The pain severity coding system from 1 (low) to 4 (high) was based on an internationally pilot study, which has shown that individuals with chronic pain category 3 or 4 level present worse health status, use more health care, and suffer more often from disability (Clarke et al., 2015).

According to Dowell, Haegerich, & Chou (2016) an estimated 20 % of Americans visiting a physician for pain-related symptoms receive prescribed opioids. Adequate pain treatment should consider the mental health factors that are associated to chronic pain. Chronic pain leads often to mental health disorders such as major depression and anxiety disorders (Ciaramella, 2017). Importantly, there was a significant increase of individuals using complementary health approaches from 2007 to 2012 in U.S. adult population (Clarke et al., 2015). The National Center for Complementary and Integrative Health (NCCIH) provides overview of complementary health practices and describes group sessions of mindfulness-based stress reduction (MBSR) and cognitive-behavioral therapy (CBT) as cost-effective treatment for chronic low-back pain (NIH, National Center for Complementary and Integrative Health: Pain, 2018).

However, there are fewer studies that have examined the effect of mindfulness approaches on chronic pain in adults. The author will describe cutting edge research, evidence-based treatments, and offer practical resources for pain and mindfulness in the following parts.

Pain and the Elderly

Chronic pain can have a dramatic effect on patient physical and mental health, with increased likelihood of depression, social isolation, and a decrease in physical activity (Brooks et al., 2018; Kwok et al., 2016). In the preceding section on depression, it was noted how depression, physical activity, and social isolation are related. Brooks et al. (2018) approached this relationship from a different perspective, investigating the health conditions present among elderly adults who are diagnosed with severe mental illness. The authors compared 183 patients over 50-years-old (mean age of 60.2 years) who were diagnosed with a serious mental health disorder (such as bipolar disorder, schizoaffective disorder, major depressive episode, etc.). One hundred twenty-two participants reported no or mild pain, while 61 reported moderate or severe pain. When compared, those with more severe pain also reported more pain-related activity interference, were older, had more mental health difficulties, and demonstrated more physical and emotional health-related social limitations (Brooks et al., 2018). Clearly, whether mentally healthy prior to developing a chronic pain disorder or whether already having a mental health challenge, chronic pain increases the likelihood of increased mental health problems and a decrease in social isolation and physical activity.

However, the question remains regarding the best course of treatment for chronic pain among the elderly. One potential course of treatment is the use of pain medications, including the use of opioids. A present concern, however, has become the growing opioid epidemic, with both doctors and patients reporting concerns over overmedication and addiction. To investigate these beliefs further, Griffioen et al. (2017) assessed physician knowledge of and attitude towards the use of opioids for pain management within older adults living in long-term care facilities. It is estimated that between 45% and 80% of long-term care facility patients report chronic pain, which greatly affects physical functioning and depression (Griffioen et al., 2017). The authors surveyed 435 elderly-care physicians (ECP) and ECP trainees to determine prescription and use of opioids among this patient population. Results indicated that the ECP and ECP trainees were not afraid to prescribe opioids, however, patients were reluctant to take opioids (83.3%). Additionally, the physicians were less likely to prescribe opioids if they did not know the degree (79.2%) or origin (51.4%) of the pain. However, questions have also arisen regarding the usefulness of opioids for treating chronic pain. Krebs et al. (2018) studied the effectiveness of opioid and nonopioid medications on chronic pain among 234 older patients (mean age of 58.3 years). The results of this randomized controlled study were that there was no significant difference on pain-related functioning over 12 months. However, pain intensity was significantly better in the nonopioid group, and the opioid group reported more adverse medication-related symptoms over 12 months (Krebs et al., 2018). While definitive conclusions cannot be drawn from a single study, it does raise the question of whether it might be more beneficial to use nonopioid interventions whenever possible among older adults struggling with chronic pain.

Other interventions have been utilized with a good deal of success. Kwok et al. (2016) investigated a self-management program's effect on the quality of life of 46 older adults (adults over 60 years of age living in Hong Kong) living with chronic musculoskeletal knee pain. The intervention program, called Arthritis Self-Management Program (ASMP), included teaching of problem-solving skills, decision-making skills, resource utilization, formation of patient-provider partnership, and adoption management practices. Because of the Chinese cultural component, the authors also added a Tai Chi component as a health management practice. The participants in the experimental group demonstrated higher levels of self-efficacy (their belief that they were able to take care of themselves), better performance in a walking test, higher reported levels of quality of life, and experiencing pain less often than the control group. It is important to note that within this intervention relaxation skills and Tai Chi were both taught to the participants. These practices are like and may have similar effects of the use of mindfulness. Thus, mindfulness may be an important component to overtly include within the ASMP program, as well as other pain-management programs which utilize self-monitoring, self-awareness, and practice of non-judgmental acceptance of current functional states as part of the program.

Pain and Mindfulness

The connection between body and mind is a long-discussed question, addressed in the 17th century by René Descartes who set the agenda of consequent dialogues of the mind-body relations. Descartes claimed Dualism, which means that the essences of body and mind are materially true and distinct (Flage, 2014). Interestingly, it was a female, Princess of Bohemia, who questioned the Descartes' idea of dualism and how the body and mind could interact. When she got sick, she even shared that she thinks her symptoms are caused by sadness as her brother caused family problems (Shapiro & Descartes, 2007).

Psychosomatic research has examined the body and mind connection and there is an increasing support that emotions can affect health by acting on the neuroendocrine and immune systems (Jessop, 1998). For instance, anxiety levels changes were equivalent in inflammation over time in cancer patients (Armer et al., 2017) and Haroon et al. (2016) found a correlation between increased glutamate in the basal ganglia and increased inflammation in patients with major depression. The connection between mind and body can explained by the influence of mood such as stress, depression, or grieving on sexual experiences (Hendley, 1996).

Considering an alternative to the mind and body dichotomy a person's physical, psychological, and sociocultural dimensions must be included. The rising visibility of neuroscience, as evidenced by discovery of brain development has pursued to build bridges of shared research and clinical practice across medical and mental health disciplines. For instance, the discovery of mirror neurons (Di Pellegrino, Fadiga, Fogassi, Gallese, & Rizzolatti, 1992; Gallese et al., 1996, Rizzolatti, Fadiga, Gallese, & Fogassi, 1992; Iacoboni & Dapretto, 2006) have led to enhanced findings about levels of empathy in individuals (Iacoboni & Lenzi, 2002; Praszkier, 2016). A recent study by Ghitani et al. (2017) identified a group of sensory neurons that can be activated by pulling a single hair.

Pain and suffering demonstrate a process resulting from a somatosensory perception, subsequently developing a mental image in the brain that creates unpleasant emotions and changes in the body (Bueno-Gomez, 2017). Pleasure can be defined as the same process resulting with positive emotions. More specifically, this process includes cognitive awareness (Eccleston & Crombez, 1999), interpretation (Merskey, 1994; Sullivan et al., 2001; Ferrell & Coyle, 2008), behavioral characteristics (Goodin, Kronfli, King, Glover, Sibille, & Fillingim, 2013), cultural aspects (Kizilhan, 2018; Lindinger-Sternart, 2015), level of education (Andorsen, Luai, Emaus, & Klouman, 2017) impact the perception of pain, which can be described as pain tolerance. Pain is complex and can be experienced at a physical or emotional level. Brain regions can be explained by their cellular similarities, according to their connectivity and physiological portions. For instance, Hayes and Northoff (2012) investigated common brain activations for painful and non-painful stimuli and found no difference in brain areas. Pain cannot be understood only by physiological areas as it affects the whole person and not only their body or their mind (Bueno-Gomez, 2017). Interdisciplinary studies of neuroscience and philosophy attempt to clarify scientific methods and conceptualize is as philosophy of science.

However, understanding all the dimensions of pain requires not only natural sciences but also social sciences and this may lead to a paradigm shift in the medical and research field. Mindfulness approaches have shifted to interactions between the mind and the body to address human perception, thinking, and action. Increasing research about the effectiveness of mindfulness practice on pain gives hope that the divide between the immaterial mind and the material existence of human beings will be dissolved. Mindfulness approaches seem promising for providing a bridge across the mind-body concepts.

Research on Pain and Mindfulness

Considering cognitive information processing that occurs either bottom-up or top-down (Eysenck & Keane, 2000), Mindfulness meditation functions rather as a bottom-up process through the stream of sensory data of visual forms, tastes, smells, bodily sensations, and arising thoughts in the mind toward the upper level of schemas and beliefs (Didonna, 2009a). Mindfulness fosters the sensory experience and leads the attention away from the conceptual judgments and schemas that influence our experiences in daily life. When practicing mindfulness, the individual becomes the observer rather than the judge about arising sensations and thoughts and strives to let it go.

Kabat-Zinn (1982) investigated the impact of Mindfulness-Based Stress Reduction (MBSR) in 51 people with chronic pain in back, neck, shoulder and headache. The outcomes showed decreased pain ratings in 65% of the participants but were limited as there was no control group. In addition to the reduced physical pain, 62% of participants reported decreased mood disturbances.

A follow-up study by Kabat-Zinn, Lipworth, & Burney (1985) compared the pain parameters of participants with chronic pain who received a 10-week mindfulness program with the pain parameters of participants who received traditional treatment such as nerve blocks and medication. The result showed significant improvements in anxiety, depression, present moment pain, negative body image and inhibition of activity by pain in the mindfulness group compared to the control group. Participants in the mindfulness group demonstrated reduced drug use and higher levels of self-esteem after participating in the mindfulness program. Except for present moment pain, all parameters remained the same after a 15-months follow-up assessment.

An increased research around the positive impact of mindfulness meditation and interventions has found significant improvements of experiencing emotional and physical pain in individuals. A meta-analysis by Veehof, Trompetter, Bohlmeijer, & Schreurs (2015) assessed 25 studies regarding their effects of acceptance- and mindfulness-based interventions in individuals with chronic pain. The researchers were interested in parameters of physical and mental health in participants. At post treatment, moderate effects were found for pain-interference and anxiety and small effects for pain intensity, depression, disability, and quality of life. To conclude, the effect sizes found in this study were equivalent to those in a meta-analysis by Williams, Eccleston, & Morley (2012) who assessed the effect of Cognitive Behavioral Therapy (CBT) for chronic pain clients.

Fahey (2018) stated in her recent review of Mind/Body Medicine that mind-body techniques such as mindfulness directly impact the genes as the body-mind connection is generated in the genes. This reinforces the idea that genes are alive and every process in the body, including the mind may influence genes. Considering the brain's plasticity, every interaction affects the genes expression.

Combs, Critchfield, & Soble (2018) investigated in their pilot study (N=19) the impact of yoga-mindfulness group interventions of veterans with a diagnosed brain injury. The researchers focused on assessing participants' reported benefit on overall health, pain, sleep, attention, mood, anxiety, and self-awareness after they received a mindfulness-based intervention. The results showed that frequency of group participation was positively correlated with participants' self-reported belief about the positive impact of mindfulness on their outcome variables. Introducing mindfulness skills as a part of multidisciplinary rehabilitation for a military population with Traumatic Brain Injury seems valuable.

Mindfulness training for chronic pain clients involves also acceptance of the sensations of pain in the present moment and letting it go as an observer. McCracken & Vowles (2014) have described the role of acceptance and shifting the focus to valued activities in life. She has written about Acceptance and Commitment Therapy (ACT) and Mindfulness for Chronic Pain and offered a model and process for this approach. ACT has its roots in learning theory and is a treatment approach within the cognitive behavioral therapy (CBT). ACT is a combination of acceptance and mindfulness approaches focusing on activation and behavioral changes. One of the core concepts of ACT is to increase psychological flexibility, which describes the capacity of continuing behavioral change when moving toward one's goals. The two sets of influences on behavior are either based on information processing such as thinking, judging, and analyzing or on direct sensory experiences. Mindfulness may strengthen the influence on behavior through direct sensory experiences and balance the tendency of cognitively based influences, which increases psychological flexibility.

A study by Hülsebusch, Hasenbring, & Rusu (2016) investigated the correlation between pain and depression in back pain considering the role of catastrophizing, helplessness, and thought suppression as potential mediating factors. The sample of 164 back pain patients who participated in this study were answering questionnaires about pain intensity, depression, and pain-related thoughts. The findings suggest that thought suppression mediated the relationship between pain and depression. This may aid future research to investigate the impact of mindfulness on pain-related cognition in individuals with chronic back pain to prevent depression.

Zautra et al (2008) examined the effect of cognitive behavioral (CB) and mindfulness meditation (M) interventions in clients who struggled with rheumatoid arthritis. The experimental study involved clients with both a history and without history of recurrent depression and targeted responses to chronic pain. Participants were randomly assigned to one of three groups as the educational only group served as a control group. The outcome variable pain was measured through a multimethod approach such as daily diaries, laboratory assessments of pain, and mitogen-stimulated levels of proinflammatory cytokine such as interleukin-6 (IL-6). Participants who received the cognitive behavioral intervention showed the highest reduction between pre- and post-reported pain levels. This result was confirmed by the greatest reductions in IL-6 in participants of the CB group. Both CB and M groups resulted in improvement of coping efficacy compared to the control group members who received only education. Depression history influenced the value of treatments as rheumatoid arthritis patients with recurrent depression showed better outcomes from received mindfulness meditation when measuring negative and positive affect and physicians' ratings of joint tenderness.

As chronic pain affects nearly one third of the U.S. population, pharmacological treatments were utilized as a common treatment. Hence, the substantial rise in prescription opioid treatment and opioid related mortality rates has increased the demand for counseling treatments.

Garland, Manusov, Froeliger, Kelly, Williams, & Howard (2014) conducted a randomized controlled trial of a multimodal intervention (Mindfulness-Oriented Recovery Enhancement MORE) to target mechanism underpinning chronic pain and opioid misuse. Chronic pain clients (N=115) were randomized to either the MORE or a support group (SG). The researchers collected pre- and post-measurements of pain severity and interference (The Brief Pain Inventory), changes in opioid use disorder status (Current Opioid Misuse Measure), and desire for opioids, stress, nonreactivity, reinterpretation of pain sensations, and reappraisal after 8 weeks. Outcomes were also measured as a 3-month follow-up. Results showed significantly reduced pain severity and interference in participants who received MORE treatment compared to SG treatment. These significant findings were maintained by the 3-months follow-up measurements and were mediated by increased nonreactivity and reinterpretation of pain sensations. Participants who received the

MORE treatment showed also significantly lower levels of stress arousal, desire for opioids, and less likely met the criteria for symptoms of opioid disorder. Nevertheless, these lower levels did not remain after 3 months. The researchers concluded that MORE treatment is an effective intervention for co-occurring prescription opioid misuse and chronic pain clients.

Herman et al. (2017) reported research about the effect of cognitive behavioral therapy (CBT) and mindfulness-based stress reduction therapy (MBSR) in individuals with chronic low-back pain as a group setting. Participants (N=342) of an integrated health care system were randomly assigned to a group who received CBT and usual care, MBSR and usual care, and the control group who received only usual care. CBT and MBSR interventions were provided in weekly 2 hours for 8 weeks. MBSR showed better outcomes than CBT when calculating the health care cost savings. The findings showed increased scores of qualities of life in both intervention groups compared to individuals who received only usual care.

Pain interferes with activities of daily life in most individuals who face health issues. Lee, Harvey, Price, Morgan, Morgan, & Wang (2017a) found in their investigation of 80 patients with knee osteoarthritis that non-judging mindfulness methods represented the strongest association with mental health. Although they did not find a significant correlation between mindfulness and pain or function, the results showed that mindfulness moderated the influence of pain on stress. They suggested future research on mind-body therapy in individuals who struggle with knee osteoarthritis.

Talaei-Khoei, Chen, Ring, & Vranceanu, (2018) investigated in 142 clients with upper extremity musculoskeletal injuries whether life satisfaction moderates pain catastrophizing that influences pain intensity. Their result confirmed that pain catastrophizing showed 35.9% of the total effect of pain intensity that impacts activities of daily life. After controlling for crucial covariates, the indirect effect of pain intensity through pain catastrophizing was differently moderated by life satisfaction. The highest satisfaction with life showed an insignificant indirect effect of pain intensity on pain interference through pain catastrophizing. The researchers concluded that life satisfaction appears to buffer the impact of pain in clients with upper musculoskeletal injuries. Results suggest that clinical interventions such as acceptance and commitment therapy (ACT), mindfulness interventions, and positive psychology methods may be beneficial to strengthen life satisfaction and decrease pain catastrophizing and pain intensity. A high satisfaction with life appears to prevent pain catastrophizing that affects the level of pain interference in clients who are experiencing an upper musculoskeletal injury. This study encourages the incorporation of integrative care involving clinical mental health counselors and psychologists who can engage clients in strengths-based interventions such as ACT and mindfulness methods.

A Holistic Approach of Chronic Pain Management

Mindfulness approaches concentrate on experiencing the present moment and accepting and letting go the experienced sensations such as pain or disturbance. When practicing mindfulness on a regularly basis, the person may refocus on participating in activities that are in alignment with individual values and life goals reduces medication. Given an example, McCracken & Eccleston (2005) found that emotional and social functioning were unrelated to pain intensity when they accepted their pain. This result was confirmed after more than 3 months and suggests that reduced attention and acceptance of pain fosters emotional and social functioning.

Considering the vast research body that supports the positive impact of mindfulness methods on chronic pain clients may influence the chronic pain management in the future. Chronic pain can be viewed as a sign that a part of the person's life is malfunctioning and is reflected in the body. Treating pain only based on the medical model through medication appears concentrating on the symptom without considering the body mind connection of a person. Integrated care with involvement of physical care professionals and mental health care professionals who can apply mindfulness approaches may offer a promising alternative in the future of pain management.

Professional counseling is based on the wellness model and can provide significant services in the care of orthopedic patients who have been mainly treated through traditional medical models that are heavily tied to pathology and deficits. In contrast, the wellness focusses on resources and strengths in clients and fosters humanistic values such as empathy and compassion. The wellness model has been adopted by clinical mental health counselors who can serve as wellness advocates and focus on the integration of the whole person, considering the individual's weaknesses and strengths. The benefit of a wellness model is to take a person's physical, mental, social, and spiritual health into consideration. To conclude, a holistic health care system may utilize both approaches to benefit the individuals who seek assistance with their health issues. Hence, multidisciplinary teams that involve physicians, nurses, mental health counselors, psychologists, social workers, speech therapists, and spiritual leaders may be the bright future concept in the health care system across the world.

The increased interest in mindfulness-based programs (MBPs) such as Mindfulness-Based Stress Reduction (MBSR) and Mindfulness-based Cognitive Therapy (MBCT) is demonstrated in a vast research body, implementation in health care, criminal justice, workplace, and educational settings. Crane et al. (2017) articulated a framework to define essential criteria of MBPs originating from the parent program MBSR. He describes MBPs as an experiential inquiry-based learning process for understanding that involves the development of merits such as compassion, wisdom, joy, equanimity, self-regulation and attention embedded in theoretical concepts from various traditions, science, medicine, psychology and education. The underlying model addresses the human experience of distress and the ways of relieving it as well as the concentration on the present moment concentration.

Day, Jensen, Ehder, & Thorne (2014) proposed a theoretical model of mindfulness-based interventions for chronic pain clients. Their implication was to guide future research to identify the broad benefits of mindfulness-based treatments and integrate it in chronic pain management. As mindfulness-based techniques have become integrated into mainstream health care settings, some studies have investigated the link between mindfulness and happiness. Bellin (2014) proposed a humanistic-oriented theoretical framework for meaning in life as a mediator between mindfulness meditation and happiness. The described major functions of mindfulness are nonidentification, choice, and compassion. The author examined these factors through the lens of meaning in life theory and offers some implications of professional counseling for clients to enhance happiness.

Treatments

Mindfulness based treatments are those which are comprised of any therapy which includes mindfulness as a component of the model or treatment process. Prominent types of MBT include mindfulness-based stress reduction (technically not a type of therapy) (van den Hurk et al., 2015), mindfulness-based cognitive therapy (Bieling et al., 2012; Cairns & Murray, 2015; Michalak et al., 2015; Shallcross et al., 2015; Worsfold, 2013), acceptance and commitment therapy (Forman, et al., 2007; Forsyth, & Eifert, 2016), and dialectical behavior therapy (McKay & Wood, 2007). All of these MBT have been used to address stress, anxiety, depression, or pain management within clinical and sub-clinical populations.

Mindfulness-based stress reduction is most often taught in an 8-week, structured group. During the group, members are taught the principles of mindfulness while engaging practices which help develop participants' mindfulness meditation skills. MBSR remains a core element within the mindfulness community and is used in both therapy and research. However, MBSR was not developed specifically for use in a therapeutic setting. MBSR has been widely used with non-clinical and clinical populations to alleviate stress, anxiety, depression, somatic symptoms of stress, mood disturbance, and chronic physical pain (Reibel, Greeson, Brainard, & Rosenzweig, 2001; Roth, 1997; Speca, Carlson, Goodey, & Angen, 2000; Teasdale et al., 2000), improvement in sleep quality, immune function, quality of life, health related quality of life, and alleviation in psychological distress and physical symptoms (Carlson, Speca, Patel, & Goodey, 2004; Davidson et al., 2003; Lawson & Horneffer, 2002).

One of the most applied and researched MB therapeutic treatments is mindfulness-based cognitive therapy (MBCT). The method was developed by Segal, Williams, & Teasdale (2002) to focus on vulnerability processes that seems to be significant in depressive relapse. The program is designed for 8 weeks and combines the approach developed by Kabat-Zinn (1990), cognitive behavioral therapy (CBT) and mindfulness meditation (MM). Research has also shown that MBCT is beneficial for clients with serious suicidal ideation when experiencing depression. According to Segal et al., (2002) MBCT teaches the core skills to recognize and change self-defeating patterns of negative thoughts and to take a position toward experience that is based on openness, acceptance, and curiosity. MBCT offers individuals to change their perspective and reshape their thoughts from negative responses toward questioning their meaning and seeking for facts. MBCT does extend the CBT focus on cognitions and encourages the client to increase awareness itself and taking a unique perspective. When the client practices awareness and being in the present moment, a shift of perspective from self-focus and analytical processes that underlies depressive symptoms toward the present moment experience occurs. As Kabat-Zinn (1994) stated mindfulness defines purposeful awareness in a specific way, without judgment in the present moment. Mindfulness means to change from acting toward being, and regular mindfulness meditation supports this state of mind.

The first stages concentrate mainly on increasing awareness and afterwards MBCT moves toward recognizing negative thoughts about her- or himself, and triggers of negative feelings in daily life (Segal et al., 2002). MBCT requires the implementation of this awareness and these skills in daily life to be effective. Usually the mental health counselor also provides psycho-education about the symptoms of stress, anxiety, depression, and chronic pain and the risk factors of relapses to the client. However, the primary focus of MBCT is on mindfulness meditation practice and the client's experiences and awareness of the present moment. These sessions help the client to increase their capacity to observe themselves and to differentiate thoughts, emotional responses, sensations in the body, and the experience of distress and suffering.

The mental health professional models' curiosity, acceptance, compassion, and openness and guides meditations from within and based on their own experience. MBCT consists of eight sessions of two hours every week and each has its own theme. Usually there are not more than 12 participants in MBCT groups. The first four sessions emphasize developing attention skills and increasing the awareness of thoughts, emotions, sensations in the body as a means of being in the moment (Segal et al., 2002). Session five to eight concentrate on the client's dealing with challenging thoughts and emotions. During these sessions, acceptance, compassion, non-judgmental awareness, and letting go of thoughts are learned, as these reduces the tendency of ruminative thinking and allowing focus on the present moment. During all eight sessions, various guided meditation practices such as body scan, yoga stretches, walking meditation, eating meditation, and sitting meditations are applied. Clients are encouraged to develop a set of applied mindfulness activities that suits their individual needs.

Mindfulness-based cognitive therapy (MBCT) has been described as part of a third generation of cognitive therapies (Williams et al., 2005). MBCT incorporates the construct of cognitive behavioral therapy with mindfulness-based stress reduction into an eight-week group program with up to twelve participants (Williams & Kuyken, 2012) to help individuals become more aware of thoughts and feelings and put them into context as mental events rather than self-defining constructs (Sipe, Eisendrath, 2012; Teasdale et al., 2000; Schwarze & Gerler, 2015). Each session of MBCT is two-hour long including one all-day practice between the sixth and seventh classes (Williams et al., 2005).

General Guidelines for Integrating Mindfulness into Therapy. According to Brown et al. (2013), counselors can incorporate mindfulness approaches into their theoretical orientation as well as to the practical application of theory in order to help clients with various issues. Brown et al. (2013) recommended that before the starting of formal mindfulness exercises in-session, counselors should help clients understand the fundamentals of mindfulness approaches in counseling, which can be achieved by offering psycho-education or by referring them to the literature providing basic overview of mindfulness practices.

Brown et al. (2013) discussed that psycho-education is a crucial aspect of mindfulness practices in counseling, which is used by counselors in the beginning stage of counseling. During psycho-education, clients learn about the basic tenets of mindfulness including human tendency to preoccupy mind with the thoughts related to past events, planning for the future, and judging everyday experiences (Brown et al., 2013). Therefore, it is important for counselors to normalize any or all these experiences possessed by clients, so that clients can learn that they are not the only ones who fail live in the present moment without judging it (Brown et al., 2013). Brown et al. (2013) suggested that the clients should also be provided with the research-based information on the effectiveness of mindfulness in counseling and healing. The focus of the research-based information can be specifically on the client's particular issue, if it is available in the literature (Brown et al., 2013).

According to Brown et al. (2013), counselors can give direct instructions of mindfulness-based meditation techniques to the clients once they learn the basic tenets of mindfulness. In the beginning stage, counselors teach clients to sit quietly while noticing anything that enters their field of awareness such as thoughts, emotions, or sensations without any emotional reaction or judgment (Brown et al., 2013). Counselors can assist clients to learn this process with their own personal or professional skills such as by helping them to imagine thoughts as clouds and letting them float in the sky of their minds without any reaction (Kabat-Zinn, 1990). Counselors can also help clients to focus on their breath and teaching them to redirect their awareness to their breathing whenever they are distracted by their thoughts (Kabat-Zinn, 1990). Accoring to Kabat-Zinn (1990), this whole process involves the intentional observation of the sensations of the natural breathing process. Thus, the counselor teaches clients to focus on their breath to keep themselves from distracting in past-related thoughts in order to live in the present moment (Kabat-Zinn, 1990).

Specific exercises. One can teach exercises such as "Take a Mental Vacation," (Altman, 2016), that takes only few moments to revitalize an individual. This practice has been utilized to improve the performance of athletes and regains resilience. The client is asked to find a quiet place where no one disturbs. Then the individual recalls a vacation or a place where s/he feels relaxed and revitalized. After closing the eyes and vividly imagining the place, all senses are activated. The client imagines the surroundings and the smell, taste, touch, sounds, and sight of this experience. For example, if a client was in the forest, s/he may imagine the smell of trees, taste some berries, touch ivy on the tree, hearing birds, and enjoying the green of the forest. After continuing this visualization for one or two minutes, the individual observes the changes in the body such as breathing, movements, energy, and respiration. The body corresponds with the visualization and supports relaxation and calming down. Afterwards, the client opens the eyes and likely feels refreshed when continuing the day.

Another example is "The Optimist's Breath and Body" (Altman, 2016). This brief exercise focuses on body posture and gaze that is influenced by feelings and the mind. This breathe, and movement practice can help to shift toward optimism in the morning or during the day. The client finds an open, quiet place big enough to stretch the arms out wide. Being outside in nature is ideal for this exercise. The person starts with a smile even if it feels fake and continues to smile during this activity. After taking a long breath in and picturing yourself inhaling all the positive and beauty that exists. Taking in the kindnesses, the compassion, the beauty of nature and the benefits of the world will be the next step in this process. The deep attention and awareness of it helps to seep it into every cell of the body. Afterwards, the client exhales and feels relaxed and soothed. Now the client takes in a second breath while spreading the arms out in front of him or her and to the sides, as if preparing to give someone a hug. This gesture is one of receiving, so it helps the client opening to, and receiving all the goodness that is available at this moment. The best is to remain open like this for up to four seconds. Afterwards, the client exhales and brings back the hands to his or her heart center and palms touching. Remaining like this for few moments, will continue to flow optimism through the body with each new breath.

A further mindfulness intervention that is also often used in reducing stress is the body scan. A study by Ussher et al. (2014) found immediate benefits of mindfulness-based body scans in clients with chronic pain that differed significantly compared to the control group. During the body scan exercise the client is guided through intentional attention to physical sensation, which begins by focusing attention at the top of head and then moving down the body or vice-versa leading to the unified awareness of the whole body (Kabat-Zinn, 1994). Clients are encouraged to practice the body scan exercise daily, and sometimes clients are provided with the recorded guided exercises including some other exercises, for instance sitting meditation. Another example of mindfulness exercise given by Kabat-Zinnm (1990) is mindful eating. Brown et al. (2013) discussed that in the mindful eating exercise, counselors encourage the clients to sit quietly and focus on their bodily sensations and then focus on their awareness on the sight and texture of the raisin or any eatable in their hand, later the smell, the taste, and so on. Once the clients swallow that eatable, they are encouraged to feel the sensations of that eatable while it is going down the throat and into the stomach (Brown et al., 2013). While doing this exercise clients might have thoughts, worries, or other preoccupations; therefore, they are encouraged to acknowledge them without judgment, and refocus on their physical experience of that eatable (Brown et al., 2013).

Counselors also help clients to live in the present moment during everyday mundane activities such as driving a car, washing dishes, ironing clothes, gardening, walking, or bathing (Brown et al., 2013). To illustrate this idea, Brown et al. (2013) gave an example of a woman driving a car: as she drives a car, she focuses her awareness to her physical sensations such as her back against the seat, her feet on the car floor, or the rhythm of her breathing along with focusing on her driving, the road, and the surrounding cars. If she notices that her attention is drifting away from the present physical sensations of her body, she gently brings her attention back to those sensations (Brown et al., 2013). For instance, if she loses the awareness of her foot on the floor by thinking about what she might eat that night, she might bring her awareness back to the physical sensation of her foot without judging her thought of dinner (Brown et al., 2013).

Challenges and Assessment of Mindfulness. However, there are few challenges that clients face while practicing mindfulness during their daily activities (Brown et al., 2013). The biggest challenge for clients is the intentional focus on the present moment, which is in direct conflict with the habitual modes of human functioning and with many cultural norms (Brown et al., 2013). Brown et al. (2013) mentioned that only after one attempt, one could experience that "our conditioned mode of operating is dominated by automatic internal processes that ultimately obstruct living fully in the present moment" (p. 98). This struggle of conditioned mode with the automatic mode needs the diligent practice to remain non-judgmental, attentive to the current thoughts and physical sensations (Brown et al., 2013). Therefore, in order to successfully practice mindfulness, clients require maintaining discipline and regular systematic practice (Brown et al., 2013). To help clients practice mindfulness regularly, they are given homework and encouraged to spend at least 5-10 minutes on mindfulness practices in the beginning stage (Brown et al., 2013). The homework in the later stages may include sitting meditation, body scanning, mindful eating, writing journals, or completing daily worksheets as a tool to support clients in developing a regular practice (Brown et al., 2013). This kind of homework might help them to develop their capacity of practicing mindfulness daily. Brown et al. (2013) cited several authors, including Chodron, Kabat-Zinn, Martin, & Welwood, who noticed that focusing on oneself without any judgment, and accepting oneself to create a state of emotional non-reactivity is a powerful healing process especially for less sever or non-pathological problems (p. 98).

Brown et al. (2013) stated that there are few standardized tools that can be used to assess mindfulness and to monitor changes in clients' mindfulness level over the course of treatment. For instance, the most widely used mindfulness assessment tools are the Five Facet Mindfulness Questionnaire (FFMQ) and Mindful Attention Awareness Scale (MAAS), which are easily accessible and free to download (Brown et al., 2013). FFMQ roughly takes 10 minutes to complete and MAAS takes approximately 5 minutes to complete, which are not too time consuming for clients (Brown et al., 2013). Brown et al. (2013) mentioned a few other instruments that are used to measure mindfulness such as Freiburg Mindfulness Inventory, the Kentucky Inventory of Mindfulness Skills, and the Cognitive and Affective Mindfulness Scale. Children's mindfulness assessment can also be done with the help of mindfulness tools such as the Child and Adolescent Mindfulness Measure, a 10-item questionnaire, which is designed for youth over age 9 (Brown et al., 2013).

Although mindfulness can be measured with the help of self-report data, this method possesses a limitation in that some clients are unable to accurately report their state of mind. Mindfulness assessment instruments are helpful in such cases (Brown et al., 2013). Moreover, these assessment instruments help counselors and researchers to assess the baseline levels of mindfulness and the change in mindfulness level after mindfulness interventions (Brown et al., 2013).

Concluding Remarks

As should be clear by now, MBT have developed from a combination of rich history, ongoing interaction with the therapeutic community, and repeated testing by the scientific community. Mindfulness therapies, while initially developed for pain management and ceasing recurring depressive episodes, now holds a prominent place as a key therapeutic intervention for both mind and body healing. And the studies on the effects of mindfulness have not slowed; mindfulness continues to be a hot topic at conferences and within journals, not to mention with researchers who hope to glean a little of the effects themselves.

Regarding the aging adult, mindfulness interventions studies continue to amass as the supportive effects demonstrate positive outcomes. MBT are increasingly used for dealing with ongoing physical health problems, such as diabetes or managing pain associated with arthritis, as well as the depression, stress, and anxiety which arises as we struggle with social isolation, loneliness, financial uncertainty, or existential uncertainty. While MBT cannot solve all of the problems of aging, mindfulness practices can clearly help facilitate increased health and wellbeing as we move into our later years.

Resources

Books

Forsyth, J. P. & Eifert, G. H. (2016). The mindfulness & acceptance workbook for anxiety: A guide to breaking free from anxiety, phobias & worry using acceptance and commitment therapy (2nd ed.). Oakland, CA: New Harbinger Publications.

Germer, C. (2007). *The mindful path to self-compassion.* New York, NY: Guilford Press.

Goldstein, J., & Salzberg, S. (2002). Insight meditation kit: A step by step course on how to meditate. Louisville, CO: Sounds True Audio.

McKay, M. & Wood, J. C. (2007). *The dialectical behavior therapy skills workbook: Practical DBT exercises for learning mindfulness, interpersonal effectiveness, emotion regulation & distress tolerance.* New York, NY: New Harbinger Publications.

Orsillo, S., & Roemer, E. (2011). *The mindful way through anxiety.* New York, NY: Guilford Press.

Sears, R. W. (2015). *Building competence in mindfulness-based cognitive therapy: Transcripts and insights for working with stress, anxiety, depression, and other problems.* New York, NY: Routledge.

Segal, Z.V., Williams, J.M.G., & Teasdale, J.D. (2013). *Mindfulness-Based cognitive therapy for depression* (2nd ed.). New York, NY: Guilford Press.

Teasdale, J., Williams, M., & Segal, Z. V. (2014). *The mindful way workbook: An 8-week program to free yourself from depression and emotional distress.* New York, NY: Guilford Press.

Williams, M., & Penman, D. (2011). *Mindfulness: A practical guide to finding peace in a frantic world.* London, England: Piatkus.

Williams, J.M.G., Segal, Z.V., Teasdale, J.D., & Kabat-Zinn, J. (2007). *The mindful way through depression: Freeing yourself from chronic unhappiness.* New York, NY: Guilford Press.

Wolf, C., & Serpa, J. G. (2015). *A clinician's guide to teaching mindfulness: The comprehensive session-by-session program for mental health professionals and health care providers.* Oakland, CA: New Harbinger.

Trainings and Websites

Websites:

www.mbct.com
www.bemindfulonline.com
www.oxfordmindfulness.org
www.bemindful.co.uk

For tapes/CDs of meditation practices recorded by Jon Kabat-Zinn:
www.stressreductiontapes.com

A website that allows you to set a bell as a reminder to be mindful throughout your day:
www.mindfulnessdc.org

Website of the Center for Mindfulness (and Mindfulness Based Stress Reduction), University of Massachusetts Medical School:
www.umassmed.edu

Mental Health Foundation: report on MBCT; Access to material on mindfulness under "Be Mindful" and "Wellbeing podcasts":
www.mentalhealth.org.uk

Acceptance and Commitment Therapy: https://contextualscience.org/act
Dialectical and Behavioral Therapy: https://behavioraltech.org/resources/resources-for-providers/
Mindfulness Based Cognitive Therapy: http://mbct.com/training/

References

Adorni, R., Brugnera, A., Gatti, A., Tasca, G. A., Sakatani, K., & Compare, A. (2018). Psychophysiological responses to stress related to anxiety in healthy aging: A near infrared spectroscopy (NIRS) study. *Journal of Psychophysiology.*

Almeida, D. M. (2005). Resilience and vulnerability to daily stressors assessed via diary methods. *Current Directions in Psychological Science, 14 (2),* 64-68.

Altman, D. (2016). 101 mindful ways to build resilience. WI, Eau Claire: PESI Publishing and Media.

American Psychological Association (2016). How stress affects your health. Retrieved from http://www.apa.org/helpcenter/stress.aspx.

American Psychiatric Association. (2013). *Diagnostic and statistical manual of mental disorders* (5th ed.). Washington, D.C.: Author.

Andorsen, O. F., Luai, A. A., Emaus, N., & Klouman, E. (2017). A prospective cohort study on risk factors of musculoskeletal complaints (pain and/or stiffness) in a general population. the tromsø study. PLoS One, 12(7).

Andreu, C. I., Cosmelli, D., Slagter, H. A., & Franken, I. A. (2018). Effects of a brief mindfulness-meditation intervention on neural measures of response inhibition in cigarette smokers. *Plos ONE, 13*(1), 1-16.

Antai-Otong, D. (2001). Creative stress-management techniques for self-renewal. *Dermatology Nursing, 13 (1),* 31-39.

Arbel, R., Shapiro, L. S., Tommons, A. C., Moss, I. K., & Margolin, G. (2017). Adolescents' daily worry, morning cortisol, and health symptoms. *Journal of Adolescent Health, 60,* 667-673.

Armer, J., Schrepf, A., Cuneo, M., Christensen, D., Thaker, P., Slavich, G., . . . Lutgendorf, S. (2017). Anxiety levels parallel changes in inflammation over time in ovarian cancer patients. *Brain, Behavior, and Immunity, 66,* E27.

Baker, N. (2016). Using cognitive behavior therapy and mindfulness techniques in the management of chronic pain in primary care. *Primary Care: Clinics in Office Practice, 43*(2), 203-216.

Bamberger, P. A., & Bacharach, S. B. (2006). Abusive supervision and subordinate problem drinking: Taking resistance, stress, and subordinate personality into account. *Human Relations, 59,* 723-752.

Barnhofer, T., Crane, C., Brennan, K., Duggan, D. S., Crane, R. S., Eames, C., . . . Williams, J. M. G. (2015). Mindfulness-based cognitive therapy (MBCT) reduces the association between depressive symptoms and suicidal cognitions in patients with a history of suicidal depression. *Journal of Consulting and Clinical Psychology, 83*(6), 1013-1020.

Barry, K. (2013). From melancholia to Prozac: A history of depression. *International Social Science Review, 88*(1), 71-72.

Baumeister, R.F., Gailliot, M., DeWall, C.N., & Oaten, M (2006). Increase regulatory success, and how depletion moderates the effects of traits on behavior *Journal of Personality, 74,* 1773–1801.

Bazzano, M. (2014). After mindfulness: New perspective on psychology and meditation. New York, NY: Palgrave Macmillan.

Beck, A.R., & Verticchio, H. (2014). Counseling and Mindfulness Practice With Graduate Students in Communication Sciences and Disorders. *Contemporary Issues in Communication Science and Disorders, 41,* 133-148.

Bellin, Z. J. (2015). The Meaning Connection Between Mindfulness and Happiness. *Journal of Humanistic Counseling, 54*(3), 221-235.

Bendixen, A. B., & Engedal, K. (2016). Anxiety among older psychiatric patients: A hidden comorbidity? *Aging & Mental Health, 20*(11), 1131-1138.

Benn, R., Akiva, T., Arel, S., & Roeser, R. W. (2012). Mindfulness training effects for parents and educators of children with special needs. *Developmental Psychology, 48*(5), 1476-1487.

Bergfeld, J. R., & Chiu, E. Y. (2017). Mediators in the relationship between minority stress and depression among young same-sex attracted women. *Professional Psychology: Research and Practice, 48*(5), 294-300.

Bernal, E., Edgar, D., & Burnes, B. (2018). Building sustainability on deep values through mindfulness nurturing. *Ecological Economics, 146*, 645-657.

Bieling, P. J., Hawley, L. L., Blotch, R. T., Corcoran, K. M., Levitan, R. D., Young, L. T., … & Segal, Z. V. (2012). Treatment-specific changes in decentering following mindfulness based cognitive therapy versus antidepressant medication or placebo for prevention of depressive relapse. *Journal of Consulting and Clinical Psychology, 80*(3), 365-372.

Blake, M., Waloszek, J. M., Schwartz, O., Raniti, M., Simmons, J. G., Blake, L., …, & Allen, N. B. (2016). The SENSE study: Post intervention effects of a randomized controlled trial of a cognitive–behavioral and mindfulness-based group sleep improvement intervention among at-risk adolescence. *Journal of Consulting and Clinical Psychology, 84*(12), 1039-1051.

Bodhi, B. (2000). *A comprehensive manual of Adhidhamma.* Seattle: BPS Pariyatti.

Boeyink, D. E. (1974). Pain and suffering. *The Journal of Religious Ethics, 2*(1), 85-98.

Bound, F. (2006). Hypochondria. *Lancet, 367*(9505), 105.

Boyle, C. C., Stanton, A. L., Ganz, P. A., Crespi, C. M., & Bower, J. E. (2017). Improvements in emotion regulation following mindfulness meditation: Effects on depressive symptoms and perceived stress in younger breast cancer survivors. *Journal of Consulting and Clinical Psychology, 85*(4), 397-402.

Bränström, R., Kvillemo, P., & Moskowitz, J. T. (2012). A randomized study of the effects of mindfulnesstraining on psychological well-being and symptoms of stress in patients treated for cancer at 6-month follow-up. *International Journal of Behavioral Medicine, 19*(4), 535-42.

Breivik, H., Collett, B., Ventafridda, V., Cohen, R., Gallacher, D., 2006. Survey of chronic pain in Europe: prevalence, impact on daily life, and treatment. *European Journal of Pain 10*, 287–333.

Brooks, J. M., Umucu, E., Huck, G. E., Fortuna, K., Sánchez, J., . . . & Bartels, S. J. (2018). Sociodemographic characteristics, health conditions, and functional impairment among older adults with serious mental illness reporting moderate-to-severe pain. *Psychiatric Rehabilitation Journal, 41*(3), 224-233.

Brown, A.P., Marquis, A. and Guiffrida, D.A. (2013). 'Mindfulness-Based interventions in counseling. *Journal of Counseling & Development, 91,* 96–104.

Brown, G. W., & Harris, T. O. (1989). *Life events and illness.* New York, NY: Guildford.

Bueno-Gomez, N. (2017). Conceptualizing suffering and pain. *Philosophy, Ethics and Humanities in Medicine, 12*(1).

Burnett, R. (2011) Mindfulness in schools: Learning lessons from the adults—secular and Buddhist, *Buddhist Studies Review,* 28 (1), 79–120.

Butler G. (1993). Definitions of stress. In: Stress management in general practice. Occasional paper 61. London: Royal College of General Practitioners.

Cairns, V., & Murray, C. (2015). How do the features of mindfulness-based cognitive therapy contribute to positive therapeutic change? A meta-synthesis of qualitative studies. *Behavioural and Cognitive Psychotherapy, 43,* 342-359.

Cannon, W. B. (1927). *A laboratory course in physiology.* Cambridge, MA: Harvard University Press.

Carhart-Harris, R. L., Mayberg, H. S., Malizia, A. L., & Nutt, D. (2008). Mourning and melancholia revisited: correspondences between principles of Freudian metapsychology and empirical findings in neuropsychiatry. *Annals of General Psychiatry,* 71-23.

Carlson, L. E. (2008). Review of the mindful way through depression: Freeing yourself from chronic unhappiness. *Canadian Psychology/Psychologie Canadienne, 49*(3), 264-265.

Carlson, L.E., Speca, M., Patel, K.D. and Goodey, E. (2004) 'Mindfulness-based stress reduction in relation to quality of life, mood, symptoms of stress and levels of cortisol, dehydroepiandrosterone sulfate (DHEAS) and melatonin in breast and prostate cancer outpatients', *Psychoneuroendocrinology,* 29, 448–474.

Carver, C.S., & Scheier, M.F. (1981). Attention and self-regulation: A control-theory approach to human behavior. New York, NY: Springer-Verlag.

Cassidy, E. L., Atherton, R. J., Robertson, N., Walsh, D. A., & Gillett, R. (2012). Mindfulness, functioning and catastrophizing after multidisciplinary pain management for chronic low back pain. *Pain, 153*(3), 644-650.

Center for Disease Control and Prevention, Division of Population Health, National Center for Chronic Disease Prevention and Health Promotion. (2016). *The state of Mental Health and Aging in America (MAHA) Issue brief #1: What do the data tell us?* Retrieved on October 15, 2018 at: https://www.cdc.gov/aging/agingdata/data-portal/mental-health.html.

Center for Disease Control and Prevention, Division of Population Health, National Center for Chronic Disease Prevention and Health Promotion. (2016). *The state of Mental Health and Aging in America (MAHA) Issue brief #2: Addressing depression in older adults: Selected evidence-based programs?* Retrieved on October 15, 2018 at: https://www.cdc.gov/aging/agingdata/data-portal/mental-health.html.

Changeux, A. R. Damasio, W. Singer, & Y. Christen (Eds.), *Neurobiology of human values* (pp. 107–123). Berlin, Germany: Springer-Verlag.

Chiesa, A., & Serretti, A. (2009). Mindfulness-based stress reduction for stress management in healthy people: A review and meta-analysis. *Journal of Alternative and Complementary Medicine, 15*(5), 593-600.

Chodron, P. (1997). *When things fall apart: Heart advice for difficult times.* Boston, MA: Shambhala.

Chrisman, J.A., Christopher, J.C., & Lichtenstein, S.J. (2009). Qigong as a mindfulness practice for counseling students: A qualitative inquiry. *Journal of Humanistic Psychology, 49,* 236-257.

Christopher, J.C., Chrisman, J., & Trotter, M. (2009). Long-term impact of mindfulness-based self-care on psychotherapists and counselors. 7th Annual International Scientific Conference for Clinicians, Researchers and Educators: Investigating and Integrating Mindfulness in Medicine, Health Care, and Society, Worchester, MA.

Christopher, J.C., Christopher, S.E., Dunnagan, T., & Schure, M. (2006). Teaching self- care through mindfulness practices: The application of yoga, meditation, and qigong to counselor training. *Journal of Humanistic Psychology, 46,* 494-509.

Chrousos, G. P., & Gold, P. W. (1992). The concepts of stress and stress system disorders; overview of physical and behavioral homeostasis. *Journal of the American Medical Association, 267,* 1244–1252.

Ciaramella, A. (2017). Mood spectrum disorders and perception of pain. *Psychiatric Quarterly, 88*(4), 687-700.

Clarke, T. C., Black, L. I., Stussman, B. J., Barnes, P. M., & Nahin, R. L. (2015). Trends in the Use of Complementary Health Approaches Among Adults: United States, 2002–2012. National Health Statistics Reports, (79), 1–16. Retrieved from https://www.ncbi.nlm.nih.gov/pmc/articles/PMC4573565/pdf/nihms720042.pdf

Coelho, H. F., Canter, P. H., & Ernst, E. (2013). Mindfulness-based cognitive therapy: Evaluating current evidence and informing future research. *Psychology of Consciousness: Theory, Research, and Practice, 1*(S), 97-107.

Coleman, J., & Trunzo, J. (2015). Personality, social stress, and drug use among college students. *Psi Chi Journal of Psychological Research, 20,* 52-56.

Combs, M. A., Critchfield, E. A., & Soble, J. R. (2018). Relax while you rehabilitate: A pilot study integrating a novel, yoga-based mindfulness group intervention into a residential military brain injury rehabilitation program. *Rehabilitation Psychology*, No Pagination Specified.

Crane, R. S., Brewer, J., Feldman, C., Kabat-Zinn, J. Santorelli, S., Williams, M. G., & Kuykens, W. (2017). What defines mindfulness-based programs? The warp and the wheft. *Psychological Medicine, 47,* 990-999.

Curtin, K. B., & Norris, D. (2017). The relationship between chronic musculoskeletal pain, anxiety and mindfulness: Adjustments to the fear-avoidance model of chronic pain. *Scandinavian Journal of Pain, 17,* 156-166.

Davidson, R.J., Kabat-Zinn, J., Schumacher, J., Rosenkranz, M., Muller, D., Santorelli, S.F., Urbanowski, F., Harrington, A., Bonus, K. & Sheridan, J.F. (2003) 'Alterations in brain and immune function produced by Mindfulness meditation', *Psychosomatic Medicine*, 65, 564–570.

Day, M. A., Jensen, M.P., Ehder, D. M., & Thorne, B. E. (2014). Toward a theoretical model of mindfulness-based management. *The Journal of Pain, 15*(7), 691-703.

Day, M. A., & Thorn, B. E. (2016). The mediating role of pain acceptance during mindfulness-based cognitive therapy for headache. *Complementary Therapies in Medicine, 25,* 51-54.

Day, M. A., & Thorn, B. E. (2017). Mindfulness-based cognitive therapy for headache pain: An evaluation of the long-term maintenance of effects. *Complementary Therapies in Medicine, 33,* 94-98.

Deterline, B. (2017). The United States of Anxiety. *HuffPost*, August 8, 2017, retrieved at: https://www.huffingtonpost.com/entry/the-united-states-of anxiety_us_5984c091e4b0bd8232029765

Didonna, F. (Ed.). (2009a). *Clinical handbook of mindfulness.* New York, NY: Springer.

Di Pellegrino, G., Fadiga, L., Fogassi, L., Gallese, V., & Rizzolatti, G. (1992). Understanding motor events: A neurophysiological study. *Experimental Brain Research, 91*, 176 –180.

Dowell, D., Haegerich, T. M., & Chou, R. (2016). CDC guideline for prescribing opioids for chronic pain—United States, 2016. *Journal of the American Medical Association, 315*(15), 1624-1645.

Droutman, V., Golub, I., Oganesyan, A., & Read, S. (2018). Development and initial validation of the adolescent and adult mindfulness scale (AAMS). *Personality and Individual Differences, 123*, 34-43.

Duggan, K., & Julliard, K. (2018). Implementation of a mindfulness moment initiative for healthcare professionals: Perceptions of facilitators. *Explore, 14*(1), 44-58.

Dutt, A. J., Wahl, H., & Rupprecht, F. S. (2018). Mindful vs. mind full: Processing strategies moderate the association between subjective aging experiences and depressive symptoms. *Psychology and Aging.*

Eccleston, C., & Crombez, G. (1999). Pain demands attention: A cognitive-affective model of the interruptive function of pain. *Psychological Bulletin, 125*(3), 356.

Ekman, P., Davidson, R. J., Ricard, M., & Wallace, B. A. (2005). Buddhist and psychological perspectives on emotions and well-being. *Current Directions in Psychological Science, 14*(2), 59–63.

Ekpenyong, C.E., Daniel, N.E., & Aribo, E.O. (2013). Associations between academic stressors, reaction to stress, coping strategies, and musculosketetal disorders among college students. *Ethiopian Journal of Health Science. 23(2)*, 98-112.

Engel, P. A., & Engel, A. G. (2002). George L. Engel 1913-1999: Remembering his life and work: Strengthening a father-son bond in a new time of grief. Australian & New Zealand *Journal of Psychiatry, 36*(4), 443-448.

Epstein, M. (1995). *Thoughts without a thinker*. New York, NY: Basic Books.

Eysenck, M.W., Keane, M. T. (2000). *Cognitive psychology: A student's handbook*. New York: Psychology Press.

Fahey, R. L. (2018). A novel approach to using mind-body therapies for chronic pain. *Integrative Medicine Alert, 21*(2).

Farb, N., Anderson, A., Ravindran, A., Hawley, L., Irving, J., Mancuso, E., . . . Segal, Z. V. (2018). Prevention of relapse/recurrence in major depressive disorder with either mindfulness-based cognitive therapy or cognitive therapy. *Journal of Consulting and Clinical Psychology, 86*(2), 200-204.

Felder, A. J., Aten, H. M., Neudeck, J. A., Shiomi-Chen, J., & Robbins, B. D. (2014). Mindfulness at the heart of existential-phenomenological and humanistic psychology: A century of contemplation and elaboration. *The Humanistic Psychologist, 42*, 6-23.

Ferrell, B. R., & Coyle, N. (2008). The nature of suffering and the goals of nursing. Oncology *Nursing Forum, 35*(2), 241-247.

Flage, D. E. (2014). Descartes and the real distinction between mind and body. *The Review of Metaphysics, 68*(1), 93-106.

Fleischman, P. R. (1986). The therapeutic action of Vipassana: Why I sit. Kandy: Buddhist Publication Society.

Friedman, H. (2010). Is Buddhism a psychology? Commentary on romanticism in "Mindfulness in Psychology." *The Humanistic Psychologist, 38*, 184-189.

Fonow, M.M., Cook, J.A., Goldsand, R.S., Buke-Miller, J.K. (2016). Using the Feldenkrais Method of somatic education to enhance mindfulness, body awareness, and empathetic leadership perceptions among college students. *Journal of Leadership Education, 15(3),* 116-130.

Forman, E. M., Herbert, J. D., Moitra, E., Yeomans, P. D., Geller, P. A. (2007). A randomized Controlled effectiveness trial of acceptance and commitment therapy and cognitive therapy for anxiety and depression. *Behavior Modification, 31*(6), 772-799.

Fuchs, C. H., Haradhvala, N., Evans, D. R., Nash, J. M., Weisberg, R. B., & Uebelacker, L. A. (2016). Implementation of an acceptance- and mindfulness-based group for depression and anxiety in primary care: Initial outcomes. *Families, Systems, & Health, 34*(4), 386-395.

Galante, J., Galante, I., Bekkers, M., & Gallacher, J. (2014). Effect of kindness-based meditation on health and well-being: A systematic review and meta-analysis. *Journal of Consulting and Clinical Psychology, 82*(6), 1101-1114.

Garland, E. L., Manusov, E. G., Froeliger, B., Kelly, A., Williams, J. M., & Howard, M. O. (2014). Mindfulness-oriented recovery enhancement for chronic pain and prescription opioid misuse: Results from an early-stage randomized controlled trial. *Journal of Consulting and Clinical Psychology, 82*(3), 448-459.

Geschwind, N., Peeters, F., Drukker, M., van Os, J., & Wichers, M. (2011). Mindfulness training increases momentary positive emotions and reward experience in adults vulnerable to depression: A randomized controlled trial. *Journal of Consulting and Clinical Psychology, 79*(5), 618-628.

Ghitani, N., Barik, A., Szczot, M., Thompson, J. H., Li, C., Le Pichon, C. E., & ... Chesler, A. T. (2017). Specialized mechanosensory nociceptors mediating rapid responses to hair pull. *Neuron, 95*(4), 944-954.e4.

Gibbons, C., Dempster, M., & Moutray, M. (2011). Stress, coping and satisfaction in nursing students. *Journal of Advanced Nursing, 67*, 621–632.

Global Burden of Disease Study Collaborators, Barber, T., Bell, R.M., Bertozzi-Villa, B., Biryukov, A.S., Bolliger, I., Charlson, F., et al., 2015. Global, regional, and national incidence, prevalence, and years lived with disability for 301 acute and chronic diseases and injuries in 188 countries, 1990–2013: a systematic analysis for the Global Burden of Disease Study 2013. Lancet (London, England) 386, 743–800.

Goldberg, S. B., Tucker, R. P., Greene, P. A., Davidson, R. J., Wampold, B. E., Kearney, D. J., & Simpson, T. L. (2018). Mindfulness-based interventions for psychiatric disorders: A systematic review and meta-analysis. *Clinical Psychology Review, 59*, 52-60.

Goodin, B. R., Kronfli, T., King, C. D., Glover, T. L., Sibille, K., & Fillingim, R. B. (2013). Testing the relation between dispositional optimism and conditioned pain modulation: Does ethnicity matter? *Journal of Behavioral Medicine, 36*(2), 165-74.

Greeson, J. M. (2009). Mindfulness research update: 2008. *Complementary Health Practice Review, 14*, 10–18.

Griffioen, C., Willems, E. G., Kouwenhoven, S. M., Caljouw, M. A. A., & Achterberg, W. P. (2017). Physicians' knowledge of and attitudes toward use of opioids in long-term care Facilities. *Pain Practice, 17*(5), 625-632.

Guang, X. (2010). The historical Buddha: A psychological analysis. In M. G. T. Kwee (Ed.), New horizons in Buddhist psychology: Relational Buddhism for collaborative practitioners (pp. 53–78). Chagrin Falls: Taos Institute Publications.

Haddy, R. I., & Clover, R. D. (2001). The biological processes in psychological stress. *The Journal of Collaborative Family Healthcare, 19*, 291–299.

Hanstede, M., Gidron, Y., & Nyklícek, I. (2008). The effects of a mindfulness intervention on obsessive-compulsive symptoms in a non-clinical student population. *Journal of Nervous and Mental Disease, 196*(10), 776-779.

Haroon, E., Fleischer, C. C., Felger, J. C., Chen, X., Woolwine, B. J., Patel, T., & ... Miller, A. H. (2016). Conceptual convergence: increased inflammation is associated with increased basal ganglia glutamate in patients with major depression. *Molecular Psychiatry, 21*(10),

Harvard Medical School, 2007. *National Comorbidity Survey (NCS). (2017, August 21).* Retrieved from https://www.hcp.med.harvard.edu/ncs/index.php. Data Table 2: 12-month prevalence DSM-IV/WMH-CIDI disorders by sex and cohort.

Hayes, D. J., & Northoff, G. (2012). Common brain activations for painful and non-painful aversive stimuli. *BMC Neuroscience, 13*, 60.

Helmes, E., & Ward, B. G. (2017). Mindfulness-based cognitive therapy for anxiety symptoms in older adults in residential care. *Aging & Mental Health, 21*(3), 272-278.

Hendley, J. (1996). Sexual problems your doctors may not have mentioned to you. *Inside MS, 14*(1), 14.

Herman, P. M., Anderson M. L., Sherman K. J., et al. Cost-effectiveness of mindfulness-based stress reduction vs cognitive behavioral therapy or usual care among adults with chronic low-back pain. *Spine.* July 24, 2017.

Herrera, S., Montario, I., & Cabrera, I. (2017). Effect of anxiety on memory for emotional information in older adults. *Aging & Mental Health, 21*(4), 362-368.

Hill, L. M., Maman, S., Kilonzo, M. N., & Kajula, L. J. (2017). Anxiety and depression strongly associated with sexual risk behaviors among networks of young men in Dar es Salaam, Tanzania. *AIDS Care, 29*(2), 252-258.

Hjeltnes, A., Molde, H., Schanche, E., Vøllestad, J., Lillebostad Svendsen, J., Moltu, C. & Binder, P.-E. (2017). An open trial of mindfulness-based stress reduction for young adults with social anxiety disorder. *Scandinavian Journal of Psychology, 58*, 80–90.

Hoge, E. A., Bui, E., Goetter, E., Robinaugh, D. J., Ojserkis, R. A., Fresco, D. M., & Simon, N. M. (2015). Change in decentering mediates improvement in anxiety in mindfulness-based stress reduction for generalized anxiety disorder. *Cognitive Therapy Research, 39*, 228-235.

Holmes, T. H., & Rahe, R. H. (1967). The social readjustment scale. *Journal of Psychosomatic Research, 11*, 213.

Holmquist, S., Mattsson, S., Schele, I., Nordrtröm, P., & Nordström, A. (2017). Low physical activity as a key differentiating factor in the potential high-risk profile for depressive symptoms in older adults. *Depression and Anxiety, 34*, 817-825.

Horwitz, A. V., Wakefield, J. C., & Lorenzo-Luaces, L. (2016). History of depression. In R. J. DeRubeis & D. R. Strunk (Eds.), *The Oxford Handbook of Mood Disorders* (1-24).

Huppert, F.A. and Johnson, D. (2010) A controlled trial of mindfulness training in schools: The importance of practice for an impact on well-being. *Journal of Positive Psychology, 5* 264–274.

Hülsebusch, J., Hasenbring, M. I., & Rusu, A. C. (2016). Understanding pain and depression in back pain: The role of catastrophizing, help-/hopelessness, and thought suppression as potential mediators. *International Journal of Behavioral Medicine, 23*(3), 251-259.

Hyland, T. (2015). On the contemporary applications of Mindfulness: Some implications for education. *Journal of Philosophy of Education, 49*(2), 170–186.

Iacoboni, M., & Lenzi, G. L. (2002). Mirror neurons, the insula, and empathy. Behavioral and *Brain Sciences, 25*(1), 39-40.

Iacoboni, M., & Dapretto, M. (2006). The mirror neuron system and the consequences of its dysfunction. Nature Reviews. *Neuroscience, 7*(12), 942-51. ICD-11 Beta Draft, (Mortality and Morbidity Statistics), (2018). MK90 Chronic Pain. Retrieved on 03/16/2018 from https://icd.who.int/dev11/lm/en#/http%3a%2f%2fid.who.int%2ficd%2fentity%2f1581976053

Idusohan-Moizer, H., Sawicka, A., Dendle, J., & Albany, M. (2015). Mindfulness-based cognitive therapy for adults with intellectual disabilities: An evaluation of the effectiveness of mindfulness in reducing symptoms of depression and anxiety. *Journal of Intellectual Disability Research, 59*(2), 93-104.

Irving, J. A., Dobkin, P. L., & Park, J. (2009). Cultivating mindfulness in health care professionals: A review of empirical studies of mindfulness-based stress reduction (MBSR). *Complementary Therapies in Clinical Practice, 15*(2), 61-66.

Jackson, T., Thomas, S., Stabile, V., Shotwell, M., Han, X., McQueen, K. (2016). A systematic review and meta-analysis of the global burden of chronic pain without clear etiology in low- and middle-Income countries. *Anesth. Analg. 123*, 739–748.

Jessop, D. (1998). Evidence for mind-body connection increases. *Lancet, 351*(9110), 1185.

Jones, L., Hastings, R. P., Totsika, V., Keane, L., & Rhule, N. (2014). Child behavior problems and parental well-being in families of children with autism: The mediating role of mindfulness and acceptance. *American Journal on Intellectual and Developmental Disabilities, 119*(2), 171-85.

Kabat-Zinn, J. (1982). An outpatient program in behavioral medicine for chronic pain patients based on the practice of mindfulness meditation: Theoretical considerations and preliminary results. *General Hospital Psychiatry, 4*, 33–47.

Kabat-Zinn, J., Lipworth, L., & Burney, R. (1985). The clinical use of mindfulness meditation for the self-regulation of chronic pain. *Journal of Behavioral Medicine, 8*, 163–190.

Kabat-Zinn, J. (1990). *Full catastrophe living: Using the wisdom of your body and mind to face stress, pain, and illness.* New York: Delacorte Press.

Kabat-Zinn, J. (1994). Wherever You Go, There You Are: Mindfulness Meditation in Everyday Life. *Hyperion,* New York.

Kabat-Zinn, J. (2003). Mindfulness-based interventions in context: Past, present, and future. *Clinical Psychology: Science and Practice, 10*, 144–156.

Kabat-Zinn, J. (2005). *Coming to our senses.* London: Piatkus Books.

Kahn, J. H., Wei, M., Su, J. C., Han, S., & Strojewska, A. (2017). Distress disclosure and psychological functioning among Taiwanese nationals and European Americans: The moderating roles of mindfulness and nationality. *Journal of Counseling Psychology, 64*(3), 292-301.

Kalupahana, D. J. (1992). *A history of Buddhist philosophy: Continuities and discontinuities.* Honolulu: University of Hawaii Press.

Kangas, M. (2014). The evolution of mindfulness-based cognitive therapy. *Australian Psychologist, 49*, 280-282.

Kelley, M. (2012). An anxiety epidemic is sweeping the US. *Business Insider*, July 17, 2012, retrieved at: http://www.businessinsider.com/an-anxiety-epidemic-has-swept-across america-and-our-broken-meritocracy-is-to-blame-2012-7

Khong, B. S. L. (2003). Buddhism and psychotherapy: experiencing and releasing disease. *Constructivism in the Human Sciences, 8*(2), 37–56.

Khong, B. S. L. (2009). Expanding the understanding of mindfulness: seeing the tree and the forest. *Humanistic Psychologist, 37*, 117–136.

Kim, B., Lee, S., Kim, Y. W., Choi, T. K., Yook, K., Suh, S. Y., … & Yook, K. (2010). Effectiveness of a mindfulness-based cognitive therapy program as an adjunct to pharmacotherapy in patients with panic disorder. *Journal of Anxiety Disorders, 24*, 590-595.

Kim, Y. W., Lee, S., Choi, T. K., Suh, S. Y., Kim, B., Kim, … & Yook, K. (2009). Effectiveness of mindfulness-based cognitive therapy as an adjuvant to pharmacotherapy in patients with panic disorder or generalized anxiety disorder. *Depression and Anxiety, 26*, 601-606.

Kizilhan, J. I. (2018). Trauma and pain in family-orientated societies. *International Journal of Environmental Research and Public Health, 15*(1), 44.

Koszycki, D., Thake, U., Mavounza, C., Daoust, J. P., Taljaard, M., & Bradwejn, J. (2016). Preliminary investigation of a mindfulness-based intervention for social anxiety disorder that integrates compassion meditation and mindful exposure. *The Journal of Alternative and Complementary Medicine, 22*(5), 363-374.

Kraemer, K. M., McLeish, A. C., & Johnson, A. L. (2015). Associations between mindfulness and panic symptoms among young adults with asthma. *Psychology, Health, & Medicine, 20*(3), 322-331.

Krebs, E. E., Gravely, A., Nugent, S., Jensen, A. C., DeRonne, B., ... & Noorbaloochi, S. (2018). Effect of opioid vs nonopioid medications on pain-related function in patients with chronic back pain or him or knee osteoarthritis pain: The SPACE randomized clinical trial. *Journal of the American Medical Association, 319*(9), 872-882.

Kwee, M. G. T. (Ed.). (2010a). *New horizons in Buddhist psychology: Relational Buddhism for collaborative practitioners.* Chagrin Falls: Taos Institute.

Kwok, E. Y. T., Au, R. K. C., & Li-Tsang, C. W. P. (2016). The effect of a self-management program on the quality-of-life of community-dwelling older adults with chronic musculoskeletal knee pain: A pilot randomized controlled trial. *Clinical Gerontologist, 39*(5), 428-448.

La Cour, P. (2015). Mindfulness and chronic pain. What is next step? *Journal of Psychosomatic Research, 78*(6), 608-608.

Lacoste-Badie, S., & Droulers, O. (2014). Advertising memory: The power of mirror neurons. *Journal of Neuroscience, Psychology, and Economics, 7*(4), 195-202.

Langer, E. J., & Moldoveanu, M. (2000). The construct of mindfulness. *Journal of Social Issues, 56*(1), 1-9.

Largo-Wight, E., Peterson, P. M., & Chen, W. W. (2005). Perceived problem solving, stress, and health among college students. *American Journal of Health Behavior, 29,* 360–370.

Lazarus R S and Folkman S (1984). *Stress, appraisal and coping.* New York, NY: Springer.

Lawson, K.L., & Horneffer, K.J. (2002). Roots and wings: A pilot of a mind-body- spirit program', *Journal of Holistic Nursing,* 20(3), 250–263.

Lear, J. (2014). Mourning and moral psychology. *Psychoanalytic Psychology, 31*(4), 470-481.

Lee, A. C., Harvey, W. F., Price, L. L., Morgan, L. P. K., Morgan, N. L., & Wang, C. (2017a). Mindfulness is associated with psychological health and moderates pain in knee osteoarthritis. *Osteoarthritis and Cartilage, 25*(6), 824-831.

Letzen, J. E., Boissoneault, J., Sevel, L. S., & Robinson, M. E. (2016). Test-retest reliability of pain-related functional brain connectivity compared to pain self-report. *Pain, 157*(3), 546–551.

Lindinger-Sternart, S. (2015). Help-Seeking behaviors of men for mental health and the impact of diverse cultural backgrounds, *International Journal of Social Science Studies, 3*(1).

Lo, H. H., Ng, S. M., Chan, C. L., Lam, K. F., & Lau, B. H. (2013). The Chinese medicine construct "stagnation" in mind-body connection mediates the effects of mindfulness training on depression and anxiety. *Complementary Therapies in Medicine, 21*(4), 348-57.

Lyons, A. (2016). Mindfulness attenuates the impact of discrimination on the mental health of middle-aged and older gay men. *Psychology of Sexual Orientation and Gender Diversity, 3*(2), 227-235.

Manuello, J., Vercelli, U., Nani, A., Costa, T., & Cauda, F. (2016). Mindfulness meditation and consciousness: An integrative neuroscientific perspective. *Consciousness & Cognition*, 4067-78.

Martin, L.L., & Tesser, A. (1996). Some ruminative thoughts. In: Wyer, RS., Jr, editor. Ruminative thoughts. Mahwah, NJ: Erlbaum. 1-47.

Martino, R. (2009, May 12). Stress - How perceived stress vs actual stress affects your health. Retrieved from http://EzineArticles.com/expert/Russell_Martino/324737

McCall, T. (2007). *Yoga as medicine: The yogic prescription for health and healing*. New York, NY: Bantam.

McCarney, R. W., Schulz, J., & Grey, A. R. (2012). Effectiveness of mindfulness-based therapies in reducing symptoms of depression: A meta-analysis. *European Journal of Psychotherapy & Counselling, 14*(3), 279-299.

McCracken L. M., Eccleston C. (2005). A Prospective study of acceptance of pain and patient functioning with chronic pain. *Pain, 118*, 164–169.

McCracken L. M., Vowles E. K. (2014). Acceptance and commitment therapy and mindfulness for chronic pain model, process, and progress. *American Psychologist, 69*, 179-187.

McEwen, B. S. (1995). Stressful experience, brain and emotions: Developmental, genetic and hormonal influences. In M. S. Gazzanga (Ed.), The cognitive neurosciences. Cambridge, MA: MIT.

McKay, M. & Wood, J. C. (2007). *The Dialectical Behavior Therapy Skills Workbook: Practical DBT Exercises for Learning Mindfulness, Interpersonal Effectiveness, Emotion Regulation & Distress Tolerance*. New York, NY: New Harbinger Publications.

McWilliams, S.A. (2014). Foundation of mindfulness and contemplation: Traditional and contemporary perspectives. *International Journal of Health Addiction, 12*, 116–128.

Merskey, H. (1994). Logic, truth and language in concepts of pain. Quality of Life Research: An International Journal of Quality of Life Aspects of Treatment, *Care & Rehabilitation, 3*, S69-S76.

Michalak, J., Schultze, M., Heidenreich, T., & Schramm, E. (2015). A randomized controlled trial on the efficacy of Mindfulness-Based Cognitive Therapy and a group version of Cognitive Behavior Analysis System of Psychotherapy for chronically depressed patients. *Journal of Consulting and Clinical Psychology, 83*(5), 951-963.

Mikulas, W. L. (2010). Integrating western psychology and Buddhist psychology. In M. G. T. Kwee (Ed.), New horizons in Buddhist psychology: Relational Buddhism for collaborative practitioners (271–287). Chagrin Falls: Taos Institute Publications.

Mikulas, W. L. (2007). Buddhism and western psychology: fundamentals of integration. *Journal Of Consciousness Studies, 14*, 4–49.

Millstein, D. J., Orsillo, S. M., Hayes-Skelton, S. A., & Roeme, L. (2015). Interpersonal problems, mindfulness, and therapy outcome in an acceptance-based behavior therapy for generalized anxiety disorder. *Cognitive Behavior Therapy, 44*(6), 491-501.

National Institute of Mental Health. (2017). *NIMH-Funded National Comorbidity Survey Replication (NCS-R) Study: Mental Illness Exacts Heavy Toll, Beginning in Youth*. Retrieved at: https://www.nimh.nih.gov/health/topics/ncsr-study/nimh-funded-national comorbidity-survey-replication-ncs-r-study-mental-illness-exacts-heavy-toll-beginning in-youth.shtml.

Newsome, S., Christopher, J.C., Dahlen, P., & Christopher, S. (2006). Teaching counselor's self-care through mindfulness practices. *Teachers College Records, 108 (9)*, 1881-1900.

NIH, National Center for Complementary and Integrative Health: Pain. (2018). Retrieved from https://nccih.nih.gov/health/pain

Nolen-Hoeksema, S. (1994). An interactive model for the emergence of gender differences in depression in adolescence. *Journal of Research on Adolescence, 4*, 519-534.

Nolen-Hoeksema, S., Wisco, B.E., & Lyubomirsky, S. (2008). Rethinking rumination. *Perspectives on Psychological Science, 3*, 400–424.

Noor, S. M., Saleem, T., Azmat, J., & Arouj, K. (2017). Mandala-coloring as a therapeutic intervention for anxiety reduction in university students. *Pakistan Armed Forces Medical Journal, 67*(6), 904-907.

Nordqvist, C. (2015, December 14). What is stress? How to deal with stress. Retrieved from http://www.medicalnewstoday.com/articles/145855.php

Nyklicek, I., & Kuijpers, K. F. (2008). Effects of mindfulness-based stress reduction intervention on psychological well-being and quality of life: is increased mindfulness indeed the mechanism? *Annals of Behavioral Medicine, 35*, 331–340.

Paulson, S., Davidson, R., Jha, A., & Kabat-Zinn, J. (2013). Becoming conscious: the science of mindfulness. *Annals of The New York Academy of Sciences, 1303*(1), 87-104.

Perez-Blasco, J., Sales, A., Meléndez, J. C., & Mayordomo, T. (2016). The effects of mindfulness and self-compassion on improving the capacity to adapt to stress situations in elderly people living in the community. *Clinical Gerontologist, 39*(2), 90-103.

Potash, J. S., Chen, J. Y., & Tsang, J. P. Y. (2016). Medical student mandala making for holistic well-being. *Medical Humanities, 42*(1), 17–25.

Praszkier, R. (2016). Empathy, mirror neurons and SYNC. *Mind & Society, 15*(1), 1-25.

PsychoNeuroImmunology Research Society meeting (Brighton, UK, 2016). Retrieved on 03/17/2018 from PNIRS-2017, the annual meeting of the Psychoneuroimmunology Research Society in Galveston, Texas, USA. Retrieved from https://www.pnirs.org/resources/docs/PNIRS%20 2016%20Program6.pdf

Rapgay, L. (2010). Classical mindfulness: Its theory and potential for clinical application. In M. G. T. Kwee (Ed.), New horizons in Buddhist psychology: Relational Buddhism for collaborative practitioners (pp. 333-351). Chagrin Falls: Taos Institute Publications.

Rapgay, L., & Bystrisky, A. (2009). Classical mindfulness: An introduction to its theory and practice for clinical application. *Annals of the New York Academy of Science*, 1172, 148–162.

Reibel, D., Greeson, J., Brainard, G., & Rosenzweig, S. (2001). Mindfulness-based stress reduction and health related quality of life in a heterogeneous patient population. *General Hospital Psychiatry, 23*, 183-192.

Rizzolatti, G., & Fabbri-Destro, M. (2010). Mirror neurons: From discovery to autism. *Experimental Brain Research, 200*, 223–237.

Rizzolatti, G., Fadiga, L., Gallese, V., & Fogassi, L. (1996). Premotor cortex and the recognition of motor actions. *Cognitive Brain Research, 3*, 131–141.

Rizzolo, D., Zipp, G. P., Stiskal, D., & Simpkins, S. (2009). Stress management strategies for students: Theimmediate effects of yoga, humor, and reading on stress. *Journal of College Teaching & Learning, 6(8)*, 79–88.

Roberti, J. W., Harrington, L. N., & Storch, E. A. (2006). Further psychometric support for the 10-item version of the Perceived Stress Scale. *Journal of College Counseling, 9*, 135–147.

Robinson, M. S., & Alloy, L. B. (2003). Negative cognitive styles and stress-reactive rumination interact to predict depression: A prospective study. *Cognitive Therapy and Research, 27*, 275-292.

Ronkin, N. (2009). Theravada metaphysics and ontology. In W. Edelglass & J. Garfield (Eds.), Buddhist philosophy: Essential readings (pp. 13–25). New York: Oxford University Press.

Roos, C. R., Bowen, S., & Witkiewitz, K. (2017). Baseline patterns of substance use disorder severity and depression and anxiety symptoms moderate the efficacy of mindfulness-based relapse prevention. *Journal of Consulting and Clinical Psychology, 85*(11), 1041-1051.

Rosselló, J., Zayas, G., & Lora, V. (2016). Impacto de un adiestramiento en meditaction en consciencia plena (mindfulness) en medidas de ansiedad, depression, ira y estres y consciencia plena: un studio piloto. *Puerto Rican Journal of Psychology / Revista Puertorriqueña De Psicología, 27*(1), 62-78.

Roth, B. (1997). Mindfulness-based stress reduction in the inner city. *Advances, 13,* 50–58.

Rybak, C. (2012). 'Nurturing positive mental health: Mindfulness for wellbeing in counseling', *International Journal for the Advancement of Counselling,* 35(2), 110–119.

Santo, H. E., & Daniel, F. (2018). Optimism and well-being among institutionalized older adults. *GeroPsych, 31*(1), 5-16.

Scher, C.D., Ingram, R.E., & Segal, Z.V. (2005). Cognitive reactivity and vulnerability: Empirical evaluation of construct activation and cognitive diatheses in unipolar depression. *Clinical Psychology Review, 25,* 487–510.

Schoeberlein, D. & Sheth, S. (2009). *Mindful teaching and teaching mindfulness* Boston, MA: Wisdom Publications.

Schure, M. B., Christopher, J., & Christopher, S. (2008). Mind-body medicine and the art of self-care: Teaching Mindfulness to counseling students through yoga, meditation, and Qigong. *Journal of Counseling & Development, 86,* 47–56.

Schwarze, M.J., & Gerler, E.R. (2015). Using Mindfulness-Based Cognitive Therapy in Individual Counseling to Reduce Stress and Increase Mindfulness: An Exploratory Study With Nursing Students. *The Professional Counselor, 5(1),* 39-52.

Sears, R. W. (2015). *Building competence in mindfulness-based cognitive therapy: Transcripts and insights for working with stress, anxiety, depression, and other problems.* New York, NY: Routledge.

Segal, Z.V., & Ingram, R.E. (1994). Mood priming and construct activation in tests of cognitive vulnerability to unipolar depression. *Clinical Psychology Review, 14,* 663–695.

Segal, Z. V., Williams, J. M. G., & Teasdale, J. D. (2002). *Mindfulness-based cognitive therapy for depression: A new approach to preventing relapse.* New York, NY: Guilford Press.

Selye, H. (1956). *The stress of life.* New York, NY:McGraw-Hill.

Semino, L., Marksteiner, J., Brauchle, & Danay, E. (2017). Networks of depression and cognition in elderly psychiatric patients. *GeroPsych, 30*(3), 89-96.

Shallcross, A., J., Gross, J. J., Visvanathan, P. D., Kumar, N., Palfrey, A. Ford, B. Q. … & Chaplin, W. (2015). Relapse prevention in major depressive disorder: Mindfulness-Based Cognitive Therapy versus an active control condition. *Journal of Consulting and Clinical Psychology, 83*(5), 964-975.

Shapiro, S., Shapiro, D., & Schwartz, G. (2000). Stress management in medical education: A review of the literature. *Academic Medicine, 75*, 748–759.

Shapiro, L., & Descartes, R. (2007). The Correspondence between Princess Elisabeth of Bohemia and René Descartes. Retrieved from https://ebookcentral.proquest.com.

Siegel, D.J. (2007). The Mindful Brain. New York: W.W. Norton & Co.

Siegel, M. (2011). *Mindsight: The new science of personal transformation*. New York, NY: Bantam Books.

Sinha, R. (2008). Chronic stress, drug use, and vulnerability to addiction. *Annals of the New York Academy of Sciences, 1141*, 105-130.

SIP Societal Impact of Pain, (2017), World Health Organization proposes new definition of chronic pain, giving hope to patients. Retrieved on March 16, 2018 from https://www.sip-platform.eu/press-area/article/world-health-organisation-proposes-new-definition-of-chronic-pain-giving-hope-to-patients

Sipe, W.E.B., & Eisendrath, S.J. (2012). Mindfulness-based cognitive therapy: Theory and practice. *The Canadian Journal of Psychiatry, 57*(2), 63-69.

Slavich, G.M., O'Donovan, A., Epel, E.S., & Kemeny, M.E. (2010). Black sheep get the blues: A psychobiological model of social rejection and depression. *Neuroscience and Biobehavioral Reviews, 35*, 39–45.

Smith, J. (2007). The new psychology of relaxation and renewal. *Biofeedback, 35 (3)*, 85-89.

Speca, M., Carlson, L. E., Goodey, E., & Angen, M. (2000). A Randomized, wait-list controlled clinical trial: The effect of a Mindfulness meditation-based stress reduction program on mood and symptoms of stress in cancer outpatients. *Psychosomatic Medicine, 62*, 613–622.

Sullivan, M. J. L., Thorn, B., Haythornthwaite, J. A., Keefe, F., Martin, M., Bradley, L. A., & Lefebvre, J. C. (2001). Theoretical perspectives on the relation between catastrophizing and pain. *The Clinical Journal of Pain, 17*(1), 52-64.

Sundquist, J., Palmér, K., Johansson, L. M., & Sundquist, K. (2017). The effect of mindfulness group therapy on a broad range of psychiatric symptoms: A randomised controlled trial in primary health care. *European Psychiatry, 43,* 19-27.

Takahashi, K., Sase, E., Kato, A., Igari, T., Kikuchi, K., & Jimba, M. (2016). Psychological resilience and active social participation among older adults with incontinence: A qualitative study. *Aging & Mental Health, 20*(11), 1167-1173.

Talaei-Khoei, M., Chen, N., Ring, D., & Vranceanu, A. (2018). Satisfaction with life moderates the indirect effect of pain intensity on pain interference through pain catastrophizing. *Journal of Consulting and Clinical Psychology, 86*(3), 231-241.

Teasdale, J. D. (1999). Metacognition, mindfulness and the modification of mood disorders. *Clinical Psychology and Psychotherapy, 6,* 146-155.

Teasdale, J.D., Segal, Z.V., Williams, J.M.G., Ridgeway, V.A., Soulsby, J.M. and Lau, M.A. (2000) 'Prevention of relapse/recurrence in major depression by mindfulness-based cognitive therapy', *Journal of Consulting and Clinical Psychology,* 68, 615–623.

Tovote, K. A., Schroevers, M. J., Snippe, E., Emmelkamp, P. G., Links, T. P., Sanderman, R., & Fleer, J. (2017). What works best for whom? Cognitive Behavior Therapy and Mindfulness-Based Cognitive Therapy for depressive symptoms in patients with diabetes. *Plos ONE, 12*(6), 1-16.

Treynor, W., Gonzalez, R., & Nolen-Hoeksema, S. (2003). Rumination reconsidered: A psychometric analysis. *Cognitive Therapy and Research, 27,* 247-259. United States Census Bureau. (2017). *Quick facts, United States.* Retrieved on April 6, 2018 at: https://www.census.gov/quickfacts/fact/table/US/PST045216.

Ussher, M., Spatz, A., Copland, C., Nicolaou, A., Cargill, A., Amini-Tabrizi, N., & McCracken, L. (2014). Immediate effects of a brief mindfulness-based body scan on patients with chronic pain. *Journal of Behavioral Medicine, 37*(1), 127-134. van den Hurk, D. G. M., Schellenkens, M. P. J., Molema, J., Speckens, A. E. M., & van der Drift, M. A., (2015). Mindfulness-Based Stress Reduction for lung cancer patients and their partners: Results of a mixed methods pilot study. *Pallative Medicine, 29*(7), 652-. 660.

Veehof, M. M., Trompetter, H. R., Bohlmeijer, E. T., & Schreurs, K. M. G. (2016). Acceptance- and mindfulness-based interventions for the treatment of chronic pain: A meta-analytic review. *Cognitive Behaviour Therapy, 45*(1), 5-31.

Walsh, E., Eisenlohr-Moul, T., & Baer, R. (2016). Brief mindfulness training reduces salivary IL-6 and TNF-α in young women with depressive symptomatology. *Journal of Consulting and Clinical Psychology, 84*(10), 887-897.

Watkins, E.R. (2008). Constructive and unconstructive repetitive thought. *Psychological Bulletin.134,* 163–206.

Watkins, E., & Teasdale, J. D. (2004). Adaptive and maladaptive self-focus in depression. *Journal of Affective Disorders, 82,* 1-8.

Weisman, A., & Smith, J. (2001). *The beginner's guide to insight meditation.* Bell Tower: New York.

Williams, A. (2017). Prozac Nation is now the United States of Xanax. *The New York Times,* June 10, 2017, retrieved at: https://www.nytimes.com/2017/06/10/style/anxiety-is-the new-depression-xanax.html

Williams, A. C., Eccleston, C., & Morley, S. (2012). Psychological therapies for the management of chronic pain (excluding headache) in adults. *Cochrane Database of Systematic Reviews, 11,* CD007-407.

Williams, J. M. G., & Kuyken, W. (2012). Mindfulness-based cognitive therapy: A promising new approach to preventing depressive relapse. *The British Journal of Psychiatry, 200,* 359–360.

Williams, J.M.G., Duggan, D.S., Crane, C., & Fennell, M.J.V. (2005). Mindfulness-based cognitive therapy for prevention of recurrence of suicidal behavior. *Journal of Clinical Psychology, 62(2), 201*-210.

Wong, Paul T. P. (2012). The positive psychology of meaning and spirituality. Abbotsford, B.C.: INPM Press

World Health Organization [WHO] (2017). Depression and other common mental disorders: Global health estimates. Retrieved from http://www.who.int/mental_health/management/depression/prevalence_global_health_estimates/en/

Worsfold, K. E. (2013). Embodied reflection in Mindfulness-Based Cognitive Therapy for depression. *The Humanistic Psychologist, 41*, 54-69.

Yeager, K. R., & Roberts, A. R. (2003). Differentiating among stress, acute stress disorder, crisis episodes, trauma, and PTSD: Paradigm and treatment goals. *Brief Treatment and Crisis Intervention, 3(1)*, 3–26.

Yoon, I. A., Slade, K., & Fazel, S. (2017). Outcomes of psychological therapies for prisoners with mental health problems: A systematic review and meta-analysis. *Journal of Consulting and Clinical Psychology, 85*(8), 783-802.

Zautra, A. J., Davis, M. C., Reich, J. W., Nicassario, P., Tennen, H., Finan, P., . . . Irwin, M. R. (2008). Comparison of cognitive behavioral and mindfulness meditation interventions on adaptation to rheumatoid arthritis for patients with and without history of recurrent depression. *Journal of Consulting and Clinical Psychology, 76*(3), 408-421.

Zautra, A. J., Davis, M. C., Reich, J. W., Sturgeon, J. A., Arewasikporn, A., & Tennen, H. (2012). Phone-based interventions with automated mindfulness and mastery messages improve the daily functioning for depressed middle-aged community residents. *Journal of Psychotherapy Integration, 22*(3), 206-228.

Zautra, A. J. (2003). *Emotions, stress, and health.* New York: Oxford University Press.

Zenner, C., Hermleben-Kurz, S., & Walach, H. (2014) Mindfulness-based interventions in schools—A systematic review and meta-analysis, *Frontiers in Psychology, 5*, 1–20.

Zimmerman, M. E., Ezzati, A., Katz, M. J., Lipton, M. L., Brickman, A. M., …, & Liptom, R. B. (2016). Perceived stress is differentially related to hippocampal subfield volumes among older adults. *Plos One, 11*(5), 1-10.

Zuojie, Z., Lingli, Z., Guorong, Z., Jianing, J., & Zhenyang, Z. (2018). The effect of CBT and its modifications for relapse prevention in major depressive disorder: a systematic review and meta-analysis. *BMC Psychiatry, 181-14.*

Quality of Life Determinants for Retirees

Fiona Sussan and Richard Hall

Introduction

As active aging, healthy aging, or productive aging have become an important agenda for policy makers (Boudiny, 2013), the conversion from active work life to retirement, voluntary or involuntary, remains an under investigated research topic (Dingermans & Henkens, 2014). At the core of this conversion is the shifting of priorities, social groups, communities, human relationships, and routine activities that impacts life satisfaction. For example, when actively working, one mainly interacts with others within the context of daily work whether that interaction be with colleagues or clients. However, once retired, that level of interpersonal interaction may suddenly and dramatically decreases, resulting in a commensurate drop in one's subjective sense of well-being that adversely impacts their perceived life satisfaction. As such, this sudden change of activities related to interacting (lack of) with people poses threat to the subjective well-being (SWB) of retirees. Interactions with others in the society while an important component of SWB, personal physical and mental health, locus of control, standard of living, spousal interactions, and social support are also key components of SWB. SWB, a subjective term, is synonymous to the objective term of Quality of Life (QoL).

QoL is an important topic for retirees learning how to adjust their priorities to attain optimal QoL. It is also an important topic for policy makers and businesses worldwide catering to this dominant demographic group of consumers. The purpose of this chapter is to investigate the determinants of QoL of this group of individuals. Based on literature that discusses various QoL determinants such as physical health (e.g., smoking, weight, blood pressure, exercise, nutrition, vaccinations, and others), mental health, income (i.e., individual income, national income, standard of living), social economic status, social interactions (both strong and weak ties), locus of control, the practice or belief in spirituality or religiosity, spousal relationship, and pet ownership, this chapter proposes a holistic model for understanding retirees' QoL. The next section reviews the literature of various concepts and their relationship with QoL. After that, an integrative model of QoL specifically for retirees is introduced. A case study of Japan is provided to illustrate the model. This chapter concludes with managerial implications.

Literature Review

The following QoL determinants were thematically recurrent in our review of the literature: Subjective Well Being, Health (physical and mental), Locus of Control, Standard of Living, Social Support, and Spirituality -- along with some less studied and potentially promising ancillary ones like touch and pet ownership. While other determinants certainly exist, the ones included in our model and subsequently discussed appear to be significant in augmenting the overall QoL. Each of the QoL determinants is reviewed below. While these QoL determinants can be viewed and studied in isolation, they seem to be interrelated and impact an individual's relative SWB and thus their QoL.

QoL and SWB

As a concept, QoL is difficult to define and quantify but it can usefully be described by the individual. An individual's description of their QoL can take many aspects of their life into account with each of those aspects viewed in terms of differences between their expectations and that of their actual experience. QoL is an objective perspective and SWB is a subjective term, and over time these two terms have come to be synonymous and are often used interchangeably (cf. for a review, see Camfield & Skevington, 2008).

QoL or SWB essentially consists of three major cross-disciplinary components as depicted in Figure 1. Figure 1 is comprised of three inter-related components of the self, others (i.e., the interactions with others such as social interactions, or the comparison to others), and societal or macro-level matters (demographics, economic status of a society).

Figure 1: The inter-relation of self, others, and society in QoL

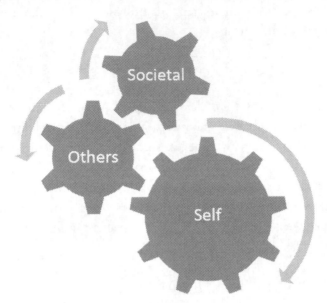

Source: Authors' own configuration

SWB is an umbrella term used by psychologists for what people report thinking and feeling about their lives. There are a range of social, economic, and social determinants associated with SWB. These factors, or determinants, of SWB are those things experienced and reported by individuals that positively or negatively impact their perceived sense of how well their life is going. A good deal of the data for SWB has cross disciplinary overlap and comes from research that used large data sets where many factors were considered and explored (Dolan, Peasgood, and White, 2008). Demographic factors include age, gender, ethnicity, education level, marital status, children, urban versus rural living, and the impact of SWB.

Demographic Differences in SWB

First, there appears to be a negative relationship between age and SWB. Researchers reported that a U-shaped curve best describes this relationship where higher SWB is found among younger and older ages with the lowest SWB occurring in middle age between 32 to 50 (Dolan et al., 2008). Second, for gender difference, women tend to report somewhat higher levels of SWB than men. Third, for ethnicity difference, Whites report higher levels than African-Americans but ethnicity may interact with age. Fourth, education seems to be a factor. Fifth, marriage and intimate close relationships are positively related to SWB, but loneliness and separation has an even lower SWB than does being either divorced or widowed. Sixth, having children seems to have a positive impact on reports of overall life satisfaction but is neutral relative to SWB while visiting and interacting with family and friends is positively associated with SWB. Seventh, living in large cities appears detrimental to life satisfaction whereas rural living appears beneficial. In fact, commuting lowers life satisfaction as does informal care-giving of aging and declining family members (Sisson, 2014). While several other factors such as climate, safety, various economic and political variables have been explored by SWB researchers, those are so far nuances and nothing conclusive as of yet been forthcoming.

Physical Health and QoL

Health is the foundation upon which our lives seem to center. Having health and vitality affords us with the drive necessary to stay actively engaged in the world and makes that engagement possible. Both health and psychological well-being are tied to physical exercise, and regular structured exercise seems particularly important for the over 60 cohort's SWB and QOL. Regular physical activity can maintain functional abilities and independence in older people, both of which contributes to their overall QoL. As the population ages, there is also a growing demand for increasingly expensive medical services and regular physical activity seems to lessen those demands when contrasted against those aged individuals who do not or cannot engage in such activity. Bouchez (2016) quotes Rita Redberg, a cardiologist from the University of California at San Francisco, and the science advisor for the American Heart Association's "Choose to Move" program as asserting, "Fitness is absolutely the most powerful predictor of deaths from heart disease and other causes." In fact, sustained physical activity in older age is associated with improved overall health. Significant health benefits were even seen among participants who became physically active relatively late in life (Mamer, Lavoie, & Bacon, 2013).

Other research by Cotman & Berchtold (2002), indicates that exercise stands to benefit overall health and cognitive function, especially in the later years of life. Voluntary exercise increases levels of brain-derived neurotrophic factor (BDNF) and other growth factors, stimulates neurogenesis, increases resistance to brain insult and improves learning and mental performance. Exercise also mobilizes gene expression profiles that promote brain plasticity. In short, exercise seems to be a readily available activity that affords us all with a simple way to maintain brain function and for promoting brain plasticity.

Good health is associated with higher SWB as is psychological well-being, and both health and psychological well-being are tied to physical exercise, and exercise seems particularly important for the over 60's cohort. Psychological well-being is discussed in the subsequent section, mental health.

Mental Health and QoL

Mental health is just as important as physical health in aging adults. Both mental and physical health are interrelated to various degrees as noted in the various QoL determinants discussed throughout this chapter. While good mental health greatly contributes to SWB, untreated mental health disorders in older adults can lead to declining function, slower recovery from illness, alcohol or substance abuse, increased mortality, and an overall lower QoL.

On the bright side, most adults enjoy good mental health throughout their golden years. For those not so fortunate, the most common psychological and neurological disorders are dementia and depression that respectively, affects about 5% and 7% of our older population (Penedo & Dahn, 2005). Also, alcohol, substance abuse, and suicide ideation in those older adults who do suffer from depression are often overlooked or misdiagnosed by physicians and mental health professionals (NCADD, 2015).

Despite inevitable age-related detriments, healthy older adults can continue to grow as people and enjoy life. Engaging in favorite activities and socializing with family, friends, and others are just a few of the activities that can be enjoyed by people at any age. Older people who engage in regular physical activity exhibit more desirable health outcomes across a variety of physical conditions. Specifically, those who engage in such physical activity show better health outcomes, better functional capacity, mood, SWB, and QoL. The bottom line is that exercising the mind and body while maintaining social connections contributes to good mental health in old age. The inter-relationship between physical and mental health is complex but from a QoL perspective Rejeski & Shannon (2001) propose that QOL for older adults is one of "Adding life to years, not just more years to life!"

Standard of Living and QoL

Seemingly axiomatic is the idea that enough income helps non-affluent people maintain an adequate standard of living and in so doing, plays some role in their reported subjective well-being. Research shows that enough income appears to produce about the same levels of happiness in both poorer and more affluent areas of the United States but at higher levels of income, there seemed to be little influence on SWB. In fact, it has been suggested that it is the national GDP per capita that is related to SWB but not an individual's own income (Dolan et al., 2008), meaning that people who have the same income but live in different countries report different SWB - with those who live in countries with higher GDP per capita report higher SWB than people who live in countries with lower GDP per capita.

On the opposite side of healthy aging, chronic disease, impaired physical functioning and decreasing mobility can result in earlier that anticipated retirement. Forced early retirements often significantly reduce the expected income of such retirees, thus negatively impacting their standard of living and lowering their QoL. Researchers found that an aging population's capacity for continued work until or beyond customary retirement age is associated with the proportional onset of medical or physical disability within that cohort and is associated with education level (Rehkopf, Adler, & Rowe, 2016). Social policy targeted towards individuals in the non-optimally aging cohort with lower levels of education could mitigate decreasing capacity for future work in that population cohort who are nearing retirement age.

Social Support and QoL

SWB in older adults is generally related to the extent to which they perceive themselves as being embedded in their family and friendships and considerably less so to their extended, weak tie, social networks. That said, social support and social interaction seem to be related. Different social interactions and activities have a differential effect on SWB in older adults and social activities with friends may become increasingly important over time and serve as a buffer against the effects of aging.

Social support specific to physical activity is an important factor associated with older adults being physically active, especially when that support comes from family members. Evidence from Smith, Banting, Eime, O'Sullivan, & Uffelen (2017) stresses the importance of having a friend who is supportive of physical activity in their aging adult friend. So far, general levels of social support do not seem to be associated with successfully encouraging or sustaining physical activity. However, there is evidence that loneliness frequently results in lower levels of physical activity levels, especially among women (Smith et al., 2017). In short, promoting the social benefits of physical activity should be a part of positive interventions aimed at older adults as a way of increasing their QoL. Also, community involvement and volunteering are activities that boost SWB as does participatory membership in religious and non-religious organizations.

Spirituality and QoL

Spirituality and religiosity are often associated with higher levels of reported subjective well- being. The term spirituality defies definition given its inherent ineffable nature which is often associated with the transcendent, connectedness, oneness, integration, and wholeness, to name but a few of its definitively elusive thematic descriptors. Spirituality consists of concepts of existential reality, experiences, meaning/purposes of life, connectedness, relationship with self, with nature, with others, and higher being, transcendence, and power force of energy (Chiu et al., 2004).

Acknowledging the influence of spirituality on health and the importance of considering the spiritual dimension in providing health care services for the aged is slowly becoming more commonplace. While traditional religions continue to be of importance to many in the aging population, Baby Boomers influenced and encouraged the migration of meditation and Eastern philosophical thought and practices into Western society (Goldberg, 2010).

This influence on the West has become increasingly apparent in health, religion, and spirituality. Specifically, this trend is reflected by its influence across popular culture such as the increasing popularity of yoga classes, meditational practice and pop music. Considering the importance of spirituality on SWB, spirituality is a determinant that could be given attention by health care providers (Vohra-Gupta, Russell, & Lo, 2007).

Spirituality is often important to many adults at the end of life. While the meaning and importance of spirituality varies among individuals at any age, it may provide acceptance, give meaning, and help the older person make needed decisions toward the end of life. Despite the increasingly evident role of spirituality in the United States, Wallace & O'Shea (2007) point out that the spirituality of older adults is still often neglected and that health care providers should acknowledge and be supportive of the spiritual health of older adults. Elderly Native Americans were found to have more faith and have more spiritual practices resulting in higher self- perceived overall health status (Wallace & O'Shea, 2007).

Locus of Control and QoL

Personality attributes play a role in that higher levels of self-esteem and a mixed locus of control seem to be associated with higher SWB. Locus of control is a concept derived from the study of personality psychology and refers to the extent to which people believe they have control over the outcome of life events (internal locus of control), as opposed to attributing such outcomes to luck, chance, or other people (external locus of control). People who are adept at handling stress and who best cope with infirmity are those who possess a favorable mix of both internal and external loci of control. While these people take personal responsibility for their actions and its consequences, they nevertheless can rely upon and have faith in outside resources. Since locus of control seems to be an attribute of the individual personality, this is a QoL determinant that is probably not amenable to significant change.

Emerging QoL Determinants

Pet Ownership. The bond between animals and people has been researched and historically documented across cultures. However, the benefit of companion animals has been undervalued and occasionally pathologized in the field of mental health (Walsh, 2009). Human-animal bonds have been reported to benefit both physical and mental health in and to have a positive influence on many people across their lifespans. Animal-assisted interventions and applications in hospital and eldercare settings is also a growing phenomenon that has been innovatively extended into settings such as schools, prisons, and some community programs. The QoL benefits that arise from human-animal interaction appear consistent with the human social support literature and to positively impact QoL socially in terms of social interaction, physical and psychological health. While there are differences between those who own pets and those who do not, there is a clear link between owning a dog and beneficial outcomes. Consequently, the value of the human- animal bond could be further explored by policy makers as a positive QoL influence in aging adults.

Spousal Interaction. New QoL of life determinants continue to emerge in the literature. For instance, there is evidence regarding the protective effect of close spousal interaction on physical health that positively impacts social and emotional support on both disease and early mortality. Debrot, Schoebi, & Perrez (2013) investigated whether a support intervention (warm touch enhancement between couples) could directly influence physiological stress systems that are linked to important health outcomes. The researchers found that salivary oxytocin levels were favorably enhanced and alpha amylase was consistently reduced in experimental group husbands and wives relative to the controls. In short, a warm touch between spousal couples was shown to have a beneficial influence on multiple stress-sensitive systems.

1. A Holistic Model of QoL for Retirees

Based on the literature reviewed, Figure 2 is proposed to depict a holistic model of QoL for Boomer generation. In this figure, the larger sized components represent the more important components of QoL. For example, physical health is a large component at the center suggesting that for Retirees physical health is the most dominant component for SWB. Immediately next to it is mental health which is also tied to physical health. Locus of control also plays a major part in Retirees SWB. Although literature suggested locus of control is a personality trait that is more-or-less pre-determined, it is possible that with spirituality practice or connections such locus of control can be improved to better SWB. Standard of living is an important component of SWB, but research also suggested a national level of standard of living is more important in impacting SWB than an individual's level of standard of living. Based on this suggestion, this component is slightly smaller in size; thus, important than physical health, mental health, or locus of control. Social support and spousal interactions are also important but not as important as physical health, mental health, and locus of control.

Figure 2: A Holistic Model of QoL for Retirees

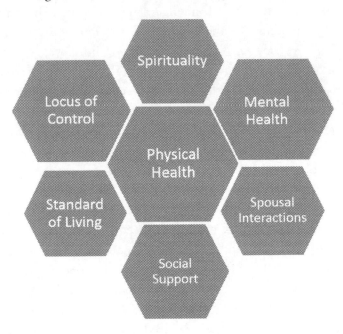

Source: Authors' own configuration

2. Case Study

To illustrate our model in Figure 2, an example from Japan is used. Based on a national survey conducted by the Japanese government (ESRI Research Note No. 24, 2014), selective SWB data of 2014 will be reported below to describe our model. Since the data is collected for the year 2014, the age group of 60-69 and 70 and above will fall under people who are retired. In Japan the mandatory retirement age is 60 years old (Kashiwagi, 2018).

First, gender and age differences in SWB are reported. Table 1 reports the age cohort of 15-19, 20-29, 30-39, 40-49, 50-59, 60-69, and 70 and above. As suggested in prior literature, female have higher SWB than male in all age cohorts. The Japanese data behave in a U-shaped curve, but the dip was for both men and women who are in their 50s, but not the 32-50 age group found in previous research. This suggests that SWB is lowest for Japanese female who were born between 1953 and 1964. For male born in the same years in Japan, they rank second lowest in SWB after male in their 20s.

Table 1: SWB in Age Groups and Gender

Age	Male			Female		
	Average	St. Dev	No. of Response	Average	St. Dev	No. of Response
15-19	6.39	2.13	116	6.88	2.01	117
20-29	6.29	1.96	224	6.72	2.01	296
30-39	6.63	1.95	230	7.02	2.04	321
40-49	6.65	1.90	282	6.67	2.06	409
50-59	6.47	1.87	365	6.65	2.01	437
60-69	6.56	1.80	374	6.81	1.80	366
70 and above	6.71	1.86	258	6.99	1.98	263
All ages	6.54	1.90	1,849	6.80	1.99	2,209

Source: ESRI Research Note No. 24 (2014), Economic and Social Research Institute Cabinet Office Tokyo, Japan

Note: First column is age group. Second major column is male SWB. Third major column is female SWB. Sub- columns denote means, standard deviation, and number of responses. The bottom role is for all age cohorts.

The comparisons of past and future SWB however vary among age groups. Female in general reported higher SWB in the present when compared to the past. People in their thirties reported the highest positive SWB when compared the past followed by people in their 20s. Female in their 40s while reporting higher positive SWB in the present than the past however were less positive than their male counterpart. While female in their 50s report higher positive SWB than those in the 60s, the reverse was true for male. The only group that reported lower SWB in the present than in the past is for people above 70.

Figure 3: Comparison of Past and Present SWB by Age Group and Gender

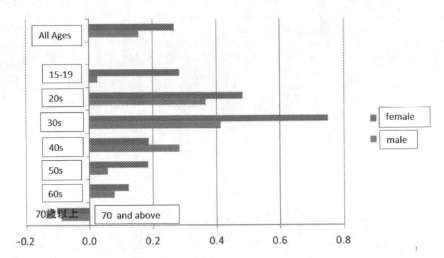

Source: ESRI Research Note No. 24 (2014), Economic and Social Research Institute Cabinet Office Tokyo, Japan

Comparing present to future SWB however tells a different story for retirees. Most retirees forecast their future SWB to be substantially lower than their present SWB with the worst among female in their 60s. Female in their 50s still believe their future SWB somewhat better than the current SWB, male in their 50s forecasts negative SWB in the future.

Figure 4: Comparison of Present and Future SWB by Age Group and Gender

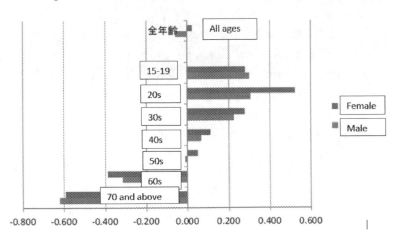

Source: ESRI Research Note No. 24 (2014), Economic and Social Research Institute Cabinet Office Tokyo, Japan

Next, the relationship between SWB and household size is reported in Table 2. While the highest SWB belongs to household size larger than 6, the second best SWB belongs to 2-person household size. The worst SWB are those who live alone, confirming prior research findings.

Table 2: SWB and Household Size

Household Size	Mean	Standard Deviation	Number of Households Surveyed
One-person household	5.71	2.13	120
2-person household	6.91	1.82	302
3-person household	6.60	1.99	153
4-person household	6.64	1.91	75
5-person household	6.42	2.13	24
6-person and above household	7.12	2.16	8
All household	6.74	1.93	682

Source: ESRI Research Note No. 24 (2014), Economic and Social Research Institute Cabinet Office Tokyo, Japan

Note: First column is household size. Second column denotes means, third column is standard deviation, and forth column is the number of responses. The last row is for all household sizes.

In Table 3, the determinants of SWB for overall population and by age cohort and gender are reported. The Japanese data confirmed the model in that physical health is the most important component of SWB. From the same Table, the determinants of SWB by age cohort and gender showed that people in their 50s, 60s, 70s and above evaluate more than 80% of the importance of physical health as a component within SWB, confirming this dimension as the dominant factor for retirees in SWB. The second most important determinants for Retirees' SWB is household budget, followed by family relationships and free time. Comparing to other age cohorts, Retirees put more weight in contribution to society and having relationship with local communities than other age cohorts.

Table 3: Determinants of SWB by Age Group and Gender

	All Age Group %	Age Group Male (Female) % of importance						
		70+	60s	50s	40s	30s	20s	15-19
Health	79	85(80)	90(90)	84(85)	70(80)	62(80)	55(70)	52(48)
Budget	73	70(50)	80(75)	80(85)	82(79)	82(80)	63(63)	38(36)
Family	70	72(68)	65(75)	70(72)	73(73)	62(80)	48(62)	45(65)
Freedom	56	50(45)	49(55)	51(47)	53(53)	51(55)	62(72)	66(66)
Friends	42	38(42)	30(45)	38(52)	30(38)	30(50)	52(72)	73(83)
Employment	35	10(8)	30(17)	40(32)	40(37)	50(40)	50(42)	20(25)
Work	31	13(13)	28(18)	45(20)	51(27)	50(30)	48(42)	10(17)
Relationships at work	22	5(5)	13(13)	30(26)	36(30)	34(30)	35(40)	12(20)
Local Comm	13	21(12)	18(18)	13(9)	12(9)	8(11)	5(5)	4(3)
Society Cont	11	20(10)	20(20)	18(11)	17(10)	11(9)	11(9)	9(1)

Source: ESRI Research Note No. 24 (2014), Economic and Social Research Institute Cabinet Office Tokyo, Japan

As Table 3 reported retirees in Japan found physical health to be the most important component in their SWB, Figure 5 depicts their self-reported physical health in various age cohorts.

Although retirees find physical health the most important in SWB, they are the age cohort that have the least percentage of people reporting being 'healthy' (at 8.2% for the 50s and 7.8% for the 60s). They are also the group who reported the most percentage being 'unhealthy.' The correlation of self-reported physical health and SWB by age group is presented in Figure 5.

Figure 5: Self-Reported Physical Health by Age Group

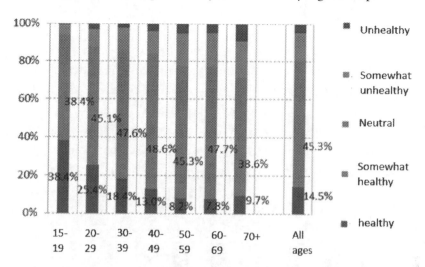

Source: ESRI Research Note No. 24 (2014), Economic and Social Research Institute Cabinet Office Tokyo, Japan

Note: There are five responses to health: healthy, somewhat healthy, neutral, somewhat not healthy, not healthy. The shade and related percentage depicted at the bottom represents 'healthy'. The second bottom shade and percentage represent "somewhat healthy". The top shade represents 'not healthy." The last bar on the right reports all age groups.

Figure 6: Correlation of Self-reported Physical Health and SWB by Age Group

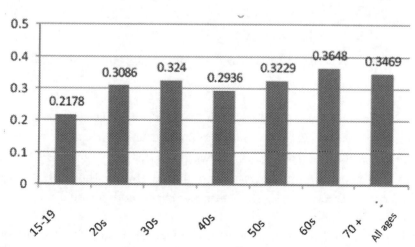

Source: ESRI Research Note No. 24 (2014), Economic and Social Research Institute Cabinet Office Tokyo, Japan

The holistic model in Figure 2 proposed that mental health is a major component of SWB for Retirees. Figure 8 depicts the self-reported mental health among different age groups in Japan in 2014. The respondents who have the highest scores are viewed as the highest mental health problem. From the results in Figure 8, people in the 60s and 70s have the least percentage within the high score bracket (15 points plus) with people in the 60s having the highest percentage in the lowest score range (0-4) followed by 70s and 50s. It can be concluded among Japanese respondents, Retirees are relatively mentally healthy when compared to other age cohorts.

Figure 7: Self-reported Mental Health and Age Group

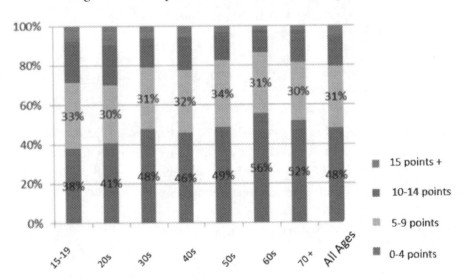

Source: ESRI Research Note No. 24 (2014), Economic and Social Research Institute Cabinet Office Tokyo, Japan

Note: The questions in this survey asked respondents their feelings in the past 30 days in questions such as 1. Feeling overly sensitive, 2. Feeling hopeless, 3. Feeling unsettled, 4. Feeling pessimistic without capability to feel optimistic, and 4. Viewing self has no value. The respondents' feelings were categorized as none, little, sometimes, almost always, always. Those who answered none will score zero, little scores 1, sometimes scores 2, almost always score 3, and always score 4.

In the following figures, gender-based relationships between work and SWB are reported in Figures 8 and 9. As Japanese workers are perceived as spending the most time in their workplace, the investigation of the relationship between work and SWB in the Japan context is important. Figure 9 shows that males throughout all age cohort except in the teens, those who work enjoy much higher SWB than those who do not work, whereas for female such a relationship only applies for those in their 40s and 50s. For younger male Retirees in their 50s, the difference between having worked and no work and their SWB is very large, but this gap narrows as they approach their 60s. Comparatively for female, the SWB for those who have worked some and those who did not work do not differ drastically throughout all age cohorts.

Figure 8: Work and SWB by Age Group for Male

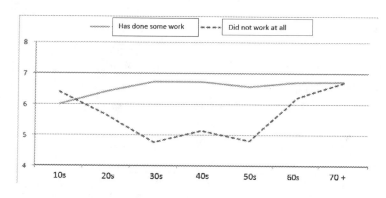

Source: ESRI Research Note No. 24 (2014), Economic and Social Research Institute Cabinet Office Tokyo, Japan

Note: Solid line represents the group that has worked somewhat, and the dotted line represents the group that has not worked at all.

Figure 9: Female Work and SWB by Age Group

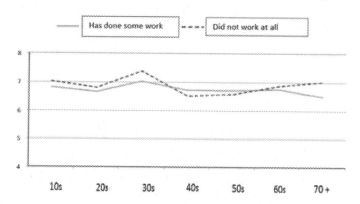

Source: ESRI Research Note No. 24 (2014), Economic and Social Research Institute Cabinet Office Tokyo, Japan

Note: Solid line represents the group that has worked somewhat, and the dotted line represents the group that has not worked at all.

Finally, Table 4 and Figure 10 report the relationship between social interactions, volunteer activities and SWB. Table 4 begins with the report of social interactions and volunteer activities based on age groups. People in their 60s and 70s interact with their neighbors most, followed by people in their 50s. In other words, Retirees are active in this dimension. The same pattern is seen in the local activities participation, local events participation, interacting with elderly, and volunteering activities. Comparing with other age cohorts, people in their 60s has the highest percentage in volunteering activities. Retirees in Japan thus fair quite well engaging in social interactions and volunteer services as reported. Figure 10 further reports the relationship between social interactions, volunteer activities and SWB with the higher (always) interactions or activities the higher SWB.

Table 4: Social Interactions and Volunteer Activities by Age Group

		Age Cohorts %						
		70+	60s	50s	40s	30s	20s	15-19
Interactions with neighbors	None	2	0	2	2	4	10	12
	Not much	5	4	7	6	12	20	18
	Sometimes	20	20	33	40	42	50	45
	Often	73	76	58	52	42	20	25
Interactions with elderly	None	12	13	19	23	38	45	40
	Not much	18	28	35	40	35	32	37
	Sometimes	40	37	33	26	18	17	18
	Often	30	22	13	11	9	6	5
Local Activities Participation	None	23	20	27	35	54	70	62
	Not much	24	25	36	35	26	20	27
	Sometimes	30	32	28	24	15	7	8
	Often	23	23	9	6	5	3	3
Local Events Participation	None	20	19	26	33	47	64	51
	Not much	26	28	32	32	28	24	32
	Sometimes	28	35	26	27	21	9	10
	Often	26	18	16	8	6	3	7

Volunteering Activities	None	44	38	48	55	68	66	52
	Not much	26	33	35	32	23	23	32
	Sometimes	20	17	12	10	7	4	12
	Often	10	12	5	3	2	7	4

Source: ESRI Research Note No. 24 (2014), Economic and Social Research Institute Cabinet Office Tokyo, Japan

Note: There are four categories of answers for the survey: 'none', 'not much', 'sometimes' and 'often'.

Figure 10: Social Interactions, Volunteerism and SWB

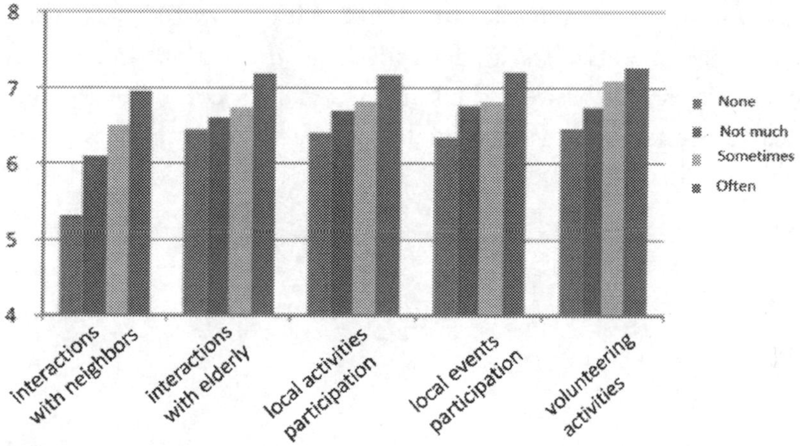

Source: ESRI Research Note No. 24 (2014), Economic and Social Research Institute Cabinet Office Tokyo, Japan

Note: On the X axis from left to right: interactions with neighbors, interactions with elderly, local activities participation, local events participation, volunteering activities. Within each activities, there are four possible answers represented by four columns: the furthest left column represents the answer "none", the second column is 'not much', the third 'sometimes' and the furthest right column represents 'often.' The Y axis represents the percentage of answers.

This chapter organizes current inter-disciplinary literature that studies QoL and SWB into self, others, and societal sub-domains, and presents a holistic model for understanding QoL for retirees. Our model posits physical health as QoL's main determinant for retirees and suggests that mental health, locus of control as major determinants, alongside with spirituality, social interactions and volunteering activities. The model finds substantial support in the case study of Japan. Same as our model's conceptualization, retirees in Japan place physical health as the most important determinant of SWB. While they have good mental health, retirees in Japan perceive themselves at the lowest SWB when compared to other cohorts. This finding contrasts with prior studies in which age cohort of 32-50 were reported to have the lowest SWB of all age groups. This leads us to the conclusion that the relative weight of the various surrounding determinants of QoL or the proposed model likely varies across individuals and especially across cultural contexts. As such, managers cannot use 'one size fits all' approach in crafting strategies toward SWB whether it is from the perspective of regional or national policy, healthcare, or education.

The proposed QoL model and the evidence from Japan however did not consider QoL from a consumer behavior perspective, future research should consider investigation materialistic consumption and QoL. Prior research (Sussan, Hall, & Meamber, 2012) has investigated the inter-relationship between the benefits of spiritual practice (e.g., meditation) and brand divorce, hinting a possible beneficial relationship between shedding materialistic consumption and improvement of QoL. Future research should investigate brand divorce practices or mindset change of materialistic consumption and QoL for retirees.

References

Bao, K. & Schreer, G. (2016). Pets and happiness: Examining the association between pet ownership and wellbeing. *Anthrozoos, 29* (2), 283-296.

Boudiny, K. (2013). 'Active ageing': from empty rhetoric to effective policy tool. *Ageing Society, 33,* 1077-1098.

Bouchez, C. (2016). *The Baby Boomer Heart: Healing Fitness. When it comes to protecting your heart, fitness plays a key role.* Accessed July 1, 2018 from https://www.webmd.com/fitness-exercise/features/baby-Boomer-heart-healing-fitness#1.

Camfield, L. & Skevington, S.M. (2008). On Subjective well-being and quality of life. *Journal of Health Psychology, 13*(6), 764-775.

Casey, T. (2016) Regular exercise may decrease healthcare costs, utilization. *Practice Management in Cardiovascular Business.* Accessed July 1 2018 from https://www.cardiovascularbusiness.com/topics/practice-management/regular-exercise- may decrease-healthcare-costs-utilization.

Chiu, L., Emblen, J. D., Hofwegen, L.V., Sawatzky, R., & Meyerhoff, H. (2004). An Integrative review of the concept of spirituality in the health sciences. *Western Journal of Nursing Research, 26*(4), 405-28.

Cotman, C., & Berchtold, N. (2002). Exercise: a behavioral intervention to enhance brain health and plasticity. *Trends in Neurosciences,* 25(6), 295-301.

Debrot, A., Schoebi, D., & Perrez, M. (2013). Touch as an interpersonal emotion regulation process in couples' daily lives: The mediating role of psychological intimacy. *Personality and Social Psychology Bulletin,* 39(10) 1373-85.

Diener, E., Sandvik, E., Seidlitz, L. & Diener, M. (1993). The relationship between income and subjective well-being. Relative or absolute? *Social Indicators Research, 28*(3), 195-223.

Dingemans, E. & Henkens, K. (2014). Involuntary retirement, bridge employment, and satisfaction with life: A longitudinal investigation. *Journal of Organizational Behavior, 35*(4), 575-591.

Dolan, P., Peasgood, T., & White, M. (2008). Do we really know what makes us happy? A review of the economic literature on the factors associated with subjective well-being. *Journal of Economic Psychology, 29* (1), 94-122.

ESRI Research Note No. 24 (2014). Economic and Social Research Institute Cabinet Office Tokyo, Japan 25 年度「生活の質に関する調査 世帯調査：訪問留置法の結果について.

Garrity, T. F., & Stallones, L. (1998). Effects of pet contact on human well-being: Review of recent research. In C. C. Wilson and D. C. Turner (Eds.). *Companion Animals in Human Health.* Thousand Oaks, CA, US: Sage Publications, pp. 3-22.

Goldberg, P. (2010). American veda: From emerson and the Beatles to Yoga and Meditation How Indian Spirituality Changed the West. New York, NY: Harmony Books.

Hayes, N. & Joseph, S. (2003) Big 5 correlates of three measures of subjective well-being. *Personality and Individual Differences, 34*(4), 723-727.

Holt-Lunstad, J., Birmingham, W.A., & Light, K. C. (2008). Influence of a "Warm Touch" support enhancement intervention among married couples on ambulatory blood pressure, oxytocin, alpha amylase, and cortisol. *Psychosomatic Medicine, 70* (November-December), 9, 976-985.

Jacobs-Lawson, J. M., Waddell, E. L., & Webb, A. K. (2011). Predictors of health locus of control in older adults. *Current Psychology. 30* (2), 173-183.

Kashiwagi, S. (2018). Japan must abolish mandatory retirement. *Nikker Asian Review.* May 07.

Accessed September 5, 2018 from www.asia.nikkei.com/Opinion/Japan-must-abolish- mandatory-retirement2.

Lun, V. & Bond, M. (2013). Examining the relation of religion and spirituality to subjective well-being across national cultures. *Psychology of Religion and Spirituality, 5*(4), 304- 315.

MacKinlay, E. (2017). *The spiritual dimension of ageing.* Philadelphia, PA: Jessica Kinsley Publishers.

Mamer, M., Lavoie, K, & Bacon, S. (2013). Taking up physical activity in later life and healthy ageing: the English longitudinal study of ageing. *British Journal of Sports Medicine.*

Published Online First: 25 November 2013. Accessed May 15, 2018 from https://bjsm.bmj.com/content/early/2013/10/28/bjsports- 2013-092993.short

Martin, C., Church, T., & Thompson, A. (2009). Exercise Dose and Quality of Life: A Randomized Controlled Trial, *Archives of Internal Medicine. 169*(3), 269-278.

NCADD (2015) Alcohol, Drug Dependence and Seniors. Accessed June 15, 2018 from https://www.ncadd.org/about-addiction/seniors/alcohol-drug-dependence-and-seniors

Penedo, F. & Dahn, J. (2005). Exercise and well-being: a review of mental and physical health benefits associated with physical activity. *Current Opinion in Psychiatry, 18*(2), 189-193.

Rehkopf, D., Adler, N., & Rowe, J. (2016). The impact of health and education on future labour force participation among individuals aged 55–74 in the United States of America: the MacArthur Foundation Research Network on an Aging Society. *Ageing and Society, 37* (August), 1313-1337.

Rejeski, W.J. & Mihalko, S.L. (2001). Physical activity and quality of life in older adults. *Journal of Gerontology, 56* (2), 23-35.

Sisson, M. (2014) The high cost of commuting. Mark's Daily Apple. Accessed July 1, 2018 from https://www.marksdailyapple.com/the-high-cost-of-commuting/

Smith, L.G., Banting, L, Eime, R., O'Sullivan, G., & Uffelen, J. (2017). The association between social support and physical activity in older adults: a systematic review. *International Journal of Behavioral Nutrition and Physical Activity, 14*(1), 56.

Sussan, F., Hall, R. & Meamber, L. (2012). Introspecting the nature of a brand divorce. *Journal of Business Research, 65*(4), 520-6.

Vohra-Gupta, S., Russel, A. & Lo, E. (2007). Meditation: The adoption of eastern thought to western social practices. *Journal of Religion and Spirituality in Social Work: Social Thought, 26*(2), 49-61.

Wallace, M. & O'Shea, E. (2007). Perceptions of spirituality and spiritual care among older nursing home residents at the end of life. *Holistic Nursing Practice, 21*(6), 285-289.

Walsh, F. (2009), Human-animal Bonds I: The relational significance of companion animals. *Family Process, 48*, 462–480.

The Creativity-Longevity Balance: A View from Asia

Kamala Rana

Introduction

Global trends have long indicated that the Asian continent is witnessing an interest pattern as far as the ageing of its populations are concerned. According to Menon & Melendez Nakamura (2009) "…by 2050, Asia will have some 922.7 million elderly, comprising 17.5% of the population. Median age will rise to 40.2 years, and the old-age dependency ratio will increase to 38.8."

Although Asia is expected to age within the first half of this century, there are marked differences in timing and speed among sub-regions. East Asia will age fastest, while Western Asia will age slowest." In view of the imbalance in ageing populations in different parts of Asia over the next few decades, it becomes important to examine some of the critical issues confronting ageing populations and analyze the multiple factors that affect longevity patterns in this vast continent. Longevity in Japan follows a completely different matrix to longevity patterns in India and other parts of South Asia. While looking at these differences, this chapter also examines the centrality of creativity in the life-spans of Asians as a whole and different cultures in their contexts.

My analysis will reflect on five major themes of the creativity-longevity balance in the lives of my case studies. First it will examine the most pressing issues facing the ageing populations of Asia. Second, I will look at the longevity patterns in a comparative perspective of the different regions of Asia. In the third section I will look at the social and cultural factors that impact ageing in Asia compared to other regions of the world. Fourthly, there will be focus on creative pursuits and processes and their link to living a long and healthy life. Finally, I will attempt to suggest the various ways in which state policy can focus on encouraging the creative process in ageing populations to ensure a better quality of life, ensuring health longevity emotionally, mentally and physically.

It is almost impossible to write on this subject and not include real life stories of those whose lives have been intrinsically woven around interests and passions that have gone beyond their working years. I examine these lives to see how the excitement for an idea or the need to serve the underprivileged has given meaning to the heroes of these stories. I have personally known the central characters of my case studies and their stories stand as an inspiration for all those who believe that creative and interest driven lives are able to sustain longer and healthier life-spans. The central theme in my interviews with my case study participants is that there was a desire to keep engaged with an interest, hobby or passion that involved an active engagement of the heart and mind, and that this focus also kept these seniors from brooding too long over their physical limitations. A sense of their own mortality kept them deeply engaged with all that they still wished to contribute to their communities and to the world. It was evident that there was deep gratitude within the participants for the time that they had been given their lives to pursue their personal and professional goals, and with still more bonus time on their side, they were determined to continue to lead rich and fulfilled lives until the very end.

Challenges Facing the Elderly in Asia

Let us begin by examining the various challenges of ageing and the dilemmas they present for government policy and for Asian societies at large. One of the most critical realities of ageing in Asia is the drastic drop in income for the post-employed population. According to one study, "In many developed countries, pensions and social security schemes are tied to employment, which cannot be easily replicated in Asia where most people work in the informal sector" (Longstreath, 2012). According to Dave Mather, head of the non-governmental organization (NGO) Help Age, "The general feeling in the Asian region is that pension schemes are simply not affordable." A loss in income can make the ageing years a struggle on several fronts, especially of those who are unable to obtain family support and are left to fend for themselves without state support. Since financial systems remain largely under-developed in many parts of Asia, it is imperative for governments to introduce schemes that will assist low-income countries in assisting their ageing populations. So, what are the regions that are ear-marked as established ageing societies that need to address income related issues? One study has identified the trajectory thus: "In Asia, Japan became the first ageing in 1970, which is much later than high-income countries. As of 2010, several Asian countries, including China, Hong Kong, Taipei, Singapore, South Korea and Thailand began to have large numbers of ageing seniors. In the next ten years, countries like Vietnam, Indonesia, Myanmar and Malaysia will join the same group. India is expected to become an ageing society by 2024 (Longstreath, 2012).

In view of the demographic transition taking place in Asia there are two challenges that the region must face: "(1) developing socioeconomic systems that can provide economic security to the growing number of elderly, and (2) sustaining strong growth in the face of ageing over the next few decades" (Longstreath, 2012). The speed with which the ageing process is taking place in Asia, puts considerable strain on the ageing population as well as the state. In the absence of strong social security systems and financial institutions that can be the pillars of support for ageing populations, the region and its people may have to face an unprecedented crisis of managing a demographic emergency. It is also essential to develop employment plans for the elderly beyond their retirement to ensure that their dependence on family or state support is not absolute. The current rigidity of Asian labor markets in not hiring workers beyond a certain age limit can have catastrophic consequences for the economy when the availability of older workers far outweighs that of younger workers. An investment in human capital is an urgent need for countries as their populations age rapidly in maintain consistent production levels.

Healthcare becomes a second most important issue affecting ageing populations. Professor Sarah Harper of the Institute of Ageing at Oxford University concludes in a 2010 report that,"greater life expectancy without the bonus of increased health may be increasing to such an extent that we are on the verge of epidemic frailty (Harper, 2010). In the Asian context, "beyond physical frailty, the number of dementia patients in the Asia-Pacific region will rise from 14 million in 2005 to 24 million in 2020 and become as high as 65 million by 2050" (Alzheimer's Disease International, 2013). Experts in the field of mental health have identified depression, disorientation, loneliness, sense of abandonment and the lack of self-worth as some common characteristics of ageing populations as they become less active in their senior years.

The World Health Organization (WHO) has published numerous reports over the past few decades indicating the dire health conditions of large numbers of the ageing population in Asia. As one report states, "Chronic diseases make up almost one-half of the world's burden of disease, creating a double burden of disease when coupled with those infectious diseases that are still the major cause of ill health in Asian developing countries (WHO, 2005). Primary and secondary prevention approaches are also woefully lacking in these countries where a "negative ageing paradigm" assumes that older people's health needs are high in cost and long-term (Lloyd-Sherlock, 2002). Primary prevention programs are necessary to ensure that old diseases do not occur at all or their onset, if not entirely preventable, can be slowed down. If disease has already been identified, then tertiary care programs need to be in place so any illness can be managed with suitable medication and therapy. WHO reports that "adherence to long-term therapy is a woeful 25 percent for Asian countries" (WHO, 2003).

Disability and requirements for quality care become the other two prominent areas of concern for ageing populations in Asia. The types of disability frequently observed in the elderly populations are limitations in walking and climbing stairs, restricted movement confined to wheelchair and the inability to manage personal care at home. These conditions interfere with the normal ageing process and require quality caregiving to those in need of it. In Asia, informal care systems have generally involved close family members who have had their elderly relative live with them and medical treatments were also administered in homes. As these trends are also changing "care provided at home is often considered the preference of the elderly, and, from a policy standpoint, is essential for managing the cost of long-term care. However, despite the increasing demand for home-based care due to population ageing, decreased fertility rates at present times means that future cohorts of elderly will have smaller networks of potential family caregivers" (Kaneda, 2006). Living arrangements also continue to change affecting the quality of care provided to the elderly. According Chamie (2017), "In the past, elderly persons generally lived with adult children and grandchildren. With rising levels of urbanization, increasingly neither the elderly nor their adult children are choosing to live together but prefer separate household with proximity." Lives separated after centuries of families living together and taking care of the elderly has an increasingly evident phenomenon in the ageing population, the problem of social isolation.

Loneliness and isolation among the elderly are increasingly observed all across Asia. One study observes: "The bodies of elderly persons, especially those aged over 85, present visible signs of time and aging and may, for some, reflect very significant experiences of loss which may contribute to isolation and/or loneliness. The feelings of loneliness that affect the elderly are not only a hallmark of those who are institutionalized (although they appear to be more common in these cases). Prevalence increases, particularly when life events occur that result in loss, or when the ability to adapt is decreased (Sa Azreado et, al 2016). It is the loss of friends and also family members closer to their own age that makes it harder for elders to have the community that once kept them socially connected. The younger generations need their busy lives and technology has succeeded in alienating the older populations even more from life as they one knew it. Gender disparities have been observed in the ageing process where women outlive men and tend to be the ones living alone a lot more often, and longer, than men. According to one study," In the Asian and Pacific region, women outlive men by at least four years on average. This difference is a high as 13.2 years in the Republic of Korea and 12.7 years in the Russian Federation…the gap between male and female life expectancy appears to be greater in high-income countries, which suggests that socio-economic factors intervene alongside the biological dynamics" (ESCAP, 2016).

The most alarming statistics related to loneliness also point toward increased thoughts of suicide or suicidal tendencies among the elderly in many Asian countries. As one such report indicates: "there is a 37 percent increased likelihood of suicidal thoughts among elderly participants with disadvantaged structural social relationships. Among the structural measurements, the strongest association with late-life suicidal thoughts was "not being married in late life" with a 44 % increase in suicidal risk, followed by living alone (39%), unemployment (36 %), without religious affiliation (35 %) and familial discord (19 %)" (Chan & Yip, 2018). The actual suicide rates reported among Asian elders are steadily increasing and this crisis is likely to assume epidemic proportions if not addressed soon.

Near loneliness and isolation is also the prospect of violence and ill-treatment often faced by the elderly within the family and in crime ridden communities where they remain the most vulnerable to physical abuse and theft of their personal belongings. This is often evident even in care facilities for the elderly. An important finding concludes, "(Chan & Yip, 2018). Violence towards older persons can take the form of physical, emotional, psychological, financial or sexual abuse." A Committee Against Torture (CAT) finding highlights this problem thus: "State parties should prohibit prevent and redress torture and ill-treatment including, inter alia, in institutions that engage in the care of the aged (de Aguri Sa Azreado and Alcina Nato Alfonso, 2016). It is a frightening prospect to acknowledge the cruelty towards elders in societies that have long cherished traditions of care and respect for their elders.

Longevity Patterns in Asia

Asia was for long held as a model for graceful and peaceful old age where longevity was ensured in the comfort and security of familial love and togetherness of extended families. The western world was inspired by the spiritual traditions of Asian countries as well as the reverence given to old age and the relevance of the elderly on important familial and social occasions. Even people who emigrated to other parts of the world in search of better prospects always returned home to their Asian context. In the evening of their lives, they were assured that they would be cared for by loving families and protected from the vulnerabilities in their adopted homelands. This no longer holds true in most countries of the Asia-pacific region. A rapidly globalizing world has levelled the entire notion of ageing in all parts of the globe and the problems faced by the elderly seem to be more similar than even before in history. Nevertheless, the next section will reflect upon what still sets the Asian paradigm of ageing apart from other areas of the world and draw a comparative analysis of cultural, social and political factors that define the ageing-longevity narrative in these different contexts. I will look closely at what explains unusual longevity in Japan over the rest of the world and how Scandinavian countries are a remarkable example of healthy ageing. We will see which traditions remain and which have faded away in time. It will also be very worthwhile to see what the Asian ageing process may still have to teach the world, and conversely what other models of state intervention can be imbibed by Asian countries in policy towards ageing which falls woefully short in several areas.

Recent projections of the United States Census Bureau and the World Bank estimate,"the entire world's population is ageing. In some countries, the number of people who are 60 years or older is expected to double by 2050. In other countries, the number is expected to triple. These projections stand as a testament to longer lifespans and better care for older adults, but they also raise important questions. How are older individuals treated around the world, and what policies are in place to ensure that they receive the care and respect they deserve (Aging Around the World, nd)? As the world ages at a faster than was possible to project earlier, it is useful to look at some statistics of the world map and a growing grey population.

An overview of some populations getting older across the globe gives the following snapshot: "The rapid increases in median age are a reflection of the rising proportions of seniors (65 and older) in the populations of all countries. In the U.S., the share of seniors is expected to increase from 13.1% in 2010 to 21.4% in 2050. But it may triple in Mexico, from 6.0% to 20.2%, and in Brazil, from 6.9% to 22.5%. The share almost doubles in Argentina, rising to 19.4% in 2050. A doubling to tripling of the share of seniors is also expected in the Middle East and Asia. The most notable gains are in China, from 8.3% in 2010 to 23.9% in 2050, Iran (5.2% to 21.5%), and South Korea (11.1% to 34.9%). Japan, where the share is already quite high, is projected to experience an increase from 23.0% in 2010 to 36.5% in 2050. European countries that are likely to track the Japanese experience include Germany, Italy and Spain. They, too, will likely find that about one-third of their population is ages 65 and older in 2050 (Pew Research Center, 2014).

As is evident from the above statistics, the Asian region has the highest statistics for rapidly ageing populations. How does the region stand out culturally, socially and politically from the other nations when it coming to issues related to ageing? According Jared Diamond: "The Confucian teaching of filial piety shapes the living arrangements of elderly Chinese, Japanese and Korean people. About ¾ of elderly Japanese parents live with their adult children, a pattern replicated in Korea and China. China's new Elderly Rights Law mandates that children visit their parents frequently, no matter how far away they live. If children do not comply, they could face fines or jail time" (Diamond, 2013). In other parts of Asia there are language and traditions still maintained that reflect the onset of senior years. According to Jared Diamond, "A culture's respect for the elderly is often reflected in its language. <u>Honorific suffixes</u> like –ji in Hindi enable speakers to add an extra level of respect to important people — like Mahatma Gandhi, who is often referred to as Gandhiji…And then there's the suffix –san in Japanese, which is often used with elders, reveals the nation's deep veneration for the old. The country regularly holds <u>Respect for the Aged Day</u>, with the media running special features that profile the oldest Japanese citizens. The Japanese also see a person's 60th birthday as a huge event. *Kankrei,* as the celebration is called, marks a rite of passage into old age (Diamond, 2013).

Cultural factors may grant a sense of relevance for the elderly in Asia, but social and political factors place them at a great disadvantage as compared to more developed regions of the world. Increasingly, the elderly question a relevance that their forefathers took for granted, as faster and younger members of society remain more in demand. Social networks remain few and far between. Political leaders in many Asian countries seek their constituents among the youthful population with little regard for improving social protection systems, infrastructure, re-employment and creative opportunities, stronger care structures, ease of travel and other benefits for ageing populations. As Heller (2006) points out, "Most of the social insurance systems that have emerged in Asia have not been designed with the anticipation of an aged population, suggesting that these countries will face difficult issues of intergenerational burden sharing and complex ethical issues associated with medical-care options for the elderly...social-insurance systems will have to grapple with the design of a zero-pillar safety net scheme to address the needs of the large number of the elderly who have resided in the urban informal sector or the rural sector, outside the coverage of formal social insurance schemes"

Asian Ageing In Comparison To Other Countries

In contrast, western countries are coping with their own issues related to longevity of ageing populations. Some of these are country-specific and others are more common among many countries. It is interesting to note that while studying longevity-related issues in industrialized nations, Japan is always included in the analysis as a highly developed nation with the longest life expectancy. In an important study of the most advanced nations of the world, the effects of population aging on health spending, retirement policies, use of long-term care services, workforce composition, and income was analyzed across Australia, Canada, France, Germany, Japan, New Zealand, the United Kingdom, and the United States (Anderson & Hussey, 2000). In defining the ageing patterns the authors highlight that "Between 2000 and 2020 the relative size of the population age 65 and older is projected to increase rapidly in all countries. The United Kingdom is projected to have the smallest rise (from 16.0 to 19.8 %), and Japan, the largest (from 17.1 to 26.2 %). In 2020 the percentage of the population over age sixty-five is projected to range from a high of 26.2 % in Japan to a low of 15.6 % in New Zealand. In 2020 more than 20 % of the populations in France, Germany, and Japan will be age sixty-five or older, while less than 17 % of the populations in Australia, New Zealand, and the United States will be in that age group (Anderson & Hussey, 2000). A significant feature associated with ageing in these advanced societies is the practice of institutionalizing the elderly. It is rare to see the elderly living with their families and being cared for by them. Most families move their elders or otherwise, to efficiently managed old age homes where they are looked after, whether infirm, or healthy and able to move around on their own. However, recent studies have shown a slight move away from these long-accepted practices to more deinstitutionalized forms of caring for the elderly. As one author describes it: "Although the organization, financing, and delivery of long-term care differ greatly among the eight countries, one common theme has been explicit or implicit: policies promoting deinstitutionalization. Despite different approaches, the institutionalization rate of the elderly is remarkably similar in all eight countries, ranging from one in fifteen elderly persons in Australia and Germany to one in twenty elderly persons in the United Kingdom. The rate of institutionalization for the elderly is not expected to change substantially between 2000 and 2020, if there are no changes in age-specific disability rates and could actually fall slightly if current trends toward deinstitutionalization continue" (Jacobzone, 1999).

An area of the globe that is often cited as a model of a progressive social welfare model is Scandinavia. Here, as in many other parts of the world, an ageing population has begun to show rapid increase over the past several years. As one report indicates: "In the Nordic countries, the highest proportion of elderly people aged 65 years and over is found in Finland and Sweden. As in all the Nordic countries, the most notable differences between age groups are found between regions and municipalities. The general pattern is that the population in urban areas is younger than that in rural and peripheral areas, which is a pattern that is strengthened by depopulation in many rural areas. The proportion of elderly people is not only increasing in all Nordic regions, but the process is continuing faster than ever before (Hornstrom & Rao, 2013). It should be noted that Nordic countries have long been preparing for the large numbers ageing in their societies and setting up models of coping with the numbers for many years.

Both Sweden and Japan have been, in many areas of research on longevity and care for the elderly, cited as models from the Eastern and Western hemispheres. Both these countries display some of the best methods and policies for the care of the elderly as well as ensuring their continued participation in activities that ensure their longevity and satisfaction. Let us examine how they can be an inspiration for other countries to follow and what are they doing right to give hope to the ageing populations in the evening of their lives. In Sweden, "life expectancy is among the highest in the world: 79.9 years for men and 83.7 years for women. In Sweden, 5.2 %of the population are aged 80, which is slightly more than the EU average of 5.1 %. Since more and more citizens in this age group are in good health, their care requirements have declined since the 1980. In 2040, nearly one in four Swedes will be 65 years or older, and most of the people in this age group will be active and healthy. Several initiatives aimed at meeting future needs are now being put in place around the country. Some of the measures the state has actively taken for the well-being of ageing Swedes include allocating 3.6% of its GDP on long-term care, each municipality provides home care for the elders of the municipality, seniors are entitled to free transportation by taxis and other transport systems that ensure comfortable mobility, home care assistance and already prepared meals are delivered to the homes of the aged and finally, comprehensive social and medical care programs ensure that no matter what the medical emergency may be, it is covered by the taxes that citizens have paid all their lives. In 2013, Sweden was ranked first for treatment of the elderly as shown by the United Nations supported study, *The Global AgeWatch Index (BBC)* (Sweden Sverige, n.d).

In the case of Japan, "policymakers traditionally expected the country's younger generation to respectfully care for their ageing parents in multi-generational households. Public long-term care programs were mostly restricted to low-income elders without family support. As the 21st century was approaching, however, Japan's family-oriented approach foundered, due to demographic and economic changes. Daughters and daughter's-in-law- the primary caregivers-grew overwhelmed by the task, especially with the trends towards fewer children and more women joining the workforce" (Farrell, 2015). The pressure felt by the state given the strains on the elderly and the caregivers prompted reforms that included a universal long-term care system established in the year 2000 funded by taxes and insurance premiums paid by everyone over the age of 40, adult day care, home assistance, respite care and visiting nurses. Employers have also begun helping families with providing care for their elders by easing the workday burden and shortening the work week.

Although Japan remains a family care-based system, the state supports younger adults with subsidized services that help them care for the aged. The initiatives of the government have been far from perfect and "the new system's expenses have been higher than anticipated, which has led to various control measures aimed at reining in costs." Despite these problems, the Japanese model is one of the most advanced care systems not only in Asia but also in the world. Sweden and Japan have both developed systems within their resource structures that have set standards for the rest of the world to emulate as they face the daunting task of rapidly ageing populations in urban and rural areas.

A final point for reflection is what different parts of the globe can learn from each other, and for purposes of our thesis here what Asia can learn from the world, and what the world can learn from Asia. We have looked at the most advanced models from the northern and southern hemispheres and highlighted what can be learnt from their structure. Low and middle-income countries, including in Asia, have begun to experiment with innovative techniques to address challenges facing ageing populations. Some of these include: devoting an entire city of Chile to experimenting with elderly care, increasing involvement of older people in democracy through old people's councils in Brazil, training armies of volunteers in elderly care, as in several south-east Asian nations, establishing job creation schemes for older people, as Finland and South Korea have both done (Hill, 2017). The western world needs to be open about ideas that it can take from countries of Asia, and those similar to it, as it designs programs for elder care. As one analyst writes, "The west could learn a lot from low- and middle-income countries about economically efficient, innovative and effective solutions to the ageing issue…But it is not (learning), because there is alot of negative bias, patronizing attitudes and prejudice from developed countries towards developing ones: a feeling that if an idea comes from a developing country, it's not worth looking at" (Kalache, n.d.)

For the Asian content, there is a lot to learn from countries such as Japan Sweden and other more advanced nations as far as preparedness for its ageing population is concerned. There is urgent planning needed by the state to ensure better methods of long-term care that is both affordable and high in quality. Second, great strides need to be made in at-home care and employers supporting employee programs that support elder care. Third, employment prospects need to be generated for those elderly that are in good health and capable of being re-employed so as to continue making an economic contribution in their societies. Fourth, infrastructure and quality housing needs of the ageing need to be met on an urgent basis, particularly in poorer nations of South Asia which very often lack even basic facilities. Fifth, communities need to encourage greater participation of the elderly in educational and cultural activities where they can continue to learn as well as contribute from their vast experience and wisdom collected over their lifespans. Finally, all measures of creative pursuits must be encouraged to ensure healthy longevity among the elderly. Many people discover new talents and hobbies in their retirement years and these must be encouraged to flourish in supportive environments.

Creative Pursuits and Ageing

The next section will look at the creativity-longevity balance with an emphasis on actual case studies that show how strongly a creative life can help create a longer and healthier life. The lives of the elderly must be kept relevant and participatory until the very end. Let us shift focus from the issues faced by the elderly and the steps needed for their care to examining the quality of life and longevity for ageing populations. We will look at facts that affect longevity as established by research over many decades and then examine the role creative involvement in work and hobbies plays in ensuring the best quality of longevity for the elderly. Although our thesis focuses on Asia, there are lessons here to be learned for other parts of the world as well.

There is an increasing amount of evidence that points to the fact that: "over the past two decades, dozens of studies have shown that seniors with a sense of purpose in life are less likely to develop mild cognitive impairment, Alzheimer's disease, disabilities, heart attacks, or strokes. They are also more likely to live longer than people without this kind of underlying motivation (Straits Times, 2014). The purpose does not necessarily need to be an overly-ambitious one and can all focus on simpler things in life that can keep the elderly going strong over the long-term. According to one expert on Behavioral Sciences: "I think people can get a sense of purpose from very simple things - from taking care of a pet, working in the garden or being kind to a neighbor. Even small goals can help motivate someone to keep going. Older adults often discover a sense of purpose from taking care of grandchildren, volunteering or becoming involved in community service work or religion. A purpose in life can arise from learning a new thing, accomplishing a new goal, working together with other people or making new social connections (Boyl, 2009).

More so than ever before, older individuals look for a sense of purpose in their remaining years. The advent of technology and the alienation that it can potentially cause the elderly makes them seek a purpose within the world that they know and live in despite the hectic pace that life around them has assumed. Those that are living a purposeful life are creating a new environment of positive energy in later life. The experience gained through an active younger life creates a sense of purpose in later years. Hopes, aspirations and unfulfilled desires seek avenues of fulfilment in later life, provided factors such as health and social acceptance support these endeavors. In Asian communities, the bedrock of the longevity of older populations has long been the social and community-based ways of living. Socializing on a regular basis is an important factor in making choices of personal engagement in community work. Successful and purposeful social engagement in later years of life requires courage and determination to ensure a longer and happier lifespan. Good health to enjoy a longer life-span become an important aspiration for the elderly. How do they make this happen? Creative pursuits, according to established research, can be the magic potion that drives seniors in their later years to literally get a new lease on life. Beyond the demands of working years where they have supported families, helped their children get established and planned for retirement years, there emerges a new creative window of opportunity to explore outlets of expression that can be enjoyable and help in establishing healthy longevity.

An expert on the subject of creativity and longevity asserted over two decades ago that the elderly themselves very often have a negative notion of ageing which is only a social stereotype and is "just plain wrong (Collins, 1981). In fact, creativity in old age "means having the opportunity to attend to parts of ourselves that we never had the time or the energy or the chance to develop earlier in life. There is the opportunity to be honest in a way we've never been able to be before-for there can be a fearlessness in the face of death that fosters truth-telling. There is a deep and different sense about human beings and situations, one that just isn't possible when one is younger" (Collins, 1981).

For the 50th reunion of his class of 1825 at Bowdoin College, Henry Wadsworth Longfellow wrote a poem where he begins by addressing a Roman Emperor "Hail Caesar (youth), we who are about to die, salute you". He urges his ageing classmates to remain engaged and active and ensure that they were not done with their labor quite yet. He ends this beautiful poem thus:

"For age is opportunity no less
Than youth itself, though in another dress,
And as the evening twilight fades away
The sky is filled with stars, invisible by day"

The idea of creative living goes as far back as Wadsworth and is not a new phenomenon. Over the ages, lives of creative people and observations on them has only verified that creative and purposeful living almost ensures a healthier and longer life. Research at the turn of the 20th century concluded that creativity can foster a sense of proficiency, purpose and self-growth-characteristics essential to successful ageing. Creative engagement leads to creative activity throughout one's life (Fisher & Specht, 1999).

Some Case Studies In Ageing

In India where it is members of the middle class have the largest in number in the economic spectrum, which are able to be creative in their old age. They stay interested in finding different avenues to engage themselves in so as to enjoy their later years to the maximum. The conscious desire to improve their quality of life in later years has led to an emerging section of the elderly who are active, healthy and therefore continue to have a productive and purposeful old age. They are committed to serve in community welfare-activities. Those who participate in social events, and friendship groups, seek opportunities to help those in need lead a healthy and longer old age than those who live in loneliness and anxiety for their future.

I decided to look at some cases of those elders that are making significant contribution to Indian society in their senior years and I share their stories of creative and happy living below. I have worked with and known these individuals for over 45 years.

Sheela Rani Gupta, 94 years (Lives in Indore, Madhya Pradesh, India)

Sheela had a difficult childhood. Her father taught in a school named Mayo College, Ajmer and her mother kept ill-health and was not able to take care of her family. Sheela completed her graduation from college and got married. She assumed all the household responsibilities in her husband's family and raised two sons. Her husband worked in the Police Department and was away a lot given his transferable job. Her sons completed their education and the older son joined the Indian army. His wife left him eventually leaving behind a one-month day old baby. The younger son's wife died and soon he also passed away leaving behind two children aged two and a half and four years of age. Sheela was suddenly left with three small children to raise without their parents. Her older son also died a few years later. Her husband still away for work, Sheela began raising three small children with no help at all. Her husband died at the sixty with these parting words: "I have lost but you should not give up. Who will take care of these children if you do?"

She looks back at those days of heavy family responsibilities and no family support as very difficult days of her life. She worked at an institution organizing eye and medical camps and oversaw all the administrative work. She faced many challenges during those long and hard years. Sheela believes in selfless service for all. She looks after the resident welfare association of her area, serves as chairperson of a woman's organization that works to empower tribal and rural women, and is on call in her neighborhood for anyone who needs her. Her dairy is full of appointments every day of the week.

Bhawani Shankar Garg, 90 years (lives in Udaipur, Rajasthan, India)

Bhawani Shankar Garg began his career in the Rajasthan Vidya Peeth (University) after completing a master's degree in political science. Following this tenure, he was appointed a Lecturer at the Janata College and Community Centre under India's first Five Year Plan. He also organized mobile libraries in rural areas for many institutions including his previous employer, the Rajasthan Vidyapeeth at night. He did exceedingly well in his work and was soon appointed Principal of Janata College. He worked on areas such as Panchayat Raj (democratic system of government) and on women's empowerment issues serving as the Director of a women's university. He retired at the age of 60. Hie main interest was promoting community work.

For the past thirty years, Mr. Garg has been advocating democratic practices in all areas of work in which he remains engaged. In his continued involvement in education he espouses the following principles: 1)Development in any society is based on maximum participation by all; 2) Education is for life, not just to obtain academic qualifications.; 3) Community centers for social development are essential for education and 4) India must continue to enrich its cultural and intellectual traditions. He continues to serve on several committees, advocating critical analysis, honey and objectivity in educational and social endeavors and is passionate about preparing the next generation to continue quality work in these areas.

Welthy Honsinger Fisher (September 18, 1879-December 16 1980)

Welthy Honsinger was born in 1879 in Rome, New York. After receiving her college education from Syracuse University, she traveled to China as a Methodist missionary to become principal of Bao Lin, a girls' school in Nanchang Province. The year was 1906, fourteen years before American women would have the right to vote. While there, she encouraged her girls to develop into new, modern Chinese women, often against the wishes of their more traditional parents. She was committed to the idea of women's independence, however, and knew that if she could give them the tools they needed through education, then there would be no stopping them from changing the face of China. In 1924, after working for the YWCA during World War I and traveling the world for pleasure, Welthy married Frederick Bohn Fisher, a Methodist bishop with a passion for life, freedom, and mutual respect among all peoples. For the next fourteen years these two amazing personalities joined forces to campaign for cooperation among peoples and cultures to eradicate suffering and promote peace. Throughout their travels, they came to realize that lack of education and poverty were the cause of much suffering in the world, and they both spoke publicly throughout the U.S. to raise awareness of such problems. The Fishers spent much of their time in India, where Fred's sermons drew standing-room-only crowds. Despite Fred's powerful Christian message, and both Fred and Welthy's dedication to their Christian faith, they had the ability to see beyond the boundaries of individual religions. They embraced all races, cultures, and faiths equally. It was this "spiritual color-blindness" that drew the attention of Gandhi, a man who would remain both friend and inspiration to the Fishers throughout their lives. In the times they met with Gandhi, they engaged in philosophical debate and discussed how best to solve the multitudes of problems

India was facing in the twentieth century. Welthy was impressed with Gandhi's dedication and self-sacrifice. "There was no one with whom I could compare him except Christ himself," she once said.

Dedicated to improving the chances of men and women's survival, advancement and independence in "new India" through education, Welthy began Literacy House, a small, non-formal school that would combine literacy with agricultural training. However, it was not long before Welthy and other literacy pioneers realized that "new India" could be replaced with "new Asia," "new Africa" or even "new America," and World Education was born in New York City, dedicated to providing literacy training to those who needed it most throughout the world. Welthy was deeply involved with World Education either as president or advisor from 1951 until 1972, when she gave up all official duties. At the age of 93 she was once again free to travel as she pleased. In 1973 she visited China for the first time in years and returned to Peking in 1978 as the oldest foreign guest of the government. She made two "farewell" trips to India in 1973 and 1977 but returned one last time in 1980 before dying at the age of 101 in Southbury, Connecticut (Our Founder, nd)

Om Prakash Pathak, 73 years (lives in Indore, Madhya Pradesh)

Om Prakash Pathak retired as a manager with the State Bank of India at the age of 58. He had no plans to work in any specific area and thought the years will somehow pass. He felt lonely and lost. In need of something to occupy his mind, he began to search for elderly who were also alone and had lost their near and dear ones, like him. He found a new way to find people who felt lonely and lost. He met a friend who lost his wife and was looking for a friend with whom he could share the joys and sorrows of his life. The two men became good friends and began looking for other lonely souls like themselves.

Om Prakash finally found fifty men and women and formed a group that shared friendships, jokes, thoughts and personal life experiences. The group expanded into an NGO with 300 members and Om Prakash arranged lectures once a month, delivered by doctors, historians, lawyers and musicians. He set up sports activities, indoor games and libraries in different areas of Indore and Ujjain, two cities for senior citizens. Members of this growing group are lonely elders who feel happy and relieved that they have each other to share their lives with and form strong bonds.

The important achievement of Om Prakash post-retirement is the unusual initiative he has taken to look for lonely people and help them evolve a meaningful life in whatever ways they desire. His greatest satisfaction comes from creating an environment of sharing thoughts, creating new interests and sharing togetherness in the group. He continues his efforts to find more members for his group and looks for ways they can all make their lives more meaningful.

As is evident from these individuals, creative pursuits and continuously challenging themselves kept them fully engaged with life and with a zeal to ensure maximum benefits to maximum number of human beings. There is a great emphasis in these lives for a striving for a greater common good and passing their torch to the next generation to enable their work and legacy to be carried on. These examples form the very essence of creative living where through the act of overcoming hurdles in their own lives, these elders saw their purpose as serving a larger humanitarian purpose because that bound them to people and communities for whom they have tirelessly worked over decades.

I, the author, at 87 years of age, look back at my life as an incredible journey for which I express gratitude every day that I am healthy and purposeful. As a young girl, I was witness to India's independence struggle from the British. My mother continuously told me that there was "no cause greater than serving humanity, family responsibilities are not enough, make sure to serve society." This message stayed with me all my life and became the bedrock of my existence for the past eight decades. My passion for social work gave me the direction and focus that I needed to begin what I considered my purpose in life-to provide hope and relief to those lives that did not have either in their lives. I was fortunate to have a supportive family of parents, husband and children that encouraged my commitment to serve those in need and felt pride in all that I was able to do for the marginal people in my country. I completed training in social work with a master's degree in social work from the Tata Institute of Social Sciences in Mumbai, and then began my career initially with the Indian Cooperative Union, then World Education and finally the United Nations Childrens' Fund (UNICEF).

Following my retirement from UNICEF I continued to give my time and skills to participating in adult education conferences, writing for various journals, and helping run the Bhartiya Grameen Mahila Sangh (Indore, Madhya Pradesh), a non-governmental organization (NGO) that empowers women in skill training and development. For the past 25 years, I am helping this organization design programs for women and girls in self-help, skill learning and empowerment through education. The response to her work has been very positive. At 87+, I am looking forward to designing an Institute for Women's Empowerment which is now helping rural and tribal women earn living through learning tailoring.

The change I see in the lives of these women is visible yet needs continuous efforts and remains a challenge for me. I will never give up because it has brought change for the better in the lives of those with whom I worked with in many communities. I feel fulfilled with this work that I continue to do as it continues to fuel my purpose for living and does not allow me to give up. The greatest moving force in my journey through life in the service of others has been my parents, husband and my children.

Recommendations and Conclusions

I have endeavored to highlight to my readers a sense of the most pressing issues that consume the ageing process today, in Asia where I live, and across the world. I have looked at the commonalities and differences in the struggles of the elderly population and the way they are able, or unable to cope with them. Then I have explored how creative thinking and work can influence healthy longevity and what may be the necessary ingredients that inform a long and fulfilling life. In conclusion, I wish to visit the many state and private initiatives that can be taken in Asia to ease the progressive burden of old-age experienced by the elderly. In particular, I will examine how creative pursuits and outlets can become the foundation of policy that can encourage senior citizens to look forward to more joy and satisfaction as they get older. There is a tremendous amount that can be done in this area and innovative policies are needed to protect the interests and welfare of a large ageing population.

The first step in working toward greater well-being is the deep study and understanding of critical areas of concern. in the ageing process As one author notes: "It is critical that we now focus on paramount public health, social, behavioral, and biological concerns as they relate to the needs of older adults. We must also distill the most important advances in the science of aging and incorporate the evidence of scholars in gerontology, anthropology, humanities, psychology, public health, sociology, social work, biology, medicine, and other, similarly related disciplines. It is time that our attention centers on areas pertinent to the well-being of adult population such as work and retirement, social networks and neighborhood, discrimination, health disparities, long-term care, physical functioning, caregiving, housing, and, end of life care. Bringing our knowledge of this understudied group in line with their needs and the impact they will have on society will be an "achievable" challenge of current and future generation of scholars" (Baker, 2014).

In Asia, there are great discrepancies in policies toward ageing populations. We have shown the model that Japan presents and it now rests on par with a developed nation like Sweden. In a four-country study of the Philippines, Taiwan, Thailand and Singapore, researchers have noted that policies towards the elderly are getting an incredible amount of attention and reform, and these nations are slated to follow the Japan model at a faster rate than other parts of Asia. New innovative programs for the elderly that encourage their participation in the arts, business and other community oriented programs are changing the very quality of life for the elderly. These will become the next tier of countries that will set new standards for the lesser developed parts of Asia. An important factor that has made this shift possible is noted by the authors of the study: "The cultural tradition in these countries of relying on families for the physical care, economic security, and emotional support of the elderly, as well as the relative recentness of the demographic shift to older age structures, did not inhibit the early establishment of these programs for the elderly. The countries were influenced in their decisions by several factors: the influence of policies developed by more industrialized countries, the far-sightedness of policymakers in recognizing changing socioeconomic and demographic trends, as well as recognition by governments that regardless of social norms, certain individuals and groups fall outside the prescribed arrangements and required special assistance" (Hermalin, 2002). It is heartening to observe that efforts are underway in these countries to enhance the quality and longevity of the lives of the elderly and indeed their model needs to be adopted in other parts of West and South Asia.

Governments, NGO's and private sector enterprises looking to work on sounder policies to encourage more creative and healthier lives for older people, need to develop policies that reach out to elder populations, instead of the reverse. Below are some recommendations that I propose that may assist those in policymaking roles to assess how best to form new and more creative opportunities for senior living.

1. Employers can plan post-retirement hiring practices that encourage those in sound health beyond the ages of 60-65 to continue to work, on part-time or full-time basis in a mentor capacity. These experienced older adults can help solve problems and provide guidance to new entrants to the organization. Remuneration may be reduced but engagement can continue.

2. Educational institutions, arts and crafts councils, theatre and film societies, writers association, community organizations and a whole host of civil society hobby initiatives can reach out to post-retirement communities and welcome their active engagement in fun as well as creative activities that be enjoyable and continue the growth of the ageing groups in nurturing environments.

3. The ageing population can be encouraged to keep fit and active by being out in nature and if access to such activities are provided for free such as nature works, guides at heritage

sites, gardening and other pursuits in which many volunteers would be more than happy to participate.

4. The Asian tradition of families being involved in the lives of the elderly must be cherished and preserved. As the rest of the world sees an increase in at-home living and care as well as more attempts at deinstitutionalization, the Asian models of several generations living together continues to have an important place in the healthy longevity of the elderly. Younger members of families need mandated state and employer policy that encourages a commitment of their time and energy to care of their elderly family members as well as providing companionship.

5. Both governments and the private sector need to identify the economic boom that can flourish with greater participation of elderly populations. They can be at the forefront of new business and technological innovations, learn new technologies and combine them with their experience of life and work to suggest more creative public-private sector partnerships. In many parts of South Asia, government are appointing several seniors in positions such as governors and chief ministers of states to ensure mature governance and proper guidance for young bureaucrats and politicians.

6. The older generation can provide the best inspiration as ambassadors of their communities and countries. They can be engaged at community levels or even at national agendas as the Asian continent continues to recalibrate its agendas to move forward in the 21st century. Ageing seniors have witnessed decades of societal transitions and are the best repositories of history that informs current efforts at policymaking.

7. Public messages must be sent out by all those committed to creative, long and healthy lives for the elderly that their participation in all areas of civic and political life is essential and welcomed. Younger generations must interact with vigor with senior populations in building together communities, families and welcome change as the world continues to shift.

8. To create creative urges within the senior population alive, competitive events in a range of areas can be held on an annual basis ranging from beauty and grace contests, writing and poetry, art and music and so on encouraging groups within the same age-range to participate fully in these fun activities. This would encourage them to strive harder to make the best impact.

9. Finally, policymakers must ensure policies that help create a healthy balance in the lives of seniors, emotionally, physically and spiritually. They must have immediate access to services that assist them in accessing their own potential. They can be trained to help others in need if counselling, intervention or therapies are required. Peer support is as important in later years to enhance social acceptability as it is in youth. The idea is to treat ageing as a normal human function and provide every sense of normalcy in the lives of those who are now on the other side of the demographic divide.

A healthy and long life is a privilege enjoyed by many but not by all. It must be our constant striving to live the happiest and healthiest lives that we can. The richness of life only shines when we engage fully with it and live with a purpose and a cause greater than ourselves. If we are fortunate, we are surrounded by loving family and friends who enrich us on the final laps of our journey. But even for those more in solitude as they age, all is not lost. For as Gabriel Garcia Marquez says in *A Hundred Days of Solitude*: "The secret of a good old age is simply an honorable pact with solitude."

References

Aging Around the World: Four Key Differences, USC Leonard Davis School of Gerontology Study, University of Southern California.

Ageing in Asia and The Pacific Overview, Social Development Division, Economic and Social Commission for Asia and the Pacific (ESCAP), Bangkok, 2016.

Aging in the U.S. and Other Countries, 2010-2050, *Attitudes About Aging: A Global Perspective*, Pew Research Center, January 30, 2014.

Anderson, G. F. & Hussey, P.S (2000). Population aging: A comparison among industrialized countries, *Health Affairs, 19*(3).

Baker, T.A. (2014). The importance of aging studies: Understanding the influence of diversity and culture. *Age Culture Humanities: An Interdisciplinary Journal,* 1.

Boyl, P. (2009). Characterizing the Behavioural Profile of Healthy Cognitive Aging, Rush University Medical Centre, Chicago.

Chamie, J. (2017). Population Ageing is One of the Greatest Challenges Facing the 21st Century, *The Wire,* New Delhi, 16 August 2017.

Chan, Q. & Yip, P. (2018). Strengthen social relationships to combat high elderly suicide rate", Insight and Opinion, *South China Morning Post*, Hong Kong, 12 February 2018.

Collins, G. (1981). Exploring the Past: Creativity in Old Age, *The New York Times*, March 2, 1981.

Diamond, J. (2013). What Its Like to Grow Old in Different Parts of the World, Ted Talk Series, November 25, 2013.

Elderly Care in Sweden: Challenge for Our Future, Sweden Sverige Online.

Farrell, C. (2015). What Japan Can Teach US About Long-Term Care, *Forbes Magazine,* August 24, 2015.

Fisher, B.J. & Specht, D.K. (1999). Successful aging and creativity in later life, *Journal of Aging Studies, 13*(4), 457-472.

Harper, S. (2010). The capacity of social security and health care institutions to adapt to an ageing world, *Wiley Online Library,* 27 September 2010.

Heller, P.S. (2006). Is Asia Prepared for an Aging Population? *IMF Working Paper WP/06/272,* International Monetary Fund, Washington DC, December 2006.

Hill, A. (2017). UK and US must learn from poor countries to solve ageing crisis, *The Guardian,* 13 November 2017.

Hornstrom, L. & Rato, J. (2013). A Nordic Agequake? Populations Ageing in Nordic Cities and Regions, *Nordregio News Issue 3.*

Hermalin, A.I. (2002). *The well-being of the elderly in Asia: A four country comparative study,* University of Michigan Press: Ann Arbor.

Jacobzone, S. (1999). Ageing and Care for Frail Elderly Persons: An Overview of International Perspectives", *OECD Labour Market and Social Policy Occasional Papers*, OECD Publishing, Paris,

Kalache, A., Co-President, International Longevity Centre (ILC BR), Brazil.

Kaneda, T. (2006). Health Care Challenges for Developing Countries with Aging Populations. Population Reference Bureau, Washington DC, April 2006.

Lee, S., Mason, A. & Park, D, (2011). Why Does Population Aging Matter So Much for Asia? Population, Aging, Economic Security and Economic Growth in Asia, *Eria Discussion, Paper Series* August 2011.

Lesperance, M. (2014). Sweden, A Role Model for Elderly Care, Global Health Ageing, Sweden.

Longfellow, H.W., Morituri Salutumas: Poem for the Fiftieth Anniversary of the Class of 1825 in Bowdoin College.

Longstreath, D. (2012). Isolation, poverty loom for an ageing population", *Irin News Report,* Bangkok, February 2012.

Lloyd-Sherlock, P, (2002). Social policy and population ageing: Challenges for North and South, *International Journal of Epidemiology 31*(4), 754-57.

Menon, J, & Nakamura, Anna. (2009), Aging in Asia: Trends, impacts and responses, *Working Paper Series on Regional Economic Integrations*, No. 25, February 2009.

Our Founder: Wealthy Consigner Fisher, World Education website, Boston MA.

Retirees with a sense of purpose do better, *The Straits Times*, Singapore, September 26, 2017.

Report of Alzheimer's Disease International (ADI), London UK, 2013.

Sa Azreado, Z. & Alfonso, M. (2016), Loneliness from the perspective of the elderly., *Revisit Brasilia de Geriatric e Gerontologia, 19*(2), March/April 2016.

World Health Organization (WHO) (2003). Adherence to long-term therapies: Evidence for action. Geneva.

Effect of Hobbies on Well-Being Leading to a Long Quality of Life

Aditya Putcha

Introduction

While virtually everyone needs to set aside at least forty hours a week of work during the week most people also place activities that they can look forward to outside of work. To take it a step further, many people trudge through those work hours specifically looking forward to these outside activities. The question becomes whether having a life filled with the much-needed recreation leads to a longer and healthier life. Recreation would not be the same for everyone. That is, some individuals may engage in competitive sports while others would find pleasure in reading books. This chapter explores whether artistic involvement can boost people's physical well-being in addition to their emotional well-being. The next section of this chapter will present the methodology that is used and cited in the literature, then present the existing literature. The latter is a different approach usually encountered in quantitative research.

Empirical Methodology

The studies often encountered in the literature use a regression analysis to examine their data and test their hypotheses. A regression equation way to determine a relationship between the independent variables (the variables that are manipulated) and the dependent variable (the variable impacted). The general regression equation is

$$y = \beta_0 + \beta_i X + e_i \tag{1}$$

where y represents the dependent variable, X represents the matrix of independent variables and e_i represents the error term which follows a white noise process $N(0, \sigma^2)$.

More specifically, y represents quality of life (considering both health and longevity), while the independent variables include: X_1 represents quantifiable devotion to art, X_2 and X_3 represent the same for quantifiable devotion to fitness and travel, respectively. Virtually all hobbies can be grouped into one of the three categories and thus the equation represents an attempt at a comprehensive snapshot. An assumption made is that the relationship each individual independent variable has to life quality is quadratic. Even the most basic things in life, such as food and water, tend to only help someone up until an ideal point, after which they cause adverse effects.

Hobbies improving someone's quality of life may seem intuitive on a broad level. As part of its Awareness Week no less an organization than the UK Mental Health Foundation has published a newsletter detailing the reduction an active, pleasurable lifestyle can beget in anxiety, stress, depression, etc. A researcher wants to delve more into the why and how though and at the risk of sounding immodest a great research mind is behind this chapter.

Existing Research

Zawadzki, Smyth & Costigan (2015) studied a large sample of people who self-reported on happiness, interest level in life, and stress level (both at the moment and regarding life in general), while their saliva (to objectively gauge stress using cortisol) and heart rate were analyzed. This study was also notable for using multivariate models, focusing on comparing people to themselves at other times rather than the standard practice of comparing them to different people, and making sure that the subjects were not engaging in social interactions for at least part of the study, to ensure the results were caused by the hobbies and not by the people with whom the subjects were communicating. The results showed a clear improvement in happiness, stress, and heart rate, albeit not in overall interest. That seems to suggest that while leisure activities can relax someone in the moment, they do not necessarily change the general outlook on life. Of course, simply taking the results to the next logical step, if someone consistently partook in hobbies one would think that the person would consistently feel relaxed and get more out of life. The latter deserves further examination. Tomioka, Kurumatani, & Hosoi (2016) analyzed subjects nearing the end of long lives. They observed among the elderly sample that having hobbies shields those nearing the end of their lives from mortality and the functional decline stress causes. In reaching their conclusion, they cited reasons both psychological and physiological: 1) Hobbies can reinforce neural networks and musculoskeletal abilities, which often fall under the umbrella of "use it or lose it" 2) Hobbies can give someone the sense of a greater quality in life, even a purpose in life, which their research objectively associated with better numbers for blood pressure and other disease risk markers 3) Stress buffering, which studies like the last one cited showed hobbies provide, provides people with the ability to integrate trying psychological events with minimal confusion.

Pressman, Matthews, Cohen, Martire, Scheier, Baum, & Schulz, (2009) got to the heart of this matter in their research by stating they had examined whether engaging in multiple enjoyable activities voluntarily in someone's free time tends to cause better psychological and physiological functioning, as few studies had looked directly at the health benefits. Their method piqued the interest underlying this research because nearly 1,400 respondents ranging in age from under 20 to almost 90 completed self-reports assessing their participation in 10 different types of leisure activities and gave their measures in resting blood pressure, cortisol over two days, body mass index, waist circumference, and perceived psychological functioning.

Something else worth mentioning about the study: leisure activities were talked about as "breathers" that provide a chance to take a break, engage in a pleasurable diversionary activity, and consequently induce positive emotions and reduce stress, and "restorers" that facilitate the individual's recovery from stress by replenishing damaged or depleted resources.

To robustly test any hypotheses quantitative measures were needed and various widely recognized scales were used for positive and negative states, depressive symptoms, life satisfaction, life engagement (very similar qualitatively to the purpose in life metric in the Japanese study), social network size, social support, stress of recent life events, physical activity, sleep behaviors, and physical functioning, all based on the respondents' self-evaluations. The total cortisol production was measured by plotting the different values recorded and then using the fundamental calculus technique of measuring area under the curve. As in equation (1), these researchers treated the independent variables as independent not only of the dependent variable but from each other.

Four different hypotheses were tested: 1) PEAT correlates with better mood states 2) More frequent leisure is associated with better physiological functions 3) PEAT activities are associated with better overall health behaviors such as sleep 4) A higher socioeconomic status would render leisure activities less important.

For the first three hypotheses, they assessed the basic association between the PEAT and the dependent variable of interest using linear regression. For the last hypothesis, a multivariate linear regression analysis was run, including education and income and co-varying age, race and study sample.

The results are impressive! Higher scores on the Enjoyable Activity Test (called PEAT due to the study's location of Pittsburgh, PA) were associated with lower blood pressure, total cortisol, waist circumference, and Body Mass Index (BMI) and better perceptions of physical function.

As far as mental effects, the PEAT was positively correlated with higher levels of positive psychosocial states and lower levels of depression. Also, despite the wide demographic variations among participations, the results withstood all controls, except for the one discussed in the last hypothesis. A better socioeconomic status does, both physiologically and psychologically, somewhat negate the effects of leisure activities, which intuitively makes sense given that people who must worry less about money and need to work less can afford better health care and have less reason to develop stress. This study did show that no one activity type had effects as positive as total PEAT, which means hobbies, in general, are more important than any one. That said, this chapter seeks to learn about the different types of hobbies in isolation, particularly the ones artistic in nature. Papers exist exploring the concepts.

Another independent variable, fitness, is also important. Research papers focusing on the link between well-being and exercise per se are difficult to find, likely because exercising improving someone's quality of life is reasonably common sense. A similar concept was explored, by Godbey (2009). He discussed how walking has been shown to have many health benefits for older adults. These include a laundry list of items, such as managing weight, controlling blood pressure, decreasing risk of heart attack, boosting good cholesterol, lowering risk of stroke, reducing risk of breast cancer and Type 2 diabetcs, preventing need for gallstone surgery, protecting against hip fracture, and inhibiting disorders as varied as depression, colon cancer, constipation, osteoporosis, and impotence, lengthening lifespan, lowering stress levels, relieving arthritis and back pain, strengthening muscles, bones, and joints, improving sleep, and elevating overall mood and sense of well-being. As he points out, this can easily be extrapolated to other forms of exercise, given that virtually all forms of physical activity incorporate walking.

More to the overall point of the paper, he cited various works by others that demonstrated the rejuvenating effects of natural settings, such as wilderness areas, parks, and even rooms with plants. So powerful is the effect of natural settings that stress reduction can even be achieved via such landscape images, according to the research! Regarding specific benefits, many studies cited show that time in parks decreases stress and relaxation, with the only thing more associated with parks being exercise and fitness itself. As we have shown, that is all related.

An interesting point drawn from a previous study is that the major causes of death for people in developed nations have shifted from disaster (starvation, war) and disease (smallpox, malaria) to decay (heart disease, cancer), individual behaviors play an increasingly bigger role in both longevity and quality of life. This stressed the importance of the sort of research discussed in this chapter and Godbey's (2009) paper overall serves as a nice segue to exploring the independent variable, travel. Strauss-Blasche, Reithofer, Schobersberger, Ekmekcioglu, & Marktl (2005) used two scales. Scale 1, called "Recuperation", was composed of seven items. Essentially, the researchers were asking the respondents how much they agreed with the following: "In comparison to the 2 weeks before vacation, I now feel mentally fitter, feel more balanced and relaxed, can concentrate better during work, feel physically fitter, do my work more easily, am in a better mood, and feel more recuperated". Scale 2 ("exhaustion") was composed of three items ("In comparison to the 2 weeks before vacation, I now feel more indifferent and apathetic, more depressed, and more exhausted"). The subject characteristics considered were age, sex, and an estimate of physical as well as mental strain of daily work, the latter two because they assumed that more strained individuals would show a greater improvement during vacation. That is like the insight from the Godbey (2009) about leisure providing greater benefits to people of lower socioeconomic status.

The previous studies delved into the different types of hobbies. With this paper focusing on one type, the researchers created different independent variables focusing specifically on it. The four different aspects of vacation considered: (1) physical vacation characteristics (duration, average temperature, time-zone difference, time to reach destination), (2) organization of the day (number of provided meals, self-determination of one's daily actions, planning of day ahead, time for one's self and needs), (3) health and social behavior (physical activity during vacation, average sleep duration during vacation, sleep quality, making new acquaintances), and (4) stress during vacation (health problems, interpersonal conflicts). Collectively these aspects of the vacations and the attributes of the respondents themselves explained an impressive amount of the variance in the two scales, as summarized in table 1.

Table 1. Summary of the Statistical Results

Block	Characteristics/Variables	Results
	Total R^2	.30***
1	**Subject Characteristics**	
	(R^2 - change recuperation.08***; R^2 - change exhaustion .00***)	
	Age	.12
	Sex	.10
	Physical Strain of Daily Work	.12
	Mental Strain of Daily Work	.17**
2	**Physical Vacation Characteristics**	
	(R^2 - change recuperation.06*; R^2 - change exhaustion .07**)	
	Duration	.09
	Temperature at Vacation Site	.20**
	Time Zone Difference to Home	-.16*
	Time to Travel to Vacation Destination	.01
3	**Individual Organization of Day**	
	(R^2 - change recuperation .08*; R^2 - change exhaustion .03)	
	Number of Meals Provided	.08
	Self Determination of One's Daily Activities	-.08
	Planning the Day Ahead	.09
	Time for One's Self and Needs	.21**
4	**Health and Social Behavior**	
	(R^2 - change recuperation .07**; R^2 - change exhaustion .01)	
	Physical Activity During Vacation	.14*
	Average Sleep Duration during Vacation	.08*
	Sleep Quality	.14*
	Meeting Acquaintances	.16*
5	**Stress During Vacation**	
	(R^2 - change recuperation .02; R^2 - change exhaustion .03*)	
	Health Problems During Vacation	-.07
	Interpersonal Conflicts	-.11

The most important point the study made is that the effect of vacation cannot merely be explained by the removal of work stress, as had been indicated in previous studies.

Instead, the way an individual organizes his or her vacation makes a difference. Having enough time for one's self and one's needs, exercising, getting good sleep, and socializing in a warm vacation climate facilitate recuperation, especially in vacationers reporting higher levels of mental strain prior to the trip.

Now it is time for the most central question of this chapter: what are the specific effects of artistic endeavors on a person's physical and emotional health? Davies, Knuiman, Wright, & Rosenberg (2014) went far beyond assessing physical and mental health by also studying social health, economic health, knowledge, and effects on identity and art itself. Within each theme, positive, negative and unintended outcomes of public and individual consequence were identified. On a broad level, interesting research had already been done. The authors cited numerous studies that collectively showed 1) Among people experiencing mental health issues, arts programs increase confidence, self-esteem and self- understanding 2) In the general population, arts engagement improves psychological well-being and life satisfaction. 3) The arts also entail inclusive processes that act as a catalyst for creating connections between people who are similar (i.e. bonding social capital) and people who are different (i.e. bridging social capital) in terms of certain characteristics like socioeconomic status and age. 4) Community arts programs expand social networks and facilitate a sense of belonging. 5) The arts have also been used in urban renewal projects to encourage community cohesion, identity and the development of civically valuable behaviors such as tolerance and respect. 6) Research conducted in the UK, the United States, and Sweden suggest that after controlling for a variety of factors, attending cultural events is positively associated with general health and longevity.

The authors pointed out flaws in previous research, however, saying it had focused on specific groups (e.g., patients, prisoners, and youth) rather than the general population and on positive consequences rather than the variety of positive, negative and unintended outcomes. The research had also focused on art therapy or specific art programs, rather than the art people do in their everyday lives as a hobby. With that in mind, they began their own research, defining arts engagement as active (as a creator) or passive (as a spectator) within a variety of art forms (e.g. performing arts, visual arts, literature).

First, to encourage a range of people from the general population to nominate, the study was advertised via the email lists of two universities, two arts organization and one health organization. Ultimately, 33 people were randomly selected for an interview using a random number generator used in Microsoft Excel. The interview questions and visual prompts are summarized in table 2

Table 2. Interview Questions and Visual Prompts

1.	Tell me about your most recent experience of engaging in the arts?
2.	Tell me about the type of art you do the most?
3.	If you were able to describe a friend or family member why you <attend>/<participate> in _____, what would you say?
4.	I'd like to introduce you to two different people (show stick card). Like you (name matched to gender of the interviewee) <attends>/<participates> in_____(interviewee's activity), whereas <Jane>/<Tim> (name matched to gender of person <attends>/participates> in the arts.
A.	How do you think that arts engagement **positively** affects <Laura's>/<John's> life?
B.	How do you think that arts engagement **negatively** affects <Laura's>/<John's> life?
C.	Do you think <Laura>/<John> would experience any unintended outcomes as a result in the arts? What would they say?
D.	How do you think arts engagement make <Laura>/<John> feel?
E.	If <Jane>/<Tim> was to start engaging in the arts, how would his or her life be impacted?

The seventeen theoretical nodes that formed the starting point for the analysis were learning, identity, economic activity, income, mental health, relaxation, stress reduction, reduced anxiety/depression, confidence, self-esteem, self-understanding, self-expression, social capital, networks, support, physical health, and life satisfaction. From there, the open-ended questions resulted in 850 individual coded- statements from which the seven aforementioned primary outcome themes of mental health, social health, physical health, economic factors, knowledge, art effects and identity effects were derived. Mental health outcomes (330 of 850 coded-statements) were mentioned seven times more frequently and social health outcomes (251 of 850 coded- statements) five times more frequently than other outcomes. Physical, mental and social factors were classified as 'health' outcomes, while art, economic, knowledge and identity factors were classified as 'health determinant' outcomes. Within each of the seven primary themes were, as mentioned, both positive/negative and individual/community outcomes. These health outcomes are summarized.

Mental Health

Twenty mental health-related themes were identified of which half were positive and most related to the individual. Overall, arts engagement made people feel happy, was enjoyable, was satisfying and resulted in the creation of good memories. Most study participants felt the arts made them more mentally resilient. Some participants felt the arts energized them, while others suggested it was relaxing and 'reduced their stress.' Arts engagement increased participant's self-efficacy (e.g., confidence, self-esteem) and was a means of self-expression and self-reflection. Participants liked that creating art sometimes resulted in compliments and recognition that in turn made them feel valued and respected, for example. In the words of one twenty something female "It encourages you to be yourself and be happy. It makes you a more confident person, especially if you are good at what you do and then you get compliments, so you feel good about yourself." On a negative side, arts engagement occasionally made participants feel marginalized for being 'arty' and sometimes led to undesirable emotions such as frustration, disappointment and anxiety.

Social Health

Social health is influenced by the strength of a person's network, his or her understanding of subjective norms and the capacity to make individual choices. Overall, 11 social health-related themes were identified, of which all were positive. Three-quarters of those interviewed suggested that the arts increased their network, as it was a way of meeting people of similar and diverse backgrounds. For example, one fortysomething female said "You build a network without even realizing. [You have] a range of people who you would never in your normal life meet. They might only see each other once a week but, it's like you are the oldest friends because you have this really strong love of something that connects you." Arts engagement reduced feelings of isolation, increased feelings of support and resulted in positive shared experiences. As the arts are a form of entertainment, it was a means of staying in touch with friends and family (e.g. attending a play together).

Interviewees also obtained enjoyment from giving and receiving art. Through arts engagement, interviewees felt they were part of their community. They felt they were more community minded, that the arts gave them a wider appreciation of society and broadened their ideas/beliefs.

The arts helped them see other people's perspectives and made them question social norms and stereotypes. Overall, the arts made some study participants feel they were more 'interesting', 'worldly' and 'cultured.'

Physical Health

Eight physical health subthemes were identified of which half were positive and most related to the individual. Interviewees indicated their arts engagement resulted in physical activity such as walking, standing for long periods of time, warm-ups and performance-based movement such as dancing. According to a fortysomething male respondent: "I walk around looking for a good [photographic] shot. Sometimes I've walked for an hour." On the negative side, participants also discussed how arts engagement could result in physical pain or injury (e.g., discomfort from repetitive movements, hearing damage from loud concerts) and that particularly in the visual arts, some materials are poisonous (e.g., solvents, glazes). As arts events are often at night, some participants experienced tiredness. It was also suggested that arts events could have negative health outcomes, as in some instances people drank too much alcohol, took drugs, smoked and breathed in second-hand smoke. According to a twenty something male "There is a negative effect of being in the arts. You might not realize how much more you start drinking."

Health Determinant Outcomes

Art

Art-specific outcomes occur via the expression and appreciation of the aesthetic through the process of making and/or experiencing art. In this study, nine art subthemes were identified, the majority of which were positive. Overall, most participants thought they had a talent for art. They liked that the arts were non-competitive and allowed them to interact with and support artists and arts organizations. Interviewees also discussed the importance of arts participation, appreciation and creativity in their lives, but felt that arts engagement was very time consuming. A teenage female said, "It can be quite time consuming and you can lose track of things …so, with a CD, you mean to sit there for five minutes in between other tasks and half an hour later you are still sitting there."

Economic Factors

Economic factors are key determinants of health and relate to the resources available to a person. In this study, five economic subthemes were identified, with most participants discussing how expensive arts engagement can be. A twentysomething female put it as follows: "It can be cost prohibitive and that's not just for the ticket. It could also be for the transport, babysitter, and the cost of food."

However, the ability to create art gave participants potential career options and opportunities (e.g. amateur exhibitions, travel). Performing or making art was a potential source of income; however, participants felt the community was not willing to remunerate highly for amateur artworks and performances. Making art also allowed some interviewees to save money, as they could create artworks for themselves and others. A twentysomething female responded, "There is a practical outcome for presents and for myself to put on the wall. You don't have to go to the shops. You can make it yourself."

Knowledge

Knowledge outcomes relate to the process of formal, informal or unintentional learning and are a key determinant of health. Overall, eight knowledge subthemes were identified, of which all were positive and most related to the individual and community. Study participants described the arts as intellectually stimulating. They discussed how the arts developed their capacities and capabilities, especially the development of general knowledge and skills (e.g. art, business, team work, problem-solving, social, communication and literacy). A simple quote from a twentysomething male: "I guess there is a learning process… It [art] expands your realms of knowledge, vocabulary and your spelling."

Identity

Identity relates to how a person sees him or herself and how others view them. Identity is influenced by a person's characteristics, thoughts and beliefs. Overall, two identity subthemes were identified. Both subthemes were positive, with interviewees indicating that the arts enhanced their connection to self and gave their life more meaning: "Who I am, is about whom I am when I am doing my art. Art gives you something that is totally yours, beyond family, commitments, work. You have a greater understanding of yourself and your life…creating art gives you that chance to express meaning for yourself and life", in the words of one fifty-something female. It's only fitting a paper all about art would contain visual aids and this figure summed up the results beautifully.

Overall, Davies, Knuiman, Wright, & Rosenberg (2014) mencapsulated their work by stating that the aim was to develop a framework pertaining to the relationship between arts engagement (for enjoyment or entertainment) and population health that would be useful to doctors, researchers, teachers, health/social care professionals, policy-makers and artists. Mental health and social health were mentioned more frequently than other outcomes by the participants and thus shown in larger font in the figure. This could suggest that arts engagement had a greater impact on mental and social health than other outcomes; however, this assumption requires further investigation.

Since interviewees more frequently mentioned individual rather than community outcomes, and positive rather than negative outcomes, this study could serve as a starting point in a campaign for more holistic solutions to health maladies. As the authors acknowledged, future research would need to identify and quantify the strength of the relationship between the arts and each outcome in the framework, explain conditions under which the health–arts relationship does or does not occur, determine if a threshold level of arts engagement (e.g. hours per week) before outcomes start to accrue, how outcomes are influenced by mode of engagement (e.g. making vs. experiencing art), type of art form (e.g. visual arts vs. literature) and whether engaging in single or multiple types of art forms differentially affects health outcomes. They suggested that the future research should explore whether there is a threshold above which art is no longer helpful and perhaps the sorts of negative effects cited above would outweigh the positive effects. If so, it would validate the hypothesis of this research that the relationships are quadratic rather than linear.

Conclusion and Final Thoughts

What matters most is how clear a positive relationship already is though. As confirmed by the literature, having activities in one's life done purely for enjoyment provides someone motivation to work hard and amass more spending money. Also, as cited in the literature, artistic endeavors have been a blessing as they provide an outlet to channel any emotions, however negative, into something beautiful that consequently gives me pride and happiness. It is great to see research bearing out the value of hobbies in general and art for a person's well-being, not only emotionally but physically due to less harmful stress, less reason to fill time with the likes of alcohol, etc. Earlier in this chapter, it was mentioned that people in lower socioeconomic status have less access to leisure and what a boon papers like the ones highlighted here have shown leisure activities to be. Given the lack of recreational opportunities in the lower socioeconomic status, it will be great to champion investing in artistic programs and other recreational opportunities for those less fortunate to promote well-being and a greater longevity of life. While there is room for more research, the current literature provided a firm foundation to explore these topics in future research.

References

Davies, C. R., Knuiman, M., Wright, P., & Rosenberg, M. (2014). The art of being healthy: a qualitative study to develop a thematic framework for understanding the relationship between health and the arts. *BMJ Open*, *4*(4), e004790.

Godbey, G. (2009). Outdoor recreation, health, and wellness: Understanding and enhancing the relationship. Available at: https://recpro.memberclicks.net/assets/Library/Public_Health/outdoor_recreation_health_and_wellness.pdf.

Pressman, S. D., Matthews, K. A., Cohen, S., Martire, L. M., Scheier, M., Baum, A., & Schulz, R. (2009). Association of enjoyable leisure activities with psychological and physical well-being. *Psychosomatic Medicine*, *71*(7), 725.

Strauss-Blasche, G., Reithofer, B., Schobersberger, W., Ekmekcioglu, C., & Wolfgang, M. (2005). Effect of vacation on health: moderating factors of vacation outcome. *Journal of Travel Medicine*, *12*(2), 94-101.

Tomioka, K., Kurumatani, N., & Hosoi, H. (2016). Association between social participation and instrumental activities of daily living among community-dwelling older adults. *Journal of Epidemiology*, *26*(10), 553-561.

Zawadzki, M. J., Smyth, J. M., & Costigan, H. J. (2015). Real-time associations between engaging in leisure and daily health and well-being. *Annals of Behavioral Medicine*, *49*(4), 605-615.

Tell Tale Templates of Longevity

Siddharth Rana

This chapter is dedicated to those who have the looks that matter. Hopefully, by the end of this chapter, we will appreciate why certain looks stand the test of time, and make us only admire their longevity. This chapter describes the general facial characteristics, and other characteristics of individuals that outlive most other people, and set them apart from most people.

The average lifespan of an individual in United States is about 79 years. One standard deviation is 15 years. This amounts to 68% of people who will be gone within the spread of +/- 15 yrs. of the average lifespan.

The focus of this chapter is on individuals who live to be one standard deviation above and beyond the average lifespan (94+ years).

Let us first look at the overall looks of an individual. There are those who have quite a long face, compared to most other individuals. These people have the standout looks that carry long ways. There is something about a long face that seems to give them an edge in life. Next time you see someone with a long face, just think that they mean business when they talk. If one considers the facial aspect ratio measurements of long faces from top of head to the eyes, to the measurements from eyes to the bottom of the chin, which happen to be about 3-3.5. These individuals live to be at least one standard deviation above the average lifespan. It is as if their faces have been stretched to the limit of human existence as we know it today. These individuals seem to be more considerate than most. They are good listeners. They can assess a situation better than most people. Case in point is the American Economist John Kenneth Galbraith. He lived to be 97 years, and was quite active till the very end of his life. Mr. Galbraith was world famous economist, ambassador and of course a professor at Harvard University. Jerry Lewis, the actor and humanitarian, was another example of someone with a long elongated face. He hosted the Muscular Dystrophy marathon for many years. Then there is Stan Lee, the Comic Book creator of Marvel Comics. More recent,

CNN Anchor, Fredricka Whitfield, also has a long attractive face. In all probability, she will live past her 90's. Her father, Mal Whitfield, was a gold medalist in the 800 meters in 1948 and 1952 Olympics. He died at the age of 91.

Longevity and long face is not correlated to height and longevity. According to an article in the Western Journal of Medicine, published in 2002, shorter stature Europeans, Asians and Hispanics, seem to live somewhat longer than the taller European origin people. This article stated that shorter stature people seem to have a lower incidence of cardiovascular diseases compared to the taller people. The heart does not have to work as hard in blood circulation throughout the body. Also, the taller people seem to have a greater incidence of Cancer.

This leads to the next aspect of facial characteristics that I believe is associated with longevity. The first of these are the size of ears that certain people have. Big ears are invariably associated with longevity. President Jimmy Carter, Senator Robert Dole, Secretary George Shultz, Prince Charles, Architect I. M Pei, Actor Louis Jordan (Movie 'Octuppussy' fame) are few of the famous people who have lived long lives. Their ears start at the level of the eyes and extend almost to the lips level. This seems to give them an edge on longevity.

Another aspect of longevity is high forehead. Individuals who have large foreheads, seem to live longer. Some famous individuals with high foreheads are Astronaut Chuck Yeager, Economist John Galbraith, Physicist Hans Bethe (who liked to take long showers at Harvard University), Physicist Edward Teller (father of the Hydrogen Bomb), President Jimmy Carter, Senator Chuck Schumer of New York, Queen Elizabeth 2, Actors Bob Hope, Kirk Douglas and Eli Wallach, Clint Walker, Clint Eastwood, Gene Hackman, Sharon Stone, Geena Davis, George Kennedy, Helen Hunt and Jon Voight. Jon Voight, is one of my favorite actors. I enjoyed his acting in the movie 'The Champ', when I was a teenager. His daughter, Angelina Jolie, also has a high forehead. I am guessing, that all of them will live into their 90's, barring some other unforeseen calamity. Gloria Vanderbilt (Fashion Designer and Socialite), and Gloria Steinem (Started Ms magazine in the 1970s). Then there is Dorothy Chandler (Dorothy Chandler Pavilion in Los Angeles). She made it her mission to build a theater where people could go to hear music performances, and see theatrical plays. Anderson Cooper, who is Gloria Vanderbilt's son, will in all probability live long. He has a high forehead and big ears. He happens to be my favorite CNN anchor. CNN correspondent, Poppy Harlow, will live long, as she has a high forehead. Finally, there is Pierrre Cardin, the perfume creator, who has a high forehead. High forehead is a sign of high intellect and somehow is associated with longevity. It has been said that if you can cover your forehead with the four fingers of your hand comfortably, with the hand held flat against the forehead, you have a high forehead.

In both Chinese as well as in Japanese culture, their designated deities of longevity have high foreheads. These deities in turn, are associated with certain star constellations, which have been around for millennia. The star Canopus, the brightest star in the Southern Constellation of Carina, is the star associated with the Chinese Deity Shouxing. He is depicted as someone with a high domed forehead and a peach that he carries as a symbol of immortality.

Another aspect of the facial features is the eyes. Deep set eyes give an edge to an individual's longevity. Some famous Americans with deep set eyes are Astronaut Chuck Yeager, Secretary George Shultz. Such people can peer far into the future and are deep thinkers.

And finally, those facial features that are very attractive, tend to live very long also. There are quite a few who are still living today. There are Hollywood icons Betty White, Olivia de Havilland, Doris Day ('Que Sara Sara' song singer from the movie 'The Man Who Knew Too Much'), Tony Bennett, Kirk Douglas. In the political arena, there are President H W Bush and wife Barbara Bush. I would like to mention something about President George H.W. Bush and Barbara Bush when they were in the White House. Their Bedroom was open to anyone seeking advice. This is something I have found remarkable to this day, and it has stayed with me. This was one defining moment in George H.W. Bush's presidency, which speaks volumes about what true public service should be. The facial placement of their eyes, ears, nose and lips are very evenly spaced, and are distinctive. Incidentally, Barbara Bush was the best First Lady that retired Secret Service Officers worked for, according to US News article, quite a few years back. Last, but not least, is Naomi Parker Finley (aka Rosie the Riveter) from World War II. She recently passed away at age 96. She personified that women could do anything that men could. She was quite attractive when she was young.

Henderson et. al, (2003) showed a strong correlation between Facial Attractiveness and Longevity. The researchers, from University of Waterloo in Ontario, Canada had shown a select group of male and female college students photographs of individuals when they were in high school in the 1920s. These individuals had long since passed. The researchers had the death records of all these individuals. The students were asked to predict who among these individuals lived a long life, based on their facial attractiveness and overall health. The researchers saw a strong correlation between facial attractiveness and longevity. Interestingly, the male subjects were much better at predicting attractiveness from the photographs compared to women. Women rated men based on their facial maturity as well. Thus, those individuals, who were rated more on their health perception, did not live as long as those who were judged on looks alone. Male subjects judged both men and women better on their attractiveness. This may be due in part to men in general choosing attractive females to pass on their good genes to their future progeny. But overall, there was a strong correlation between facial attractiveness and longevity.

Now, let us turn our attention to individual characteristics of both men and women that predisposes them to live long lives. In the book *The Longevity Project*, authors Howard Friedman and Leslie Martin, outline the following characteristics that predisposes individuals to live longer lives. To begin with, individuals who are characterized as worriers seem to live a lot longer than the happy go lucky ones. Being a worrier, makes you some type of a warrior in life. It gives one the courage to go on fighting in life, and live a relatively long life.

Another characteristic of longer lived lives of individuals is their desire to succeed in life. Men and women who strive to make something of their lives, and overcome adversity, tend to live longer. These individuals are far more conscientious than their peers. These individuals are more meticulous in their daily habits. They are more prudent in their spending habits. They tend to be happier with their lives, and tend to live longer. So the three characteristics of successful people who live long lives are prudence, dependability and perseverance. This applies to men and women, well past their working lives. In the book *'The Longevity Project'*, psychologist John Holland divided society into six different types based on individual personality and type of profession one chooses. These six types are as follows:

1. **Artistic** people and artistic occupations include actors, musicians, designers and artists.

2. **Realistic** occupations are the ones where people do things i.e. engineers, firefighters, pilots, machinists, doctors, veterinarians etc.

3. **Investigative** occupations involve a lot of thinking i.e. economists, professors, and scientists.

4. **Social** occupations include helpers i.e. clergy, nurses, teachers, and counselors.

5. **Enterprising** careers generally involve persuasion i.e. insurance, politics, and general sales.

6. **Conventional** occupations emphasize organizational skills i.e. administration, financial sector, and auditing.

There are always people who will end up in some of these professions, even though their interests maybe different than their chosen profession. But in general, these 6 professions define a good job match to individual interests. These individuals were studied over time. Those people, whose profession most closely matched their interests, were less likely to have more stress in their lives, and lived longer than their peers.

The researchers, expected that people who were artistic, would be the happiest and thus healthiest. However, this expectation did not necessarily correlate to the individuals studied. Among the Enterprising group, those with high correlation between personality and occupation died sooner. Assertive, persuasive men who worked in occupations such as sales management were at a greater risk than assertive, persuasive people working in other professions like law and research.

Men who were less enterprising, but found themselves holding enterprising jobs were also at relatively high mortality risk. The stressful enterprising jobs brought out latent unhealthy tendencies and they faced more stress and poorer health habits. But the less enterprising still did not do all that badly as the 'always-on' type A personalities working in jobs that required them to be go getters i.e. car salesperson.

The one case in which the there was a good correlation between career and personality match which was helpful in predicting longevity was the Social category. Individuals with social personality types i.e. cooperative and having good people skills, and working in professions like counseling did live longer. I would like to include here a Social Worker by Profession. Her name is Mrs. Vrinda Knapp, who just turned 94 in January 2018. She retired at the age of 60 from the Children's Hospital of Los Angeles. She has been a social worker all her life. She has willed part of her estate for a scholarship to University of Southern California's School of Social Work. Vrinda Knapp earned her Ph.D from USC. She has done muchwork in the field of juvenile delinquents, and their problems. She had a famous client once, singer Tina Turner, who had some issues with her daughter. After Vrinda Knapp finished counseling Tina Turner's daughter, Tina Turner gave her a Maltese puppy dog as a gift for counseling her daughter successfully. Vrinda Knapp happens to be my Aunt. I remember the dog who lived to a ripe old age. The dog was like the child of both my Aunt and her husband, Christopher Knapp. They did not have any children of their own. I had very fond memories of my time spent at their house in Hollywood Hills, over the course of my studies as an undergraduate. Unfortunately, Vrinda Knapp now has advanced Alzheimer. She lives in an assisted living facility in Pasadena, California. She has always been on the thin side throughout her life. She has also helped all her siblings and her nieces and nephews.

In summary, those individuals who are well-educated, and who are most diligent and creative, seem to be the happiest and healthiest, and thus live the longest.

This leads to the next important aspect of society which seems to point to longevity. This important aspect of society is religion. It has been recorded in the United States, that people who are religious tend to live longer than non-religious people. These individuals tend to be happier with what they have. They feel blessed with their needs being met. They reach out to others in their religious congregation on a daily basis, and try to give support, mostly moral and sometimes monetary. This kind of help enriches their own life, and they feel happier and thus stay healthier.

I would like to include here the life of a couple who are deeply religious and are in their mid-eighties. The next case I would like to discuss a couple in their mid-eighties. They come over to our house sometime early last year and trying to talk about Christianity and wanting us to come to their Jehovah Witness Church. We indicated to them that we are not very religious. But something about their desire to go out every day, and try to help people with their problems, struck a chord with me. So I decided to interview them over the course of their visits to our house. Their names our David and Ruth McCaslin. They are both devoted to each other. Ruth talked about how hard her life was during the 1945-1948. There was rationing because of the Second World War. So that period of her life was very hard. David, on the other hand, had a very good childhood. They did not have any rationing of food. David lived on a farm, and they could run around the farm. They met in Seattle, Washington, and were married in 1956. David wanted to be a baker, and got into management. After marriage, both of them moved to Los Angeles in 1960. They are both very spiritual. David wanted to get away from bigotry that existed during that time all over United States. Their two sons are both pastors. They live a very simple life. But both of them are very committed to helping people in need. They both tried to get along with others all throughout their lives. They do not argue about things for the most part. Ruth's mother developed Alzheimer's as she got old. Her mother died at 88 years. Both David and Ruth stay very busy, by going out every day. They are very particular about what they eat, and avoid sugars in their diet. David's father passed away at 72, while his mother lived to be 92. David told me that his father was always very angry. Maybe that is why his father died of a stroke. So lifestyle does sometimes affect you in a negative way.

What I got from interviewing both David and Ruth McCaslin, that because of their spirituality, they can help people. They go to homes where people are dying, to give comfort to the family members. This is not easy to do for anyone. Both David and Ruth have had lifelong friends, who they have stayed in touch all throughout their married life. They stay in touch with their kids, which is important.

In the book, 'The Longevity Project', religious women tend to live longer. According to the long-term study done by Stanford Psychologist Terman (Terman IQ Test), in childhood, these women were more prudent, generous, and unselfish than the typical child. When they were teenagers, their parents described them to be full of tenderness and sympathy and having affectionate relations with their families. They grew up happier, although somewhat more likely to conform to the authority of others, less likely to smoke, abuse alcohol, or take illegal drugs. More importantly, in addition to being religious, these women tended to be socially involved and outgoing. Interestingly enough, men religiosity did not matter much to men, in their behavior patterns, and did not play a big part to their longevity.

Although, religion played a relatively minor role on men's longevity, their social interactions, on the other hand, played a much bigger role in predicting their longevity. Men who had friends and met up frequently, lived a relatively long life, whether they were married or not. Thus, it seems social connectedness is the key to longevity, for both men and women. In the book 'The Longevity Project', Terman discovered that the people who lived long were the ones who were persistent, prudent and having a desire to help others. That is what kept them on a path to good health, even when faced with adversity or depression. It was this characteristic to stay socially interactive, that played a key role to their longevity.

Paffenbarger et al., (1993) studied the lifestyles of Harvard College men and their mortality based on their lifestyles. Two sets of questionnaires were sent to a large group of Harvard College graduates in 1962 or 1966 and again in 1977. The threshold age was 85, after which the subjects were dropped from the study.

The main conclusions of this long term study was that the men who maintained a steady exercise regimen i.e. walking, maintained a steady BMI (Body Mass Index) between 24-25, had a normal systolic blood pressure 130 mm or less, and who did not smoke had significantly less probability of dying at a younger age. Coincidentally, those men who replied if any one or both parents died before age 65, there was not a significant probability of dying young from this genetic trait. This study does prove that lifestyle changes play a much more significant role in extending one's life than genetics alone.

This is for all of us who think that physical activity is not important in a person's longevity. I will mention one person, who's parents did not live to be very old, yet she has survived to age 96. Although she has dementia now and is living in an assisted living facility. Her name is Mrs. Florence Zengler, and is still quite attractive. She had been active into her late 80s, when she had a minor stroke while playing tennis. It was after this stroke that she started to slow down. She played tennis regularly. She did pottery as a hobby. I am friends with her son Victor Zengler from college. She always made me stay for lunch when I was visiting Victor at their house, throughout my college days and even years later. I had interviewed her not too long back, about her lifestyle all throughout her younger days and then middle and later years. She described them as very active. She worked well into her early 70's when she retired as a radiology tech in a doctor's office. She has outlived both her parents by a number of years. She has outlived her two sisters by well over 20 years. In the interview she indicated that she used to eat out quite often, both when she was working and as a family, they ate out quite often.

Nir Barzilai, Director of the Institute for Aging Research at Albert Einstein College of Medicine in New York city, believes the answer to longevity lies in mutations of genes associated with longevity that are two or three times more common among centenarians than in people who don't live so long. Scientists estimate that up to a third of longevity is determined by genetic variations and two-thirds by environment and lifestyle.

Life expectancy throughout the world has increased in the twentieth century, and some researchers believe that humans can live to be around 114 years, by the end of this century. However, not all researchers believe that life expectancy will continue to increase indefinitely. Public Health researcher, Prof. S Jay Olshansky, at the University of Illinois Chicago, believe's that life expectancy will reach a plateau. In 2005, in a study published in 'The New England Journal of Medicine,' Olshansky predicted that life expectancy might actually go down in the future because of long-term effects of childhood obesity. Already more than 60% of adults in the United States are overweight or obese. "Those who forecast indefinite increases in life expectancy close their eyes in the living population, they look at historical trends", says Olshansky. Incidentally, Prof Olshansky, is working on a face aging project, that can predict how a person ages, and how long one will live. But another researcher at the Max Planck Institute, demographer Vaupal predicts life expectancy will continue to rise indefinitely at about three month's per year. "The future is going to be turbulent, but the past was also turbulent," he says. "In the 20th century we had a smoking epidemic that killed a lot of people, many more than obesity will. Nonetheless, life expectancy went up a lot."

Meanwhile, Stanford University's Bortz, and others are working to persuade insurance companies to offer incentives to their customers to adopt lifestyles that would bring many more years of good health to older people.

Finally, this chapter would be incomplete without referencing the age old question related to the 'battle of the sexes', as it relates to who came first. According to the research done by scientist Peter Underhill and colleagues at Stanford University, it has been established that the first humans were in fact women. The X chromosome has stayed unchanged throughout generations. It is only the Y chromosome that has shown mutations over generations and continues to evolve. The male and female genitalia have evolved from the same sexual tubercle, at the embryo stage. The reason the penis developed at all is the need for testosterone in human beings to make things happen, one of which is human reproduction. There is no wonder that the first woman can be traced back to 143,000 years ago, while the first man can be traced back to 59,000 years ago. There is the age-old hypothesis that women feel inside out, while men think outside in. Women's body is indeed more complex, and more sensitive than men. But there are things that women are not as adept as men are, i.e. hunting, building. So, it seems quite natural that women's chromosome underwent some changes to accommodate for the Y chromosome due to some genetic mutation, which gave way to the male XY chromosome. It is possible, that once the male female copulation started, the female reproductive cycle could only give birth by this copulation process. There are some species of vertebrates, i.e. Komodo Dragon, Hammerhead Sharks, Blacktip Sharks, Whiptail Lizards, Frogs and Salamanders, where the female can give birth without the male counterpart being present. Researchers have shown, it is because of resistance to diseases over centuries, that the process of mitosis (sexual reproduction) evolved and replaced meiosis (asexual reproduction). Women, for the most part stay attached to their children, far more than men. This could be partly explained by the evolutionary process of men moving around, and not being attached to anyone, versus women, who carry their kids to full term delivery. For women, it is akin to something that they have created inside their bodies. They show more empathy for their offspring, compared to men, who tend to discipline them more often. Breast feed their young, while men have nipples that cannot lactate. This is another rudimentary biological reminder that women indeed evolved before men. It may be, that men evolved to perform certain tasks, in each time period. Men get ready much faster and can finish a task more or less in a given time period. They are not so good about nurturing nature. Women are more inclined to work in a group setting versus working solo, which is indicative of a nurturing nature.

The population increased exponentially over time since human population is first recorded, goes to show how polygamy was quite prevalent in the Neolithic society, as the males of the predominant tribes would get to mate with the females of the subjugated tribes. The male or female sex determination is a complex chemical process, beyond the humans mating practices. Sometimes, couples have a string of boys or girls, before they have a child of the opposite sex. Men and women will continue to be different, because they evolved quite differently, and for quite different purpose. Women seem to have a higher degree of survival instinct than men. It is no wonder, that they outlive men in most parts of the world. The average life expectancy around the world shows that men live less than women, by six to seven years. Nevertheless, life should be lived well. There is no way of guaranteeing heaven. Lifespan can be roughly compared to a river flow. When it starts out, it wants to just run, much like our childhood. As it reaches the mid flow, it starts to meander around obstacles, much like our middle age, where we try to avoid confrontations, and settle for compromise. As the river reaches the delta, it slows down and gently flows and joins the sea. The sea comes in at high tide, and then receding back. This is what happens to us in old age. We cannot seem to move quickly and are slow in our reaction. And just as the tide coming and then receding, we have our good days (incoming tide), and not so good days (receding tide). If we could somehow extend each phase of our life, we could last longer, give back longer, and like the sea, could feel better by going to shore with more regularity. There are quite a few scientific researchers, working on increasing lifespan. People living in this century might be able to see lifespan increases in big leaps with gene research, supplements and mind body study. This, in turn, will enhance our abilities, and use of these abilities to bring happiness to others, and help foster other abilities to improve mankind. We can't just give up. That would mean we are quitting just because there is nothing more to discover. Mankind has developed in spurts, followed by complacency. The age of discovery happened because some humans ventured further than before, and discovered a new place, or a new way to curing disease or a problem. They were not complacent and tried hard to find a solution to the problem for survival of mankind. The age of inventions and modernization happened because we were curious why certain things could be done faster and simpler. There was a critical mass of people, who need things to live. And along came a few individuals from all walks of life to find a solution. Most were working in factories or home labs, and just stumbling upon things either by doing experiments, or improving some factory process, where they worked. So, there is this notion of discovering by association. So, no one never knows why certain things are better than others. But it is only because one tries, can one know.

Longevity is the single greatest test of patience. You learn to compensate for strength, looks, eyesight, hearing and recall. One can tell meeting a person, how passionate they are about life. You can tell, whether they still want to do for others, just by talking to them. When we become grandparents, we will do for our grandkids more than we did for our kids. We want to compensate for our discipline for love. This is classic compensation.

Late bloomers, sometimes live long. One could have a propensity for art, music, writing or doing any group activity i.e. travelling, hiking, dancing, gardening or cooking.

Women who have children in their 40's, tend to live long too. They have this innate ability to overcome age related problems of getting pregnant. Stubborn people also tend to live long. They have this ability to do things in a very set pattern. They eat at a certain time, sleep at a certain time. They buy only things that they like, and they will wait until they get what they want. So, these people have a tremendous patience. This somehow gives them the extra ability to build up a resistance in their system, to stave of mortality for a long time, and live long. Robert Engelman, Executive Director of Worldwatch Institute, an environmental research organization based in Washington, says that generally, living longer translates into later childbearing, which has a good effect. "When you raise the average age of childbearing, you slow down population growth even if women have as many children," he explains, "because you are slowing down successions of generations." Moreover, scientific evidence suggests that the same genes that likely allow centenarians to live so long also may protect their health. If researchers can mimic those genetic mutations in others, better health might result. "If you look at real data from CDC [Centers for Disease Control and Prevention], the medical costs in the last two years of life for people who die when they are 100 are about one-third of those who die in their 70's,"says Albert Einstein's College of Medicine's Barzilai. "Not only do they live longer, their medical costs were less". Now, wouldn't it be nice, if somehow we could all pass on without incurring a lot of medical bills, so much so, that our children have to mortgage our own homes that we worked all our lives to pay off.

Dan Buettner, the author of *The Blue Zones*, identifies nine behaviors that he believes contribute to healthy longevity:

- Incorporate movement into your everyday routine;
- Eat about 80% of your normal diet;
- Limit meat and processed foods;
- Regularly have a drink or two of wine or beer;
- Have a sense of purpose;
- Make time for relaxation and socialization;
- Join a spiritual community; and
- Make family a priority and surround yourself with others who share these behaviors

A paper by Dr. Kawas MD, at the American Association for the Advancement of Science Annual Conference in Austin, TX, give other tell-tale signs of what people who live to be 90+ seem to have in common.

The following are some of the habits of people who live long seem to share:

- Subjects who drank about two glasses of beer or wine a day, were 18% less likely to experience a premature death than those who abstained from alcohol.
- Participants who were slightly overweight, but not obese, cut their odds of dying early by 3%, compared to subjects who were normal or underweight.
- Subjects who kept busy with a daily hobby two hours a day were 21% less likely to die early, while those who drank two cups of coffee a day cut that risk by 10% compared to non-coffee drinkers.
- Subjects who exercised 15-45 min. a day cut the risk of premature death by 11%

Other research suggests that drinking plenty of water can increase longevity. The minimum daily water consumption should be 1/2 the body weight in ounces. So a 160 lb person should drink 10 glasses of water (1 glass = 8 oz). Half the body weight = 80lbs. So 80lbs/8oz/glass = 10 glasses of water a day.

The final bit of good news for all of us is the recent research conducted by Dr Sinclair at Harvard Medical School, on reversing aging at any age. In a recent study in the Journal CELL, Sinclair and his team at Harvard Medical School's Center for the Biology of Aging boosted NAD (Nicotinamide

Adenosine Dinucleotide) levels in the blood vessels of old mice. The old blood vessels are young again. These same old mice, and even the young mice, can run up to 50%, sometimes two times as far on a treadmill without getting tired. Human trials have been underway in Boston. A dietary supplement, Basis is available for humans. It was developed by Elysium Health, a company co-founded by Dr. Leonard Guarante, Director of the Glenn Center for Biology of Aging Research at Massachusetts Institute of Technology. "Over two months of the trial, NAD levels went up in people who were taking Basis. They went up higher in people who were taking double dose of Basis, and they stayed elevated for the duration", according to Dr Guarante. So, there is finally hope to enjoy the elixir of youth for a long time.

All of us in our lives get attached to something or someone and tend to make these things or individuals their favorites. This form of attachment is a sub conscious trait that makes us want to have and keep what we cherish. So, we all have this desire for long term attachments, and thus want to live as long as possible. I do not subscribe to try and be good to all people around you. There will be individuals who do not like you for no apparent reason. They may have had a bad experience with someone who was similar to you in their past, that may make them more prone to not liking you. You just have to leave these people alone. There are other people in your life who will give you more happiness. Just live for those people. They will bring far more happiness in your life.

When there is longing, there is belonging, and vice versa. Pyramids belong in Egypt, so people go to see them. Stonehenge belong in England, so people go to see them. Similarly, people pass on heirlooms, because they want these heirlooms to last as long as possible. Ultimately, longevity is a feeling, which gives one greater satisfaction, for having outlasted many historical events. Preservation is in our DNA. That is our only connection to our past. Staying young at heart is what we all want. Women's intuition is generally correct. So women should not be underestimated. They are more detail oriented. Therefore, they have evolved earlier. There is truth to beauty and aesthetics. All this took time. So there may have been a period in evolution, when only women were there, albeit for a short time, before men came about. Women cannot live without men, as they say!

Every day is a brand new day. The planet Earth is zipping through space at such a fast speed, that any date in the future cannot coincide exactly with the same date the previous year, or the next year. We all have to find a purpose in life, free of strife. The biggest strife of all is War. War is one factor in human history that has brought nothing but unnecessary death and destruction. If somehow, the leaders of all the countries could somehow not talk of war as tool to solve any economic, social or territorial issue, then people will not think negatively of each other. As the resources in the world are dwindling, and as different species of animals are fast disappearing, it falls on us humans, to stop wars, and look for a better way to improve mankind for the future generations. When other beings from outer space, can be so far more advanced, that they can do inter stellar travels, then surely we can learn something from them. The only way to advance is to live in peace as long as possible.

One reason to live longer, is to see how advances in Medicine can help you heal faster and better. There has been recent advances in wound healing being conducted at Harvard Medical University. A team of researchers, led by Kit Parker, have been able to create a bandage made from Fibronectin, a naturally occurring substance found in fetal skin. So they have been able to harvest Fibronectin from stem cells of fetuses, and then spin it into a fibers to make bandage. Parker and his team of researchers, including Christopher Chantre, have successfully applied these dressings made of Fibronectin to wounds in mice. The wounds healed with very little scarring. And they healed a lot faster. The wounds treated with Fibronectin closed at around 11 days, while the control group closed around 14 days. The most significant part of the wound healing was, the treated skin was similar to healthy skin. It even contained hair follicle, which are not found in scar tissue. The team reported their findings in the Journal Biomaterials, in March 2018. In a second study, published in the Journal Advanced Healthcare Materials recently, researchers from Parker's lab showed that another type of nanofiber could also help wounds heal faster. This nanofiber is made of cellulose and soy protein, according to Seungkuk Ahn, another team leader involved with the skin regeneration project. "The soy based dressing does not decrease scarring as effectively as Fibronectin dressing", says Ahn. But the soy based dressing is far easier and less expensive to make, and could be more suitable for very large wounds, ie burn wounds. "The new wound dressings are an advance", says Parker. This is a far cry from Parker's days working as an Army Civil Affairs officer in Afghanistan during the Afghan crisis in the early 2000's. Kit Parker was unable to save a 5 year old boy who died of extensive burn wounds on his body in a hospital in Kandahar, Afghanistan, in 2003. This is what made him redouble his efforts when he returned to Harvard after his stint was over in Afghanistan, to try and find a dressing that could save not only burn victims, but other surgery patients with wound healing.

The theory of UFO's visiting our Earth goes to show how our curiosity seems to give credence to a magic show. The mere fact that other civilizations exist, is intriguing in itself. The fact that these UFO's are being sighted all the time on Earth, as they come and then disappear, is nothing short of a magic show, which all of us have witnessed at some point in our lives. The concept of instant millionaire status, whether by winning the Lottery, or winning at a Casino, gives everyone a sense of elation. This magical choice gives everyone hope. Hope is what keeps mankind forward looking, and outward reaching. To visit other planets, beyond what we can see, is all in the hope of preserving ourselves for years to come, in case Earth becomes unsustainable for mankind.

But like everything, every show must come to an end. We are visitors on this planet. We experience what we can, before we need to disappear like a magic trick.

Research has shown, that the happiest countries here on Earth are the Scandinavian countries, year after year. This is because they live in more compact houses, have fewer belongings, and thus a better quality of life. Ultimately, happiness is what we are all looking for in this life, and happiness is achievable at the cost of cooperation, and some sacrifice of concern and discipline.

One often hears older people advising youngsters to be more patient. Situations change over time for the better. Just like 'Time and Tide Wait for None', so too 'Time and Tide Waste for None'. According to author Till Roenneberg, in his book *Internal Time*, starting school later, is a good idea, if everyone i.e. the administrators, parents and teachers agreed. Better understanding of the subject matter would mean better future for the students. This in turn would mean longer lifespan and less stress on these students later on in life. Stressful life, can cut short a life by a good many years. Not knowing how to plan one's future, can lead to a lot of stress on an individual, early in their formative high school years. Roenneberg points out that doctors and teachers by nature, are early chronotypes. They start their day earlier than most people. Thus, the type of chronotype one is, determines what profession one chooses. In 2017, the Nobel Prize in Physiology and Medicine, was awarded to Jeffrey C. Hall, Michael Rosbash and Michael W. Young, who have studied internal time clock gene that determines an individual's behavior pattern, and ultimately the lifespan. Ultimately, longevity depends on how you feel, how thankful you are, and how much you let go. It can be summed up in a simple equation. Longevity is a function of Attitude, Gratitude and Lattitude (Adapt)

Longevity = A* Attitude + B* Gratitude + C* Lattitude, where A, B, C are Factors of Safety variables. If you substitute 1.5 or 2 for any of these variables, A, B or C, it will add years to your life. If you have a good attitude, gratitude and lattitude, then you can be a good motivator. This is the best combination. If you have a bad attitude, no gratitude and no lattitude, then you are a sore loser. And if you have average attitude, gratitude and lattitude, then you will be a follower. So, it all depends, which of these three categories you fall under. All the ailments one gets, are as much a function of all three of these characteristics. If you are too stressed, then change your attitude. If you are too impatient, then change your lattitude. And if you take things for granted, have more gratitude. Gratitude is like 'Lady Luck'. Luck has a big part in Longevity.

I would like to end this chapter with a small poem I wrote on what a good life should be:

Live Life Just As Well
There are looks that define you,
Then there are looks that defy you,
You can tell, both looks will last long,
Both have the will, to just pull strong

Some have in their eyes and ears,
Others with long faces are seers,
Some wear it on their forehead,
And all perfect faces, stay way ahead

We all just come, we all want to be,
We all just wish, so much to see,
But few survive, the sands of time,
Those who do, know how to rhyme

They say there is one, who gives life,
They also say, that one brings strife,
Why can't we all, our beloved God,
Live out long, if you just give the nod

We should all, just live life as well,
Don't think too much, don't try to dwell,
Just try to do, and get as much done,
And try to give, and have more fun

Some Memorable Photos of Memorable People

Vrinda Knapp (b 1924 -) 94+ yrs	Florence Zengler (b 1922 -) 96+ yrs

Ruth & David McCaslin (b 1936 -) 83+yrs

Acknowledgements: I would not have been able to finish this chapter without the invaluable help of me wife, Manjari Dutt Rana. She helped in researching the photographs, and arranging them for this chapter.

References

Batmanghelidj, F., & Page, M. J. (2012). *Your body's many cries for water.* Tantor Audio. Available at: http://www.cci-coral-club.okis.ru/file/cci-coral club/knigi/FereydoonBatmanghelidj_Your_Bodys_Many_Cries_for_Water_eng.pdf,

Buettner, D. (2012). *The blue zones: 9 lessons for living longer from the people who've lived the longest.* National Geographic Books.

Friedman, H. S., & Martin, L. R. (2011). *The longevity project: surprising discoveries for health and long life from the landmark eight decade study.* Hay House, Inc.

Henderson, J. & M. Anglin, J. (2003). Facial attractiveness predicts longevity. *Evolution and Human Behavior. 24.* 351-356. 10.1016/S1090-5138(03)00036-9.

Paffenbarger Jr, R. S., Hyde, R. T., Wing, A. L., Lee, I. M., Jung, D. L., & Kampert, J. B. (1993). The association of changes in physical-activity level and other lifestyle characteristics with mortality among men. *New England Journal of Medicine, 328*(8), 538-545.

Roenneberg, T. (2012). *Internal time: Chronotypes, social jet lag, and why you're so tired.* Harvard University Press.

The Quality Adjusted Life Years (QALY)

Chandra Putcha and Brian W. Sloboda

The [QALY] evolved from being a concept intelligible to and supported by only a small handful of economists, to being part of the day-to-day language of most health managers and policy makers and many clinicians. (Smee, 2005: 91-92)

Introduction

Several approaches to valuing changes in health and mortality risks have been developed to determine the net effect of a policy on health is positive or negative. Consequently, these measures often aggregate disparate health risks, which may be fatal or nonfatal, cause cancer or other disease, and vary by other characteristics.

The most prominent of these measures are the "quality adjusted life year" (QALY) and "willingness to pay" (WTP). QALYs are used in the medical and public-health fields, and the WTP is widely used in evaluating environmental and transportation-related risks.

The approaches of QALY and WTP share similarities because these two approaches represent the preferences of individuals and aggregated across individuals to represent the social value of a change in health and safety risks. However, the specific assumptions underlying these approaches differ that produce systematic differences in the relative values of changes in risks. As such, these differences may lead to different conclusions about whether a policy increases or decreases aggregate the health and safety risk.

The aim of this chapter is to review the concept of the QALY, which is a widely used measure of health improvement that is used to guide health-care resource allocation decisions. QALY was first used in 1976 by Zeckhauser & Shepard to indicate a health outcome measurement unit that combines length and quality of life (Zeckhauser & Shepard, 1976). The QALY was originally developed as a measure of health effectiveness for cost-effectiveness analysis, a method intended to aid decision-makers charged with allocating scarce resources across competing health-care programs or as a "health status index "(Fansel and Bush, 1970; Torrance, Thomas, & Sackett, 1972; Weinstein & Stason, 1977). In fact, an earlier study of the treatment of chronic renal disease and used a subjective adjustment for quality of life (Klarman et al. 1968). More specifically, the purpose of this paper is not to be prescriptive about how to use and what approaches of QALY should be used, but we leave it for others to make their judgements about the normative significance based on the content of the literature.

The chapter is organized as follows. Section 2 reviews the concept of willingness to pay (WTP). Section 3 delves into the QALY by examining the implications for valuing current mortality risk and aggregating values of mortality-risk changes across individuals under QALY. Section 4 provides some empirical issues arising in the estimation of QALYs. Section 5 concludes the chapter.

Willingness to Pay (WTP)

Willingness to Pay

When doing cost-benefit analysis, many government agencies often developed estimates of the benefits of avoided injuries and fatalities based on the economic concept of the willingness-to-pay (WTP) to avoid a marginal increase in the risk of a fatality or injury. The WTP approach assigns a value to the risk reduction that is used to estimate what risk reduction is worth to individuals who will benefit from the prevention of illness or injury. In principle, the value of avoided injury should be measured by what an individual is willing to pay to avoid it. Individuals would be willing to accept a small level of risk for some finite benefit. For example, an individual would be willing to watch a movie in a crowded with the risk of catching some contagious disease. That is, the individual would suffer from harm and later regret the decision. WTP does not capture the realized damages to the individual from their decision or capture the *ex post* valuation of the change in the individual's health. The latter would describe the cost of illness (COI) which will not be delved in this chapter. The WTP is appropriate for the evaluation of the health and injuries that could strike with some degree of randomness meaning that we do not know which workers will receive the injury or illness and the amount of the benefits that they will receive. In sum, the willingness to pay (WTP) refers to the maximum amount an individual is willing to pay to acquire a benefit. It is measured as the reduction in income required returning an individual to the level of utility, he or she enjoyed prior to receiving the benefit.

Schelling (1966) provided a general approach in the valuation of risks to life. He further acknowledged that the individual is the best determinant for the status for what should be done to prevent injuries and illnesses. In the monetizing of the benefits, the WTP is considered the appropriate measure of the economic benefits to reduce the risk of a health effect and the effect of injuries.

Viscusi & Aldy (2003) examined 40 studies using the WTP estimates of injury risk premiums derived from wage differential analyses. The selected studies examined the nonfatal job risks based on the injury rate, the rate of injuries to result in a loss of a workday, and the total lost workdays. In contrast to the estimates by the cost of injury and quality of life, the WTP estimates do not distinguish costs for injuries of different severities. Across these studies the value of injury ranged from approximately $20,000 to $70,000 (measured in 2000 dollars).

Disadvantages for Using the Willingness to Pay

Despite the use of the WTP methods, the WTP methods suffer from two serious measurement biases that may not provide satisfactory decision-making outcomes. First, WTP responses tend to be undersensitive to the magnitude of the benefits (Bateman et al, 1997, Baron et al, 1996, and Kahneman et al 1992). This includes both 'scope effects', involving different quantities of the same good, and 'nesting effects', involving one good incorporated within a larger bundle of goods. Scope effects are particularly strong in relation to health risks. Using high quality contingent valuation survey designs, and rigorous experimental methods, researchers have found that respondents tend to state a similar amount approximately $50 for any given magnitude of reduction in the risk of death or injury (Beattie et al, 1998).

The second reason is that the WTP methods tend to inflate valuations of the specific intervention that respondents are asked about, relative to interventions that respondents are not asked about (Kemp and Maxwell, 1993). In other words, when respondents are asked about an intervention in isolation, they are willing to pay sums of money far in excess of what they are willing to pay when asked to consider the same intervention in relation to a range of other interventions. Consequently, they may be unable to budget simultaneously for the entire range of possible public and private goods and services they require. So, valuing each item in isolation can lead to sum totals of WTP in excess of the available budget.

Given the measurement problems in the WTP, these WTP approaches tend to be biased in favor of (1) interventions that deliver smaller benefits, and (2) the intervention being evaluated, as opposed to other ones not being evaluated. Given the latter, these are serious flaws to healthcare policy-makers, where the majority of the economic evaluation is the examination of the reimbursement decisions about costly new technologies and diseases (Cookson, 2003).

Quality Adjusted Life Year (QALY)

Historical Background of QALY

The earliest work on the QALY was by Klarman, Francis & Rosenthal (1968) in which they calculated what they termed "quality-adjusted life expectancy" based on quality adjustment weights. They referred to this earliest measure as the quality of life. Subsequently, an influential article by Weinstein and Stason (1977) connected QALYs with utilities, specifically expected utility, rather than the "weights" of the earlier literature. Weinstein and Stason formally recognized the framework of QALY. Why was the concept of QALY introduced? There are several reasons for the introduction of the QALY:

- What is the most cost-effective treatment for a patient?
- Which patient should be treated?
- Context in the 1970s of crisis:
  - o Scarce resources vs growing demand for health
  - o More efficient allocation
  - o Economics becomes part of decision-making

Valuing the Life Years: The Concept of a QALY

The QALY combines "the effects of health interventions on mortality and morbidity into a single index," that enables a common value to make comparisons across disease. Over the life cycle of an individual, they experience different health states, in which each of the health states are weighted according to the utility scores elucidated from the individuals are collected for each diseases and injury. The idea of combining the survival of the individual from the disease or an injury combined with the utilities is illustrated in Figure 1. Figure 1 illustrates that the QALYs that can be gained by an individual from receiving treatment as opposed to receiving no treatment. The area under each curve measures the total value of QALY. The lower curve shows the health profile if the individual receives no treatment. Thus, the value of the utility decreases over time until death (Death A). The higher curve shows the individual receiving the treatments and achieve a higher utility and living longer until death (die at Death B). Hence, the total area between the two curves indicates the number of QALYs gained by the treatment.

Figure 1: QALYs Gained from Treatment.

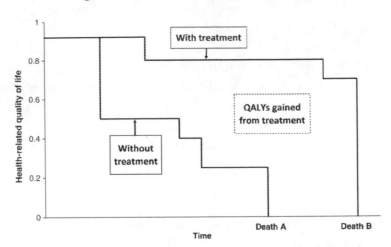

Source: From: Health outcomes in economic evaluation: the QALY and utilities *British Medical Bulletin.* 2010, 96(1), 5-21 (Published with permission)

Introduction to the Analytical Framework of QALY

There are many instruments that are readily available to measure the quality of life (QoL): the Short Form Health Survey (SF-36) developed by Ware, Snow, Kosinski, & Gandek (1993) and the Sickness Impact Profile by Gibson et al. (1975). Some QOL instruments are often developed for particular medical aliments: the Arthritis Impact Measurement Scale by Meenan, Gertman, & Mason (1980) and the Asthma Quality of Life Questionnaire by Juniper, Guyatt, Ferrie, & Griffith (1993). Furthermore, some QOL instruments are based on the symptom states scales: Faces Pain Scale (Wong & Baker, 1988), the Fatigue Scale (Chadler et al., 1993), and the Functional Independence Measures Scale (Keith, Grainger, Hamilton, & Sherwin, 1987). Each of these instruments can be combined with global QOL measures and health-related quality of life measures to capture emotional, social, and physical well-being, along with the effect a certain disease process has on the totality of a life.

Each of these instruments mentioned allow the research to describe or quantify the quality of life, but these are not measured in economic terms. Researchers may often be interested to quantify the quality of life in economic terms, and QALY is that measurement that combines quantity and quality to calculate outcomes based on treatment or other activities that influence health. QALY has three major components that support validity and reliability of this measure. First, actuarial data, experimental data, or modeling is used to study a given population. Secondly, healthy life years are weighted the same; and lastly, the weights for health states are derived from studies of individuals with the specific condition in question. The difference between QALY and QOL measures is the dynamic of measurement. QALY attempts to provide a method of measurement for the impact of disease or treatment on an individual's ability to function which can be equated to an economic scale. QALY measures differ from the QOL measures that provide subjective information describing individuals' self-perception of their health status at a point in time (Graham, 2003). The QALY measure describes the cost of producing one year of quality living existence. The scoring range of QALY is from 0 (death) to 1 (perfect health).

Like any economic model, there are underlying assumptions that are part of the model. These underlying assumptions for QALY are elucidated by Pliskin et al. (1980). They demonstrated that the QALY maximization criterion is justified in a multi-attribute utility theory framework under the following conditions: utility independence between life years and health status; constant proportional trade-off; and risk neutrality on life years. These conditions and the utility theory foundations of QALYs were further discussed in several contributions, including those of Myamoto & Eraker (1985), Loomes & McKenzie (1989), Mehrez & Gafni (1989). An extensive review published in 1992 counted 51 economic evaluations using QALYs as the outcome measure (Gerard 1992). Only a few years later the QALY framework was widely accepted as the reference standard in cost-effectiveness analysis (Gold et al. 1996; McPake et al. 2002; Drummond et al. 2005), amid a continuing debate on its theoretical underpinnings and practical implications (e.g. Bleichrodt & Johannesson 1996). Today, QALYs are used in most economic evaluations, and by many regulatory agencies which have made cost-effectiveness analysis an integral part of their decision-making processes.

With no uncertainty, no temporal discounting, and no changes in health over time, the value of a health gain from treatment for an individual, $QALY_G$, is

$$QALY_G = T_1 Q_1 - T_0 Q_0 \qquad (1)$$

where T is the number of years of survival, Q represents health state values, and the subscripts 1 and 0 represent health with and without treatment, respectively.

Modifying (1) by introducing uncertainty and temporal discounting, and assuming discrete time so changes in health occur only when moving from one period to the next, the QALY becomes

$$QALY_G = \sum_h \sum_t p_{1ht} Q_{ht} - \sum_h \sum_t p_{0ht} Q_{ht} \qquad (2)$$

where P_{1ht} and P_{0ht} represent the probabilities of an individual finding himself in health state h in time period t with and without treatment, respectively. Q_{ht} is the value of health at time t (the subscript t allows for the temporal discounting of each state of health via a discount rate). A practical calculation of the QALY using patient level data is

$$QALY = \sum_{t=0}^{n} \left[\frac{(Q_1 + Q_{t+1})}{2} * \frac{(T_{t+1} - T_t)}{T} \right] \tag{3}$$

where, n is the number of utility measurements over a period of time such as one year, Q_t is the individual utility value obtained in the tth measurement, T is the total length of time expressed as the total number of time units in a year, and T_t is the time period in which the tth measurement takes place, again expressed as number of time units in a year.

A QALY is an expression of the value to an individual associated with a given intervention. If the quality of life associated with 'full health' were to be assigned a value of 1, then the QALY could be expressed in health gains as measured in 'objective physical units' i.e. life years. Any state of health less than this is adjusted for its quality and would be assigned a lower value. Against a background based on expected utility theory, Pliskin, et al (1980) set out a set of sufficient assumptions for this model to represent individual utility over health states and duration as mentioned earlier in the chapter.

How Does the QALY Relate to the Cost-Effective Analysis (CEA) and Cost-Benefit Analysis (CBA)

In the health economics literature, some have suggested that QALYs are intended to measure health without considering the value of its uses and the distinctions between CEA and CBA go beyond whether an explicit dollar value is assigned to health outcomes (Weinstein, 1999). A decision makers' willingness to pay (WTP) for a QALY depends on the decision context, making it unlikely that a unique threshold value per QALY to determine whether interventions are cost-effectiveness exists. As a remedy, Bleichrodt & Quiggins (1999) established a set of sufficient conditions for the equivalence of CEA and CBA that enables the existence of plausible expressions for a WTP for a QALY. There is a void by the lack of what constitutes the appropriate decisions rule for the CEA that resulted in arbitrary standard. Some studies, e.g., Gyrd-Hansen et al.' and Whynes et al define an intervention or program as cost-effective if its cost-effectiveness ratio compares favorably with that of a specific intervention that has become widely accepted. For example, Gyrd-Hansen et al. (1998) and Whynes et al (1998) argue that colorectal cancer screening is cost-effective because it compares favorably with the breast cancer screening. Johannesson and Meltzer (1998) have posited any program can be made to be cost-effective by comparing it with some alternative as given by the latter example.

Because of the limitations in the estimation of the cost-effectiveness, a common approach is the use of the arbitrary, round-number thresholds, e.g., interventions costing less than $50,000 per QALY are often considered cost-effective (Lee et al., 1997 and Salzman, et al 1997). Laupacis et al. (1992) laid out a systematic scheme to determine the round number thresholds based on the previous literature. Their approach though systematic still appears to be rather arbitrary. Based on the previous literature, they conclude that evidence for adoption of an intervention is strong if the cost-effectiveness ratio is less than $20,000 per QALY, moderate if the ratio lies between $20,000 and $100,000, and weak if the ratio exceeds $100,000. As Weinstein (1995) points out these round-number thresholds established by Laupacis et al (1992) are the same thresholds suggested by Kaplan & Bush (1982).

Based on the arbitrariness in the past literature, Johannesson & Meltzer (1998) posited that more information about the willingness to pay (WTP) per QALY gained to establish a useful decision rule for cost-effectiveness analysis is important. As a remedy, they suggested to obtain an empirical basis for such a decision rule was to convert results from the value-of-life literature. Hirth et al (2000) applied the approach by Johannesson & Meltzer (1998) to derive the implied value of a QALY in each reviewed paper and to determine the range of QALY values that could be supported by the existing literature. To examine whether results were consistent across different methods that have been employed in the value-of-life literature and to determine whether data from studies of differing national origins can be pooled, they examined whether the variation in WTP per QALY across studies could be explained by the study method and by U.S. versus non-U.S. data sources.

There is no dearth of literature on the value-of-life. The main objective for the value of life is to provide a baseline for the estimate of the QALY and the upper and lower bounds of this estimate for use in sensitivity analysis. The primary methods to estimate the value of life includes the human capital (HC) approach, contingent valuation (CV), and the revealed preference (RP). The RP approach infers the value of life from the actual behaviors with respect to the willingness-to-pay to accept payment to face a risk. That is, riskier jobs will often command higher wages that provides an observable measure of how workers implicitly value their lives.

The value-of-life literature is not without its critics. That is, there are limitations to the use of the value-of-life. The human capital (HK) approach to valuing life has a long history dating back to the works of Petty (1699) and Farr (1876). The later research by Fein (1958), Mushkin & Collings (1959), Weisbrod (1965), and Klarman (1971) improved the practical applications of the human capital (HC) approach. The HC approach includes both market (paid) work and nonmarket (household and volunteer) work, which is typically valued using wage data. Unlike the contingent valuation (CV) and revealed preference (RP) approaches, the HC approach is not a measure of individual WTP. Thus, the HC estimates incorporate a zero value for persons without labor income, e.g., retired individuals with only investment or pension income. The HC approach focuses on the economic value as it is included in the national accounts, so the HC approach ignores the dimensions of illness and death as well as nonmarket activities that may be more important to an individual than economic loss. In addition, there is criticism for the use of pay as a measure of value. At the same time, valuing benefits in terms of pay neglects the health benefits that accrue to people who are not employed, e.g., non-working wives and retired people. Also, the use of pay ignores the non-financial costs of pain, suffering, and grief, which are often associated with illness and injuries. From an economist's perspective, the main criticism of the HC approach is that it is not based on an individual person's valuations of benefits. Indeed, a third-party view is taken about people's "worth" to society in terms of their productive potential. The latter viewpoint is not consistent among economists that the individuals are the best judge of their own welfare. The conceptual problem with the HC approach is the assigning of more weight to wealthy individuals, and the perception by individuals that use pre-tax income or after-tax income. In fact, those with riskier jobs, they are likely to willingly accept these jobs based on the reflection of after-tax income. Despite the conceptual problems associated with the HC approach, this approach is widely used because it is quite easy to obtain the data.

Because of the inadequacies associated with the HC approach, alternatives have been proposed. Contingent valuation (CV) provides a response to a direct question about how much one values a given product, safety measure etc. or their willingness-to-pay or their willingness-to-accept. Given the direct responses to the questions, it is quite easy with the CV to give rise to bias results. To ameliorate the biased results in a CV survey, the researchers need to devote a lot of time and effort to create a good survey that will generate the necessary results (Kling et al 2012 and Boardman et al, 2011). How the structure of the questionnaire is built up is important, especially how risk and uncertainty is presented. Kahneman & Tversky (1979) presented the concept of prospect theory in 1979. From their assessment, individuals are risk-seeking when it comes to avoiding losses and risk-averse for gains. Using the latter can explain some differences in the WTP from different studies since individuals may be willing to pay differently for health gain compared to avoid health losses.

Revealed preference theory is typically wage-risk studies (a.k.a. hedonic wage, compensating wage differentials) that examines the relationship between wages and risks across industries and occupations, controlling for other influencing factors.

Issues in the Estimation of QALY

Imbalance of the Estimates

The estimation of QALY can be rather straightforward. QALY is often not a single measure of health outcomes. That is, the patients often receive follow-up visits regarding patients' health states or direct utilities. The problem is that the follow-ups in the data regarding patients' health states or direct utilities are collected at discrete time points. In fact, there could large time intervals between the assessments with the patients. Consequently, the latter raises the issues how to handle these discrete changes in the measuring of quality of life. Billingham et al. (1999) discussed three general methods to handle discrete changes in patients' quality of life between assessments which could be used to handle changes in utility values: linear change, earlier level maintained and change at the midpoint of the two measures of QALY. Of the three approaches, the linear change is the most commonly used while no application of the other two methods exists in the literature. Despite the latter approaches to estimate QALY, patient-level QALYs are typically estimated using the area-under-the-curve (AUC) method as espoused by Matthews et al (1990), which is sums the areas of the geometrical areas obtained by linearly interpolating between utility scores provided by patients during a designated study period. The large time intervals between the assessments would lead to baseline utility imbalance and earlier estimates of these estimates would generally ignore these utility imbalances and proceed to estimate the QALY.

Hypothetical Example of the Utility Imbalances in QALYs

We present an example of the standard QALY calculation for two hypothetical patients receiving different treatments with a follow-up for nine months. During this nine month period, each patient provides three utility measurements: at baseline, six and nine months. Their utility values for each of these time periods 0.68, 0.68 and 0.75 for the standard treatment, and 0.58, 0.68 and 0.75 receiving the new intervention. Table 1 summarizes the utility values.

Table 1. Summary of Utility Values

	Standard Treatment	New Treatment
Baseline	0.68	0.58
Six Months	0.68	0.68
Nine Months	0.75	0.75

Assuming linear changes in utility values over time, the typical QALY calculation using the AUC approach using equation (3) would give 0.51875 (standard treatment) and 0.49375 (new treatment) QALY. Equations (4) and (5) shows the calculations of the $QALY_{standard\ treatment}$ and the $QALY_{new\ treatment}$.

$$QALY_{standard} = \left[\frac{(0.68+0.68)}{2} * \frac{6}{12}\right] + \left[\frac{(0.68+0.75)}{2} * \frac{3}{12}\right] = 0.51875 \qquad (4)$$

$$QALY_{new} = \left[\frac{(0.58+0.68)}{2} * \frac{6}{12}\right] + \left[\frac{(0.68+0.75)}{2} * \frac{3}{12}\right] = 0.49675 \qquad (5)$$

If the cost-effectiveness of the two interventions were being assessed on the basis only of these two patients, the differential in the QALYs would favor standard treatment (0.51875-0.49375=0.025) despite that the two patients only differ in terms of the utilities that were ascribed to their health states before they received the treatment. Because each of the patients will have baseline utilities the differences in the QALYs estimates would manifest itself when the QALYs for a treatment are averaged over a sample of patients that are randomized to a treatment group. That is, the imbalance in mean baseline utilities needs to be allowed in the calculation of the differential effects between these trial groups. Earlier empirical studies merely estimated the differential QALYs by subtracting the QALY$_{standard\ treatment}$ and the QALY$_{new\ treatment}$ calculated as shown in the previous hypothetical example. Consequently, these studies disregarded any baseline imbalance in mean utilities between treatment arms.

Patient-specific change in QALYs

The approach in the calculation of the QALYs in the preceding section essentially aggregated the utility estimates and estimated the QALYs which ignored the utility values by each patient. So equations (4) and (5) can be modified to incorporate the changes by patient. Equations (6) and (7) show the QALY estimates using the utility values from table 1.

$$QALY_{standard} = \left[\frac{(0.75-0.68)}{2} * \frac{3}{12}\right] = 0.00875 \qquad (6)$$

$$QALY_{new\ treatment} = \left[\frac{(0.68-0.58)}{2} * \frac{6}{12} + (0.68 - 0.58) * \frac{3}{12} + \frac{(0.75-0.68)}{2} * \frac{3}{12}\right] = 0.05 \qquad (7)$$

In other words, instead of using the absolute utility value at follow up to calculate an individual QALYs', Equations (6) and (7) uses the difference between baseline and follow-up utility rather than the absolute utility values as shown in equations (4) and (5). Put in another way, the treatment effect is obtained as the difference in the mean change in the QALYs in the alternative arms of the trial rather than the difference in mean absolute QALYs. The approach in the preceding section is flawed because it fails to control for baseline imbalances that occur. More specifically, those individuals with a lower (higher) utility than the mean will usually experience a higher (lower) improvement at the follow up. So the patient's future utility scores will be negatively correlated with their baseline value, which could be considered a strong predictor of future utilities and that impact the estimates of the QALYs. The subsequent section presents a remedy to correct these imbalances in utility values.

The Use of Regression as a Remedy to Correct Imbalances in Baseline Utility Values of QALY

The use of regression analysis would be the appropriate way to deal with the imbalance in mean baseline utilities. The use of the regression analysis allows for the estimation of the differential in QALYs as well as the prediction of adjusted QALYs, while controlling for baseline utility values. Equation (8) shows the regression

$$QALY_i = \beta_0 + \beta_1 * t_i + \beta_2 * Q_i^b \tag{8}$$

where the index i identifies the patient (i=1….N); t_i is a treatment dummy variable (0=control; 1= intervention), and Q_i^b is the patient-specific baseline utility value. β_1 represents the adjusted differential QALY after controlling for the imbalance in the mean utility at the baseline.

The use of the equation (8) generates an unbiased estimate of differential QALYs between the different periods of the trials, but the use of equation (8) also increases the precision of the treatment effect estimate (Vickers & Altman, 2001; Vickers, 2001). If equation (8) is not specified correctly to include $\beta_2 * Q_i^b$, will inflate the underlying error, which impacts the treatment effect as captured by β_1 as well as the sampling uncertainty surrounding the estimate.

Conclusion and Summary

The measures of "quality adjusted life year" (QALY) and "willingness to pay" (WTP) were presented in this chapter with WTP serving as the background leading to the discussion on QALYs. QALYs are used in the medical and public-health fields, and WTP is widely used in evaluating environmental and transportation-related risks. More important, the issues in the empirical estimation of the QALYs was presented, and two approaches were provided. Though both approaches seem legitimate, the first approach ignores the true utility values by the patients while the second approach clearly shows summarizing the mean utility values in each arm of the trial at the baseline and for each of the follow up periods. That is, the first approach did not control for the baseline utility in the differential QALY estimates. Controlling for baseline utility in the differential QALY estimates should be a good practice when evaluating the effectiveness of QALYs on patient care and in the assessment of their quality of life.

References

Baron J, & Greene J. (1996). Determinants of insensitivity to quantity on valuation of public goods: contribution, warm glow, budget constraints, availability and prominence. *Journal of Experimental Psychology, 2,* 106–125.

Bateman I, Munro A, Rhodes B, Starmer C, & Sugden R. (1997). Does part-whole bias exist? An experimental investigation. *Economic Journal,* 322–333.

Beattie J, Covey J, Dolan P, Hopkins L, Jones-Lee M, Loomes G, Pidgeon N, Robinson & Spencer A. (1998). On the contingent valuation of safety and the safety of contingent valuation: part 1-caveat investigator. *Journal of Risk and Uncertainty, 17*(1), 5–26.

Billingham L.J., Abrams K.R., & Jones D.R. (1999). Methods for the analysis of quality-of-life and survival data in health technology assessment. *Health Technology Assess, 3.* 1–152.

Bleichrodt H. & Quiggin, J. (1999). Life-cycle preferences over consumption and health when is cost-effectiveness analysis equivalent to cost-benefit analysis? *Journal of Health Economics, 18,* 681-708.

Boardman, A. Greenberg, D. Vining, A. & Weimer, D. (2011), *Cost-Benefit Analysis: Concepts and Practice* 4ᵗʰ Edition, Pearson Education Limited: United Kingdom.

Chadler, T., Berelowitz, G., Pawlikowska, T, Watts, L., Wessely, S., Wright, D, et al. (1993). Development of a fatigue scale. *Journal of Psychosomatic Research, 37,* 147-153.

Cookson, R. (2003). Willingness to pay methods in health care: a skeptical view. *Health economics, 12*(11), 891-894.

Gyrd-Hansen D, Soggaard J, & Kronborg O. (1998). Colorectal cancer screening. Efficiency and effectiveness. *Health Economics, 7,* 9-20.

Fanshel S. & Bush J.W. (1970). A health status index and its application to health services outcomes. *Operations Research, 18,* 1021–1066.

Gibson, B.S., Gibson, J.S., Bergner, M., Bobbitt, R.A., Kressel, S., Pollard, W.E., et al. (1975). The sickness impact profile: Development of an outcome measure of health care. *American Journal of Public Health, 65*, 1304-1310.

Graham, J. D. (2003). Cost-effectiveness analysis in health policy. *Value in Health, 6*(4), 417-419.

Hirth, R. A., Chernew, M. E., Miller, E., Fendrick, A. M., & Weissert, W. G. (2000). Willingness to pay for a quality-adjusted life year: in search of a standard. *Medical Decision-Making, 20*(3), 332-342.

Johannesson M, & Meltzer D. (1998). Some reflections on cost-effectiveness analysis. *Health Economics 7*, 1-7

Juniper, E.F., Guyatt, G.H., Ferrie, P.J., & Griffith, L.E. (1993). Measuring quality of life in asthma. *American Review of Respiratory Disease, 147*, 832-838.

Kahneman D, & Knetsch J.L. (1992). Valuing public goods: the purchase of moral satisfaction. *Journal of Environmental Economics and Management. 22*, 57–70.

Kahneman, D. and Tversky, A. (1979). Prospect theory: An analysis of decision under risk, *Econometrica, 47*(2), 263-291

Kaplan, R. M., & Bush, J. W. (1982). Health-related quality of life measurement for evaluation research and policy analysis. *Health Psychology, 1*(1), 61.

Keith, R.A., Grainger, C.V., Hamilton, B.B., & Sherwin, F.S. (1987). The functional independence measure: A new tool for rehabilitation. *Advances in Clinical Rehabilitation, 1*, 6-18.

Kemp M.A., & Maxwell C. (1993). Exploring a budget context for contingent valuation estimates. In Contingent Valuation: A Critical Assessment, Chapter 5. Hausman, JA (ed.) Cambridge Economics Inc: Cambridge MA, 217–265.

Klarman, H. E., & Rosenthal, G. D. (1968). Cost effectiveness analysis applied to the treatment of chronic renal disease. *Medical Care, 6*(1), 48-54.

Kling, C. Phaneuf, D. & Zhao, J, (2012). From Exxon to BP: Has some number become better than no number, *Journal of Economic Perspectives 4*(26), 3-26.

Lee, T.T., Solomon, N.A., Heidenreich P.A., Oehlert, J, & Garber, A.M. (1997). Cost-effectiveness of screening for carotid stenosis in asymptomatic persons. *Annual Internal Medicine, 126*, 337-46.

Matthews J.N.S, Altman D., & Campbell M.J. (1990). Analysis of serial measurements in medical research. *British Medical Journal, 300*, 230–235

Meenan, R.F., Gertman, P.M., & Mason, J.H. (1980). Measuring health status in arthritis. The arthritis impact measurement scales. *Arthritis Rheumatology, 23*, 146-152.

Pliskin J.S., Shepard D.S., & Weinstein M.C.. (1980). Utility functions for life years and health status. *Operations Research, 28*(1), 206-224.

Salzmann P, Kerlikowske K., & Phillips K. (1997). Cost-effectiveness of extending screening mammography guidelines to include women 40 to 49 years of age. *Annual Internal Medicine. 127*, 955- 965

Schelling, T.C., (1966). The life you save may be your own. *Problems in Public Expenditure Analysis* edited by Samuel Chase. Washington, DC: Brookings Institution.

Torrance G.W., Thomas, W.H., & Sackett D.L.. (1972). A utility maximization model for evaluation of health care programs. *Health Services Research, 7*, 118–133.

Vickers A.J., & Altman D.G.. (2001). Analysing controlled trials with baseline and follow up measurements. *British Medical Journal, 323*, 1123–1124.

Vickers A.J. (2001). The use of percentage change from baseline as an outcome in a controlled trial is statistically inefficient: a simulation study. *BMC Medical Research Methodology*, 16.

Viscusi, W. K., & Aldy, J. E. (2003). The value of a statistical life: a critical review of market estimates throughout the world. *Journal of Risk and Uncertainty, 27*(1), 5-76.

Ware, J.E., Snow, K.K., Kosinski, M., & Gandek, B. (1993). *SF-36 health survey manual and interpretation guide.* Boston, MA: New England Medical Center, The Health Institute.

Weinstein M.C. (1999). Theoretically correct cost-effectiveness analysis. *Medical Decision Making 19*, 381-382.

Weinstein M.C. & Stason W.B. (1977). Foundations of cost-effectiveness analysis for health and medical practices. *New England Journal of Medicine, 296*, 716–21.

Wong, D.L. & Baker, C. (1988). Pain in children: Comparison of assessment scales. *Pediatric Nursing, 14*, 9-17.

Whynes D.K., Neilson A.R., Walker A.R., & Hardcastle J.D. (1998). Faecal occult blood screening for colorectal cancer is it cost-effective? *Health Economics, 7*, 21-29

Zeckhauser R, & Shepard D. (1976). Where now for saving lives? *Law and Contemporary Problems, 40*, 5–45.